SAINTS, SCHOLARS,
AND SCHIZOPHRENICS

TWENTIETH
ANNIVERSARY
EDITION,
UPDATED AND
EXPANDED

NANCY SCHEPER-HUGHES

Saints, Scholars, and Schizophrenics

MENTAL ILLNESS
IN RURAL IRELAND

UNIVERSITY OF
CALIFORNIA PRESS

BERKELEY
LOS ANGELES
LONDON

University of California Press
Berkeley and Los Angeles, California

University of California Press, Ltd.
London, England

Library of Congress Cataloging-in-Publication Data

Scheper-Hughes, Nancy.
    Saints, scholars, and schizophrenics : mental illness
in rural Ireland / Nancy Scheper-Hughes. — [20th
anniversary ed., rev. and expanded].
            p.   cm.
    Includes bibliographical references and index.
    ISBN 978-0-520-22480-3 (pbk. : alk. paper)
    1. Mental illness—Ireland—Clochan. 2. Clochan
(Ireland)—Social life and customs—20th century.
3. National characteristics, Irish. I. Title.

RC450.I732 C637 2001
362.2'09419'6—dc21   00-060379

16   15   14   13   12

11   10   9   8   7   6

To the memory of

HORTENSE B.
POWDERMAKER

teacher, friend,
and tribal elder,
and in hopeful celebration
of the Good Friday
Peace Agreement . . .
and to all the rebellious
and "scandalous" youths
of the new Ireland and
to the liberation theology-
inspired priests of Maynooth

CONTENTS

LIST OF TABLES

WHEN THE EDITORS at University of California Press contacted me about their intention of preparing a twentieth anniversary edition of *Saints, Scholars, and Schizophrenics*, their call coincided with an expected trip to Ireland in the summer of 1999 following a brief season of fieldwork in South Africa. I had planned to spend a few weeks in Dublin with our son, Nathanael, who was studying Irish theater at Trinity College (see Hughes 1999) and, after that, to head out to the west of Ireland for several more weeks. I had been for some time negotiating a return to "Ballybran." After witnessing some remarkable experiences of reconciliation in the new South Africa (see Scheper-Hughes 1999b), I had high hopes for a "negotiated settlement" between the anthropologist and the villagers of An Clochán, the true Irish name of the village that I took the liberty of naming Ballybran.

The return was shorter and more traumatic than expected. In the new prologue, Writing Ireland, I comment on some striking changes, especially the remarkable prosperity of Ireland today in the wake of globalization and the effect, on community life, cultural identity, and national consciousness, of Ireland's membership in the European Union. The epilogue, Crediting An Clochán, tells the story of my naive and aborted efforts at peacemaking and of my hurried, even comical, departure from the village, sad as it was for me and for those in the village who were intimidated into silence and complicity against their own better judgment. I find myself revisiting questions about anthropological ethics and the politics and poetics of "writing culture" and especially about the difficulties of balancing one's responsibility to honest ethnography with care and respect for the people who shared a part of their lives and their secrets with me.

ONE SOURCE of ethnographic data frequently absent in anthropological analysis is the response of the people studied to the ethnographer's description and interpretation of the meaning of their lives.[1] For the most part, anthropologists (as well as the communities studied) have been shielded from any local repercussions

Description is revelation. It is neither
The thing described, nor false
facsimile.

It is an artificial thing that exists,
In its own seeming, plainly visible,

Yet not too closely the double of our
lives
Intenser than any actual life could be.
—WALLACE STEVENS

and aftershocks resulting from publication because we have traditionally worked in what were until recently "exotic" cultures and among preliterate peoples. In most cases the "natives" never knew what had been said about them, their patterns of kinship and marriage, their sexual practices, their beliefs and values or—God help us!—their basic personality structures. The anthropologist might, as a professional courtesy, send a village headman or a mestizo *mayordomo* a copy of the published ethnography, which was often proudly displayed in the village. Its contents, however, normally remained as mysterious as the private life of the "masked" white man, that professional lone stranger, who would periodically reappear (sometimes bearing gifts) and then just as inexplicably vanish (not infrequently at the start of the rainy season). Within this traditional fieldwork paradigm our once colonized subjects remain disempowered and mute.

Such local invisibility (and hence invulnerability) has not been the fate of those who have studied "modern" cultures, and in particular that most literate and self-reflexive people, the rural Irish. Irish reaction to, analysis of,

NOTE: Some portions of this text were originally presented as the Margaret Mead Award address at the 41st Annual Meeting of the Society for Applied Anthropology, Edinburgh, Scotland, and later appeared as "*Cui Bonum*—For Whose Good? A Dialogue with Sir Raymond Firth" in *Human Organization* 40, no. 4 (1981): 371–372.

and commentary on anthropological writing generally has been swift, frequently harsh, and (at least for the ethnographer) most unsettling.[2] Although, for example, Conrad Arensberg's *The Irish Countryman* (1937) was well received in the Republic as a sympathetic portrait of rural lives, the Irish did *not* like the image of themselves as an appropriate subject for anthropological inquiry. Hence, it was not too long before an enormously popular book by the Anglo-Irish novelist Honor Tracy (*The Straight and Narrow Path*, 1956) appeared and parodied the anthropologist protagonist in an Irish village as a naive, bumbling, and pompous fool of uncertain moral principles, given to inept interpretations of local custom, and prone to the perpetration of malicious gossip. Fair enough: the anthropological looking glass reflected back on ourselves. And very reminiscent of the rather blunt warning offered by one resident of "Ballybran": "Ye'll only know how it feels to have your whole family history spilled out for the whole world to see when it's been done to yourselves."

At an early stage in the writing of this book I was tempted to entitle it *The Confessional Conscience*, so struck was I by the rigorously self-critical mode of the Irish villager. I trust that a touch of that same reflexivity and introspection has rubbed off on me as, over the past three years, I have had ample time and opportunities to observe the impact of publication on the lives of those who "so kindly took us in" as total strangers on that stormy day in 1974 and who, during the ensuing months, entrusted to my keeping a few of the "darkest secrets" of their souls.

The ethical dilemma that has gradually emerged through an exchange of letters, a series of review articles and replies in the Irish press,[3] and through a brief return to Ballybran, was most succinctly stated by the village schoolmaster: "It's not your science [i.e., your accuracy] I'm questioning, but this: don't we have the right to lead unexamined lives, the right *not* to be analyzed? Don't we have a right to hold on to an image of ourselves as 'different' to be sure, but as innocent and unblemished all the same?"

If our anthropological code of ethics can be said, minimally, to reflect the medical profession's proscription to "do no harm," then it would be fitting on this occasion of a second edition to reflect on the fundamental question raised by Sir Raymond Firth[4]—*cui bonum?* To whose advantage or for whose good do we cast what is so often a critical gaze on the contradictions and paradoxes implicit in the character of human relations, institutions, and organizations?

What have they lost, what have they gained in "Ballybran" as a result of the publication of *Saints, Scholars and Schizophrenics,* a book that clearly departs from the traditional anthropological stance of cultural relativism in order to examine the social and cultural contributions to psychological suffering? I will relay here what I have learned by a moving and often painful return to "Ballybran" during the spring of 1981, our first visit since 1976.

They have lost a hitherto unchallenged native interpretation of the meaning of their lives as ones based on the implicitly cherished values of familistic loyalty, obedience, and sacrifice. I was told that one village lass has not been the same since identifying herself in the following pages. Until that time she herself (and the parish at large) viewed her decision to give up a disapproved "love match" in order to stay at home and care for her widowed father and unmarried brothers as the good, moral, "Christian" thing to do. As was said: "her father and brothers 'had right' to claim her." But now there is an alternative view, and a hint of pity has been introduced: "Oh, what a shame, the poor creature." Worse, a suggestion of something subliminal: "Could she be overly attached to them?"

I intruded into their "commonsense world" with an alternative and sometimes shattering vision — that provided by psychological anthropology. And they are angry at me, not so much for exposing their lives to the larger world outside, but rather for exposing their hurt and pain to one another. So, I was scolded: "Why couldn't you have left it a dusty dissertation on a library shelf that no one would read, or a scholarly book that only the 'experts' would read? Why did you have to write it in a way that *we* could read it and understand exactly what you were saying?"

There is an irony here and a "double bind." The irony is that my colleagues in the Society for Applied Anthropology honored me in 1981 with the Margaret Mead Award in recognition of a work that "interprets anthropological data and principles in ways that make them meaningful to a broadly concerned public." Probably the most immediately concerned part of that "public," the villagers of Ballybran, rather wish I had kept my mouth shut or else had said what I did in a jargon so confounding that *they* would not have had to deal with it. Committed as I am, however, to writing for "the public" rather than for a scientific elite, the mandate from "the people," so to speak, to render myself inaccessible and unintelligible posed a real paradox.

While it would be implausible to expect that the members of a community would wholeheartedly agree with the outsider's perspective, with his or her rendition of their social, cultural, and psychological situation, that same rendition should not be *so* foreign or removed from their commonsense interpretation of the meaning of their lives as to do violence to it. Any ethnography ultimately stands or falls on the basis of whether or not it *resonates:* it should ring true, strike a familiar (even if occasionally painful) chord. It should not leave the "native" reader cold and confused. Angry and hurt, perhaps, but not confused or perplexed.

When I protested in Ballybran during my return visit that there should have been no surprises in the book, that I revealed no "personal" secrets, but only commonly known and widely shared "community" secrets (such as the questionable status of the community as an Irish-speaking or *Gaeltacht* parish, the depressions and drinking associated with the lonely winter months, the difficulty of keeping an heir on the land, and the distance and alienation between the sexes), I was told pointedly: "There is quite a difference between whispering something beside a fire or across a counter and seeing it printed for the world to see. It becomes a public shame."

There were other objections and responses to what I had written, among them:

She should be shot.

There's a lot of truth in what she said, you can't deny that. But did she have the right to say it, so?

'Bad 'cess to anyone from here who throws good Irish pounds after a copy of that Yankee work.

To be accurate there was also the quite predictable praise from the young emigrés of Ballybran, reporting back from their new homes in America or from University College in Cork or Dublin. As one young scholar wrote to his distraught mother, already fearful for the loss of his soul at University College, Dublin, ". . . and you can tell Da that '*that* book' is the first one to speak the truth about this secret Ireland of ours." And there was also the silence—the traditional Irish cut-off—from many of those closest to us and, hence, most stunned by my candor.

I never did learn exactly how many villagers had "thrown away good Irish pounds" after the book since one of the best kept secrets in Ballybran today is just *who* owns a copy, and after that, who has actually read it. Most deny both. The *Irish Times* correspondent Michael Viney reported after his investigations in Ballybran that "two or three copies of the book have been passing from house to house, [with] hurt and anger flaring up like a gunpowder trail"(see note 3 to this Preface). My village friends, however, tell me that there are a good forty or fifty copies in private circulation through the parish: "Everyone is curious, of course, to see if they are in it, and everyone is ashamed to *look* curious by borrowing it. So most have their own copy. It is difficult to say what the 'public consensus' is because '*it*' is never discussed openly and in public, but only privately and among kin."

"How do they get '*it*'?" I asked, falling into the local term of reference.

"Oh, they're cute, mind you. They won't go walking into a Tralee [in County Kerry] bookseller and ask for it. They'll get it through contacts going to Cork or Dublin. Or they'll have relatives send it from America the same way we did."

When I argued, somewhat lamely, that it would be pointless for individuals to try to identify themselves since I carefully constructed *composite* characters that would defy any attempts at labeling or identification, I was silenced:

Nonsense! You know us for better than that. You think we didn't, each of us, sit down poring over every page until we had recognized the bits and pieces of ourselves strewn about here and there. You turned us into amputees with hooks for fingers and some other blackguard's heart beating inside our own chest. How do you think I felt reading my words come out of some Tom-O or Pat-O or some publican's mouth? Recognize ourselves, indeed! I've gone on to memorize some of my best lines.

Sensing a possible wedge, I asked my friends whether they could not at least see through to my affection for them and for their way of life. I was brought up short with the answer: "Affection, appreciation, we could see that all right. But wasn't it a case of 'Look, I can love you warts and all'? Isn't love more generous than that? Couldn't you have overlooked the warts?"

Cui bonum? For whose good? What, if anything, has been gained? The "problem of the aged," discussed in the following pages, is being actively debated and a local village association has been formed to look after the solitary elderly to prevent their premature hospitalization. One villager confided that for the first time in their years of friendship she and another wife and mother have been able to discuss family and marital problems they share in common: "A kind of great burden has been lifted. There's no need to hide it and worry over it alone — it's part of the public record, now, anyway."

My suggestion that the *Gaeltacht* status of the community is debatable wounded deeply, and has been met by an even fiercer attempt to revive and restore Irish usage. The new curate, who takes a rather dim view of the Irish revival and who has refused to celebrate the Mass in Irish, has been firmly ignored by the once docile parishioners who have weekly attempted to shout down his English liturgy with their bold Irish responses and Seán O'Riada hymns. "Now, make sure you record *that* next time," I was told. And so I have.

Finally, a new (I will not say better) insight into themselves has been gained. "We are less naive now," said a village teacher.

We can see more clearly what our problems are, and how deep the roots of them go. Your book made me very sad. After all, it isn't a very pretty picture. But I have said to myself, "Let's stop grieving over it, and let's get on with what has to be done." Quod scriptum est, scriptum est. *There are old lives that need caring for, and new ones still in formation. And I was wondering what might be done for some of our young bachelors, before it's too late. A small, informal marriage information bureau, do you think that might work?*

Quod scriptum est, scriptum est. Therefore, as advised, I leave the original work intact, although the impulse to cut and paste, to excise this phrase or that section, to erase those few words now known by me to have caused pain to one individual or another in Ballybran, is strong. I had already in the original Prologue (see p. xxvii) asked villagers' forgiveness for "exposing the darker and weaker side of their venerable culture." I now understand that this forgiveness is not forthcoming. And while I can never ask my fellow travelers in Ballybran to "bless the work" in the characteristically Kerryman fashion, I can pass on to them what I was told upon leaving Ballybran by a "village elder" when I asked whether it would be at all right for me to accept the Mead award in Scotland for a book that had caused so much local controversy. He thought long and hard about it. "Take it," he said finally, "but take it for Ballybran, and for what you have learned from us. For better or for worse our lives are inextricably linked." And he cited the Celtic proverb: *Ar scáth a chéile a mhaireas na daoine* — In the shadows of each other we must build our lives.

Chapel Hill, 1983

ACKNOWLEDGMENTS

MY FIELD RESEARCH in County Kerry was supported by a predoctoral grant from the National Institute of General Medical Sciences (No. 1224). Throughout the years in Berkeley I enjoyed the intellectual stimulation and moral support of a great number of professors and friends; among them, I wish to thank in particular Gerald Berreman, Margaret Clark, David Daube, May Diaz, George Foster, and Eugene Hammel. To whatever skills and insights in psychological theory I may lay claim I am most indebted to two very special people, Leonard Duhl and George DeVos. The scrupulous review of this book in manuscript form by Robert Coles, an anonymous reader, Robert Kennedy, Jr., Nancy Lawler, and my editor, Grant Barnes of the University of California Press, resulted in many substantial revisions for which I am deeply appreciative. My colleagues in the anthropology department of Southern Methodist University provided a congenial and frequently animated environment within which the final drafts of the manuscript took place. Special thanks are due to my typists, Vicki Davidson and Mary Coleman, for their careful work in the preparation of these pages.

Older and more personal debts are owed: the open and inquiring minds of my parents, George and Anne Scheper, and of my brother and first mentor, George Louis Scheper, Jr., awakened my curiosity about the world from a very tender age. For the pleasure of their friendship and encouragement over years that had many trying moments, I am particularly grateful to Susanna Hoffman, Grita and Allan Kamin, Richard Day and Nadine Robles-Day, Margaret and Richard Lock, and Rob and Janice Wasserstrom. For my husband and best friend, Michael Hughes, lighter of turf fires, gas lamps, and not infrequently of the darker corners of my soul, no words of thanks suffice. To my children, Jenny, Sarah, and Nathanael, I offer my apologies for the weeks and months I was but half a mother to them: scribbling notes at the breakfast table, typing during their naps, and revising in the evenings when I should have been reading aloud from *Winnie the Pooh*. I can only say, in the words of another colleague, "Thank God, it's over—let's go out and play!"

Within Ireland, my work was both aided and inspired by Professor Séan O'Súilleabháin of the Irish Folklore Commission, Professor Dermot Walsh of the Medico-Social Research Board, and Dr. David Dunne of St. Stephen's Hospital, Cork. My greatest debt is, of course, to the people of Ballybran. They are a modest, private people who would not like to be mentioned by name, but I should like to thank in particular the dynamic and dedicated young curate, the warm and perceptive schoolmaster and schoolmistress, the national-school teachers, the village tailor, the publicans and shopkeepers, and, above all, the storytellers and mythmakers who fired and inspired us with a love, and perhaps even a little understanding, of the Irish tradition.

December 1977

I AM EXTREMELY GRATEFUL to Conor Cruise O'Brien and to Máire Mac an tSaoi for their unfailing support, wise counsel, brilliant company, and their warm hospitality in Dublin. Jamie Saris, Lawrence Taylor, and their colleagues and students in the anthropology department at Maynooth are creating a congenial space for "the difficult science" to take root in Ireland and I wish to thank them for their warm reception. Micheal Mac Gearailt, Aongus O'Caoimh, and Eithne Nic Gearailt's assistance with local archival materials is greatly appreciated. William Coventry of the University of Vermont sent me useful bibliographic and demographic data and source materials. Sheila and Aiden Mucahy will always be teachers, guides, and "confessors" in the best Irish scholastic tradition. I will carry with me the harsh lessons imparted by several village critics and I hope their words and actions will make me a better person and a better anthropologist. Seamus and Moira, Jazz Woods, and James Kinsella (of Dublin) offered shelter up through and including the final storm. Their kindness will not be forgotten. Naomi Schneider, Laura Cerruti, Marielle Leon, Nola Burger, Frances Bowles, and Randall Goodall went out of their way in the final preparations of this new edition. To the many students of anthropology and aficionados of Irish culture who have taken the time to write and share your own stories, recollections, and insights with me, thank you. I hope you will continue to write and respond.

Berkeley, May 2000

LÉVI-STRAUSS ONCE conferred the infelicitous title of necrographer upon those anthropologists who, like himself, were rushing in to record the death rattles and attend the wakes of those cultures sadly but rapidly on the wane. "We must study them," he said, "before they disappear." And, in like fashion, fresh from a year at play in the green, green fields of Ireland and attendance at no less than thirty-eight wakes in the tiny parish of Ballybran, I see myself today in the uncomfortable role of crepehanger, yellow journalist, grave-watcher, and procession follower. For I am here today to announce, among other things, that while I was so busy and preoccupied attending all those funerals and burials of ancient, gnarled, lonely old bachelor farmers, something far more serious happened right behind my back — so silently, gracefully, and unpretentiously that I almost missed it. That is, I bear the sad tidings that on a certain gray, windy day in March in the year of Our Lord 1975, Ireland passed away. She died with the grace and good manners of those very old yet cultured ladies who sense the time when it might be considered in poor taste to linger on any further. And she died with but the faintest trace of an Irish curse upon her lips.

Her name was Mag Moriarty; she was ninety-three, and in her lifetime she had seen the last of the *curachs* brave the Atlantic for mackerel, the Irish storyteller turn his back to the hearth and refuse to translate his tales and proverbs into a despised foreign tongue, the end of the Wren Boys and the bawdy fun of the pre-Lenten Skellig Lists, and finally the dispersal of the hard-won family lands among strangers — ironically, English tourists — while each of her first six children emigrated to America, and the seventh, her heir, remained home, an arthritic bachelor.

Death took her, or She, Mag, Ireland took death, as the old Celtic prayer would have it, not sudden or unprepared or peacefully dazed in sleep, but planned, calculated, tensely aware with full faculties of sense and reason. It was a long, slow, not unpainful suicide, but under the circumstances there was a Christian burial after all.

I make this prologue in order to introduce a book that is one of the most difficult pieces of writing I have undertaken; for in it I say things that would distress the people who quite literally took us in from the storm—total strangers on the day of our arrival—and who without introduction or fanfare warmed us by their fires and fed us the first of an innumerable succession of cups of tea and fresh baked bread. We entrusted to their grown and single daughters the care of our three small children, who thrived and flourished where their own did not. To them we owe the greatest debt and ask pardon for exposing the darker and weaker side of their venerable culture.

SAINTS, SCHOLARS,
AND SCHIZOPHRENICS

Writing Ireland

Time is the best story-teller.
— Irish Proverb

ON A DAMP summer evening in 1968 at a Catholic youth club dance held in a cheerless church auditorium in one of the new and hastily conceived suburbs of Dublin, stirrings were afoot of the mighty changes that would, during the next three decades, transform Ireland from a half-mythological creature — the "misty green isle" of Irish and Irish-American tribal longings — into the modern, prosperous, relentlessly materialist, and almost thoroughly secular (if not altogether humanist) European nation that it is today.

A dour parish priest slipped into the dance hall from a side door to find the lights turned down dangerously low, the music slow and dreamy, and several couples locked in mortally sinful, body-hugging embraces. On cue, the priest set into motion a clichéd pastoral drama that had been hounding the Irish "body sexual" since the late nineteenth century when the Irish Catholic Church turned into an alternative state and then into a state of mind that I had described in this book (see page 207) as "anti life, bitter, gloomy, and sexist." The church hall lights were rudely switched on, the needle scratched angrily across the plastic record, and the dancers interrupted, chastised, and sent home with a stinging reminder to return the following Saturday to confess the sinful acts in which they had been caught.

But something snapped in the youths on that evening. Perhaps it was the sad lyrics of the Beatles' song about gloomy old Father McKenzie or perhaps it was the life-affirming, zany lyrics of the "Yellow Submarine." The dancers did not, as usual, break up and run home burning with shame and sick with fear that "the Da" find out what had just transpired. Instead, they plotted a house rebellion. They did not confess their sins on the following Saturday afternoon and on Sunday, at the 10 o'clock Mass, the dancers walked quietly together into the Church and took up their places in the first few pews. As the elderly priest entered the pulpit and was about to begin one of his quietly devastating and guilt-inducing sermons, the rebellious dancers rose in unison and walked out of the church, loudly clomping their ungainly adolescent boots down the central aisle to the startled gasps of their parents, anxiously fingering their "Sunday morning special" pink crystal rosary beads.

We are told (see O'Toole 1998: xiii) that the young rebels were eventually knocked back into line and cut down to size. They returned to church a few weeks later, shamefaced, heads bowed, and spirits defeated. But, without their knowing it, from the moment they had dared to stage their collective strike against the mean-spirited parish priest, the old Irish world of unquestioned obedience to priestly authority was doomed in that parish and, soon after, elsewhere on the island. It was a strike against the bully, and as significant in Ireland as the 1969 "Stonewall Riots" were in the United States. In each case, a public act of refusal and insubordination signaled to a younger generation the possibility of a very different kind of world.

In the spirit, then, of a book that violated, or perhaps I should say *sinned* against the *ancien régime* of patriarchal Ireland by telling the story of the Irish Countryman—as so eloquently told first by Conrad Arensberg in 1937—from the point of view not of the old men sitting snugly and confidently at the hearth and the pub, at the very center of family, church, and village authority, but from the resentful, distanced, and slant-eyed view of their often browbeaten, unhappy, and constrained young sons, the bachelor boy-os of County Kerry, I dedicate this edition of *Saints* to all the rebellious and "scandalous" youths of the new Ireland *and* to the liberation theology-inspired priests of Maynooth who have at last found ways of loving God other than by hating sex, reviling the body, and disparaging women.

Sheep fair, An Clochán; summer 1974. Outsiders—"Black Protestant" middlemen—engage in active bidding while anxious and embittered local farmers and shepherds avert their faces and turn their backs on the auctioneers.

Twenty-five years have elapsed since a young and somewhat brash anthropologist and her offbeat, countercultural family—shaggy-haired, gentle "hippie" husband and their three rambunctious babies and toddlers—stumbled somewhat dazed and almost by default into the relatively isolated, rugged mountain community of Ballybran just over the spectacularly beautiful Connor Pass through the Slieve Mish mountains past the Magharees and nestled on the shores of Brandon Bay, a cul de sac on the eastern end of the Dingle Peninsula in West Kerry.

We had reached the end of the line, figuratively *and* literally. Having spent several weeks in a rented car canvassing villages in West Kerry and West Cork in search of an Irish-speaking (though bilingual) community kind enough to accept our presence for a year of live-in fieldwork, it was Ballybran or bust. We would begin our tentative inquiries about securing housing with the local postmistress or the resident curate or parish priest

"On through the silent land": Main street, An Clochán, at high noon in July 1999.

only to be told that people living in this or that community would not much fancy being observed by a resident stranger.

Our meager research funds were disappearing. We could not afford to continue to live like American tourists housed in a succession of big-breakfasted farm homes and guesthouses. Worse, our precious supply of American Pampers—disposable nappies had not yet crossed the Atlantic—stuffed into two green Salvation Army duffel bags was almost depleted. With two "babas" still in diapers and no access to coin-operated washing machines in rural areas, what would have been a minor inconvenience turned into a daily anxiety. No one in the guesthouses ever thought to inquire just *how* we managed to take care of our babies' basic physical needs. For our part, there seemed no appropriate way to broach the indelicate subject. I once made the mistake of inquiring whether anyone in a particular village took in washing. The question was taken as an insult. Did I think there were country people of less social worth than ourselves who would stoop to such a thing? Did I think the village was made up of char women? Couldn't I take care of my own family's

Sheep graze on lower pasture lands formerly reserved for cows; 1999. Sheep raising survives only by dint of subsidies from the European Economic Community.

"dirty work"? Abashed, I retreated. How easy it is to instill a sense of shame. But along with this, I was already beginning to take note of Irish attitudes toward the body and its incessant and apparently shameful needs.

Ethnographic fieldwork was still a new and alien concept for a country people known both for their spectacular hospitality and for their fierce family loyalty and sense of privacy. Tourists who came and went for the brief salmon-fishing season on the Dingle Peninsula were one thing, and bothersome enough in their own way; a resident writer-anthropologist was something else again. In a country dedicated both to banning books *and* revering the written word—local farmers in West Kerry could recite endless verses about the Siege of Limerick or the flight of wild geese—any writer learns to tread lightly and to have a quick exit plan.

People in West Kerry were still angry in the 1970s about the publication in 1942 of *The Tailor and Ansty*, a book by Eric Cross, about a remarkable old Irish-speaking couple from mountainous West Cork who spent their days quarreling amiably with each other, their fellow villagers, and God himself.

Banned in Ireland: The Tailor and Ansty, whose rough-and-tumble speech and western Irish folkways scandalized the up-and-coming rural and urban Irish bourgeoisie in the early 1940s, when Eric Cross's book about the robust country couple first appeared.

They were a robust and earthy pair, free thinking, mischievous, and unburdened with the moral rigidities of Jansenist Catholicism. They were, in short, exemplary Celtic Irish peasants. Although initially greeted with rave reviews, *The Tailor and Ansty* was banned in 1943 by Mr. de Valera's government following an acrimonious four-day debate in the Irish Senate during which the protagonists of the book were all but pilloried. The Tailor was condemned as a "sex-obsessed" peasant and his wife, Anastasia (Ansty), was cruelly dismissed as a village moron. The author, Eric Cross, was accused of participating in an anti-Catholic campaign originating in England and financed by American (Protestant) capital (see O'Connor 1964: 8–9).

But the public outcry was most devastating for the Tailor and Ansty themselves, who had to live through it all. The couple was shut out and cut off by the rest of the village. Because of their advanced age and limited resources, they had nowhere to hide except in their tiny cottage on a mountain road near the lake at Gougane Barra. A policeman checked in on the pair from time to time and tried to discourage local ruffians from venting their anger against the old ones, their cottage, or their single milk cow. The Tailor complained to the policeman about the appearance one morning at his doorstep of three priests who had forced him to his knees and made him burn his only copy of the book in his hearth. Ansty fussed that the flames had consumed "eight and sixpence worth of book," an enormous expense and a "bleedy" waste of paper, it being a fair and warm day.

The banning of *The Tailor and Ansty* was preceded and followed by a succession of real and metaphorical book burnings in Ireland. Several days of rioting and looting followed the opening performance in January 1907 of J. M. Synge's *Playboy of the Western World* at the Abbey Theater in Dublin. The looters were protesting a play written by an *Anglo*-Irishman and portraying Irish peasants as a wild, violent, and lawless white tribe of peripheral Europe. Subsequent performances of *The Playboy* had to be protected by a small army of police stationed in and around the theater (Miller 1977: 130–134). Frank O'Connor's translation, published in 1945, of Brian Merryman's *Cúirt an mheán oiche (The Midnight Court)*, an early Irish poem rich in earthy and ribald verses, was banned by the Irish government representing the sensibilities of an emerging urban bourgeoisie. The filming of

Ryan's Daughter in Dunquin on the Dingle Peninsula caused an uproar there. And, as we leaned over a fencepost during the annual sheep dipping, soon after I began my own research in An Clochán, I was given due warning by Steve Hennesy, a ruggedly handsome, middle-aged sheep farmer. He told of local reactions to the "shockingly immoral" stories and novels of Edna O'Brien.[1] "They ran that woman out of her village in County Clare," he said, a conversation I had reason to recall in 1999. Meanwhile, my close association with another tailor, the agnostic and freethinking Tailor Dean of Ballybran, would likewise incite the ire of the rural Irish.

On arriving for the first time in Ballybran, I introduced myself and my family to the young curate of the spectacularly beautiful "half parish" with some trepidation. We had checked ourselves into the one local inn in Ballybran for a few days. We tried to keep out of the way of serious English anglers and keep our toddlers out of the formal parlor where they might be tempted to pull leather-bound volumes of local folklore, fishing, and mountain climbing off the tidy bookshelves. We were quickly using up our welcome in that fussy house. Among the letters of introduction that I presented later that day to the amiable but distracted Father L. were the standard doctoral research letters, each embossed with the official University of California gold seal meant to dazzle local bureaucrats anywhere in the world into granting access to local informants, archives, and libraries.

My official documents failed to dazzle this down-to-earth curate. What did make a difference were a letter from our local university chaplain stating that Michael and I were "good enough" Catholics, if perhaps a bit wayward in our post-Vatican II enthusiasms for the transformation of Mother Church, and an almost illegible note from an older friend and informal mentor, David Daube, the late scholar of canon law, vouching that we were trustworthy and decent people. The priest accepted these two letters and agreed to introduce us on Sunday morning during the Irish Mass. Though we never knew just what was said about us, we were approached after Mass by a few local families who quickly worked out a complicated but feasible series of rental arrangements that would carry us through most of the year.

And so, ironically, with the sponsorship and blessing of the same Irish Catholic Church that I would take to task in the following pages, we settled into Ballybran a few weeks before the feast of Corpus Christi in June 1974 and stayed until a few weeks after Saint Bridget's Day in late spring the following year. During that period we lived in three different houses. The first was a cottage in the IRA-dominated mountain hamlet of Ballynalacken and our second house was an unfinished vacation bungalow tucked between the thatched hut of the old widow, Bridget McCarthy, and the small stone church dedicated to St. Brendan, from which I derived the composite pseudonym, "Ballybran," referring both to Bran, an ancient pagan Celtic deity associated with the village and Saint Brendan, the fifth-century seafaring Catholic saint.

Our last house was wonderfully situated within shouting distance of the village primary school and just above the blacksmith's forge, an old institution that the young curate was trying to revive. The two comely and swarthy young men recruited by Father L. as apprentice village smithies helped us to attract a few nubile high school girls from the village to baby-sit for us part of each day. The clanging, fire-breathing blacksmith's forge served as our children's first daycare center. It was also a youth club for young adults in the parish, who had few other places or opportunities to meet.

Some critics of *Saints and Scholars* have suggested that Ballybran (like Hugh Brody's Inishkillane) does not exist at all, and that it represents a composite made up of bits and pieces of dozens of rural communities, both real and imagined. If anthropologists had the literary skills to create imaginary communities, I dare say we would take to writing commercially successful novels rather than our more pedestrian and less widely read ethnographies. By inclination and by training anthropologists are natural historians of social life; without our notepads and our proverbial boxes of field notes we would be utterly out of our depth and out of our jobs. In any event, soon after the book appeared the true identity of Ballybran was found out by Michael Viney, a persistent journalist who worked for the *Irish Times*.

In September of 1980 Viney headed out along the Dingle Peninsula, pedalling his ten-speed mountain bicycle and buffeted by gale winds and pelting sheets of rain, in search of what he later described in one of his columns as the "mythical valley of Ballybran." After a few false starts and cases of mistaken identity reminiscent of a Shakespearean comedy of errors, Viney rejoiced on hitting the mark and reaching his desired goal as he slipped inside the snug materiality of Peig's Pub. "Yes," said the publican identifying herself, "I was one [in the book] who didn't believe in socio-logical statistics!" "Mrs. Scheper-Hughes had sat here often," Viney mused, with a pint of Guinness in his hand, "as I was doing now, with the rain hosing down from the mountains beyond the open door."

In a subsequent column, Viney pictured himself as he thought the anthropologist might have seen him: "Sometimes—cycling over the hill to the post office, past the rusty, crumpled bracken and the lichen-crusted walls—I look down at the little houses (which are for my writerly purposes crouched in Atlantic mist) and wonder what the anthropologist would make of our community (or indeed, *of me*, a squinting, unkempt figure in black oilskins and dripping cap, alienated irretrievably from his own urban peer group, the epitome of *anomie* on wheels). Would [she] decide that our remote half parish [should] have a whole new perspective on [its] right or ability to exist?"

Over the past two decades since Viney's peregrinations in the early 1980s Ballybran has been host to a small but steady stream of anthropologists and sociologists from Europe and North America—little red paperback of *Saints* in hand—searching among the dispersed mountain hamlets for some of the protagonists of the book. The drama of hide-and-seek played by villagers, their various defenders, unabashed curiosity seekers, and global interlocutors continues to this day.

Were I to be writing this book for the first time and with hindsight, there are things that, of course, I would do differently. I would be inclined to avoid the cute and conventional use of pseudonyms. I would not attempt to scramble certain identifying features of the individuals portrayed on the naive assumption that such masks and disguises could not be easily decoded by villagers themselves. I have come to see that the time-honored practice of bestowing anonymity on our communities and informants fools few and protects none—save, perhaps, the anthropologist. And I fear that the practice makes rogues of us all—too free with our pens, with the government of our tongues, and with our loose translations and interpretations of village life.

Anonymity makes us forget that we owe our anthropological subjects the same degree of courtesy, empathy, and friendship in writing that we generally extend to them face to face in the field, where they are not our subjects but our companions and without whom we quite literally could not survive. Sacrificing anonymity means we may have to write less poignant, more circumspect ethnographies, a high price for any writer to pay. But our version of the Hippocratic oath — to do not harm, insofar as possible, to our informants — would seem to demand this. A hermeneutics of (self-)doubt could temper our brutally frank sketches of other people's lives as we see them, close-up but always from the outside looking in, "through a glass darkly."

In keeping with this, I now identify the village by its true Irish name and I have restored a few personal names in the new material where it seems appropriate and not invasive. In other cases I am not sure what is the proper thing to do, either because the individuals I am discussing are dead and cannot defend themselves or because the topic itself is so intrinsically painful. There I continue the custom of bestowing ethnographic pseudonyms. From the perspective of most villagers of An Clochán, the only proper thing for me to do is to stop writing altogether, a position I took once with respect to another community, Picaris Pueblo in northern New Mexico (see Scheper-Hughes 1987). But I cannot move away so easily from An Clochán, even as it wishes to distance itself so thoroughly from me. The die has been cast, we are tangled up with one another, and the tangle has lasted these many years, involving now the adult children and grandchildren of some of my key informants. The original text, warts and all, is again presented here as it was first written. Nor, despite my reservations, can I even change the title, which villagers and some Irish scholars find offensive in its witty alliteration: "The stuff of tabloids, really," scolded Riobard, a former villager now living and working in Limerick. *Saints, Scholars, and Schizophrenics* was written from a particular perspective, at a particular moment in time, by a particular sort of anthropologist-ethnographer.

Today, Ballybran, anthropology, and the ethnographer are not what they were in the mid–1970s. Twenty-five years on, the village is barely recognizable. The last of the real thatched farmhouses have been razed and modern suburban ranch-style homes have appeared in their place. The only thatched cottage in evidence is Nellie Brick's former tea-rashers-butter-and-

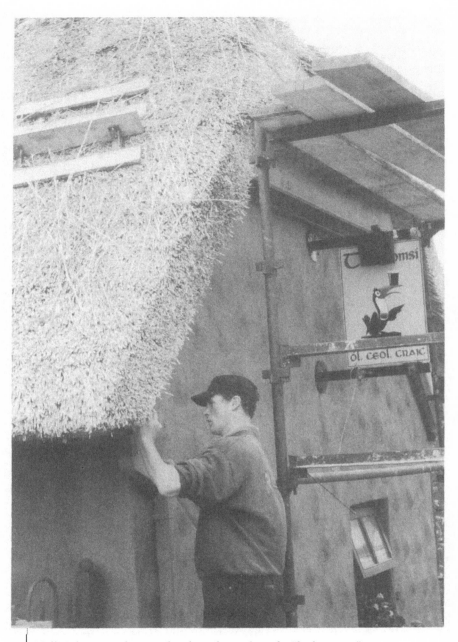

Nellie's butter-and-egg-and-rashers shop, where the "lucky penny" was returned for every purchase no matter how small, is now being converted into an "authentic" tourist pub; summer 1999.

*On the road from An Clochán to Breanainn: an old stone cottage in ruins;
summer 1999.*

bread shop, which is now being renovated as a snug and romantic pub for
the pleasure of tourists. The interior is rustic English countryside and the
thatch has been imported from Poland. But the thatchers, at least, are from
Killarney even if they learned their traditional trade on a development grant
from the European Union. Still, the thatch smells as sweet and inviting as
ever, and some kind soul had thought to stick a cardboard sign on a win-
dowsill indicating "Nellie's window," the vantage point from which the
wonderful old wag had once kept tabs on the village world.

As I had predicted, family farms are no more; little parcels of land, some
arable, some useless, have been sold off, piecemeal, to summer tourists from
the outside and to citified ex-villagers wanting to keep a summer home and
a toehold in the natal village. A former villager, now resident in the city,
took a shine to Tailor Dean's sturdy little cottage and after the old man's
death purchased it and spiffed it up, painting it a *post-moderne* teal set off by
an eye-catching rose trim. "Yuppified," some villagers, the older ones, say,
with a sniff and a note of disdain. The once-welcoming cottage that rarely
saw a closed door is today bolted shut, possessed but not inhabited. As I pass
by, I think I can still see the Tailor resting himself on a three-legged stool at

The clattering of hooves, wooden wagons, and tin milk containers announced the definitive ritual of the farmer's workday in 1974: the return from the village cooperative creamery, seen at the far left.

the open door, pipe in the crook of his mouth and dressed in his gentlemanly soiled gray vest, waiting to hail passersby and invite them in for a supeen and a few stories told in his deep, resonant, Celtic-accented voice amplified by the empty, fireplace-sooted walls. "Yerra, there was a story told in these parts about a spoiled priest and a beheaded nun. I've half a mind to share it with ye. It's a longish story now . . ." Or, after a vexing discussion of some aspect of village life, I can hear the Tailor's firm obliteration of any commentary or further discussion: "Well, let's leave that there now."

A few individuals still keep sheep, coaxing the shaggy, long-haired creatures down from the mountains where they used to rough graze to gentler pastures near the sea, land once kept for milk cows. Sheep have been subsidized by the European Union, in part to allow the mountains to recover from centuries of overgrazing. Cows have not. Consequently, the village creamery, once the dead center of the village, is today simply dead. There are no more rattling horse-drawn carts carrying large tin jugs spilling over with thick yel-

Once dead center of the village of An Clochán, the creamery is now simply dead; summer 1999.

The end of things: milk tin, rusty and abandoned; summer 1999.

The blacksmith's forge today, a tangle of overgrown weeds; 1999. The young smithies, trained in the mid-1970s as part of a village cultural revival, spearheaded by the local Irish-speaking curate, have long since left the village and their trade. The beloved curate is now a Roman Catholic missionary in East Africa.

low milk, rich in its high caloric, fatty goodness—unless, that was, the old "witch" Bridie McCarthy (as *she* called herself), had managed to steal the top of the cream by casting out her apron along with her widow's curse. No Bridie, no cream, and the only curses are those that fall now on my head.

*Mackerel fishermen leaving from the quay at Bhréanainn, in a naomhóg,
a traditional, tarred-canvas canoe similar to the ones used by fishermen of
the Great Blasket Island and their neighbors on the mainland; date unknown.*

Despite these changes and my own dire predictions, An Clochán has
thrived in recent years as a prosperous little tourist mecca with booming
property values, the construction of summer vacation homes, a tiny fishing
industry, and the arrival of a few new settler families. Still, the resident population has continued its steady decline to little more than three hundred people today. The transient summer population has expanded, but few tourists
spend more than a few days in An Clochán once they learn that it offers only
a series of arduous hikes and mountain climbs without the assistance of local
guides. New tourists are handed a detailed book mapping a variety of daunting trails along with a cheerful warning, "Watch out for mountain mists; they
can be deadly to the new hiker. Good luck; see you at dinner time. If you're
delayed, we won't wait up. The key is hanging on the door post."

The last of the mackerel fishermen bringing in their naomhóg; *exact date unknown, mid-twentieth century, Brandon/Bhréanainn.*

The empty quay at Bhréanainn; summer 1999.

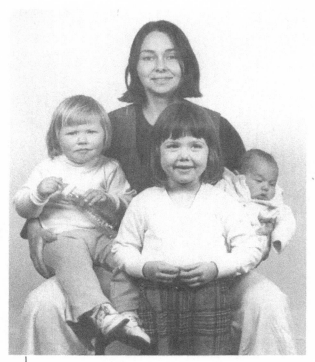

*Irish visa and U.S. passport photo: Nancy, Jennifer,
Sarah, and Nathanael, April 1974. Twenty-five years
have elapsed since a young anthropologist
and her countercultural family stumbled into the
remote mountain parish of Ballybran.*

If the Ballybran I describe in the following pages is no more, neither is the kind of anthropology that I practiced in the late 1970s. Today we no longer approach the field as if it were a private laboratory of human behavior in which to test scientific hypotheses or an untapped reservoir of unconscious material waiting to be seized upon and analyzed. The anthropologist as "skillful pathologist of the human condition" has given way to a researcher with a healthy skepticism in the field toward all grand and ultimately reductionist paradigms. We no longer believe, as did the young woman who wrote this book, that it is possible to sum up the key dilemmas that present themselves to, for example, young people coming of age in a rapidly modernizing village or to diagnose just what ails a community and then prescribe a few magic, silver-bullet solutions. I blush today at my naiveté in arguing as I did once the merits of introducing a local marriage bureau — a mail-order groom service as it were — to match shy and disappointed bachelor farmers from Ballynalacken and Ballyguin with eligible young women from towns and cities in Ireland or even from Canada, Australia, and the United States.

The young woman in short skirts and leather sandals who intruded, pencil and notebook in hand, into the lives and deaths of a great many old timers in Ballybran, themselves sensibly and defensively wrapped in layers of aprons, off-white woolen sweaters, and sturdy Wellington boots, looks and sees the world more and more like an old timer herself. The young mother — one baby stuffed into a Gerry-pack on her back, another strapped into a Snuggli-pack on her front, and a third pushed along in a portable stroller as she visited far-flung households, confident in the powerful collaborations between Margaret Mead and Benjamin Spock to bring aspects of the Western Enlightenment into the nursery — is now a grandmother and a lot less certain about what kinds of "critters" children are and what they need.

Why Ireland — of all places? *Why schizophrenia* — of all topics? These are questions I am still asked by readers of *Saints, Scholars, and Schizophrenics*. The assumption is often that only someone of Irish descent could possibly be interested in a small village in the western *Gaeltacht*. Even our village neighbor, Bridget McCarthy, would often introduce us to visitors to Ballybran as "Mike and Nancy, our 'Yanks' [here meaning Irish-Americans] who have *come home* for the year." I soon learned not to fight it. Michael, too, acquiesced by submerging what was left of his Midwest German Lutheran background in his new-found Catholicism and hauling out on more than one occasion stories about his quasi-mythological Irish "Healy" ancestor. To a great extent the early controversy surrounding *Saints* represented a native response. Of the twenty-six published reviews of this book, fourteen were written by self-identified Irish, Irish-American, or Irish Catholic critics. A few were written by Irish Catholic priests. Meanwhile, insofar as social anthropology is practiced in the Republic of Ireland, it has been nationalized and taught in the context of the Irish Catholic national seminary of Maynooth. And, to be sure, my twelve years of mostly Irish Catholic education in New York City gave me a certain psychological entrée into the sense and sensibility of Irish village life.[2] Once we arrived in the "back of beyond" of mountainous West Kerry, I felt the clanging of the consecration bells reverberate in my very bones. So, perhaps Bridget McCarthy was right, and I *had* "come home" after all. And research was just that, an act of recovery and rediscovery.

Similarly, I have often encountered the suspicion that an anthropological interest in madness must be derived from some prior personal trauma. It sometimes felt as if the only proper answer to the question, "Why schizophrenia?" would be an admission that I was a recovering schizophrenic myself. In these times of intense identity politics—so much at odds with the classical anthropological imagination—I recall the words of my early mentor, Hortense Powdermaker, who in her last public lecture in Berkeley, California, in May 1970 (she died in June), warned against what she saw as a new spirit of "cultural separatism" in research: The study of social groups or cultural minorities was encouraged only if conducted by members of the same group. Powdermaker reminded younger anthropologists that cross-cultural understanding was only a more complex and challenging version of understanding any other human being, including members of one's own family. We are always *others* to one another.[3] She advised younger anthropologists, like myself, to use their intuition—today we might say their "emotional intelligence"—in the field, but always disciplined by the practice of a critical self-analysis. Empathize freely, Powdermaker charged (1970), but remain ever vigilant against the dangers of countertransference and psychological projection, a difficult mandate and one I am not sure I have always lived up to.

Nonetheless, I did not go to Ireland with any intention of seeking out madness, i.e., schizophrenia in clinical jargon. At the time my primary research interest concerned another equally problematic issue, Irish sexuality and gender. I had an open field before me, so to speak. Very little cultural anthropology preceded this study. In addition to Conrad Arensberg's little gem, *The Irish Countryman* (1937), and Arensberg and Kimball's more empirical and prosaic *Family and Community in Ireland* (1940), there was John Messenger's controversial psychological portrait of the Aran Islanders, *Inis Beag* (1969), a book that alerted the Irish to a new danger: ethnography and anthropological writers. Robert Cresswell's *Une Communauté rurale de l'Irlande* (1969) introduced the subject of anomie and "cultural decline" in the west of Ireland and then, in 1974, just as I arrived in western Ireland, Hugh Brody's excellent monograph, *Inishkillane*, appeared, to be followed by Elliott Leyton's, *The One Blood* in 1975.[4] So, in addition to the small corpus of available anthropological writings, I steeped myself in Irish literature — from the novels of James Joyce and the plays of W. B. Yeats and J. M. Synge to the pastoral poetry of the young Seamus Heaney and Irish folklore and fairy tales.

Each ethnographer before me touched on a few generative cultural themes that I — perhaps somewhat uncritically — took up: decline and demoralization; late marriage, celibacy, and sexual abstinence; competition and conflicts over farm inheritance. Among these the so-called problem of Irish sexuality seemed most compelling. In rural Ireland, following and in response to the Great Famine (1845–1849) and up through the 1970s, Irish erotic culture seemed to go underground and a sexual amnesia to have settled into the bodies of a once wild and sensual people. To see what was denied, one need only dip into the corpus of early and early modern Irish poetry, preoccupied as it is with the fleshy life, with sex, human cruelty, love, birthing, and death.[5]

I wondered how Irish practices of sexual control and asceticism were taught and internalized so as to feel altogether normal, expected, and unremarkable. Trained in psychological/psychodynamic anthropology, I felt certain that the "antieroticism" of modern Ireland went against the grain and was extracted at high cost. Only a very powerful ideology and a severe socialization process would be capable of turning "raw" and wild Irish children into "cooked" docile and obedient adults willing to sacrifice themselves to the demands of family and community.

But certain serendipitous events altered the original focus of my study. We left for Ireland in early May 1974, a few days after a rash of IRA bombings in London. Fears of retaliatory bombings led our air carrier, Aer Lingus, to advise all families traveling with small children to deplane at

Shannon Airport rather than risk Dublin Airport, which was perceived as a likely target of retaliation. All my scholarly contacts, researchers attached to various medical and social and economic institutes, were in Dublin. But in my knapsack I found the name and address of a psychiatrist, David Dunne, the director of a psychiatric unit in a general hospital in Cork, who had been referred to me as an insightful therapist and as receptive to outsiders. Upon landing in Shannon we rented a small car and drove directly to Cork, where David graciously and spontaneously received us, babies and all. He was very much a family man himself.

Before the end of the day, Dunne had convinced me to shift the topic of my research. Handing me the latest Irish psychiatric hospital census (O'Hare and Walsh 1974), in which it was reported that the Irish have the highest "first admission" mental hospitalization rates—particularly for schizophrenia—in the world, Dunne coaxed: "You Americans are so obsessed with sex. Why not take a crack at *this* puzzle instead?" Although vaguely biological models of etiology dominated psychiatric thinking in Ireland then, as today, Dunne was one among a small but influential coterie of Irish psychiatrists with an interest in existential psychiatry, an influence of the writings and clinical practice of R. D. Laing, then at the Tavistock Institute in London.

Whatever the *ultimate* sources of Irish madness, Dunne suspected that social factors contributed to the overproduction of young adults in severe distress whose very real problems in living were perhaps too readily diagnosed as schizophrenia. People in certain social categories were particularly likely to be hospitalized: young and middle-aged bachelor farmers and bilingual Irish speakers from small villages along the rugged western coast of Ireland and, in particular, County Kerry, the very heartland of Celtic culture and civilization. What in the world, Dunne mused, was driving so many young Irish men and some young women to the brink of madness?

I took up Dunne's challenge and, armed only with the psychiatric hospital census, I arrived in the west of Ireland with a relatively straightforward research problem: What was going on in these idyllic, peaceful, bucolic villages that might be contributing to the excessive hospitalization? What were the particular stresses that afflicted certain high-risk groups, the young people, bachelor farmers, and so on? Were there aspects of Irish culture, family dynamics, religion, child rearing, and so on that were pathogenic? Granted, this was not a very flattering way to approach an alien culture. Alternatively, I wondered whether inflated hospitalization rates reflected a highly developed intolerance for bizarre, eccentric, or deviant behavior. Did the straight and narrow path in rural Ireland lead, for some, to a straitjacket?

Saints, Scholars, and Schizophrenics documents the uneven path I took to explore Irish madness from numerous and shifting vantage points, beginning with — and never straying very far from—the history and present-day experience of family and community survival strategies, a term that makes me a bit uncomfortable today. These strategies were produced in the context of English colonization and later forms of economic and cultural vassalage to Great Britain that not even the Irish land war of 1879–1883 or the political rebellion of 1916 and its aftermath have been able to destroy completely.[6] The survival of rural Catholic Ireland depended for generations on the forced emigration of surplus children from disadvantaged areas and on struggles between parents and adult children and among siblings over rights to land and responsibilities for the care of the old ones.

What follows are a few crib notes to help the reader navigate the original text by reference to some of the more dramatic changes that have occurred over the past quarter of a century in Irish social life and cultural identity, in psychiatry, and in anthropology and related disciplines. These should cast new light on some of my original descriptions and interpretations of rural Irish life and Irish madness.

The ethnohistorical traditions that I treat in chapter one, In Space and in Time, represent what remained in the mid–1970s of an exceedingly rich Celtic Irish aristocratic culture as it was imperfectly preserved, adapted, and transformed by a repeatedly colonized and disenfranchised Catholic peasantry. In the late nineteenth century this highly syncretic folk tradition was simultaneously rediscovered and reinvented by the Gaelic League (*Conradh na Gaeilge*), which tried to substitute images of rustic dignity and rural virtue for earlier stereotypes of rural Irish indolence, dirtiness, and brutality.

The leaders of the Gaelic Revival, a powerful social movement, elegized the simple beauty of whitewashed cottages, the versatility and richness of the Irish tongue, the cute wisdom embedded in traditional folklore, and the robust vigor (and sexual energy) contained in Irish step dancing and *ceili* music. In the early twentieth century these cultural representations of Mother Ireland fostered a powerful national political culture of resistance to British colonization.

In opening this book with reference to the material and symbolic icons of ancient Celtic culture and civilization still found in An Clochán, I may have fallen prey to the romantic bias of the ethnographers of Ireland since the days of Arensberg and Kimball in the 1930s: the search for an authentic Irish locale and authentic Irish voices, always to be found in such outposts on the fringes of the Atlantic as the Aran Islands, Tory Island, the west of Galway, the now depopulated Blasket Islands off the southwest coast of Kerry, and the Dingle Peninsula, which Lawrence Taylor (1996) has called the "Gaelic Ur-ground" (p. 216) and the "very heartland in the symbolic geography of Irish identity" (p. 219).

It never occurred to me, following earlier generations of anthropologists and Irish folklorists, to do anything but "go west," my movements dictated by an Irish collective unconscious, a symbolic march of the anthropological lemmings to the [Atlantic] sea. Of all possible Celtic fringe sites, the Dingle Peninsula represents "the west of the west" of Ireland and, in adopting the mood and the vocabulary of the Irish cultural nationalists, I could only perceive the west—that is, the *real* Ireland—as endangered, as a "world on the wane" and a way of life (as villagers often put it) "the likes of which shall never be seen again." Consequently, *Saints and Scholars* contributed to the national conversation about Irish cultural identity, even when it took the form of a dialogue *in opposition to* the interpretations of the anthropological "stranger," the "false friend" who "betrayed" them, that damn pencil-scratching, note-taking "Yank in the corner" (Viney 1983).[7]

Nothing in recent Irish history—as in the history of any other nation— has been unambiguous, and every struggle and every achievement had its price and its darker side. But it was that darker side, the vulnerable and soft underbelly, that I emphasized and that became the bone of angry contention. ("Why didn't you give us credit, girl, for what we did right?") Any anthropologist writing today would certainly have a great deal more to say about the history and experience of colonial and postcolonial relations in rural Ireland and about the signatures that that vexed history has left on the three bodies of Ireland: the lived, existential body self (and cultural self-identity); the representational body social; and the restless, champing-at-the-bit Irish national body politic. As a critical medical anthropologist today, I would put a great deal more emphasis on the cumulative effects of the Great Hunger (Kavanagh 1964) as a socially produced famine, the last straw, really, of British colonial history. It was the Black Famine that brought about the radical reorganization of rural Irish family life described in these pages as well as the diaspora that produced a far-flung and politically sophisticated global Irish culture abroad, but which left at home devastated, hollowed out rural communities that have never recovered.

What remains today of that romantic Celtic folk tradition in An Clochán? In the summer of 1999 one could hardly find a person willing to tell an old tale, recite a Celtic prayer, or sing the praises of good, strong poteen—homemade and illegal Irish whiskey. When one older woman was gently coaxed by a local friend into singing a few lively verses about "village slavery"—referring to the community work projects demanded of those villagers dependent on the dole or state pensions—her daughter-in-law interrupted the merriment, giving the singer a cool and pointed stare meant to dissuade her, while she fussed around the older woman, adjusting the doilies on the living room sofa. The verbal antics of the older generation are greatly out of step with the fiercely bourgeois requirements of the new dominant generation.

Later, when I made my surreptitious rounds of the graveyards in An Clochán, both old and new, to pay my respects to the only villagers who might have understood what I was about, then as well as now, I was brought up short by the absence of a familiar face—an ancient stone, the remains of the pagan Celtic god, Crom Dubh ("the dark, crooked one"), which had "forever" stood watch in the churchyard next to the ruins of a medieval

Artist's sketch of Crom Dubh's head. Until it was stolen from the "old graveyard" near the ruins of a medieval church in An Clochán, in August 1993, Crom Dubh's head was the only ancient Celtic stone carving discovered in the southwest of Ireland.

Crom Dubh ("the dark crooked one") was a pre-Christian god of the Irish Celts. Local people would kiss the stone to cure a toothache and the image was always visited during the rounds made in procession with the casket prior to burial and at the start of the annual pilgrimage to the summit of Mount Brandon that took place on Crom Dubh Sunday, part of the ancient festival of Lughnasa marking the beginning of the harvest. The pilgrimage wedded pagan and Christian traditions and Crom Dubh with Saint Brendan. One represented the creative forces of darkness, the other, of light; one wild and irrational, the other, tame and scholarly, but both remain the undisputed co-patron saints of An Clochán. (sketch by Eileen Hout)

church. Gone. Disappeared. "Presumed stolen," I was told later that evening by the husband of the owner of the cozy B&B where I was then staying. Crom Dubh gone? Just now when I *most* needed him? "What?" asked a curious villager. "Yes, *now* of all times and with me suffering the worst toothache of my adult life!" [8]

The view presented in chapter two, "The People Left Behind," of Ballybran as a microcosm of a dying Ireland can be corrected, as it were, in various ways, but especially by reference to the Irish diaspora. For "She, Mag, Ireland" — as I had called her in my prologue — did not so much expire as become transmogrified into all those cheeky young Irish men and women in exile, the map of Ireland imprinted on their faces, who have made their way up the various social, religious, political, and economic ladders of St. John's,

Newfoundland, Toronto, Sydney, and Cape Town, not to mention Montauk, Long Island, Cairo, and Catskill, New York, and even Shamrock, Texas, a truly God-forsaken town in the Panhandle where my family and I, while crossing the United States in a battered and tattered Volkswagen bus, were nearly blown to smithereens by a relentless Chinook wind in the mid–1980s. "Welcome to Shamrock—your

> *Keep yours dirty tongue off Ireland! You're a fine one to sneer with the map of it on your face!*
> —EUGENE O'NEILL,
> *Long Day's Journey Into Night*

home away from the 'Old Sod'" the local billboard announced as we drove into the nearest KOA campground ("Home at last!").

A map of Ireland that doesn't include all its "elsewheres," suggests O'Toole (1998) is hardly worth anything because it "leaves out the places where Ireland is always landing and returning from" (p. 5). The people and the land are no longer coterminous and "the lie of the land is that there *is a place* [at all] called 'Ireland' inhabited by the Irish people . . . [when] over the past 150 years much of [Irish history] has happened elsewhere . . . The central fact of that culture is that it knows no borders . . . it is porous and diffuse" (ibid., 4). And so, the death of rural Ireland that I describe here has been accompanied by the rebirth of Ireland (and Irish culture, language, ethos, and values) elsewhere and "off island," the ultimate postmodern paradox.

A second correction, however, is that not everything about life in Bally-bran/An Clochán, even in 1974–1975, was sad, demoralized, and anomic. But the few spaces of vitality, passion, and camaraderie were largely channeled into covert activities on behalf of the local IRA. In my erasure of this vital feature of local social and political life I joined a long (and distinguished) tradition of anthropological ostriches, beginning with Robert Redfield, who weathered the Mexican revolution in Tepotzlan without writing a word about it, lest it disrupt his description of a placid, harmonious peasant village, and including Conrad Arensberg, who failed to address the events of the Easter Rising and the effects of the new Irish Free State on his static portrayal of the timeless Irish countrymen of Clare. There is, it seems, a tradition among anthropologists that Orin Starn (1992) has somewhat playfully described as "missing the revolution."

In this instance, the missing was in part intentional, a self-blinding meant to protect the cover of local activists in the community, some of whom were operating very close to where we lived. It has taken me more than two decades to confront acts of overt political violence (see Scheper-Hughes 1994, 1995, 1999) as an anthropological subject that, given my choice of early field sites — Ireland in the mid–1970s and Brazil during the military years — must have also required a massive dose of denial. While studying the madness of everyday life in Ballybran, and primarily concerned with *interior* spaces and with the small dark psychodramas of scapegoating and labeling within farm households that was driving so many young bachelors to drink and bouts of depression and rage, I paid scant attention to the mundane activities of the neighbor from whom we rented our cottage and who used our attic to store a small arsenal of guns and explosives that he and a few of his comrades were running to Northern Ireland.

In reviewing, for example, the original responses to the Thematic Apperception Test (TAT) in preparation for a talk a few years ago, I noted a subtext that I had overlooked: the many asides and fleeting references to killing, guns, and political violence, as in the following responses [emphasis supplied] to the blameless and innocent card number 1, the image of a young boy and a violin:

This boy is pondering over a . . . *can it be a gun?* And he's very . . . he's in another world altogether, not really here at all. [Girl, age 17]

This is a little boy and he is trying to play *some kind of game with a gun.* [Village girl, age 15]

A studious boy who is thinking about all the people who were killed in this way. [Village boy, age 16]

Why, *he is dead in thought.* What's this? A gun? . . . I'm in spirit with him. And what is that article? It has me baffled. *Is that a skull there?* Perhaps *it might be a gun and he sees death or life in it.* [Older village woman]

I think this young boy is *thinking about shooting with a gun* or something. Is that a gun? [Me, "Anything you like."] Yes, a gun, I think. He will go out and kill some birds. [Middle-aged bachelor, hospitalized]

I left unexamined the possible links between the political violence in the North and the tortured family dramas in West Kerry that I so carefully documented and which certainly had a violence of their own. It now seems that some, even passing, reference to those activities — of which some villagers are very proud — would have modified the unremitting images of demoralization and anomie.

Meanwhile, the economic climate in Ireland has been subject to many fluctuations over the past few decades. In 1974–1975 when the research for this book was being conducted, there were real grounds for pessimism in Ballybran as in Ireland at large. Soon after Ireland reluctantly joined the European Economic Community in 1973, the global oil crisis caused havoc throughout the world and Ireland was especially hard hit. Inflation, recession, high interest rates, reduced work weeks, widespread layoffs were commonplace. There were many strikes; dissatisfaction was rife; the cost of living soared. The rural Irish, in particular, felt as though they had been sold down the river, instructed to retire and sell off their idle properties to make way for agricultural capitalism. In 1978 the then Taoiseach (prime minister) of Ireland, Jack Lynch, stated that his government did not deserve to be reelected if it allowed the unemployment level to rise to a hundred thousand, but by the mid–1980s Ireland had to accommodate itself to a level more than twice that. In 1993 registered unemployment for the first time surpassed three hundred thousand or 21 percent of the labor force (Sweeney 1998; Kennedy 1993). Keiran Raymond Crotty, who gave up farming in Kilkenny to become an influential angricultural economist and rural development specialist, could launch a book as late as 1986 decrying the devastating effects of "colonialist underdevelopment" in an Ireland that he described as "in deep crisis."

Then, suddenly, in the mid–1990s, the logjam broke and things began to move very quickly. Employment soared, property values increased, and money, for the first time, became plentiful. An Irish "economic miracle" unleashed the so-called Celtic Tiger[9] and Ireland began to show signs of becoming the single greatest beneficiary of the European Community. At the time of this writing Ireland leads all the Community member nations in almost every economic sphere; Irish growth rates, averaging 7.5 percent in the late 1990s, are the highest. Over two hundred thousand new jobs were created in Ireland between 1994 and 1999. National interest rates are low, industrial production is booming, foreign investment has grown considerably, and living standards have risen rapidly (see Sweeny 1998, chapter 1). With a substantial drop in birthrates, Ireland's living standards will soon exceed those of Britain.

Unprecedented prosperity and a self-conscious materialism have followed as Ireland, once the remote and stand-offish "western island," joined Europe, eventually shedding its ambivalent economic dependency on Britain. The changes are dramatic and striking. Rather than exporting her children and future workers, Ireland has become a receiving nation to a great many foreign guest workers, political asylum seekers, and economic refugees, who have been drawn to the country by its reputation for tolerance, its newfound prosperity, and the growth of Irish industry, especially electronics, pharmaceuticals, and computer technology. Ireland became known among many political and economic refuge-seekers from Asia and Africa — largely through contacts with Irish Catholic missionaries in the third world — as a nation of relative equality, nonracialism, and compassion (Valarasan-Toomey 1998, chapter 7). So, today Ireland, too, must deal with being a multiracial, multicultural nation and accept that bilingualism may refer to French, German, or Wolof as the second language rather than to the special status of Irish.

The shifts in Ireland's economic fortunes have been accompanied by equally dramatic political and social changes, including the signing of the Northern Irish Peace Accords, the acceptance of Sinn Fein, the political wing of the Irish Republican Army, as a legitimate political party, the growth of environmentalism and the electoral strength of the Green Party, the democratic expansion and extension of university education to working-class youths and, most notably, the decline in the once-dictatorial power of the Irish Catholic Church. With the legalization of divorce and birth control, the growth of feminist and gay social movements in urban areas, and the secularization of daily life in both rural and urban areas, a throughly Europeanized Ireland has emerged.[10] Only the continued ban on abortion remains a heavily defended vestige of the old, relatively culturally isolated, Catholic Ireland.

Whether these positive (not just economic) changes will be sustained over time and what they will mean for the west of Ireland beyond the proliferation of vacation homes and singing pubs to serve foreign tourists remains to be seen. But, once the last piece of good pasture land is sold off and developed for tourism, the ultimate renewable resource of the countryside has been spent. So far, in An Clochán there is little evidence of the promised expansion of a revitalized and capitalized agriculture. There is some talk of reforestation subsidies through the European Union and the potential commercial prospects but, in fact, very few young people in the current generation have taken up farming or related rural occupations and those who have explain their choice as a temporary, stopgap measure.

Declan is a case in point. After completing high school in Ballybran in the mid–1970s, young Declan joined his cohort in leaving the village. Some went on to university, others found work elsewhere in urban Ireland, America, or the United Kingdom. Declan had sheep farming in his bones and he went off to Australia to pursue his dream there. A few years ago he returned, lured back by the promise of EC subsidies for sheep. A more romantic and solitary figure would be hard to find as at dusk each evening Declan jumps from his tractor and orders his sheepdogs to round up the recalcitrant herd grazing on a lovely stretch of pastureland in the center of the village. But the young man is a realist for all that. When the subsidy goes, he will go too, he says. And that day is fast approaching. Economic miracle or not, one still cannot survive as a working farmer in Ballybran/An Clochán.

▪ Schizophrenia — The Irish Malady?

More than one reader of *Saints, Scholars, and Schizophrenics* has suggested that, despite its provocative title, one should not be misled—this is a book about rural Ireland, not about schizophrenia. They are correct. It is a book about the state of rural Ireland in the mid–1970s, written from the point of view of some of its casualties and, therefore, through the prism of disappointment, sadness, anger, and madness; about Ireland then "as told" by those for whom the costs of loyalty to family and village — of staying behind—proved very high, indeed.

In the 1960s, when the Irish government began to pay close attention for the first time to the rates and treatment of mental disorders (Healy 1994:15), it came as a shocking revelation to discover such a high proportion of rural Irish showing up in the mental hospital registers, the majority burdened with the heavy and discrediting label of schizophrenia pinned to their medical charts. As one Finbar McTernan, a middle-aged Irish Catholic so-called schizophrenic told the young anthropologist Jamie Saris a few years ago: "We are, in fact, the lowest, on the lowest rung of society there is. Even the really mentally handicapped people . . . are more appealing to people . . . and [people think that] manic-depressives are all geniuses . . . [while] the attitude people have to lunatics or schizophrenics is that, you know, they are dangerous, they're sort of . . . horrible" (1995: 43).

The statistical evidence indicating a possible Irish vulnerability to schizophrenia was treated in the Irish media throughout the late 1970s and 1980s as an embarrassing national scandal, a stain on the national and cultural identity. The data seemed to confirm ancient folk beliefs and stereotypes of mad Ireland. Some of the earliest Gaelic poems and legends refer to a kind of madness that afflicted those who went into battle, a kind of premodern Post-Traumatic Stress Disorder (PTSD) as it were. The *Buile Suibhne*, for example, an early Irish epic poem (first translated by J. G. O'Keefe for the Irish Texts Society in 1913 and much later by Seamus Heaney in a graceful version under the title *Sweeny Astray*) treats the legend of King Sweeny, who went mad at the battle of Moiar in 637 and who was subsequently transformed into a bird—free, mad, and exiled—by a curse laid on his head. Western County Kerry, in particular, had long carried the stigmatizing designation as the "glen of the madmen." It was into this cultural, political, and emotional context that my study of Irish madness was problematically inserted.

Although biomedical models of mental illness predominated, when I set to work in the mid–1970s it was still not automatically thought by Irish psychiatrists and country people that *every* form of mental distress was rooted in biology, in "bad genes" or "faulty wiring." Madness was also understood socially in terms of the relative deprivation, poverty, and social isolation characteristic of rural, western Ireland at that time. Some, both specialists and laymen, believed that generations of emigration had siphoned off the cream and left behind a "weaker" and "vulnerable" population. It was oft noted that older people from rural areas—especially those without claims to a strong network of kin —were sometimes "put away" permanently in the "madhouse" in order to free their land and farm holdings to distant relations. More frequently, the unattached elderly were seasonally warehoused in mental asylums ("wintering out") and then returned home in summer to lend a hand with farm chores. The expansion of modern health and welfare programs into the west of Ireland at midcentury were seen as destroying traditional forms of care and support for the elderly, the frail, and the psychologically vulnerable, leading to their otherwise avoidable hospitalization.

So, when I approached the personable director of St. Finan's mental hospital in Killarney with my proposal to study a small number of young schizophrenics through open-ended, conversational interviews and storytelling through the TAT, I was well received and given access to patients and even some staff collaboration in conducting part of my research there. *Saints, Scholars, and Schizophrenics* was the first ethnographic study in Ireland to explore the meanings of *going* and *being* mad by moving between asylum and village. I hardly realized then how daunting it would be to develop empathic rapport with institutionalized people who, in addition to being cognitively and emotionally different, were also suffering from personal histories of profound social rejection. I learned to slow down, to be comfortable with long silences, and to communicate solidarity by merely standing by and being willing to be present in an undemanding way.[11] Communication once removed, through drawings and TAT pictures, proved to be an ideal medium, for which I am thankful to George DeVos. "If nothing else," DeVos said jocularly in urging me to take a set of TAT cards along to the field, "they break the ice. They give you and the people you want to get to know better something to do."

I share with the Italian psychiatrist, Franco Basgalia (see Scheper-Hughes and Lovell 1987), an understanding of madness as a polymorphic phenomenon that should not be reduced to a medical problem alone. Even if most mental illness proved to be biological at its base, it is devastatingly social in its consequences. It made sense to refer, as Dr. Basaglia had, to the "disease and its double" (ibid., chapter 3). The "master" psychiatric problems such as schizophrenia or deep depression inevitably produce a double in the social relations that cluster around the disease —all the layers of social rejection, exclusion, marginalization, isolation, confinement, and experimental and sometimes painful medical treatments. While we are waiting for the elusive biological key to schizophrenia to materialize, it seems reasonable for cultural anthropologists to continue to try to understand the double, the social dis-ease that is at times difficult to distinguish from the original disease. The mentally ill in any society give the anthropologist a privileged vantage point. One way of learning rather quickly about the nature of any society is to pay attention to its human refuse — the people who get rubbished (see Scheper-Hughes 1997b) —and to how and why they are defined and treated in that way.

Rural Ireland in the 1970s was a place where it was rather difficult to be altogether sane. Indeed, the responses of average and normal villagers to the TAT often seemed more deviant than those given by the various social misfits institutionalized in St. Finan's. In An Clochán even rather marked eccentricity was allowable and sometimes coddled, especially if it could pass as harmless tomfoolery or came wrapped in the mantle of Irish asceticism or Catholic spirituality.

I think back, for example, to a particularly haunting story once told by locals in what was then still the small village of Dingle (see McCabe 1980). It concerned an odd fellow who had moved in the 1970s into a remote hamlet on the outskirts of town. He was a ventriloquist who had for many years traveled with a small rural circus in the company of his wooden dummy. A neighbor commented: "Every day your man would go into the village with his motorbike about ten in the morning. He'd go into the village shop and he would buy just one thing. And that was the smallest can of the smallest peas that the shop sold. He would tie this onto the back of his motorbike and bring it back to the cottage." Of course, people watched him and they wondered among themselves what a man like him would be wanting with a small can of peas each day. "We all got used to him. And all of the villagers would wait along the road to see if the can of peas was strapped as usual to the motorbike and they remarked daily how much the man likes his peas."

The man never talked to anyone very much though he was said to have a pleasant enough smile. Then one day he was riding his motorbike and was killed instantly by a large delivery truck. One of the women reported: "Since he seemed to have no friends or relatives, ourselves and the rest of the villagers went down to the cottage to sort things out and pack up his belongings. In the kitchen we found hundreds of unopened small cans of small peas." And next to the cans in the kitchen cabinet was the little wooden dummy, sure enough, that had for so many years made a living for the old ventriloquist. One wonders what the man said to his dummy when he fed him with a can of peas that he would not be able to eat. But he died alone and very quickly so that the mystery of his life vanished along with him. And he was, the poor saint, soon forgotten.

An Clochán, across Connor Pass from Dingle, also had its share of saints, those odd but cherished mountain people who often lived alone, following (people would sometimes say) the hermit's calling, often forgetting ("poor creatures") to mind the body, to eat, or to bathe, and to take proper care of the self while doting on their favorite cows. The relations of some of the older bachelors of Ballynalacken hamlet toward their cows—the lavish and personalized care shown to them as if they were extended family members — is perhaps characteristic of herders and pastoralists everywhere. One thinks, for example, of the East African cattle complex, referring to a close identification with the creatures that is not too far removed from attitudes in these parts of mountainous West Kerry.

There was Michael, for example, who after the death of his old mother had virtually moved into the barn to keep his cows company, praying aloud and singing lullabies to them through the night. And there was Conor and his brother who took turns "standing the cows" in the evening, as vigilant as Biblical shepherds watching over their flocks by night although, in the back of beyond of Ballynalacken, it was hard to imagine what danger lurked to threaten the existence of those dumb animals. Down the road a piece, Jack, much doted on by villagers despite his ferocious pack of near-wild sheep-dogs, doted in turn on his small herd of "thieving cows" that respected no man's stone boundaries.

As I did the rounds of Balynalacken in 1999 in the company of Aiden, a village mentor and retired schoolmaster, I found that Michael was long since dead. But "Jack," his neighbor, was at home, hardly changed at all over these past twenty-five years, and still surrounded by his pack of snarling dogs that greeted us by jumping and knocking themselves against the car, snapping at the tires and threatening us from the other side of our quickly rolled-up windows. Aiden was unsure of what to do when Jackaleen (little Jack) himself came out, angrily brandishing his walking stick at the dogs or at us. "Away! Away!" he said, approaching our vehicle until his pale narrow face and watery, cloudy blue eyes were at the car window. Though very nearly blind, the old fellow recognized me right off. "I do think that I know ye, girl!" he said, sounding very much like an accuser. "Tell him who you are! Tell him," Aiden prompted. But before I could say anything Jack had already guessed: "Is it Nancy? And how's himself? How's your Michael? The babas are all grown, I suppose?"

From the safety of the car, we queried Jack about his and his animals' well being. "The cows are not still bedding down in your kitchen?" asked Aiden. "No, they are *not!*," Jack replied, offended. "There's been *no more* of that. Not at all." "Did you go out and vote today, my man?" asked the schoolmaster teasingly. "I did. I did. And before you ask me, I hope I still have the right to a secret ballot," the old man chided as he waved us off with another flourish of his staff. Later I learned that Jack had not only brought his cows into his large, barnlike kitchen to "winter out" close to the hearth, but also when a couple of the animals had died there, little Jack, lacking the strength to move them, had simply made do, continuing his daily life around the remains until the neighbors notified public health officials. To guard against any future incidents, the public health nurse had a turnstile installed inside Jack's front door so that his cows – even the skinniest of them – could not get in and out of the house.

Then, at the sturdy farmhouse of the brothers, Conor and Derek, the story was told of the night some ten years earlier when, while both men were sound asleep, thieves broke into the house making off with several thousand Irish pounds that the brothers had carefully saved and stashed away for their old age. The theft seemed to mock the brothers' pointless hypervigilance that had consigned one or the other to guard duty night after night for so many years. Not a hair on the hide of one of the precious animals had been touched, but the brothers' entire fortune was whisked away from right under their noses. Ah, the misery of it all, agreed Conor, shaking his gray head while feeding the smallest piece of turf into the smallest fire that gave off the barest bit of light and warmth in his traditional kitchen-hearth room. "But sure it made TV stars of you," teased the former schoolmaster, referring to a news feature about the theft that led to the brothers being flown to Dublin to tell their story to the nation on the celebrated Saturday night Gaye Burne show. "And, I believe, some marriage offers came in after that show," joked Aiden. The painfully shy bachelor blushed and retreated into himself as I remember his doing so often in the old days whenever the subject turned dangerously close to marriage or women.

We also stopped at the homestead of Jeremy and his old Aunt Maire who, senile and querulous in 1974, was *still* senile and querulous in 1999, only more so. Jeremy, the good son and devoted nephew, was still taking care of her though at the time of my visit he was busy preparing for a flight to New York City with some local lads to help celebrate the wedding of a former villager. It would be his first real voyage out of County Kerry. Aunt Maire suspected something, and she was mightily distraught. "They've all gone! All gone!" she yelled anxiously at us, as if we were as deaf as she. "Where's Jeremy? Where's Jeremy?" she repeated incessantly. Though we tried to reassure her that her nephew would be gone from her side only very briefly, the old woman shook her head and called after us as we left, "They'll poison me yet!"

* * *

Since the first publication of *Saints* there have been two decades of debates over the validity and reliability of the Irish psychiatric hospital statistics showing an excessive case load for schizophrenia in the Irish population (see Torrey et al. 1984; Keatinge 1987; Waddington and Youssef 1994; Ni Nuallain, O'Hare, and Walsh 1987; Kendler et al. 1993; Torrey 1994; Walsh 1994; Walsh and Kendler 1995). Most significantly, key staff of the Irish Health Research Board, Aileen O'Hare, Mairin Ni Nuallain, and

Dr. Dermot Walsh, coauthors of the annual (1977, 1978, 1979, 1980, and 1981) reports on the *Activities of Irish Psychiatric Hospitals*, disowned their own statistics, which I had used as my statistical baseline, referring to them as false and misleading.

The Irish researchers had come to realize that first-admission rates for schizophrenia —supposedly referring to the number of people hospitalized for a first episode of illness—were unreliable. Irish medical directors tended to overdiagnose schizophrenia and many hospital administrators would interpret a first admission to mean first admission to *their* hospital whether or not the patient been previously hospitalized elsewhere. Incidence was confused with prevalence. Meanwhile, more recent psychiatric hospital censuses were beginning to show a steady decline in new admissions for schizophrenia, which is not surprising given the Irish government's new policy of deinstitutionalization, which began to take effect in the 1980s (Smyth et al. 1997).[12] Dermot Walsh and his colleagues at the Irish Medico-Social Research Institute in Dublin noted that medical and social science researchers from Europe and the United States (myself included) had long attempted to demonstrate high rates of insanity among the Irish, beginning with Malzberg and Lee's epidemiological data (1956) showing excessively high admission rates of Irish immigrants to New York State hospitals at the turn of the century.[13] Was there an unconscious bias against the Irish at work in these studies of Irish insanity?

My own conclusions as reported here confirm, and I like to think, contributed to Walsh and O'Hare's later rethinking. Schizophrenia was, I argued, a label too readily affixed to patients suffering from transient psychoses. At the time of my original study, the revised Present State Exam (used in Britain) and the American DSM-III (Diagnostic and Statistical Manual), which established more rigorous criteria for psychiatric diagnoses, especially for schizophrenia, had not yet appeared. The deinstitutionalization policy had yet to challenge the long-standing tradition of warehousing the unwanted. But the "labeling" process had its origins not so much in diagnostic manuals or in anti-Irish bias but in the moral judgments of Irish villagers who were willing to consign large numbers of troublesome and surplus people — especially bachelors, single women, disinherited sons, and the unattached elderly — to a variety of total institutions (Goffman 1961) from the workhouses of the mid- nineteenth century to the Catholic seminaries and convents that proliferated after the Great Famine in the late nineteenth century to the district mental hospitals and Church-run special institutions for the "mentally handicapped" and the "infirm" that emerged in the early twentieth century.[14]

Meanwhile, the regimen of early child rearing (as described in chapter five) contributed to patterns of adult behavior that lead to considerable social isolation. I described, for example, the tendency among villagers to avoid touch and to react to hurt, disappointment, and anger by withdrawal and denial, evasiveness in speech, and defensiveness in body language and posture. While this rural Irish propensity is perhaps well adapted to the lives of future priests and nuns, monks and scribes, and to certain hermetic bachelor farmers, it was destructive to more physically and emotionally expressive villagers, some of whom (like the village bachelor and sexual outlaw who had exposed himself on a parish hall dancefloor in a fit of sexual frustration) became ready candidates for the mental hospital. Once institutionalized, they would tend to remain there, their numbers growing over time. The social immaturity and dependency of rural Ireland's surplus males contributed to their long-term institutionalization as did Irish Catholic values of monastic asceticism. Hence, the saints, scholars (and schizophrenics) of my impolitic but apt title.

Despite a more critical and discerning view of Irish mental hospital statistics, there is still evidence of excessive mental suffering in rural, western Ireland (as there is, also, in rural Finland, Norway, and Sweden) that cannot be explained away as an artifact of sampling or other deficiencies in the statistical data. Obviously, public records of any kind — including hospital census data — are not pure, accurate, or objective sources of information Nor are they politically, let alone scientifically neutral. Public records and the statistical inferences drawn from them are less mirrors of reality than filters and collective representations. At best, official records and national statistics reveal a society's particular system of classification and some of its basic values. Reality is always more complex, contradictory, and elusive than our limited and partial theoretical models and methods allow. Quantitative data needs validation and contextualization through qualitative methods that are more sensitive to the actual lived social reality. Here the interpretive method — an "epidemiology without numbers" (see Almeida Filho 1989; Scheper-Hughes 1997a) — is invaluable.

The everyday experience of mental and social suffering can best be gleaned through participatory immersion in the very scenes and spaces where psychiatric labeling originates and by documenting, not only the individual life histories of distress and dis-ease but also the stories of ordinary people — the village folk demographers and organic epidemiologists — who take part in the practical calculations around marriage, reproduction, education, and farm inheritance that take into account evidence of family histories of mental stability or instability.

As a village demographer and "clerk of the records" (see Scheper-Hughes 1992: 26-30), I had gathered enough stories and been present at enough family and community crises to know what a great many ordinary village genealogists knew without ever going to the university — that something was gravely amiss. There were too many psychological tragedies to be accounted for, some taking the form of madness ("schizophrenia"), a greater number expressed in deep clinical depressions and, in more recent years, a shocking number of young adult suicides. There was trouble in the system, a very nervous system, indeed (see Taussig 1992).

Beneath the quaint thatched roofs of the rural farmhouses an extraordinary drama of masked violence and sacrifice was taking place. Up through the 1950s, when family farming was still a valued and productive way of life, the firstborn son would have inherited the farm. By the time I arrived in An Clochán the first born were being reared for export and rural parents were faced with a new problem: how to retain at least one son for the farm and for the care of themselves in their dotage. The new family selections paradoxically privileged the firstborn children by *disinheriting* them, thereby allowing them to leave the village with honor, and victimized the designated heirs in relegating them to the status of pathetic leftovers and stay-at-homes, good enough for the village, a place not then generally thought of as very good at all.

This family dynamic (as described in chapter six) involved considerable

A *much loved neighbor from Ballynalacken warms himself by the tiniest of turf fires to chase away the damp and gloom of a cool morning in the summer of 1999.*

symbolic violence: a cutting down to size of the designated farm heir; a sacrifice of his manhood and reproductivity to permanent celibacy, and exploitation of his labor. All this was accomplished silently and through considerable shaming and ridicule toward these captive men. The moral economy of farm inheritance constituted what Pierre Bourdieu (1977) would have called a "bad faith economy," one based on lies and secrets and concealing the true state of affairs. "Blessed are the meek," it is written, "for they shall inherit the earth." And with it, too, I was tempted to add, a life of involuntary poverty, chastity, and obedience, a monastic and saintly life, but without any recognition of the sacrifice that was entailed.

The situation I described here was similar to that, described by Pierre Bourdieu (1962, 1989), of the bachelor peasants of the Béarn, his own home region of France. Bourdieu once recalled a simple village scene — a small dance on Christmas Eve in a rural tavern — that had haunted him for more than thirty years. Later, he reflected: "I witnessed a very stunning scene: young men and women from nearby towns were dancing in the middle of

Two generations—alone together. Outside An Clochán, 1979

the ballroom while another group of older [local village] youths, about my age at the time, all still bachelors, were standing idly on the sides. Instead of dancing, they were intensely scrutinizing the hall and, unconsciously, moving forward so that they were progressively shrinking the space used by the dancers" (Bourdieu and Waquant 1992: 163). The resentment of the village bachelors who had been sidelined at the dance (as in life) spilled over into their angry, nonverbal challenge to the "townie" dancers.

The spurned rural farm heirs of the Béarn, like the bachelor farmers of An

Clochán, both once privileged under an earlier system of primogeniture, suddenly found themselves victims of their privilege, fated to permanent bachelorhood and virtually, in Bourdieu's terms, forbidden to reproduce. At the time of his observation this situation was still new and viewed by older villagers as "scandalous" and profoundly sad. Why were local village girls fleeing the countryside? Why couldn't a handsome young farmer find a wife? What was so wrong with settling into a nicely arranged marriage on a small but comfortable farm?

The aggressive behavior of the village bachelors at the tavern dance was, in effect, a symbolic protest against the new matrimonial market that had emerged among the emancipated factory workers from nearby towns. The older, rural system of matchmaking, controlled by the elders, had since given way to a free market in which young men were now expected to manage their own marital and reproductive affairs counting on their own personal assets including their symbolic capital: the ability to dress, to dance, to present oneself, to talk to girls, and so on. The new system had almost completely disenfranchised the rural class of shy bachelors who had always depended on intermediaries to arrange their personal and romantic affairs.

The transition from arranged marriages to free exchange signaled the demise of an entire class of small peasant farmers that the French state, beginning soon after World War II, was actively trying to eliminate through various modernization projects (Bourdieu and Waquant 1992: 165). Although this war on the class of peasant farmers was accomplished without overt violence and bloodshed, the brutality of the process was grasped intuitively by the young anthropologist who observed with mounting horror the shame and impotent rage of the bachelor wallflowers sidelined at that poignant Christmas Eve dance in the Béarn.

He wept for all that would no longer happen.
He wept for his mother making potato fritters.
He wept for her pruning roses in the garden.
He wept for his father shouting.
He wept for never being able to leave the farm for a single day.
He wept for the farm where there were no children.
He wept for the hay, still to be brought in.
He wept for the forty-two years that had gone by, and he wept for himself.
—JOHN BERGER,
Once in Europa

In a nutshell this was also the situation of the young, angry bachelors of An Clochán.[15] Still, one is often struck by the resilience of the human spirit despite the violence that culture and society visit upon it. And there were some compensations and rewards for those who stayed behind and who were recognized as dutiful, loyal saints: "Sure, Paddy's a saint the way he takes care of his old mother." A great many bachelor farmers adjusted quite well, thank you, to the new system, making their daily little accommodations to it without complaint. Others, a minority, could not bring themselves to do so and, over time, they grew into angry, isolated, hurt, and bitter individuals, cut off from the flow of human life. Some of these became the depressed and alcoholic bachelor farmers who populated the several village pubs that catered to the village; others become the saintly hermits who retreated to their barns and sought companionship in their dogs and cows; still others became mental patients at St. Finan's hospital, men who were often obsessed with paranoid fears of bodily encroachment or possessed by unfulfilled and unruly sexual and generative needs and fantasies.

It was never my intention to point a finger or to blame individual parents or households for what was clearly a collective social tragedy. I had hoped only to bring out of the shadows a hidden dimension of social life and to prick the defenses of the rural Irish collective unconscious so that, once a harmful rural family dynamic was recognized, the emancipation of its victims — the good sons of An Clochán — could be imagined. Although motivated by an admittedly odd identification and solidarity with the lonely bachelors of Ballynalacken, Ballyguin, Clonshurach, Faha, Lisnakealwee, Mulloch, and all the other almost vanished hamlets of An Clochán, my attempt at "writing against violence" had a violence of its own. Blinded by an overinvestment in the subject, I was unable to anticipate the effects my words might have on some of those same young men and women who recognized their lives and could now clearly see the nature of their dilemma, thus exacerbating their sense of entrapment in a no-exit, double-binding situation. Insight without the power to change the conditions of one's existence is cruel indeed.

Two young villagers among several who took their lives in recent years — and here my discussion shall necessarily be circumspect — exemplify the entrapment to which I am alluding. We knew "Maureen" as well as we knew anyone in the village, she being our children's daytime baby-sitter throughout the fall and winter of 1974–1975. A buxom and handsome young woman of seventeen with a ready laugh and bright blue eyes that would flash with indignation at a perceived slight or insult, Maureen was a graduating senior of the local high school and a champion *camogie* (Irish field hockey) player. Maureen stood out among her peers for her ability to speak her mind directly and to express her feelings freely. She was highly principled, a devout Catholic, and a Pioneer for Total Abstinence (from alcohol), and yet she was, at times, quite impulsive. She could quite suddenly break away from a gaggle of giggling school girls or jump from the school bus without warning even if it meant walking some six or seven miles to her distant home by herself.

At the time we knew her, Maureen was hopelessly in love with a shy and inarticulate village artisan. She did her best to engage "Fintan" in small talk and to prod him toward initiating a dating relationship, but the young man always looked slightly terrified when Maureen, bouncing one of our babies on each hip, would approach him at his workplace. She asked my advice on several occasions: Should she stay here in the "back of beyond" waiting for the lad of her dreams to notice her and respond appropriately, or should she follow her teachers' and her mother's advice and seek out her fortunes elsewhere? She was scheduled to enter nurses training at an English hospital after the new year.

I don't remember how I advised her but I understood both her attraction to, and frustration with, the dark-eyed country lad who was utterly lacking in what Bourdieu would have called the necessary "social capital" to participate in the "dating game" of the new matrimonial market. Paralyzed with shyness, Fintan withdrew ever more deeply into the cocoon of his workshop, and Maureen finally threw up her hands and left for England in the spring of 1975. We communicated for a while through chatty letters and it seemed that she was enjoying her new life away from the village. But then the letters stopped arriving and news about the young woman came from others in the village. It was said that she had suffered a bad period of homesickness, that she was deeply depressed and had stopped eating. The diagnosis of anorexia nervosa was new to villagers, and one that made little sense to them. "Why, she was such a great big lovely girl altogether. What would make her do that to herself?"

When Maureen returned to Ireland after a period of hospitalization abroad she was, villagers said, utterly changed: her strong, athletic limbs were wasted and her demeanor was strange. She sometimes dressed inappropriately in flamboyant clothing and she wore too much makeup. She laughed and cried without rhyme or reason. "The poor girl just lost her level-headed self," an older villager commented sadly. "And we no longer knew how to reach her." Her lonely death when it finally came was not a great surprise, though none the less mourned for that.

The suicide of young "James" a few years later, however, sent out shock waves that reverberate to this day. An elder son in a large and talented family, James was neither the best of scholars nor was he drawn to farming or to the small family shop, which was left to a younger brother. So, after leaving school and floundering for a bit, James fell into the role of village hackney (taxi-van) driver, ferrying people back and forth to Dingle and Tralee markets on Saturdays and to Mass on Sundays. Soon he was also the school bus driver carrying students to and from the small high school that served the rural families of the peninsula. James's maroon van was a fixture in the area and people thought that, after all, he had settled nicely into his local niche. He was a bit of a rebel, however, and wore his hair long and bushy, a local Bob Dylan, and dressed in the style of British and American hippies. He was popular with the lads and had his circle of young cronies at a village pub. But as more and more of his friends moved on and out of the village to make their fortunes elsewhere, James harbored deep resentments, feeling that life had passed him by while favoring his outward-bound friends and siblings.

In the months before his death James spoke often of having been an unfavored child. His life, so limited in comparison with that of his vanishing cohort, seemed to be going nowhere and he feared becoming a clownish sort of village mascot. Sometimes, during a night of heavy drinking at a local pub, James would threaten suicide, but his friends discounted his words as "rubbish" brought on by the drink and would do their best to cheer him up. On the evening that James did take his life —the day before the beginning of the new school year when, villagers say, he should have been home polishing his van — he treated his friends to a few extra rounds at the pub, telling them to remember him after he was gone, a story they had heard once too often.

Then James went home, played with his dog, teasing him with a little bean-bag frog that was the animal's favorite toy, and stepped inside the old van that had increasingly defined the parameters of his existence. In that van—inherited from his father who had once used it to carry his mother, a local midwife, to her deliveries—James delivered himself to the other side. In his hand was the dog's toy frog.

Leaving and staying home both carry risks for the young adults of An Clochán, caught between old and new social systems and moral economies and between conflicting interpretations of the values of autonomy, industry, intimacy, and generativity. James's story resonates with similar ones in John Berger's collection of vignettes and short stories about the vagaries of love in a peasant community, *Once in Europa* (1983). In recent decades, depression (sometimes resolved in suicide) has become the symptom of choice among young adults in distress, not only, as we know all too well, in the United States, but also in one of the most socially conservative rural areas of Europe.

Although official suicide rates were always very low in Ireland compared with those of other European countries, at least some of the difference was the result of underreporting, especially in rural areas where the stigma of suicide was great (see Kirwan 1991; Connolly and Cullen 1995; Kelleher, Corcoran, and Keeley 1997). Over the past twenty years, however, with changes in attitude and new reporting laws, the ratio of suicide to undetermined death has increased tenfold in Ireland from 2.2 to 28.6 percent for males, and from 2.3 to 29.9 percent for females. But more accurate reporting accounts for only about 40 percent of the rise. Most Irish demographers and psychiatrists agree that there has been a real increase in suicides over this time (see Connolly 1997; Kelleher 1998). The main rise in suicide rates has been among young men, like James in the twenty- to twenty-four-year-old age group. Among fifteen- to twenty-four-year olds, young men are seven times more likely than young women are to commit suicide. Youth suicide rates are highest in the south and west of Ireland and among the unemployed and young people denied access to higher education or professional training because of low scores on their school leaving certificate examination. In other words, blocked and frustrated aspirations seem to play a critical role as they seem to have in the case of James. Maureen's suicide reflects another form of blocked aspirations — the forced emigration of young women who, under slightly different social and economic conditions, would have gladly stayed behind and married into the village.

Given the observable values conflicts and threats to social self-identity that were already apparent in An Clochán in the mid–1970s (see chapter two), I might have anticipated this diagnostic and experiential shift from schizophrenia to depression and suicide. Indeed, the villages of rural western Ireland offered an almost classic Durkheimian paradigm of anomie, the loss of moral force, meaning, and certainty, accompanying the transition to a more secular, industrialized, and materialist society in which the rights and demands of the individual would begin to conflict with those of family, Church, and community. In the older generation many individuals were prevented, perhaps even protected, from knowing they might have aspirations in the first place. The older villager who said, when asked if his arranged marriage had been a good match, "Well, she had the cows, didn't she?" exemplifies the older system in which personal happiness and sexual fulfillment were beside the point. But for the younger generation, including Maureen and James, such instrumental and collectivist sentiments toward marriage would make no sense at all. Both were thoroughly modern and therefore thoroughly romantic about life's ultimate meaning.

Almost ten years after the publication of *Saints* (see Scheper-Hughes 1987), I found myself studying two native American pueblos in northern New Mexico, where I was I surprised by strong resemblances in the sense of social entrapment expressed by Pueblo youth and by the young people I had known in An Clochán. Depression, alcoholism, and so-called heroic suicides were prevelant in the Pueblo community among adolescents, especially those who had completed kiva training and Pueblo initiation. Young initiates spoke quite freely of feeling trapped between the generations and between the highly compromised Anglo world chosen by their acculturated fathers and the romanticized Indian world of their traditionalist grandfathers. One Indian youth told me that his suicidal preoccupations were driven by a desire to join the older generation: "I miss my grandfather. He's dead now and I don't know how to be a Pueblo without him." As in An Clochán, the options for young Pueblo men were so restricted and double binding that every choice seemed to be a bad one. Leave and you are a traitor; stay behind and you risk being caught in a cycle of economic and psychological dependency. Opting out of the dilemma by suicide could seem preferable, an honorable escape, and a modern-day equivalent of the Ghost Dance.

In Ireland suicide among the young increased most dramatically in rural areas where the changes in family life, sexual mores and practices, marriage, and childrearing were experienced most profoundly. Secularization and a loss of confidence in the moral authority of the Catholic Church resulting from revelations of sexual scandals among the Catholic clergy[16] — most of these the predictable and ordinary failings of the flesh, but others verging on the criminal — have been especially devastating to rural people whose faith in the traditional church had been profound. National surveys show that, in recent years, the number of Irish people attending Mass, receiving Holy Communion, and confessing their sins has decreased precipitously. In the rural communities of County Kerry parents have ceased sending their sons into the priesthood, and today the figures on priestly vocations have reverted to levels obtaining in the early nineteenth century, before the famine.

Hence, the relationship between the decline in religious practice and the increase in suicide in Ireland appears to be a significant and meaningful correlation. In the old faith, a suicide was an almost unforgivable mortal sin, a blasphemy against God that put one beyond the pale, graphically represented in the refusal to grant such deaths a Catholic burial. With the decline of the older Catholic orthodoxies and the rise of more enlightened attitudes toward mental distress, more young men in trouble may allow themselves to consider suicide as an acceptable, even heroic, solution to their existential dilemmas and one that would not weigh as heavily on the next of kin as it did in times past.

▪ Irish Erotics: Lost and Found

Finally, what can be said of Irish sexuality today, the problem that first captured my imagination? Chapter four, Brothers, Sisters, and Other Lovers, which treats the pummeling that the Irish libido took at the hands of a repressive, puritanical version of Jansenist Irish Catholicism, reinforced by sanctions imposed after the famine against premarital sexuality and early marriage, and by loyalties within rural farm families that made almost any marriage a betrayal of one's kin at any age, remains the most locally contested section of my book.

"How *dare* you suggest that there is something not quite right with those God-fearing households of brothers and sisters?" I was angrily challenged while trying to purchase a *Kerryman* newspaper at a village shop in 1999. "What gave *you* the right to say those things?" Not only "Tomas," but a great many other villagers, were affronted by my "experience-distant," neo-Freudian interpretation of what had been viewed until then as normative farm households composed of unmarried adult siblings.[17] My suggestion, based on my reading of key themes from the Thematic Apperception Test, of incestual preoccupations and anxieties underlying and "troubling" those same brother-sister households (see especially pages 195–202) had a chilling effect on villagers who saw this discussion, above all, as an unforgivable breaching of a public, if closely guarded and unspoken, secret.[18] My attempts to reassure villagers by pointing out the enormous difference between conscious acts and unconscious fears and fantasies had no effect. "Those who have seen themselves in the book won't make those fine, scholarly distinctions. They will have to live with the hint of scandal for the rest of their lives."

And, yes, I would now eat my words if I could. But "published and read, published and read"—as I was so often reminded during my last brief stay—the words have already done their damage to the equanimity of some villagers who *have* lived all these years with an abiding sense of shame after confronting for the first time some stray fragments of the collective unconscious of everyday life in An Clochán. Had I been a better anthropologist I might have considered that to the notorious confessional conscience of the rural Irish there was not, at least in those days, a great deal of difference between "bad thoughts" entertained and "bad deeds" enacted.

Perhaps Paddy, a talented writer and poet in his own right, can even the score by putting his fine way with words into a sea of verses that bowdlerizes the stray Americans who wandered into the village in 1974. If you like, Paddy, you can say that these unconscious themes of incest anxiety were also my own, and made me acutely sensitive to them as they floated to the surface of the stories told through the medium of the TAT.

Years ago George Devereux (1977) suggested that the anthropologist in the field was every bit as susceptible as the psychoanalyst in his office to the dangers of countertransference, of projecting one's own needs, fears, frustrations, and fantasies onto the significant other, whether one's patients or one's informants. Ethnographic work is exceedingly complex and dangerous insofar as the anthropologist is often in situations in which she must observe, record, and interpret certain primal social scenes that are inherently anxiety producing, in this instance, situations such as the institutionalized scapegoating of a designated farm heir or the exploitation of the labor of an excess adult daughter or son for whom marriage and an independent adult life have been made "impossible." And the field site itself can loom as a huge Rorschach or TAT for the naive anthropologist.

We now realize that there is no escape, no exit from the deeply subjective component of ethnographic research and writing. What is minimally required is a continuous and relentless form of self-criticism through which the anthropologist takes stock of her "object relations" in the field and later throughout the process of writing culture. But the real dilemma is this: How can we know what we know other than by filtering our observations and field experiences through the subjective categories of thinking and feeling — call them biases, if you will — that represent our particular ways of being in the world, such as the post-Vatican II radical Catholic feminist woman I was at the time of my first encounter with the mostly conservatively Catholic villagers of An Clochán, County Kerry, Ireland? But it is often in the very clash of interpretations between anthropologist and her subjects that a richer and deeper insight into the human condition is forged. If I did not believe that anthropology could also serve as an instrument of peace and as a tool for human conviviality, in Ivan Illich's sense of the term, I would have long since renounced this uncomfortable and difficult science and somewhat marginal way of life.

In an article provocatively entitled "The Erotics of Irishness" and published in *Critical Inquiry* (1990), Cheryl Herr revisited my thesis on Irish sexuality from the perspective of Irish literature and popular culture. While agreeing that a characteristic feature of modern Irish self-representation in art, film, and literature is one of hostility toward the body and sexuality, Herr argues that the concept of sexual repression begs the question. Just what powerful impulses, desires, and practices had to be erased and banished from view? Following the lead of James Joyce in his monumental *Finnegan's Wake*, Herr invokes the archeological remains of Ireland's vanquished Celtic culture — the more than fourteen hundred megalithic mounds, standing stones, and subterranean passage tombs — as an alternative, somatic text of early Irish erotics: "Tracing the sources and meanings of his pain, anger, exile and dualism took Joyce unerringly along the channels of Irish psychohistory — back to Ireland as body: the mounds, cairns, tumuli, and generally massive circular field monuments visually organizing large portions of Irish geography. In the *Wake* Joyce allows these womb-grave-body-parts to stand in for a missing link in Irish identity, the moment that might replace the perception of [bodily] paralysis with a celebration of movement" (ibid., p.7). These Celtic remains dating from four thousand years ago, large, circular mounds of earth and standing stones found on hilltops overlooking beautiful vistas, can be read as sacred icons to pre-Christian Celtic sexuality.

From the air and to the eye of the poet they take shape as breasts, vulva, and phalluses. From underground they appear to the night crawler as womblike tunnels and caves. To local country people, however, they are magical and dangerous fairy forts, homes of seductive female spirits who can lure men and children away. Country people tend to give the mounds and stones wide berth, especially those that crop up while one is digging in one's own field. For Herr they represent everything sexual that had to be erased and repressed in the modern Irish experience of self, mind, body, and culture. Tellingly, she refers to an odd encounter that I had in An Clochán with an old farmer (see p. 83) who, in response to a question about the meaning of the three ancient standing stones that could be found in the parish, replied: "Those were the kinds of altars we used to have before the priests laid them flat." There are many ways one could read this startling reply (in which I saw the collapsing of historical time with the present), but Herr saw in it the history of sexual flattening by the Church as well as the possibilities for national sexual recovery, rediscovery, and transformation.

Clearly, this recovery of the body is just what has been going on in the past two decades. Among the most striking changes to be observed throughout Ireland and even in small rural villages such as An Clochán is the acceptance, albeit begrudging at times, of sexuality, even premarital sexuality and its consequences in single parenthood. Once Ireland claimed the lowest recorded rates of illegitimacy in the world—from 1871 through 1970 marital fertility accounted for 96 percent of all births in Ireland (see Keiran Kennedy 1973). By 1996 a quarter of all births (24.8 percent or 12,484 births) were to single mothers (see Central Statistics Office, Dublin: http://www.doh.ie/statistics/health_statistics/index.html). Among younger women and for first births that percentage is, of course, much higher.

In the past quarter of a century there has been a return to earlier, eighteenth-century demographic patterns of relatively high illegitimacy, low rates of celibacy, and few priestly vocations (see Connell 1962; 1968).[19] Official statistics show that the Irish have had the lowest rates of recorded illegitimacy in Europe since the 1890s, but a fairly routine solution to premature pregnancy in rural Ireland from the turn of the century through the mid-twentieth century was travel to Britain where Irish girls gave birth in English Catholic institutions for so-called unwed mothers. Meanwhile, Irish seasonal laborers "fathered more children in Glasgow and Liverpool than they did in the Rosses or Achill; abortion and infanticide were sometimes practiced; priests, parents, and public opinion did their bit to make legitimate births of all illegitimate conceptions" (Connell 1968: 119). As with suicide, the stigma of illegitimacy was so much greater in Catholic Ireland than anywhere else in Europe that it is impossible to state with certainty what the rates of illegitimate births really were up through the mid-twentieth century.

But what has certainly changed is the extent to which single parenthood can be openly discussed as marginally acceptable. In An Clochán some seasoned teachers have assumed the responsibility of convincing the parents of pregnant daughters to allow their grandchildren to be born and welcomed into the village "as their birthright" and to coax them into coparenting so as to allow the girls to continue their educations. Where the father of the child has come forward, some teachers have tried to support the couple but also to delay the marriage until the boy has taken his school-leaving certificate and is in a better position to help support a family. I could no more have anticipated these remarkable changes in village life from my limited and myopic vantage point of 1974–1975 than I could have predicted the florescence of a vibrant and celebratory gay culture in Dublin in the past decade. As dedicated historians of the ethnographic present (and therefore wedded to a particular representation of local and national life and culture), anthropologists are poor at predicting new trends, let alone cataclysmic ruptures and transformations in social and cultural life, such as these represent.

Still, much of my description of life in An Clochán in the mid-1970s resonated, although anxiously, with villagers as with the Irish at home and overseas more generally. They have written me many lengthy and impassioned letters, at times to praise and at times to condemn, what I have written, but more often to ask advice about a troubled family member, an alcoholic younger brother, a schizophrenic daughter, an elderly aunt living alone in County Clare. From time to time I also hear from men who describe themselves as "an Irish bachelor from . . ." who want to share their feelings of isolation, longing, or frustration with me. At times I have served — I hope with empathy, compassion, and care — as a kind of anthropological Miss Lonelyhearts. So, in the end, I regard *Saints, Scholars, and Schizophrenics* as falling into that large and forgiving category I have called the good enough ethnography, a book that captured *something* true about the country people of County Kerry in the mid-1970s while it obviously missed a great deal as well.

Mental Illness
and Irish Culture

Things fall apart;
The center cannot hold;
Mere anarchy is loosed upon
the world.
—W. B. YEATS,
Collected Poems

EACH TIME I have been asked to give a lecture to a university audience on my research, I have approached it with some amount of trepidation. Usually I begin by asking the group (often a lecture hall of two hundred to four hundred people) how many of them are at least partly of Irish descent. Depending on geographical region, from one-quarter to one-third will normally raise their hands. My next response is some version of the theme "*You're* the reason why western Ireland is underpopulated and in distress!" If there is a certain amount of discomfort engendered in the process of addressing an audience about problematic themes from their own cultural background, there is also some satisfaction in demonstrating that anthropologists can bring the exotic home to roost. In learning about the plight of a small Irish village, trapped by circumstances into a state of cultural decline and widespread anomie, we can learn something about ourselves. For it was from such isolated little communities of the western coast that has come a succession of our statesmen and leaders, our local police and our teachers, our clergy and our bartenders—in short, many of those who have guided public and private morality.

The high morale and stunning accomplishments of the Irish abroad are, ironically and sadly, often contrasted to the demoralization of the Irish at home (see Brody 1974; Healy 1968; R. Kennedy 1973; Lynn 1968). There is little doubt from available statistics (World Health Organization, 1961; 1968) that the Republic of Ireland has the highest hospitalization treatment rate for mental illness in the world. A recent census of the Irish psychiatric hospital population (O'Hare and Walsh 1974) indicates that schizophrenia is the core problem—more than half of the patients are so diagnosed.

The association between Irish ethnicity and mental illness has perplexed the Irish medical profession (see Walsh and Walsh 1968) and social scientists at large (Lynn 1971; Malzberg and Lee 1956; H. B. M. Murphy 1975) for nearly half a century, and they remain divided on the basic issue of etiology: genetic, biochemical, or environmental. In this book, based on a year of fieldwork in a representatively small, isolated rural community of the Kerry Gaeltacht* I attempt a broad *cultural* diagnosis of those pathogenic stresses that surround the coming of age in rural Ireland today. I explore the particularly high vulnerability of young and middle-aged bachelor farmers to schizophrenic episodes in light of such social and cultural problems as the current disintegration of village social life and institutions; the remarkable separation and alienation of the sexes; a guilt- and shame-oriented socialization process that guarantees the loyalty of at least one male child to parents, home, and village through the systematic scapegoating of this (usually the youngest) son; and, finally, cultural attitudes toward the resolution of stress *outside* of family life and through patterns of dependency upon "total" institutions.

This work can be placed within the tradition of earlier "culture and personality" studies (e.g., Benedict 1928, 1934; Erikson 1950; M. Mead 1928, 1935; Powdermaker 1953), which attempted to delineate the cultural parameters of personality development and adult behavior. In addition, it falls into that relatively newer field called transcultural (or ethno-) psychiatry, which explores the interplay of culture and social structure upon the form, frequency, severity, diagnosis, and treatment of mental disorders (e.g., Aberle 1952; Benedict 1935; Boyer 1964; DeVos 1965; Hallowell 1934; H. B. M. Murphy 1965; Opler 1959).

---

*One of several small enclaves within the Republic where Irish is still the spoken language in many homes.

My orientation is both psychological and social structural, insofar as I shall examine the interplay of historical circumstance and economic determinants with the largely symbolic spheres of beliefs, values, and behavior. Throughout the book I shall emphasize the importance of the antithetical social spheres of the sexes to the quality of the emotional life, as well as the oppositional role of older to younger siblings—both grounded in the basic economic strategy of rural farm families. It is a major hypothesis that these preordained age and sex statuses are pivotal in defining parental expectations for their children, and result in entirely different socialization and later life experiences—weighted in favor of the mental health of girls and earlier-born sons, and against the chances for healthy ego-integration of later-born male children.

I share with other recent ethnographers, among them Hugh Brody (1974) and Robert Cresswell (1969), the belief that rural Ireland is dying and its people are consequently infused with a spirit of anomie and despair. This anomie is expressed most markedly in the decline of the traditional agricultural, sheep grazing, and fishing industries and in the virtual dependence of the small communities of the west upon welfare schemes and the ubiquitous "dole"—this despite marketing improvements through membership in the Common Market and government inducements to production through cattle, dairy, and wool subsidies. The flight of young people—especially women—from the desolate parishes of the western coast, drinking patterns among the stay-at-home class of bachelor farmers, and the general disinterest of the local populace in sexuality, marriage, and procreation are further signs of cultural stagnation. Finally, the relative ease with which a growing proportion of the young, single, male farmers are able to accept voluntary incarceration in the mental hospital as a panacea for their troubles is a final indication that western Ireland, one of the oldest and most continually settled human communities in Europe, is in a virtual state of psychocultural decline.

In chapter one I set the parish of Ballybran (which, like all personal names used, is a pseudonym) in space and in time, examining vignettes of its history from the oral tradition of legend, myth, and folktale. This section is, more properly speaking, an ethnohistory insofar as I allow the villagers to select and order the significant events of their past as they themselves perceived and remember them. In this way I introduce the reader not so much to an objectively accurate history of the locality, which can be gotten elsewhere,[1] but to the ways in which villagers attempt to validate themselves in terms of a "corrected" and "rewritten" past. Chapter two looks at the present situation of Ballybran: its demographic and economic patterns, the failure of the initially enthusiastically embraced language-revival movement, and its perhaps irreversible decline as a viable and self-sustaining community.

In chapter three I focus on the most visible effect of cultural disorganization and demoralization as I sketch an epidemiological profile of mental illness in the rural west. I suggest that the high psychiatric hospitalization rates must be discussed within the context of what has been called "labeling theory" (see Scheff 1966)—that is, through an examination of community definitions of normal and abnormal behavior, variations in diagnostic usage, and cultural attitudes toward treatment and institutionalization.

Chapter four discusses the relationship between celibacy and mental illness through an ethnographic description of relations between the sexes both within and outside the institution of marriage. I attempt to answer the oft-raised question concerning the source of the Irish antipathy to sex and marriage, and I offer an explanation grounded as much in current social and economic determinants (e.g., the refusal of women to marry into the small farms of Kerry) as in psychological predispositions (including a regressed adult sexuality seemingly fixated on early brother-sister incestual longings).

In addition to participant observation in the lifestyle of Ballybran, two groups of villagers were singled out for particular study—mothers and children. Twenty-eight village parents representing twenty nuclear or extended households were interviewed and observed on the norms of child rearing, following a modified version of the interview schedule outlined in John Whiting, et al., *Field Guide for a Study of Socialization* (1966: 78–82). Like the anthropologists involved in the seminal "six cultures" study of child rearing (see B. Whiting 1963), I was primarily interested in the values and beliefs of the society as revealed through socialization techniques. But beyond that, I was problem oriented, attempting to determine if certain rural Irish child-rearing practices might be contributing factors in the etiology of mental illness.

The "children" interviewed ranged in age from newborns to middle-aged bachelors and spinsters still living under the roof and under the thumb of the "old people." The parents interviewed, consequently, spanned three generations and gave me the opportunity to add a historical dimension and note some dramatic changes in child rearing over the past forty or fifty years. In addition I examined, with the help of Professor Sean O'Sullivan, relevant material on child rearing collected in the form of proverbs, folktales, and "old *piseogas*" (i.e., superstitions) by the Irish Folklore Commission in Dublin. Likewise, I read with care and with relish all the autobiographical literature to have come from the recently defunct culture of the Blasket Islands — once just a short canoe trip from the little market town of Dingle. From the bittersweet and poetic recollections of Peig Sayers (1962), Tomás O'Crohan (1951), and Maurice O'Sullivan (1957), I gleaned a picture of Irish attitudes toward children and the principles of child tending "uncorrupted" by sustained contact with outsiders and prior to the decline of Gaelic culture.

Chapters five and six examine current socialization practice and raise this question: Is there something in the nature of parent-child interactions in Ballybran that might be defined as psychogenic, or more exactly, as schizophrenogenic? A qualified yes is suggested by the data, and in chapter five I discuss the cultural pattern of minimal handling and isolation of the infant, and the absence for the very young of what some psychologists call necessary attachment or maternal bonding behavior (see Bowlby 1969, 1973). The casual aloofness and seeming emotional inadequacy of mothers toward infants observed in some rural homes seem to be related to the austere and puritanical cast of Irish Catholicism with its many restrictions on physical expression, and to the, at times, excessive reliance on corporal punishment both in the home and in the classroom. For the more psychologically fragile, the end product of such a socialization experience, I suggest, may be a tendency for the individual to withdraw from painful interactions into the characteristic delusional state of schizophrenia.

In chapter six I attempt to distinguish the "vulnerable" children from the "less vulnerable" in terms of the differential treatment of daughters and sons and of later- to earlier-born siblings. The pattern of fixed statuses — pets, left-overs, whiteheaded boys, and black sheep — attendant to sex and birth order is discussed in terms of the economic requirements of farm succession and its ultimate effect on the emotional and mental health of the chosen heir.

As the research progressed, I became directly involved with the rural young adults themselves and with the succession of conflicts, stresses, and ultimate decisions that resulted in emigration, in stoical resignation, or in cyclical maladjustment expressed in mental illness and alcoholism. In order to probe largely repressed attitudes of late adolescents toward marriage, sexuality, achievement, and generativity, I administered a variety of projective tests — among them the Thematic Apperception and Draw-a-Person Tests, and the Values Hierarchy Scale — to a sizable number of young adults in the parish. In addition I assigned essays and compositions on a number of relevant topics to the students at the parish secondary-school. These essays covered a myriad topics, such as "Why Does a Good God Allow Suffering and Sickness?" "Is Violence and Aggression Natural to Man?" "How Does the Idealized Image of Marriage Presented in Films Differ from a Realistic Approach to Marriage?"

Most fruitful of the instruments, and to be discussed in greatest detail, was the Thematic Apperception Test (TAT),[2] which was initially administered to thirty-six average village youths between the ages of fifteen and eighteen (twenty-two young women and fourteen young men). Each was tested individually while I transcribed the responses by hand. Whenever possible, the youths were interviewed following the test, on general topics of life history: schooling, family relations, vocational and other goal orientations. Nine of the fourteen boys tested (ages fifteen to eighteen) were potential, if reluctant, farm heirs, while the remaining five had serious designs for higher education or emigration. By contrast, all but three of the twenty-two girls tested expected to leave the village within the next few years in order to pursue a nursing or teaching career or to work abroad. These differences were not selected for, but were a natural reflection of, demographic patterns in the area.

Finally, one day each week for a period of three months I observed, interviewed, and tested young patients of the district mental hospital in Killarney and at the psychiatric clinic in Dingle. Through intensive interviewing of these young adults, already demonstrating early signs of a basic inability to cope, I hoped to identify the major stresses surrounding the coming of age in rural Kerry today. A total of twenty-two patients—eleven of each sex— were tested and interviewed on their life histories. These patients were selected at the discretion of the clinic and hospital directors. My only stipulations were that the patients be young, come from a rural Kerry background, and volunteer for the testing. The latter stipulation (in order to comply with federal regulations for the protection of human subjects) necessarily resulted in a "natural selection" of the most sociable, outgoing, cooperative, and least disturbed patients. The average length of hospitalization for these patients was short—just under one month—and for most it was their first admission to a psychiatric institution. Ten of the twenty-two were diagnosed as schizophrenic or paranoid.

There was a decided advantage to using written and verbal projective testing among the rural Irish. Forced to generalize, one could say that Irish villagers are extremely reserved and unused to, as well as uncomfortable with, the task of discussing feelings and attitudes relating to personal relationships. If asked directly, for example, how he got along with mother or father, the rural Kerryman will invariably answer with a stylized "Yerra, nothing to complain about," or will reverse the question into a question of his own: "And why would ye be wanting to know that, may I ask?" Needless to say, direct questioning often resulted in stalemate. However, the Kerryman is particularly adept at innuendo, ambiguity, and metaphor. All but two of the fifty-eight respondents *thoroughly* enjoyed the testing, which gave them an opportunity to express, indirectly, their feelings on topics such as family relations and religious beliefs, which would have been socially taboo were they brought up in a direct manner.

The fifty-eight youths told a total of 835 Thematic Apperception Test stories, which were later coded according to the ten basic motivational concerns suggested by George DeVos (1973: 20–21). Five of the dimensions are instrumental (goal-oriented) and five are expressive (directly related to feeling).

Instrumental Concerns
Achievement-Anomie
Competence-Inadequacy
Responsibility-Negligence
Control (Dominance-Submission)
Mutuality (Competitive-Cooperative)

Expressive Concerns
Harmony-Discord
Affiliation-Isolation
Nurturance-Deprivation
Appreciation-Disdain
Pleasure-Suffering

Each story is characterized by one dominant theme, but often contains from two to five additional subthemes, depending on length and complexity of the tale. In coding the stories I avoided themes that were implied and relied only on material that was expressly stated. In addition to thematic coding, I noted the sequences and outcomes of the stories and paid particular attention to the roles played by family figures. The results of the test are used illustratively throughout the book, and in detail in Appendix D (tables D-I to D-6).

In general the Irish records reveal large areas of feeling and motivation locked into conflict. Ambivalence is a dominant psychological mode for all the youth, as village lads vacillate between achievement orientation and anomie, and as village girls and boys debate their responsibility to home and parents versus their own personal drive for escape from home and village. A sense of shame and incompetence blocks male strivings for achievement, and an oppressive guilt often interferes with their need to excel *or* escape. A certain superficiality in interpersonal relations is expressed in the desire of village and hospitalized males to be affably sociable without the pressures of intimacy. And throughout all the records runs a strong current of sexual repression and personal asceticism—one that interferes not only with intimacy between the sexes, but with the nurturant and generative aspects of personality as well. With the exception of the schizophrenic patients, whose stories are readily distinguished on the basis of their more idiosyncratic themes, the greatest statistical differences were found between the sexes, rather than between the "average" and hospitalized villagers. Given the separate social realities occupied by males and females in County Kerry (see chapter four), it is the culture of sex rather than the culture of mental illness that is most recognizable in the TAT records. Most poignantly, the tests illustrate the differential stresses experienced by girls, often forced into premature emigration, and by village boys, frequently the casualties of this same female exodus.

The research team was the family—myself, my husband, and our three children: Jenny, aged five, Sarah, aged two, and Nathanael, five months at the start of fieldwork. We could hardly avoid being *participant* observers in the community as we shared with the hardy villagers day in and out their lifestyle, their celebrations, their ennui and depressions during the seemingly endless winter, their fear of the truly awesome wind storms that rocked the peninsula, and their joy at the coming of spring—the flowing of cow's milk and the birth of the calves and lambs. We worshipped with them on Sundays and holy days; we confessed our sins to the same curate; we visited their old and sick, and mourned with them their dead. My elder daughter attended the local primary-school, where she learned bilingual reading, math, her prayers, sewing, Irish dancing and music, and how to duck the bamboo rod. She admired her strict Scottish highlands-trained teacher and enjoyed her peers. Although for the first few weeks Jenny was able to relate fascinating tidbits of information to me about school and yard activities, before very long she was socialized by her friends to the extent that she adopted their worldview and joined the conspiracy of silence that separates Irish children and their parents. From that time on I lost her as a prime "informant." All the children, however, served as "rites of entry" into the normally closed lives of villagers, and remarks and criticisms of the way in which we handled our children, as well as comments on their behavior vis-à-vis their own children's, were an invaluable source of information with regard to socialization.

My husband was the second member of the team to withdraw somewhat from the research, particularly after he was given the highly sanctioned role of secondary-school teacher. His identification with the school and the Church and his shared perception with some of the villagers that there was something a little sacrilegious about the way I took notes at wakes and enquired about personal and intimate aspects of religious belief, sexual practice, and emotional life made him a rather reluctant coworker and informant—particularly when it concerned sharing with me the jokes, stories, and opinions exchanged with village men at the pub. As Jenny was socialized into the children's world, Michael joined the circle of "round"-drinking and tale-swapping bachelor farmers. And my presence at the pub, silent though it was (with the exception of singing an occasional ballad), put his companions ill at ease. So, after a few months, I resignedly left the pub mates in peace. I had in any case learned by then all that I wanted to know (and then some) about the "culture" of Guinness stout. Nonetheless, my husband with the cooperation of the schoolmistress gave me free access to his secondary-school classes and agreed to assign the essays and compositions on topics that I suggested. He accompanied me on the long trip each week to the county mental hospital, where he assisted in interviewing and testing mental patients. Finally, and most importantly, Michael's natural sensitivity and kindred spirit with the reserved rural Irish served as a foil and a censor, correcting me when I delved too far or pushed too hard or too quickly, and constantly reminding me that my primary obligation was not to "science" or to the academic community at large, but to the community—protecting the villagers' dignity, reserve, and sensitivities, and guarding them from embarrassment or emotional injury of any kind. And for these gentle reminders I am grateful to him beyond words.

There was, at first, some confusion over the nature of my research. When one village publican learned that I was in Ballybran to conduct an "anthropological survey," he informed me that this had already been done some twenty years before, and to come right to the point, he did not want to have his nose and lips and skull measured again! While at first I explained to villagers in the broadest of terms that I was a social anthropologist interested in the culture and way of life of the parish, I was soon pressed by some of the village schoolteachers to give the exact nature of the research and to inform them in advance the title of the book I would write and its contents. To this just enough demand, I would reply as honestly as I could at the time: "Interpersonal Relations in a Rural Irish Community." Like most anthropologists,

I began my research with the broad areas of interest mapped out, a "sense of problem," and a rather flexible methodology that would allow for that fortuitous creative process, which some call "serendipity," to take over at will. As it became increasingly apparent that I was concentrating on mothers, children, and adolescents, the village seemed to relax somewhat.

However, there were a few very tense incidents with regard to the research—both occurring in a pub during the summertime, and both taking place under the encouragement of outsiders—specifically Irish tourists from Dublin. In one rather trying experience, a local shepherd made belligerent by alcohol and losses at the local sheep market announced to all and sundry that he had been told by some Dubliners that "the anthropologist" was only interested in the villagers' sex practices and that I would write a book that would convert "people into numbers," and that I would ultimately degrade the Irish way of life. When my attempts at reversing the accusation into jovial banter failed, I promised Brian the shepherd a copy of Arensberg's *The Irish Countryman* (1939), which I thought might be to his liking, and told him that part of my aim in coming to Ballybran was to "modernize" the Yankee's image of Ireland because there had been such vast changes since Arensberg's time. Brian read at least parts of Arensberg, asked to keep the book, and offered magnanimously, "There's lots of truth in that book; the man didn't lie." From that day on, Brian and I were on a first-name basis, and the shepherd even offered to recite some political verses and songs into my tape recorder.

The second incident occurred some weeks later when a Dublin tourist himself offered to "introduce" me to my drinking mates of some time by explaining at a pub session the basic thesis of Irish Catholic sexual repression presented in John Messenger's recent ethnography of the Aran Islands, *Inis Beag* (1969)—a book that incurred the wrath of several Irish social scientists and received a bad press in Dublin papers as well as censorship at libraries in the west. Luckily for me, the villagers were embarrassed by the flamboyant personality of the Dubliner and, as confirmed celibates, could not relate at all to the outsider's brash charges that "anthropologists are 'peeping Toms' who write that the Irish take only the 'missionary position.'"

The perhaps apocryphal days of yesteryear, when the anthropologist was accepted and adopted as "hero" into the local kinship of an innocent and guileless people, are over—for the best, I am certain—as once isolated villages and small communities throughout the world become more enlightened as to the uses and abuses of anthropology. Today each anthropologist must confront the awesome task of slowly proving himself or herself blameless and worthy of acceptance and confidence, despite the increasingly "bad press" accorded the profession. Hence, I became keenly aware of the sensibilities of the people in Ballybran, who were not only suspicious of social science research, but who were still angered over the "stage Irishman" impression given by the films *Playboy of the Western World* and, more recently, *Ryan's Daughter*—both of which were filmed in part on the Dingle Peninsula. I worried about their reaction to a book dealing with the death of the countryside, anomie, and mental illness, topics that were not designed before the research had begun, but that grew naturally out of immersion within the depressed community.

After a particularly revelatory and intimate conversation with a village mother for whom I had a great deal of affection, I returned home one evening in Ballybran to fall into a fitful sleep during which I dreamed that a villager invited me in for tea and insisted upon giving me a suit of armor that had belonged to the family for generations, since the time of the Norman Conquest. I reluctantly accepted the unwieldy present, but as I was walking home through the bog with it, a group of strangers appeared and began to chase me, yelling that I had "stolen" the armor of the village. The dream brought to consciousness my still-lingering anxiety over whether it is defensible behavior to befriend and ultimately "disarm" a people and "steal," as it were, their guarded secrets. While I never asked intimate questions of villagers until I felt that they had extended to me the role of "confessor," knowing that what passed their lips to my ears would be considered a sacred trust and used with discretion, yet often even the closest of friends would laugh at the impertinence of a particular enquiry: "What?" demanded the tailor of Ballybran with false gruffness, after I had asked him why he had never chosen to marry, "What, my girleen? Will you even have the darkest secrets of my soul?"

One could hardly discuss data gathering among villagers without mentioning the Irish love of *blas*—skill with words—and the recreational arts of blarney (flattery) and codding (teasing). What about the reliability of my data given that peculiarly Irish form of banter that says one thing and means another? Wouldn't the naive anthropologist, notebook in hand and indiscreet question on tip of tongue, be a sitting duck for the tall tale and other useful evasions of the Irish?[3] Without a doubt, communicating with the Irish is tricky for the plodding, literal-minded Saxon, and in many an initial encounter I would think myself to be following a linear path of conversation, only to find myself lost on a forked road, waylaid by shortcuts and switchbacks, and invariably led up a blind alley or cul-de-sac. In short, I was being *had*, Irish style. Well, no matter. Reputation of the Irish aside, I'd also been had in the past by Mexican and Brazilian peasants (and more than once found myself on the wrong bus en route to nowhere), and I had eventually learned to crack *their* code. Yes, the Irish lie, and lie they do with admirable touches of wit and ingenuity. Add to the normal defensiveness of the peasant, a folk Catholic moral code that is quite "soft" on lying, and a lack of tolerance for *overt* acts of aggression, and you have a very strong propensity to "cod" (sometimes rather cruelly) the outsider. Beyond cross-checking information, the only safeguard the fieldworker has against "converting the lies of peasants into scientific data" (as one critic of the participant-observation method commented) is simply getting to know the villagers well enough to read the nonverbal cues that signal evasiveness or lying. Unfortunately, those villagers who are most eager to talk to the outsider from the onset are often the most mischievous informants. Weeding out the "unreliables" from the initially small coterie of "gifted informants" can be a painful procedure. An important point, however, and one that statistically oriented social scientists often miss, is that lies *are* data, and very essential data at that. Once I am able to figure out to what extent villagers lie, when and to whom they are most likely to lie, and who in the community have the dubious reputations of being the greatest liars, I go about systematically analyzing the values of villagers as demonstrated by what they want to believe about themselves; what they want me to believe about them; and what they think I want to believe about them. I compare these findings against my own observations and perceptions of what actually does go on in the village—the way people behave "as if" things were, even though they may define the situation quite differently.

No anthropologist likes to depart from his time-honored conventional stance of "cultural relativity" in order to ask the kinds of questions that come more easily to the clinical psychologist, the medical doctor, and the social worker, such as, What has gone wrong with this organism (or this society)? or, What is so pathogenic about the quality of interpersonal relations in this family (or in this village)? The anthropologist is the product of a historical tradition and a moral commitment dedicated to seeing the "good" in every culture. Few colleagues today would defend a traditional "functionalist" view of human societies, such that whatever exists in the culture is there by virtue of its necessity to the operation of the whole, and hence if it exists it is by definition "good." Yet there is still some calling into question the objectivity of those social scientists, such as Oscar Lewis (1951), Edward Banfield (1958), and George Foster (1967), who noted dysfunction as well as function and who, in particular, describe peasant social life as often characterized by suspiciousness, greed, envy, uncooperativeness, and interactions as charged with hostility and aggressiveness.

Even more difficult is it to embark on an ethnographic study of a subject as delicate and normally shielded from the gaze of outsiders as mental illness. In raising such questions as whether there is something in the nature of rural Irish socialization practices that might be diagnosed as schizophrenogenic, some may wonder whether I am looking to assign blame on parents, teachers, priests, and social institutions. They may ask whether I am engaged in a perverse, cultural witch-hunt. It might be wise, therefore, for me to begin with a few caveats regarding my orientation and choice of subject matter. My interest in Irish madness is an outgrowth of an earlier research interest in rituals of racial and sexual pollution (Scheper-Hughes 1973). The following pages should be taken not so much as a thesis on mental illness as a book about rural Irish society seen in part through the eyes of its indigenous outsiders. By this I mean that I am not so much interested in the phenomenon of schizophrenia, the disease, as I am in schizophrenics, the social outcasts or social critics (as the case may be), and in the rituals of definition, inclusion, and exclusion that surround them.

In this regard, I am heir to the insights of Michel Foucault, who has suggested that madness be seen as a projection of cultural themes. In his brilliant work *Madness and Civilization* (1967), Foucault documents Western society's search for a scapegoat—the leper, the criminal, or the madman—whose existence emphasizes, by contrast conception, the "normalcy" of others. Madness, like racial and caste categories, is one of the ways of drawing margins around the psychological reality of a social group. But even as a society refuses to recognize itself in the suffering individuals it rejects or locks up, it gives eloquent testimony to the repressed fears, longings, and insecurities of the group. And that particular configuration of Irish schizophrenia, as revealed through the life histories of young mental patients, expresses the continuing dialogue between the repressed and unfulfilled wishes of childhood, and the miseries of adult life in devitalized rural Ireland.

The "madhouse" of Killarney is not altogether dissimilar from the menstrual hut of Lesu or the "Blacks Only" entrance at the back of the dentist's office in Selma, Alabama. And, just as Black sharecroppers from Gees Bend taught me more about rural economics than the county extension agent (Hunt and Scheper 1969), I thought that I would learn as much or even more about Irish society from the patients of the district mental hospital than I might from the village curate or schoolmaster. Every culture has its own "normality threshold," and a society reveals itself perhaps most clearly in the phenomena it rejects, excludes, and confines.

Others may question to what degree fieldwork observation and analysis are influenced by the personality of the researcher. Ralph Piddington observed in this regard that "a critic once remarked that the Trobriand Islanders are very much like Malinowski and the Tikopia very like Professor Raymond Firth" (1957: 546). Similarly, when Reo Fortune published his *Sorcerers of Dobu* (1963), in which he described a tribal people torn asunder by seemingly paranoid accusations and counteraccusations of witchcraft and when Oscar Lewis published his contradictory restudy (1951) of Robert Redfield's original ethnography of Tepotzlan (1930), critics were quick to make reference to the largely subjective element in the interpretation of behavior. Redfield defended his original description of an almost idyllic social life in Tepotzlan (1955) by offering that, where he was concerned with villagers' enjoyment of life, Lewis was concerned primarily with their woes and sorrows. By implication, Redfield was a romantic optimist and Lewis was an unremitting pessimist in search of the evil and tragedy of human existence. However, the question of subjectivity based on the personality dispositions of researchers should not be so simply dismissed. Social scientists, despite their biases and temperaments, should be able to describe with some amount of objectivity the actual nature of social relations in any given community.

Certainly, psychologically oriented anthropologists tend to look with a more studied eye on the unconscious content of interpersonal relations, child rearing, religious institutions, and so forth, and thereby introduce sets of data different from those of a social structuralist looking at the same community. My own biases—grounded in the experiences of growing up in a New York City slum, community organizing among sugarcane cutters of Northeast Brazil, and civil rights work in rural Alabama—can be summarized in the belief that nowhere is the human condition very good for the great number, nor free from pain, either physical or psychological. Yet, I maintain a faith in the possibility for positive change and social healing so long as individuals can be alerted to and moved by the needs of their fellow human beings. To romanticize, ignore, or whitewash the darker side of the life of the peoples we study contributes to the perpetuation of social ills.

Finally, there is the question of the degree to which the remote little parish of Ballybran is representative of the Irish, or even of the rural or western Irish—terms I use interchangeably with the more restrictive terms parishioners and villagers. Are not anthropologists notorious romantics, drawn to the exceptional and exotic in human societies? How peculiar, then, to the rest of Ireland are the Seans and Paddys and Peigs written about here? While not wishing to overextend my expertise on the Irish, my observations, psychological testing, and interviewing went beyond the parish of Ballybran. Through the weekly visits to the mental hospital and psychiatric clinic, I had in-depth exposure to the lives of individuals and their families from villages throughout rural Kerry. In addition, I shared my perceptions on "the rural Irish" with psychiatrists who worked with patients throughout the western counties. In a culture area as small and homogeneous as western Ireland, I feel relatively confident in generalizing, within limits, from the village I know best. Unfortunately, Ballybran is not an exception—there are hundreds of Ballybrans just like it up and down the rugged coast of western Ireland.

In the final analysis, I am less concerned with what my anthropological colleagues and critics will think and say than I am about what my friends in Ballybran will *feel* about what is written here. I trust they realize that although I stress some of the more dismal aspects of their life—the death of the countryside, the seemingly irreversible desertion by young people, the alienation between the sexes, the high rates of anxiety and depression—that they will accept the large measure of my concern for their physical, emotional, and spiritual well-being, and my appreciation of their warmth and double-edged humor. Their children were beautiful—their scrubbed ruddy faces and perpetually muddy Wellington boots, their quixotic smiles and shocks of hair that refused to stay in place, their bread and jam sandwiches—and are engraved permanently in my memory. I only lament that in another decade there will be so many the less of these beautiful children born into Ballybran—a loss not so much for this little community as for the world at large, which has been, for generations, the recipient of some of the best of these lads and lasses as they reached adulthood.

CHAPTER ONE

In Space
and in Time

A *man who is not afraid of the sea
will soon be drownded, for he will
be going out on a day he shouldn't.
But we do be afraid of the sea, and we
do only be drownded now and again.*
—AN ARAN ISLANDER'S COMMENT
TO JOHN MILLINGTON SYNGE

A SINGLE, twisting road leads
through the eastern half of the Dingle
Peninsula—the ancient barony of
Corca Dhuibhne—in southwest Kerry,
from the bustling, almost modern,
market town of Tralee, over the Slieve
Mish mountain range, through deep
glens, alongside the "wild" coastline, past low sand dunes and steep cliffs,
ending at the sheltered bay of Ballybran. The central village of the parish is
today but a double row of two-story stone houses, half of them shuttered and
deserted—overlooking the bay with its last remaining *naomhóg** in a state of
melancholy disrepair and tied idly to the quay. A primary- school, a chapel,
a creamery, three pubs, four small dry-goods shops, the forge, a guesthouse
house, two graveyards, and the ruins of three churches complete the inven-
tory of public and social institutions of the community.

Most of the 461 parishioners of Ballybran do not live on the single paved
street of the central village; they live in the eleven sister villages or hamlets
scattered around and halfway up the sides of sacred Mount Brandon, site of
pilgrimage in midsummer each year. The mountain villagers are a hardy,

---

*The lath and tarred canvas canoe traditionally used by fishermen of the Great Blasket
Island and their mainland neighbors. *Curach* is the term used elsewhere in western Ireland.

long-lived race of shepherds, fishermen, and dairy farmers who claim ancestry and continuous residence in the parish as far back as the first settlement by seafaring Mediterranean Celts. Their physical type, however — long, lean, and finely sculptured — and their fair Norman complexions, belie their Celtic heritage.

The more "urbane" families of the central village provide for the educational, religious, and recreational needs of the resident farming and fishing population. Here reside curate, schoolteachers, publicans, postal workers, hackney drivers, nurse, auto repairman, shopkeepers, and housebuilders. Parishioners come to the central village from the surrounding hamlets and "townlands" to purchase canned goods, cigarettes, sugar, and tea, to gather gossip after Mass on Sundays and holy days, to bury the dead, to make telephone calls, and, on rarer occasions, to watch a television program in one of the four homes sporting a new antenna. Equality and classlessness are strongly defended ideals in Ballybran, but the children of teachers rarely play with the children of shopkeepers, and the children of shopkeepers even more rarely with the children of farmers, and almost no one plays with the children of shepherds. But, ironically, it is the shepherds' children who know intimately and who "own" the holy mountain that gives the village its social and religious charter.

No public transportation leads to the parish today, with the exception of the school bus that carries a handful of adolescents to and from the technical school in Tralee each day. The railroad that once crisscrossed the peninsula, carrying villagers and occasionally their livestock to the open-air cattle and sheep markets of Castlederry and Dingle, closed down in the late 1950s after only a generation of service. Ten years later, the daily public bus to and from the parish to the county seat in Tralee was discontinued. With its passing, the temporary truce of Ballybran with the rest of County Kerry ended, and the parish was allowed to lapse once again into its historical mode of isolation. Yet, as I shall discuss in the following chapter, the isolation is of a psychological nature, for the economic and political structure of the parish is one of hostile and unwilling dependence upon the outside world.

So naturally secreted and difficult of access are the small communities of the Dingle Peninsula that the worst horrors of the Black Famine (1845–1849) bypassed the hidden glens and hollows of Corca Dhuibhne, where the staple diet of spuds was ever varied with oats, turnips, milk, and butter, with salted mackerel and fresh salmon, with cockles and salty *duileask* (seaweed). The west Kerryman today, as then, is oriented primarily to his townland of two to twelve households, beyond that to his parish, and beyond that to the sea and to that other side of the Irish strand, where for generations the "Yanks" of the community have come and gone. For at least two centuries the streets of New York and Boston have been more familiar in anecdote and closer in experience to the Ballybran parishioner than have the roads to Cork, Galway, and Dublin. Central to the "mythology" of the proud community is the firm conviction that from the shores of its bay Saint Brendan the Navigator set sail across the stormy Atlantic to discover Tir na nOg (the legendary Land of the Young in the West) ten centuries before the birth of Christopher Columbus. To the imaginative minds of not a few of the villagers, America was once Saint Brendan's Isle, only a colony of the mighty Kingdom of Kerry.

The inhabitants of Ballybran share a stance, a worldview, and an ethos similar to other perennially isolated mountain and hill communities in Europe (see Bailey 1973) who fear and mistrust outsiders, are intensely familistic and tightly endogamous, who view their terrain as a holy geography, their past as a religious history, and their language as a sacred tongue. Although the lame, itinerant tailor of Ananalacken townland settled over thirty years ago into the parish and into his teasing role as village agnostic and iconoclast, his neighbors never let him forget that he is not one of them. "Sure, we should have stoned the man out of this holy village three decades ago," comments the bedridden poet laureate of Ballybran, "for it's himself is leading our young lads down the paths of wickedness and paganism." Similarly, while every married woman who was rightfully born, baptized, and married within the parish goes familiarly by her maiden name, or by a pet nickname such as Nellie Tommy (i.e., Tommy's Nellie), women who have made so bold as to marry into the parish from elsewhere are known ever by the distant and slightly contemptuous title of Missus.

In the highly personalized world of the villager every field and pasture, every spring and well, every rock, hill, and resting place is endowed with a name, a personality, a story, and a lesson. On Mount Brandon alone can be found Macha an Mhil (the Beast's Pasture), Faill na nDeamhan (the Demon's Cliff), Com na Caillighe (the Hag's Recess), Loch na Mná (the Woman's Lake), and Cnoc an Tairbh (the Bull's Head)—names suggestive of myths and legends that recur as well in other parts of Ireland. Each semiautonomous rural community claims the legends as the social charter and true history of its own people. And so it is that the people of Ballybran can point to that particular bit of mountain, or that exact lake, or stone, or well, where it all began "long ago." Near the flat mountain bog of Comm an Áir, it is told, a great battle took place between the

Have not all races had their first unity from a mythology that marries them to rock and hill?
—W.B. YEATS
Collected Works

mythical Giant Fenians and the Tuatha de Danann, and the arrowheads from the battle are still to be found and collected for a quarter of a mile surrounding the locality. Older villagers attribute the postpartum wasting sickness of cows to these "fairy darts," which they believe find their way from Comm an Áir into their pastures by night.

Beside the river called Abha Mac Feinne is a huge boulder that the folk hero Florin Mac Cumhail is said to have hurled from Connor Pass to kill a giant who was terrifying the people of Ballybran. A neighboring cromlech, or circle of monoliths, is known locally as the Giant's Grave and is associated with this same legend. The small lake of Loch Geal at the base of Mount Brandon holds captive a wicked *piast*, a demon-serpent that Saint Brendan confined there during his stay in the parish and that demonstrates its continued presence by hurling all the fish onto the shore once every seven years. The now deserted townland of Saus Creek, an almost inaccessible cliff where three or four families lived on small shelves overlooking the water, carries the melancholy tale of the woman who died in childbirth because the midwife, who slipped into the sea on her way down the cliffs by night, never reached her. The midwife's body was not reclaimed from the sea, and fear of her powerful curse as well as sadness over the triple death (mother, child, and midwife) caused the remaining townlanders to abandon their ancestral hillside homes. The lesson remains and is oft repeated today; it is wrong to isolate oneself too far from one's neighbors: "In the shelter of each other, people must make their lives." Saus Creek, because of its powerfully negative associations, is visited only by mountain-climbing tourists, despite the many warnings of villagers that the place is "unsafe." Peddler's Lake also carries a story and a lesson, for it was into that bit of water far below Connor Pass that an itinerant peddler was thrown by his companion following a money squabble on their return home from Dingle Fair: "Greed is the root of all evil."

An intense rivalry separates Ballybran from its larger, sister parish of "Castlederry" (i.e. Castlegregory). Until five years ago, Ballybran suffered the perennial humiliation of second-class citizenship, as it was tied administratively and ecclesiastically to the larger parish. Where Castlederry is English-speaking, Ballybran is identified as Irish-speaking; where Castlederry is oriented to the crowded, lively indoor cattle market of Tralee, where the language of hard cash is spoken, the inhabitants of Ballybran traditionally drive their calves and sheep by foot over the mountain pass into the sleepy little open market of Dingle, where barter and the "lucky penny" are still known. Where Castlederry is neatly divided into class, religious, and ethnic boundaries, sporting a few token Protestant residents, the people of Ballybran like to make the "proud boast" that there was never a "Black Protestant" to dig his heels permanently into their native turf. Finally, where men from Castlederry frequently contract matches with women outside their parish, the men of Ballybran feel that a match with a second cousin or no match at all is preferable to marriage with a stranger.

Villagers divide up their history as they do their geography and their social world into neat oppositional boundaries: all before their patron saint, Brendan, is dark, pagan, and forbidding; all afterward is holy, enlightened, and Christian. With a similar passion for the dialectic, villagers view their generations of struggle and opposition against the encroaching, foreign, Protestant landlord. Yet one of the outstanding characteristics of rural Irish culture is its ability to survive through compromise and syncretization, and perhaps nowhere is the pagan element in European civilization more distinctively alive than in the small villages of the western coast, and much of the heritage of the hated Puritan invader Cromwell remains in the sermons delivered and morality extolled from the pulpit of the parish church of Ballybran.

As the local tradition would have it, the "history" of the parish begins with the landing of Noah's granddaughter on Dún na mBarc on the Dingle Peninsula. She was accompanied by fifty virgins and three young men, all seeking refuge from the Great Flood. Village mythographers point for evidence to the three prehistoric standing stones (*gall* *áns*) occupying a central position in Tommy Murphy's field, each with its odd lines, which storytellers say represent a prehistoric alphabet predating the more familiar ogham script of the early Celts. A literary source of this folk belief can be found in the ancient *Leabar Gabala*, the Irish "Book of Invasions,"[1] which was written by the monks of the early Christian period, and parts of which are still committed to memory within the oral tradition of Kerry.

Despite this venerable legend, there is as yet no evidence of the Old Stone Age period in Ireland, and modern scholars agree (see Chadwick 1970; Curtis 1970) that Ireland was first peopled by mesolithic men and women (circa 6000 B.C.), users of copper and bronze tools, builders of stone monuments, and worshippers of the mother-goddess Dana. The few remaining *scéalaí* of the parish (storytellers specializing in the old Irish sagas) can be persuaded to tell about this first semidivine race of Ireland—the so-called Tuatha de Danann—who were conquered in the great battle of Slieve Mish on the coast of southwest Kerry, only a day's walk from Ballybran. The invading conquerors—a small, dark race of "gloomy sea giants" known as the Firbolg—landed on the coast of Kerry to spring a surprise attack. The wily Tuatha de Danann, however, persuaded the invaders that the attack was unfair, since their people were not prepared to meet it. In a gentlemanly gesture the Firbolg agreed to reembark and return "nine waves out to the sea" in order to give the Tuatha de Danann time to ready themselves for battle. The only gratitude the Firbolg received for their military fair play was a magical storm brewed up by the sorcerers of the coast; but the seafaring invaders were victorious in any case. Such is the legendary rendition of the arrival in Kerry about 350 B.C. of the original ancestors of the parish, the Milesian Celts of northern Spain. Fear of retaliation by the defeated tribe lingers on, however, in the still extant belief that the fairy forts, stone rings, and mounds to be found in every hamlet of the parish are the hiding places of the spirits of the angry Tuatha de Danann.

Although villagers shy away from discussing or venturing too near the prehistoric relics that abound in the parish—the monoliths (standing stones), souterrains (underground dwellings), *clochán* (beehive huts), and burial mounds—they are willing to grant religious validity as well as magical power to these monuments of their early ancestors. When in the course of general conversation with the wife of a village shepherd I had occasion to mention the three curious standing stones of the parish, I inquired of her, with

Noah floated west after the flood until he saw the top fourteen feet of the Macgillycuddy's Reeks above water. Then he stepped out of the Ark grumbling about the weather, and a Kerryman greeted him by saying, "What a fine, soft day it is, thanks be to God!"
—VILLAGE ANECDOTE

feigned naiveté, whatever were they for? The wife in her ready reply collapsed the two-thousand-year history separating the religion of her Druidic ancestors from the Catholic faith of her own times: "You mean those tall stones up in Inismore? Those were the kinds of altars we used to have before the priests made them flat."

The prehistory of the parish also merges with modern times in the persistence of at least three ancient culture traits: the mortarless form of stone architecture called corbelling; the custom of heaping rocks over the site where death or burial took place; and the open-air mountain assembly at the top of Mount Brandon on the eve of the Celtic quarterly feast of Lughnasa. The first waves of Mediterranean Celts brought to Ireland the method of constructing stone beehive-shaped dwellings by placing rows of flat stones so that each row projects further into the preceding one until the sides meet the top, the roof being a continuation of the walls. O'Riordan (1965: 82) points out that whole villages built in this manner are still to be found in the heel of Italy. The best example of the beehive hut in Ireland surviving from the early Christian period is the Gallarus Oratory on the western side of the Dingle Peninsula. It is still intact, fifteen hundred years after it was constructed, despite the ravages of Atlantic wind and rain storms, testifying to the architectural genius of the early Celts. This same architectural technique continues to be employed by a few elderly farmers of the region (as it is nowhere else in Ireland) in their construction of stone outhouses for livestock. The ancient pan-European custom of marking the spot where a death occurred by a pile of stones or sticks to which each passerby adds a bit likewise survives in the village practice of adding a stone over the grave of a loved one on each visit to the graveyard.

The historical period of the parish begins in the fifth century with the introduction of Christianity into the village by Saint Brendan the Navigator. According to the most important origin myth of the community, Brendan with his small band of holy and ascetic monks spent the winter in Ballybran on the pinnacle of the mountain that is consecrated to his memory, and later converted by trickery the despotic local pagan chieftain, Crom Dubh. Although the remains of Brendan's oratory atop Mount Brandon attest to the historicity of the monk's visit to Ballybran, the earliest written record of the life of the patron saint comes from the eleventh-century manuscript the *Navagatio Sancti Brendani Abbatis*[2] and the somewhat later medieval Vitae,[3] and it is apparent that by this time much that is legendary had already crept into the life history of the patron saint. Serious scholars, however (see M. MacNeill 1962), accept that Brendan was born during the last quarter of the fifth century—in 484 if one is to accept the Vitae—near Tralee in County Kerry, that he belonged to the then ruling tribe of the Ciarraighe (from which Kerry derives its name), and that he traveled at least as far as Scotland, Wales, and Brittany before his death in 557.

As a monk and a self-designated "wanderer for Christ" (*peregrinator pro Christi*), Brendan belonged to that particularly austere early monastic tradition in Ireland that demanded of its followers silence and solitude, celibacy and seclusion, fasting and self-mortification. It was a tradition that has left its imprint on the character of Irish Catholicism as well as on the ascetic personality of the Irish countryman.[4] Sea voyages for the discovery of new lands and conversion of pagan peoples were central to the disciplined life of these early monks and were a means of prolonging the necessary periods of isolation from the world and the opposite sex. In between voyages Brendan and his monks built a series of monasteries—clusters of beehive-shaped stone cells—on almost inaccessible rocks off the western coast, such as that of the famous Sceilig Mhichil, or on mountain peaks, such as the one in Ballybran. Here the monks pursued the early scholarly tradition of Ireland, producing the first national poetry.[5] When they were not fasting, the monks lived on fish and snared seabirds as well as on donations of oats, bread, and milk, which they received from fishermen and peasants eager to win the blessing of holy men such as themselves.

Legend has it that while Brendan was praying and fasting on top of Mount Brandon, he received his divine commission to sail westward, where he would be led to discover a Promised Land, which was called alternatively Hi-Brazil and Saint Brendan's Isle. News of Brendan's discovery of a New World spread the monk's fame to all maritime districts around the Irish coast and to as far away as Portugal and Spain, and soon Brendan became the patron saint of sailors. It is part of the folk tradition of west Kerry that Christopher Columbus on his maiden voyage across the Atlantic paid a visit to Galway in order to research the manuscripts of Brendan's *Navagatio*, which were kept in a monastery there. Interestingly, Brendan's logbook describes land and vegetation that can be matched along Columbus's route.

Throughout the Dingle Peninsula, Brendan occupies the place reserved elsewhere in Ireland for Saint Patrick—that of the champion of Christianity over paganism. However, what is most interesting about the saint is his role as mediator of the dual pagan and Christian traditions in Ballybran. Wherever possible Brendan used and Christianized—or, as local people are wont to say, "baptized"—the essential aspects of pagan Celtic worship that survive to this day: the rounds at holy wells, the assembly for sun worship at sacred mountaintops, the devotion to sacred rocks. In fact, the monasteries of Mount Brandon, Sceilig Mhichil, and Reask[6] on Corca Dhuibhne most certainly served as a meeting ground between the early Christian monks and the Druidic priests, themselves occupied with the sacred task of preserving the law and legends of the Celts. The meetings between the two cultures, pagan and Christian, bore fruit: Church Latin mixed with the vigorous phrasing of the Celt to produce a rich literary tradition famed for centuries throughout Europe and winning for Ireland the title Isle of Saints and Scholars.

Despite the historicity of his person, it is the mythical quality of Saint Brendan that invests him with power in the community, and his "life history" reads as a continuation or fulfillment of the ancient Celtic sagas. According to the Vitae, Brendan's father's name was Fionnlugh, which Márie MacNeill (1962: 102) interprets as a joining together of the names of two important divine heros of Celtic mythology—Fionn the warrior, and Lugh the sun god. Brendan's own name may be a fortuitous reworking of the name of the Celtic sea god, Bran, of whom Robert Graves (1961) has written so eloquently in *The White Goddess*.[7] The fact that Saint Brendan the Navigator was, like Bran, a divine messenger of the sea, makes him an appropriate Christian replacement for the pagan water god. An elderly publican of Ballybran, well versed in local mythology, argued one evening in his shop that the rock promontory at the edge of the parish, now called Brandon Head, was really a misinformed translation of the original Irish place-name Bran's Nose.

Márie MacNeill (1962: 104), in her detailed study of the survival in western Ireland of the pagan harvest festival called Lughnasa, suggests that Brendan may be identified with the sun god Lugh in whose honor the festival and mountaintop pilgrimage at dawn was originally celebrated. Support for this theory comes from the villagers of Ballybran themselves, who explain that in "the old days" people climbed the mountain to worship the sun, but that ever since Brendan outwitted the pagan chieftain Crom Dubh, the pilgrimage has been made in honor of the Christian saint. And ever since the conversion of the village to Christianity, it has rained on the day of the pilgrimage, hence giving annual testimony to the victory of the gloomy and ascetic Brendan over the pagan sun god. The chieftain, Crom Dubh, who occupies so central a position in the mythology of Ballybran, and whose stone head carving is to be found in the ancient cemetery of the community, is in fact an important god in the Gaelic pantheon and a son of Lugh, the Father-Creator and sun god. The essential origin myth of the parish—the defeat of Crom Dubh by Brendan—told to me in many of its variant forms, bears retelling since it demonstrates so well the syncretism between the two opposing religious traditions of the parish. The following version was given to a representative of the Irish Folklore Commission by the father of a villager upon whose land stands the ruins of the very church built by Brendan in the tale. As owner of the field, the narrator was undisputed heir to the true version of the story.

> The date of the Catholic Church being built is unknown, but a miraculous incident happened during the course of its construction. A pagan named Crom Dubh lived in the parish at the time. The monks in charge of the building approached him for some help. He first refused but afterwards told them that he had a bull in Glenahue about three miles distant if they wished to take him as his donation. The beast was known to be wild and mad and nobody dared to come near him. St. Brendan sent for the beast, caught him and brought him like a lamb to the slaughter. His flesh was used as food and his blood used in the mortar. When Crom Dubh heard that the beast was captured and slaughtered he was furious with rage and demanded payment in cash for the beast. Nothing else would satisfy him. However, he consented to have the flesh weighed and the value given to him. St. Brendan procured scales, put the flesh on one side, wrote the "Hail Mary" on a slip of paper and placed it on the other side. The slip of paper with the "Hail Mary" outweighed the carcass and Crom Dubh was immediately converted to the Catholic Faith. A Pattern [i.e., a patron saint's day] to Crom Dubh's honor is held in the village of [Ballybran] on the last day of July ever since. It is called in Irish Dómach Crom Dubh (Crom Dubh Sunday). (Irish Folklore Commission Archives, MS 202: 177–181)

Some villagers add in the telling that the "pattern" (patron saint) day of the village is celebrated to honor the baptism of Crom Dubh, signifying, as it were, the acceptance of the mythical pagan god into the Irish Communion of Saints. Other variants of the tale make mention of the stone head of Crom Dubh found in the cemetery and add that "long ago" the pattern-day festivities took place in the graveyard around the head of the pagan. It was believed that those in the parish suffering from a toothache could be cured by kissing the stone head on that day. Márie MacNeill (1962: 426), who photographed the stone carving, attests to its antiquity as a third- or fourth-century representation of the god Crom Dubh. She surmises that the stone was part of the pagan ritual and was possibly carried to the top of Mount Brandon for the harvest festivities of Lughnasa, which took place then, as the Christian pilgrimage does today, on Crom Dubh Sunday — that Sunday on or closest to the first day of August.

In effect, the parish honors two patron saints on its "pattern day," the pagan god Crom Dubh and Saint Brendan, founder of Christianity in Ballybran. The ambiguity of the tradition puzzles a few of the parishioners, and a village shopkeeper once remarked after completing the tale, "It's hard to understand why we celebrate our 'pattern day' in honor of that black pagan, Crom Dubh. He was a nasty fellow really, from the likes of the story: a kind of 'false god' if you like."

Not only does the most important ritual event of the parish — the annual pilgrimage up Mount Brandon — commemorate the Christian reinterpretation of a pagan custom, but also the pilgrim to the summit follows many of the same prescriptions adhered to by his Celtic ancestors. He stops midway for a drink at the holy well, leaving behind perhaps some piece of ribbon or red cloth; once on top, he encircles the peak in nine "rounds" from east to west, imitating the course of the sun in the sky and dropping a pebble marker at each round; finally, before making the descent, the pilgrim knocks his back three times against the holy rock called Leac na nDrom (Rock of the Backs) in order to ward off backaches for the coming year. The Church, of course, has long since Christianized the old symbols, and the curate patiently explains that the holy well sprang magically from a rock that Brendan struck with his rod; that the pagan "rounds" are followed today in imitation of Jesus' ascent up Calvary; and that the knocking of the back against Leac na nDrom is a penitential symbol whereby the pilgrim renounces the desires of this world.

But elements of both traditions are held concurrently by the hundreds of pilgrims who make the arduous climb, fasting and many of them barefooted, up the rough eastern ascent of the 3,127-foot mountain. They do it, in their own words, "because Brendan went up there, didn't he?" "for the *craic* of it"; "to do penance"; "for a kidney cure"; "to fulfill a promise"; "for the view"; "because Brendan is our patron and we 'have right' to honor him"; "for fair weather for the hay"; "to give example to the children"; "for a safe mackerel season"; "for a special intention"; "for God to take me before another winter"; "for peace in Ireland."

The villagers of today, like their Celtic ancestors, have a healthy respect for the vagaries of the sea and sky, both of which still dominate their livelihood and well-being. An appeal for fine weather and calm seas can most auspiciously and dramatically be made on the summit of a mountain closer to the heavenly home of their patron and overlooking the vast Atlantic, which their sailor saint conquered so many centuries before. Brendan is the apex of the villagers' account of their history. He represents all that is *right* about themselves and their austere lifestyle. Brendan and his monks, like many of themselves, were celibates and bitten by the same wanderlust that carries today's villagers on periodic peregrinations to England, Scotland, and America. And, like themselves, Brendan had that chameleonlike quality that allowed him to adapt easily to the cultural milieux of strangers, taking and borrowing what seemed useful, and yet able to return home seemingly unscathed and thoroughly Irish at base.

Predisposed as they are to stories of trouble, persecution, tragedy, and death, the remaining ethnohistory of the parish falls into five historical periods: the blood-bath that crushed the rebellious earl of Desmond; the Penal Times and the persecutions of Oliver Cromwell; the Black Famine; the "Troubles" and horrors of the English Black-and-Tans; and the shipwreck in Brandon Bay of a California frigate, the *Port Yarok*. The stories for each are associated with particular times of the year, and certain villagers are known to have the whole or "best" version of the tale, ballad, or poetry through which the history and its moral lesson are communicated.

The Dingle Peninsula witnessed one of the bloodiest deeds of Queen Elizabeth I, who charged Lord Grey and later Sir Walter Raleigh with the task of crushing the rebellious Irish earl of Desmond. In November 1580 some six hundred Italian and Spanish troops came to the aid of the Catholic Desmonds, and all were besieged by the English in the tiny cove called Dún an Oir, near the tip of the Dingle Peninsula. Over six hundred Irish resisters were slain, and the despised Sir Walter Raleigh was awarded by the queen a grant of forty thousand acres in Ireland in gratitude for his "brave deeds." The following centuries saw the Irish of Corca Dhuibhne, as elsewhere, persecuted by brutal English oppression. Irish lords were dispossessed, and the Irish poet and scholar was banished to wander in exile. His ragged verses survived, however, on the nimble tongues of the cottage storytellers, the *scéalaí*.

Sean Og, the parish clerk, has the stories of Penal Times and the ruthless persecution of the priests. Since the tradition of house masses, or "stations," originated during Penal Times, Sean Og finds a receptive audience for his stories at the breakfasts following stations each fall and spring. In the days of the Black Protestant Cromwell (circa 1649), tells Sean, there was a five-pound bounty on the head of every Catholic priest. At this time there was a much beloved curate in Ballybran who was captured and beheaded by one of Cromwell's men. His headless body is buried outside the graveyard and under a mulberry bush in the space once reserved for unbaptized babies. Late one night, about ten years ago, himself (says Sean) and old Father Boyle were late coming home from a sick call in Drom when they heard a terrible racket — a rumbling and banging like metal barrels rolling over the ground. The pair ducked for safety into the home of a villager, who said not to mind the noise, that it was nothing but the warning of the "beheaded priest," who comes up from his grave in search of his head each year on his anniversary. Other village legends about Cromwell tell how he died in Ireland, but that his body could not be disposed of: Irish soil refused to receive it, and the corpse bobbed atop the Irish sea until it finally sank to the bottom, causing the waters to be rough and angry ever since.

When the potato famine struck in 1845, Cork and Kerry were among the hardest hit counties, but the little fishing villages of Corca Dhuibhne served as a refuge for many fleeing even worse starvation and disease in the inland parishes. Mag, one of the oldest parishioners, "has the famine stories," since her own mother lived through those times (1845–1849). Mag is most inclined to tell these stories in the spring when there is a vestigial anxiety about the rapidly diminishing supply of potatoes in every villager's barn or back kitchen. In her at first halting and gentle voice she will tell of the stranger her mother met dying by the wayside, his mouth hanging open and the juice of the stinging nettle dripping from his blackened lips. Mag's voice rises into quivering anger as she tells of the hunger that forced men, women, and children to the roads and to a diet of the spiny nettles. The man died before Mag's mother could find help, and because he was a stranger and his religion and state of soul unknown, the man was buried in the common grave in the sandbanks of the bay, making his soul's entry into heaven all the more difficult. Years later, Mag's mother once again encountered the old man at the same spot upon her return from Mass on All Soul's Day. As he raised his hands in supplication, the old woman realized that he was the poor forgotten soul let up from Purgatory on the Day of the Dead to beg a prayer from the only friend he had in the parish.

Summertime, as the Ballybran crews are being selected for regattas and mackerel fishing, is also the "proper time" for the telling of the 1896 wreck of the *Port Yarok* and the drowning of its crew in Brandon Bay. The story has several versions, some narrative, others in ballad form, but the underlying message is the same: no salvation for those like the crew of the *Yarok* who die suddenly, unprepared and unshriven ("It's not a death without a priest").

The "war" for Irish liberation was particularly savage in southwest Kerry and Cork. Heroes were made and burned alive in Tralee. A Dingle man, Thomas Ashe, became one of the period's greatest martyrs, fighting in the Easter Rising of 1916 and then dying during a hunger strike while a British prisoner. The Anglo-Irish patriot, Sir Roger Casement, was captured by the Royal Irish Constabulary during an abortive attempt to smuggle twenty thousand German rifles to members of the IRA on a beach not far from Ballybran. No village gathering would be complete without the soulful singing of the ballad "Banna Strand," immortalizing the event. The period of "the Troubles" and the brief occupation of the parish by the hated English mercenaries, the so-called Black-and-Tans (circa 1920), is told most eloquently in verse, and the shepherd Dermot upon urging from his pub mates can be persuaded in summertime to launch into the forty-minute recitation of the trials and tribulations of the folk hero of the day, "Seamas O'Brian," without a single pause or a stumble.

In the light of their sacred history villagers have traditionally interpreted

the present. If the rural Irish are a spiritual people, they are equally pragmatic and are well seasoned in the survival arts of adaptation and change.
Their lives have often depended on it. As folk Catholic philosophers they
know that "forms" can change while the essential "substance" remains
immutable. Yet the past three decades have witnessed the most profound
changes in the western countryside, not only in the "forms" but in the very
"substance" and meaning of village social life: in the disintegration of familism; the devaluation of farming and rural trades as an acceptable way of life;
and in the growing acceptance by the young of the alien ethos of urban capitalism and secularization.

Peter Tuohy shakes his head with disbelief as he watches the rented bull-
dozer cover over the remains of Saint Flan's holy well so that the foundations for a modern tourist "singing pub" can be laid on the main road of
Ballybran. "Yerra," he says with a shrug of his shoulders, "we must go on
with the world, even when it takes a bad turn."

CHAPTER TWO

The People
Left Behind

"Wasn't a great thought Columbus had," said a man to me once as we lay gazing out over the Atlantic, "to find America? For if there wasn't America, the Island wouldn't stand a week."
—ROBIN FLOWER,
The Western Island

N E L L I E , the mother of eleven children and one of several village matriarchs, is at ninety-two a shut-in. She is tended to by her only child to remain in Ireland, and sixty-eight-year-old Mikey is today almost as feeble as herself. Mikey's marriage was arranged late in life, and his wife, a wealthy widow from "west o'Dingle" several years his senior, died early and childless. Nellie delights in telling visitors about her sons and daughters abroad, their gains and successes—a small square in Springfield, Massachusetts, named after her eldest and "pet" son, a city park commissioner; newspaper clippings of local elections won and occasionally lost by other sons and sons-in-law; colorful Penney's Department Store portraits of "Yankee" grandchildren in bountiful number. When urged, Nellie will tell some of the stories for which she has gained local renown—tales of the "Black Protestant" Cromwell, of the Penal Times, of the "Troubles," and of her son who was shot in error by his own companions during a local IRA skirmish—but in the midst of the telling, the animation vanishes from her voice and she begins to stare aimlessly out her window and over the wild Atlantic coastline. "Wisha, I should have gone off to America, too," she muses. "But, Nellie," I coax, attempting to bring her back, "look at the beauty of the place: the sea, the grass, the mountains. . . ." She laughs, cutting me off. "Sure, girlie, there's the sea and the mountains all right. But what is this miserable rock of land but a curse on us?"

The quality of social life in western Ireland today is so unrecognizably different from that described by Arensberg and Kimball (1968) in the late thirties that one is tempted to accuse the pair of unabashed romanticism. To be sure, the gay strains of the melodeon and the primitive beat of the goatskin *bodhran* can still be heard at a spirited session in the village pub on a long summer's evening. But the melodeon players are more than likely city cousins come home to visit their native turf from Liverpool or Dublin, where they are now permanent residents, and the lively crowd at the pub are most certainly German or English tourists in the area for backpacking and salmon fishing. The winter "regulars"—the solitary tight-knit group of permanent parish bachelors—sit grimly in a row, neither sure of how they feel about the invasion of their normally silent card-playing and round-drinking "club," nor how they should act in the presence of outsiders, some of them women.

During the first few weeks in August when the hay is normally cut, raked, and stacked into the traditional "wine cocks" by a *meitheal*, or cooperative work force of fathers and sons attending each man's fields in turn, what can be heard in the summers of 1974 and 1975 but the repetitive lament by solitary bachelors as they watch their fields of hay rot from rain: "Where are the people?" A few attempt to do alone or with the help of an aged wife the work that was once done by ten, fifteen, twenty pairs of hands. Others, with remittance money sent from relatives abroad, hire tractors and part-time summer help. Still others seek solace at the pub and utter, "Bad 'cess to the hay!" hoping the "dole" will get them through the winter and enable them to buy feed for their cows and calves.

The fabric of a social life once rooted in intense familism—a dependency upon and reciprocity within wide circles of near and "far out" kin—is rent beyond recognition given the virtual disappearance of the necessary relations. Family farms without the labor of extended families are inoperative today, although villagers still attempt to work within the same economic model.

▪ Demographic Decline

The rural population is vanishing and with it is vanishing the Irish race itself. Rural Ireland is stricken and dying, and the will to marry on the land is almost gone. — CORNELIUS LUCEY, *Bishop of Cork, 1953*

Prior to the Great Famine of 1845–1849, the population of Ballybran parish was 2,772. Church records indicate that early marriage was the norm and families were large. The land of the Dingle Peninsula was ever stony and inhospitable, and the excess population was forced up the sides of the Kerry Mountains to plant their spuds and turnips. The remains of stone fences still outline the old hillside plots in Ballybran, although they have, in the words of villagers, "gone back to mountain." The population was reduced to half by the famine, and as in the rest of rural Ireland, this was followed by an initially adaptive reversal of marriage and birth patterns,[1] and a spiraling emigration rate.[2] Whereas in 1965 the parish *gardaí* (civil police) census recorded a population of 645, today the community is just barely holding together at 461 souls. The thirty-eight deaths and fifteen emigrations of the past year (1974–1975) were offset by only four births. During this same period, one three-year-old girl died in a fall from a horse cart, and one adolescent died from postoperative complications. There were no matches, engagements, or marriages, and only the most furtively hinted at and fleeting courtships. The last marriage took place in 1972 and has yet to produce an heir; childlessness is a common consequence of late marriage. The average age at marriage for Ballybran couples is considerably later than for elsewhere in the Republic:[3] thirty-four years for men, and twenty-eight years for women, and only one in every three adult males is married. Few married

Tailoring is a dying trade in the countryside. When I came here forty years ago there were three times as many people in the parish. I was friends with the gardaí; *and that's how I learned there were sixteen hundred people within the local jurisdiction of the barracks. Not that all these sixteen hundred were ready for tailoring. Some were still in the cradle, and others were a day from dying. But there were enough to keep me busy from morn til night.*
— THE VILLAGE TAILOR

YEAR	MARRIAGES	BIRTHS	DEATHS	EMIGRATIONS
1970	0	10	15	11
1972	2*	6	18	16
1974	0	4	38	15

*One of these was contracted outside the parish.

couples today value the seven- to nine-child household once so prevalent in the parish, and a very successful form of birth control—total abstinence—is practiced by several village couples since they have achieved their desired limit of two or three children. Table 1 illustrates the imbalance in births, marriages, deaths, and emigration that is symbolic of the decline of the community.

The predominant household of Ballybran in the current generation is a nonconjugal unit. As marriage becomes increasingly uncommon, the majority of middle-aged adults today live alone or with one or more members of their family of origin. Given the reluctance of women to marry out of their families, and the hesitancy of young men to bring in a "stranger woman," one might be tempted to label this altogether curious situation the triumph of extreme familism at the expense of community survival. Of the one hundred and thirty-eight households of the parish, only forty-one are fully conjugal and generative, and have *any* possibility of replicating themselves in the coming generation.

In order to gain a perspective of Ballybran household structure over time, it might be helpful to consider the life cycle of the domestic group[4] as a series of bell curves,

Q. Is the lack of foresight among the Irish as great as it is said to be?
A. It is extreme. They marry at sixteen or eighteen. Very often they have to borrow to pay the priest. The more intolerable their poverty becomes, the more they seem to live from hand to mouth.
—ALEXIS DE TOCQUEVILLE, *Journeys to England and Ireland*, 1835

beginning with the marriage of a couple, reaching a peak when all children born to the couple are still at home, and gradually descending again as most of these children leave home, marry, and begin a new cycle and curve. In Ballybran the curves become fixated at the second stage—with unmarried adult children staying on in the parental household, or they end abruptly as children not only leave their natal families but leave Ballybran as well. The curve increasingly rarely takes the all-important upswing that propels the parish into the next generation. Table 2 illustrates the radical process that is

■ TABLE 2: DOMESTIC CYCLES IN BALLYBRAN HOUSEHOLD COMPOSITION

STAGES (TOTAL N = 138 HOUSEHOLDS)		CLASSES		PERCENTAGES	
I.	Simple conjugal groups; nongenerative or postgenerative (21)	A.	Husband–wife childless (by preference or sterility) (11)	A.	8.0
		B.	Husband–wife childless (by emigration of all children) (10)	B.	7.2
				Total	15.2
II.	Fully conjugal and generative; parents and young or still marriageable children (41)	A.	Nuclear households (20)	A.	14.5
		B.	Extended households (21)	B.	15.2
				Total	29.7
III.	Transitional households: conjugal-generative becoming nonconjugal, nongenerative (13)	A.	Husband–wife-middle-aged bachelor son(s) (11)	A.	8.0
		B.	Husband–wife-middle-aged spinster daughter (2)	B.	1.4
				Total	9.4
IV.	Nonconjugal or postconjugal and nongenerative: consanguineal domestic groups (63)	A.	Solitary bachelor (16)	A.	11.6
		B.	Bachelor brothers (7)	B.	5.1
		C.	Adult brothers-sisters (12)	C.	8.7
		D.	Widow–middle-aged son (9)	D.	6.5
		E.	Widower–middle-aged son (8)	E.	5.8
		F.	Widower–middle-aged daughter (1)	F.	.7
		G.	Widower–aged mother (1)	G.	.7
		H.	Widow alone (9)	H.	6.6
				Total	45.7

transforming the community of Ballybran from a healthy conjugal community to a sick and dying celibate community.

The steady erosion of the human community can be witnessed in the "death" of three ancient townlands, or hamlets of the parish, over the past ten years alone: Slieve Druicead, which in 1966 had three households with eighteen people; Farne, which had one household with three people; and Slieve Glas, which had two households with eight people. Each of these ancient hamlets is deserted today—death claiming most and emigration the remainder.

▪ Rural Exodus

> *They are going, shy-eyed cailins, and*
> *lads so straight and tall,*
> *From the purple peaks of Kerry, from*
> *the crags of wild Imaal,*
> *From the greening plains of Mayo,*
> *and the glens of Donegal.*
> —ETHNA CARBERY

The flight of girls and marriage-aged women from the small villages of the west of Ireland is at once the cause and the result of rural decline (see R. Kennedy 1973: 66–85). Although rural women have been emigrating to the United States and Britain since the period of the Great Famine, the character of the emigration has changed since World War II. Where previously village girls spent periods of from two to five years abroad in order to accumulate dowry money for a suitable match back home, today's girls leave with no intention of returning. The shyness and reluctance of village boys in romantic matters ("the lads around here are 'desperate'; they haven't a notion about women"), the boredom and lack of entertainment during the winter months, and the low social status of the in-marrying woman in patrilocal Kerry are inducements to leave. The more equitable opportunities for both sexes in British and American cities, and the relative independence and higher social status of women abroad, keep the Irish lasses from returning home. Also contributing to the massive exodus of rural girls is the vocal dissatisfaction of their mothers, who want a better life for their daughters than they themselves had. Table 3 demonstrates the general trend in western Europe toward an excess of males in rural areas and an excess of women in urban areas. Nowhere is this phenomenon more pronounced than in Ireland.

The result of this trend can be witnessed in the virtual absence of eligible females in Ballybran. We find in the parish today a total of sixty-four bachelors over age thirty-five, and only twenty-seven unmarried women in

■ TABLE 3: CONTRASTS IN RURAL AND URBAN SEX RATIOS IN EUROPEAN COUNTRIES, 1947–1962

MALES PER 100 FEMALES

COUNTRY AND EXACT YEAR	TOTAL POPULATION	RURAL AREAS (A)	URBAN AREAS (B)	"EXCESS" MALES IN RURAL AREAS (A–B)
Ireland, 1961	101	113	89	24
Denmark, 1960	98	114	93	21
Iceland, 1950	101	114	96	18
Sweden, 1960	100	112	95	17
Northern Ireland, 1961	95	106	89	17
Finland, 1960	93	102	86	16
Norway, 1961	99	108	93	15
Switzerland, 1960	96	102	91	11
Austria, 1960	87	93	82	11
Portugal, 1960	92	94	84	10
Luxembourg, 1960	98	102	95	7
Belgium, 1947	97	102	95	7
France, 1962	95	99	92	7
Scotland, 1961	92	97	90	7
England and Wales, 1961	94	99	93	6
Netherlands, 1960	99	103	98	5

Source: Robert Kennedy 1973: 68.

the same age bracket (nine spinsters and eighteen widows). Even more dramatic, where there are more than thirty still hopeful and eligible young men between the ages of twenty-one and thirty-five, there remain only five unattached young women between these years—and none of these seems inclined to give up her freedom. Although there are occasional fleeting courtships and flirtations between adolescent secondary-school pupils during the year, there is a trail of broken romances left each summer at graduation time when the vivacious and mobile young women migrate. They leave behind a large proportion of their beaux who are committed—as the girls are not—to carrying on the family farm and name, a task rendered more absurd each year as these men come to realize that they are not likely to produce any heirs of their own.

Although Ballybran, because of its unfavored location in isolated and mountainous west Kerry, is idiosyncratic insofar as it represents the extremes in demographic imbalance, similar tendencies toward an aging rural population, an absence of farmers in the productive age groups, and an inequal distribution of the sexes exist in the rest of the country as well. A comparison of the male and female farm population in County Kerry—including both farm owners and those involved on a wage basis in agricultural occupations—shows that males outnumber females in all except the over-seventy-five age group (table 4). While the aggregate ratio of male to female farm

■ TABLE 4: PERCENTAGE DISTRIBUTION OF COUNTY KERRY FARM POPULATION BY SEX AND AGE

YEARS	MALE	FEMALE	TOTAL
14 or less	14.3	13.5	27.8
15 to 19	4.6	3.8	8.4
20 to 44	14.2	8.7	22.9
45 to 64	14.0	11.2	25.2
65 to 74	5.9	4.4	10.3
Over 75	2.7	2.7	5.4
Totals	55.7	44.3	100.0

Source: *County Kerry Agricultural Resource Survey* (1972: 63).

SUCCESSOR STATUS	PERCENTAGE
(a) Definitely no heirs	23.0
(b) Heirs doubtful	12.0
(c) Heirs emigrated and unlikely to return	6.0
(d) Total farmers without prospective heirs (a + b + c)	41.0
(e) Farmers with heirs	59.0
Total	100.0

Source: *County Kerry Agricultural Resource Survey* (1972: 67).

children is approximately five to four until age eighteen, afterwards males
outnumber females by roughly three to one (Kerry County Committee of
Agriculture 1972: 72). Such demographic imbalance is immediately implicated in the serious problem in Kerry of the numerous farms without successors: 23 percent of all farmers over fifty were reported (ibid., 67) as
definitely without heirs and another 18 percent with doubtful or unlikely
heirs (table 5). Putting this into the national perspective, the *Macra na
Feirme Survey* reported that approximately one-quarter of *all* farms in the
Republic are without successors—a total of between forty-four and fifty
thousand farms (Commins and Kelleher 1973: 74). These represent the
farms of bachelors or of those married couples without children or with all
children emigrated. The celibacy, childlessness, and aging of the Irish farm
population has important implications for agricultural development. The
elderly bachelor farmers of County Kerry, for example, are neither change
nor production conscious, the former because they are old, the latter
because they are without wife or children and their own needs and wants
are minimal. Agricultural advisers in the county seat complain that the old
farmers resist the adoption of modern innovations and, although comfortable with traditional patterns of cooperation with extended family members,
are suspicious of participating with non-kin in agricultural cooperatives fostered by the Ministry of Agriculture. Village agriculture, to be described

below, is increasingly unproductive and uneconomic. Given the central position of agriculture in the economics of County Kerry, this decline is synonymous with total rural decline.

▪ Village Economics

"Too bad there isn't an export market for stone," I said. "Ah, sure," said the old man. "If it were worth anything, strangers would have carted it off a long time ago." — LEON URIS, *Ireland, A Terrible Beauty,* 1975

For most of its history, the problem of sheer physical survival has dominated the lives of Ballybran villagers, situated as they are between rough sea and eroded mountain. Over three-quarters of the parishioners list their occupation as "farmer"; however, farming is but a vestigial occupation. Land, when it is in use at all, is given to pasture and to growing animal feed. Although most villagers grow some potatoes and a little cabbage, as much of their diet comes from the sea and from canned and packaged goods in the local shops as from the land. And during the winter and spring months almost every village family qualifies for welfare under Unemployment Assistance. In essence, the holding of land today has more symbolic than utilitarian value.

The average-sized farm in Ballybran is between five and twenty acres, much of it fragmented and divided among pasture, bog, rough mountain grazing, tillage, and commonage. The village dairy farmer has an average of ten head of cows, and the sheep farmer between fifty and seventy-five sheep. Although since the establishment of the Irish Free State in 1922, and continuing under the Republic, the prevailing land tenure system is based on almost universal occupier-ownership of land, the fragmentation of fields frequently results in underutilization. One village farmer, for example, has his twelve acres divided among seven lots, a few of these more than two miles apart. He has no means of transportation other than a horse cart. Other farmers have their lots sandwiched between a neighbor's adjoining fields—a situation often resulting in enmity between households. Over the years, some farmers have made gentlemanly trades of fields between themselves in order to consolidate holdings. It was estimated by a representative of the Land

Commission in Tralee that over 20 percent of the farm holdings in Bally-bran — many of them traded without recourse to legal procedures — are without registered titles. Since 1922 the Irish Land Commission has worked to "restripe" villages, combining scattered plots into more productive holdings. The process has been slowest, however, in the Gaeltacht (Irish-speaking communities), where farmers debate endlessly about the relative merits of one plot over another, and where individual fields are often even personalized with a name.

The almost fierce pride and independence of the west Kerry farmer is both a proud boast of the Irish government and a hindrance to its plans for regional development. Land equals status in the village, and a sharp watch is kept on those farmers who attempt to rise from the ranks of ordinary farmers to the admired but greatly envied status of "strong" farmer. Many bachelors and childless couples say they would rather die without *any* plans for farm succession than live to see a "greedy" neighbor buy up their unused lots piecemeal in order to consolidate his farm and win status. The selling of a field outright to a neighbor is so preposterous a notion by village standards that the commonly heard expression "Well, today I 'sold' a field to Jimmy B" means only that the farmer sold the rights to harvest the hay or oats from his field for one season. A "limited good" worldview (see Foster 1967: 122ff) allows for the selling of village lots to "harmless" and neutral outsiders (e.g., English tourists looking to build summer vacation homes) but not one another — this despite strongly nationalistic counter-sentiments of Irish soil for the Irish. In effect, a balance is struck with the lesser of two evils: let the "strangers" have it rather than see the O'Flahertys step over the O'Donnells in the perpetual squabbles over land, which the poet Patrick Kavanaugh once referred to as "the net of all earthly intrigue."

What has occurred in western Ireland during the intervening forty years between Arensberg and Kimball's analysis (1940, 1st edition) and this study is not only a radical shift in demography, changes in technology and marketing, but also, and more important, changes in the consciousness and self-definition of the younger rural populace, and a reevaluation (even by elders) of the values of traditional country life. Arensberg and Kimball's vivid description of a lively farm family life in which patriarchal father delayed retirement and set son against son in the spirited competition for the "old fellow's" favor and eventual birthright of the farm has not only colored the "official" anthropological view of Irish family life, but also has even dominated the Irish government's conception of the mechanics of farm succession. As recently as 1973 the Macra na Feirme committee of the Department of Agriculture published a report,[5] widely distributed through small shopkeepers of the west, urging farm owners to retire early, select and name an heir as soon as feasible, and free *all* children for marriage at a reasonable age. The report was guided by a number of assumptions—that fathers still rule imperiously over their children, that competition over inheritance of the land is intense, that women are eager to marry into farms, that farming is valued as a priceless, if not a profitable, way of life—assumptions that, if they were once true, no longer hold today. For at least three decades the selection of an heir for the land has been governed by the process of elimination rather than by choice. That is, the last one to escape (usually the youngest son) gets stuck by default with an unproductive farm and saddled with a lifestyle of almost certain celibacy and service to the "old people."

▪ The Common Market versus the Kerry Farmer

The processes of modernization and rapid change have affected small communities in the world at large and are by no means unique. However, the small farmers of western Ireland were among the last in western Europe to experience the impact of agrarian capitalism, world marketing, and secularization, and they are still smarting from the blow.

As almost any villager will eagerly relate, it was the fateful entry of the Republic into the European Economic Community (EEC), or Common Market, on January 1, 1973, that sounded the ultimate death knell of traditional Irish familistic farming. Through participation in international agriculture, the village farmer is shamed and exposed—forced to measure his worth in terms of acres, heads of cattle, the English pound, and the American dollar. Judged in these capitalistic terms, the Kerry farmer with his "grass of three cows and six sheep" has begun to look upon his work as a failure and an embarrassment to the changing, modern image that Ireland wishes to project to the world. He need only, for example, look to the scolding tone of the chief inspector of the Department of Agriculture and Fisheries, who introduced a report on Kerry agriculture with criticism for the resistance of local farmers to the new mode of agricultural capitalism within the EEC.

> *As we face this new situation we cannot but realize that the full benefits of EEC membership will be achieved only if Irish agriculture is up-to-date and* competitive. *The persistence of low farm incomes in agriculture, particularly in the western region, has* hindered *the* general economic development *of the country up to the present. Membership of the EEC, of itself, will not change this situation. A major effort will be required of the farmers themselves in finding lasting solutions to the low income problem. (Kerry County Committee of Agriculture 1972: vii, emphasis my own)*

The first step toward modernization was that of ridding the land of nonproductive small farmers. Under the impetus of a Common Market recommendation (see Commins and Kelleher 1973: 76) the Irish Department of Lands initiated a program in the winter of 1974 concerning the large-scale transfer of lands away from the marginal or "transitional" farmers of the west to the hands of development-oriented agricultural capitalists. The vehicle for this transfer was the formal announcement of the New Voluntary Retirement Scheme (alternately called the Farm Modernization Scheme), which called for all nonviable, low-production farmers to surrender their land to the Irish Land Commission for the purposes of "restructuring" (Department of Lands 1974, 1975). The scheme divided farms into three categories: *commercial* farms, those 15,000 viable farms of the Republic with at least one hundred acres and an annual income of £1,800 per adult worker; *development* farms, those 35,000 intermediate farms that the Land Commission hopes can reach commercial status within a six-year development plan; and *transitional* farms, those 120,000 farms with less than forty-five acres and less than an annual income of £1,800 per labor unit. Since the average-size farm in Ireland is forty acres (thirty in County Kerry), the majority of Irish farmers were being asked to retire.

In exchange for his land, the retiring farmer would receive the market price of the land plus a small weekly pension for life. In addition, each complying farmer would be allowed to keep two acres for a garden plot, but he was prohibited from ever taking up farming again as an occupation. Neither age nor successor status had bearing on the qualifications for retirement, and those with young heirs as well as those without them, and the young and able-bodied along with the elderly and feeble, were to be pensioned off together. The Minister of Lands, Mr. Fitzpatrick, reported to the Dail (*Irish Times*, November 24, 1974) that of the first thousand retirement applicants received, 14 percent were under fifty-five years, 61 percent were between fifty-five and sixty-five, and only 25 percent were from farmers aged sixty-five or over. One of the most vocal critics of the farm modernization scheme, Dr. Ivor Browne, Chief Psychiatrist of the Eastern Health Board, expressed his alarm that such widespread early retirement not only would "set farmer against farmer" but also could contribute to "premature senility" and add to the already staggering geriatric problems of the dispirited rural areas (*Irish Times*, November 14, 1974: 2).

A representative of the Irish Land Commission in Tralee estimated that over 90 percent of the farmers on the Dingle Peninsula would qualify for retirement under the scheme, which was all but compulsory insofar as noncomplying farmers would be severed from the grants and subsidies necessary to the survival of all farmers. Transitional farmers would no longer qualify for sheep and beef premiums, and they would be disqualified from the grants for equipment and livestock purchase, farm buildings, and land reclamation. In all, the farm scheme was a move designed to facilitate the transfer of land from small to big farmers, rather than from father to son. In Ballybran, the EEC retirement scheme was interpreted as a vote of no confidence in traditional familistic farming.

Throughout the long and discouraging winter, Ballybran farmers gathered in clusters at the pub or at one another's homes to listen to radio or public television reports decry and deride the "backwardness" and "conservatism" of the western coastal farmers, who were characterized as living like parasites off welfare handouts, grants, and subsidies, who were opposed to progress, and who hung greedily and tenaciously onto their unproductive and miserable farms. The spectre of forced and early retirement hovered over the nightly pub sessions in Ballybran, and a puritanical gloom settled like a mist into each man's pint of bitter porter. "Well, lads, 'tis we're finished up now for sure" was a commonly heard refrain. The local residents read about their lives and livelihoods discussed in national papers as so much debris and dead weight. The following defense of the Voluntary Retirement Scheme from a letter to the editor in the *Irish Times* (November 20, 1974) illustrates the about-face of the urban consensus from a nationalistic pride in traditional patterns toward an enthusiastic acceptance of the international capitalistic model.

It is highly presumptuous to conclude that these 120,000 farmers (slated for early retirement) are all commercially oriented to farming with a desire to maximize profits. In fact, for the majority of small farmers agriculture is more a way of life than a means of livelihood, and a livelihood that is increasingly uneconomic. Hasn't the time finally arrived to relieve the urban taxpayer of the burden of underwriting an antiquated way of life?

The dissatisfaction of the western farmer with the EEC retirement scheme was expressed through a number of opinion surveys. In one, cited by the Macra na Feirme report (see Commins and Kelleher, p. 76), when three hundred and eighty-five farmers over fifty-five were asked whether they would avail themselves of such a scheme, the response was as follows:

	Percentage
Would adopt scheme	22.7
Would consider it	6.1
Would not adopt it	67.3
Could not say	3.9
Total	100.0 (n = 385)

The small farmers of southwest Kerry united in their protest of the forced retirement, and until our departure in the late spring of 1975, only one farmer in all of west Kerry had signed up to retire — and he was held up to vicious ridicule.

Traditional rural Irish society recognized no such status or role as "retired" farmer. Even after the aged farmer had eventually "signed over" legal ownership of the land to his heir, the old man usually maintained a managerial role in the affairs of the farm until death (Arensberg and Kimball 1968: 118). Even the *word* "retired" only begins to creep into the occupational listings of the deceased in the Ballybran death register during the mid-1960s. Not only does a deep-seated and pervasive fear of idleness keep young and middle-aged farmers busy at tasks that outsiders might consider unproductive, but the same Celtic work ethic drives elderly and already pensioned farmers and shepherds to keep up at least the pretenses of the daily round. Inactivity is associated with immorality ("idleness is the devil's workshop"), and retirement is associated with death in the mind of the Kerryman; many a rugged old shepherd attributes his longevity to a life of hard work and "no idling." Villagers are particularly fond of repeating stories of the miraculous cures of ancient farmers who struggled out of their deathbeds at the last moment to check up on a favorite old cow or newborn calf, only to discover that they felt better once on their feet and involved again in the business of the farm.

While older villagers valiantly attempt to cling to their tried and familiar, if rapidly failing, patterns, village adolescents and young adults are only rarely today motivated by the same "friendly" (i.e., kinship-based) values as their parents and grandparents. The ethos of individualism and capitalism has made steady inroads into *their* worldview. The following example illustrates the clash of values between generations in Ballybran.

The summer of 1974 was a particularly wet one, and anxiety was rampant as villagers worried about "saving" the hay that would feed their cows and calves through the winter and part of the spring. At least three consecutive dry days and several helping hands are needed in order to cut, turn, and stack the hay. Less than a decade ago this task would have been done unquestioningly by "cooring," or farmers taking turns in each other's fields. Children and adolescents would be recruited for lighter tasks, and women would take turns bringing the tea and fresh bread to the fields. It was an occasion for conversation, storytelling, poetry recitation, and drinking. Boundaries would be adjusted, and old disputes and hard feelings softened by the porter and spirits. But increasingly today connotations of "low class" and "small farmer" are attached to those few "backward" farmers who participate in "cooring." The more prosperous and "stronger" farmers hire tractors and pay village adolescents to help with the hay.

Tomás and Maire, however, are an aged, childless couple who observe the older customs, and they sent out word that a *meitheal*, or cooperative work force, was needed for the haying. My husband and I and our children showed up at their fields the next sunny day to find the seventy-year-old couple bickering about how best to do the job alone. They were surprised and grateful for our offer of help, and we worked until the sun set that evening. Later in the pub we enquired of the "idle" young lads of the village why they hadn't gone up to Ballydubh to lend a "friendly" hand to their distant cousins. The boys were incredulous to think that anyone would be so "stupid" as to work for nothing. "That old pair is so backward and miserly," offered one young man, "that they expect a dinner of dry spuds and a bottle of ale is pay enough for a day's work in the fields." Other youths in the pub protested that the old farmer was pensioned and had enough to make do on. Finally, the young men pointed out the absurdity of time spent harvesting the hay needed to feed the old couple's "herd" of two sick old cows kept up out of affection for the creatures rather than for profit. The consensus of the youths was that the cows should be destroyed and the old couple accept the inevitability of retirement. Old Tomás's face grew red with anger as I relayed the message to him, and he replied, "I helped their fathers and their grandfathers, and now they 'have right' to help me." But no such help was to be forthcoming that season, and my husband and I were ridiculed for continuing to "coor."

▪ Constriction of Village Institutions

The low fertility and decreased productivity of the parish have resulted in a gradual constriction of the major social institutions in the community. Twenty years ago there were two elementary schools in the parish, each with a matriculation of nearly two hundred pupils. Today there is one elementary school with a total enrollment of fewer than eighty pupils. During 1974 the Ministry of Education decided it could no longer justify the salaries

of four full-time teachers and consequently transferred the dynamic bilingual kindergarten teacher, and some months later an elderly pillar of Ballybran education was retired without replacement. Mothers and fathers
began nervously comparing the parish situation with that of nearby Dunquin, which has been bitterly struggling to keep its last teacher for the
remaining handful of pupils.

The government policy of amalgamation (read *closure*) of isolated rural
schools in the Gaeltacht also affects the Ballybran secondary-school,
which must fight annually for the meager government funds needed to
keep its doors open to the sons and daughters of the small farmers on the
peninsula. Established in 1963 in the home of a dedicated married couple
just then returned from lay missionary work in Africa, the aggressively
bilingual school opened with an enrollment of only thirty-eight pupils.
Over the past five years, it has averaged a hundred pupils per annum.
While the children of relatively prosperous farmers are still sent to boarding schools for secondary education, "the bungalow," as the Ballybran
school is fondly called, serves the children of those parish families who traditionally have not aspired to higher education for their children. In one
recent survey of Dingle Peninsula villagers (see Riordan 1973), it was found
that only 39 percent of the women and 19 percent of the men had gone any
further than primary-school.

The attitude of the Minister of Education has been to support verbally
the concept of village-level Gaeltacht schools, while simultaneously with-
holding financial support to them on the basis of their relatively low attendance (reflecting, of course, the low population density of the Gaeltacht).
In January of 1972 An Braine Forbairte (the development branch of the
Ministry of Education) made its policy quite clear in a letter circulated
among the managers (principals) of all small secondary-schools in the west:
no future financial support would be granted, and students midway in their
high school careers were to be transferred to the nearest *town* secondary-
school if they wished to receive a leaving certificate (diploma). The mandate infuriated village parents, for whom it demonstrated both the lack of
sympathy and the ignorance of the basic geography of the region on the part
of the Ministry of Education. The other secondary-schools nearest to Bally-

bran are located in Dingle, which no local school bus can reach through the narrow mountain pass, or in Tralee, thirty miles away and over a road often impassable during winter rains.

During the furor over the threatened closure, Siobhan Riordan (1973) surveyed one hundred families on the Dingle Peninsula on their feelings about the school situation. Of the hundred families questioned, 82 percent said that the closure of the secondary-school would be a "great loss" to the community, and gave these reasons: "It would lead to a general decline" (29%); "The school is an essential village institution" (20%); "It is better to educate the young locally than elsewhere" (51%). The latter opinion was related to parents' mixed feelings about the emigration of village youth, which often begins with secondary education beyond the parish. In Riordan's sample of peninsula families, 32 percent of the children who have already left school are currently working abroad in the United States, England, and Australia, while another 31 percent are employed in cities elsewhere in Ireland. Hence, almost two-thirds of the working child population of the area are presently employed outside their native district. The bilingual community school was seen by many village parents as a means of at least temporarily delaying the rural exodus of their children. The fact that there was never any government consultation on the local level concerning the proposed downgrading and eventual closure of the Ballybran secondary-school increased villagers' sense of hopelessness, powerlessness, and alienation. Although a temporary reprieve was granted to the school as a result of pressure exerted by the curate, the amiable bishop of Kerry, teachers, local politicians, and parents themselves — some of whom became members of the ad hoc Smaller Post Primary Schools Parents Organization — trust in the central government was thoroughly undermined. Eighty-five percent of those surveyed by Riordan said that the government was either totally ignorant of, or simply hostile to, the needs of the small Gaeltacht community.

Near the end of our stay, the village creamery closed down. The number of parish farmers making the daily or biweekly trip (depending on the season) by horse cart, donkey cart, or automobile to deliver milk and cream to the Kerry Dairy Farmer's Cooperative had steadily dwindled from one hundred and eighteen subscribers in 1940 to the current seventy-eight farmers. More important, the production of milk had halved in the same amount of time, from approximately 5,500 gallons per day in the late 1940s to only 2,295 gallons per day in 1974. The village creamery was to be replaced by a single tank truck, which would deliver the milk to a larger, more centrally located creamery for the processes of testing, separating, and pasteurizing. The retiring creamery manager, while lamenting the passing of the most vital social institution in Ballybran for bachelor farmers (with the possible exception of the pub), defended the decision as inevitable. The decreasing production of milk, he believed, was directly related to the increasing celibacy of local dairy farmers. In his years of experience, the manager found single farmers to be the least motivated to production and the least interested in modern standards of quality and hygiene. Married men with small children still at home, noted the manager, kept the healthiest cows and produced the greatest quantity of milk. Both production and quality tended to decrease for families in which the children had grown and left home, were still lower for married but childless farmers, and were altogether inadequate for the bachelors.

Apparently, degree of involvement in economics and production is a reflection of the central value of work in rural Irish society—its role in the perpetuation of families. The elderly, like Tomás and Maire, work because they are farmers and because farming is, or was until recently, an unquestioned vocation—a calling from God. If they work, however, in a listless, dispirited, and inefficient manner, it is because the farmers of the parish are, for the most part, childless or without heirs, and the essential meaning of work is lacking.

▪ Constriction of Village Trades

Dairy farming is not the only village occupation rejected by the majority of emigration-minded youth. Mackerel fishing, which had been the economic mainstay of a large segment of the parish since the Great Famine, "died" during our stay when not a single *curach* crew could be assembled from the usual father and son teams. While the elderly fishermen were willing to face the erratic and stormy northwest Atlantic, their sons ridiculed the primitive technology of the tarred canvas canoes and hopelessly aspired to the modern schooners used by foreign crews near Dingle Bay. And so, the winter of 1975 was the first mackerel season since the inception of the trade in the late nineteenth century that not a single canoe set off from the slip. This was in marked contrast to the verbal reports of several villagers who remembered the days in the height of the fishing industry boom between 1914 and 1920 when between four hundred and five hundred men would leave the slip in the evening and fish through the night. The industry employed women and children at the curing station, who cleaned and salted the fish and packed them into huge barrels for export to the American midwest. Several elderly men of the village were skilled *curach* and net makers, and younger men were employed in significant numbers as coopers, or barrel makers.

The first blow to the Ballybran fishing industry came in the early 1930s when both the demand for and the price of mackerel fell sharply—the former because Americans had begun to lose their taste for salted fish, and the latter because of competition with Scandinavian fishermen. Although World War II boosted the mackerel industry somewhat, by this time fewer village men were willing to risk their lives at sea for such small gain, and consequently each year until the present fewer *curach* set out. In the meantime the last *curach* maker of the parish died a decade ago, and there are only a handful who know how to repair the remaining canoes. Similarly, there are no coopers left in the village and few men who know how to make and repair fishing nets.

Neither does shepherding attract the village youth as a viable future trade. The romance of a life lived half within the bosom of the hearth and half in a "primitive" stone cabin or lean-to in the mountains close to the sheep represents to many adolescents the epitome of a lifestyle and moral virtues from a

Then there were coopers, which was a great job in those days. They made barrels for holding salted fish. For curing the mackerel there were sheds, and water poured over the mackerel to clean them. The women were employed to gut the fish at half a crown a day. Next day they would salt it, and get the barrels ready. There would be twenty women in each shed, laughing and singing and telling lies— each one better than the last. Oh, we did so love the fishing season!
—VILLAGER'S
RECOLLECTION

bygone era. The hardy shepherds of Ballybran are the least marrying of a population inclined toward celibacy: a full three-quarters of all parish shepherds are bachelors. According to the count of a district sheep-dipper, there are ninety-three bachelor shepherds on the eastern half of the Dingle Peninsula. To the shepherd his occupation exudes a "maleness" that is antagonistic to the opposite sex. Like the folklore of fishing, shepherding is protected by many proscriptions against women accompanying, observing, or assisting men in their work. Pub banter among shepherds often concerned the "rough and ready" nature of their work, and sexual teasing often ensued: "Johnny, sure you drive the womenfolk away with your smell of sheep and the wool stuck to your jacket."[6] One shepherd explained why he thought his occupation was antithetical to marriage:

> *A man must be willing to give half his life in the mountains. He must be there for the mating and the births, and he must gather them up for the "dipping" and carry them down for the fairs. Some nights he doesn't come down at all. He likes his food plain and simple, and his evenings given to cards and a few drinks with the boy-os.*

While the ascetic lifestyle of the shepherd is scorned by the youth of Ballybran, the survival of the occupation under new Common Market conditions is questioned by the shepherds themselves. In the first year of Common Market membership, the price of sheep at the annual open-air fair in Ballybran was artificially inflated from an average price of £2.76 in 1972 to almost £4 ($10) per head in 1973. The elated shepherds, unaccustomed to the fluctuations of world marketing, made the error of dramatically increasing flock sizes, with the result that the annual sheep market in 1974 was a disaster. Although the main street of the village was thronged with out-of-town buyers, with flocks of frightened and disoriented sheep, and with scores of taciturn shepherds attired in their high boots and woolen capes (over seventy-five shepherds arrived from the eastern half of the peninsula with more than 2,500 sheep), half the shepherds turned angrily on their heels and returned home in protest, refusing to sell their two- and three-year-old wethers for the going price of £2 and under per head.

Village housewives observing the sheep auction from a required "lady-like" distance "codded" and taunted the shepherds with their observation that lambs were selling for less than chickens. While the women teased, the shepherds became increasingly belligerent and directed angry comments under their breaths at the main buyer—a "Black Protestant" from the north. The ugly mood continued that evening at the village pubs, where I observed the first in a long cycle of despondency drinking. A woman publican commented to me privately, "Well, now you see how it is. When the lads are happy, they come by to celebrate, and when they're miserable they come to drown their sorrows. I'm the only winner, for I never touch the stuff."

The solution to the immediate burst of the sheep market followed a familiar pattern as throughout the winter and spring the prices for wool, young calves, onions, carrots, and other marketable products of the community dropped: more and more villagers relied on one or more forms of public assistance as their only form of income that year. Virtually every member of the community is supported by one of the following welfare programs: Widow's Pension; Old Age Pension; Unemployment Assistance ("the dole"); Children's Allowances; Disabled Persons Maintenance; and Gaeltacht housing and language subsidies. While most farmers and old people, in characteristically Irish fashion, made light of the dole line, which queued up early each Tuesday morning outside the door of the village post office, I often noted an accompanying mood of embarrassment and humiliation as the money changed hands. The dependency was a hostile and unnatural one for the fiercely independent Irish peasant.

▪ Tourism and the New Entrepreneur

As the traditional trades—tailor, shoemaker, cooper, *curach* builder, net maker—die out one by one, and as the main occupations of farmer, fisherman, and shepherd are threatened by emigration, lack of heirs, and Common Market innovations, one lucrative new trade has come to the fore: tourism. During the relatively dry summer months of July and August a small but steady stream of German, French, and English sportsmen come to conquer holy Mount Brandon or fish from the famed

Owenmore River, and have created in their wake a tight-knit circle of "farm and guesthouse operators" who give bed and board to travelers at a modest fee. By and large, married women serve as mediators and cultural brokers to the foreign tourists, as village men tend to feel awkward in the presence of outsiders. The tourist season is short, however, and creates no secondary economic linkages. The normally small profits from the business are looked upon as "windfalls" by most guesthouse women, analogous to their old "butter and egg" money.

A second tourist-based industry, however, threatens the future viability of the parish. This "industry" comes in the form of a new class of local entrepreneurs, or "gombeen men,"[7] who make their living by buying up the farms of lonely bachelors in order to build vacation bungalows to service the budding tourist trade. While there is no old farmer who would allow his lands to be sold during his lifetime to a rival farmer, there is a destructive mood of "one-upmanship" among bachelor farmers in their assurance that only the socially alienated gombeen man will make use of the lands. The entrepreneur, for his part, exploits the isolation and loneliness of the old men. In exchange for sale of all or part of his farm, the gombeen man promises to visit and feed the old bachelor when he becomes incapacitated and agrees to supervise the man's funeral arrangements after his death. And so the last decade has witnessed some of the finest village lots and fields transformed into summer playgrounds for visiting English tourists.

In addition, the presence of outsiders in the normally closed and secretive community creates psychological conflicts. Villagers are painfully aware that it is their "quaintness" that attracts tourists and their money. Hence, during July and August the pubs and the main street are fairly buzzing with "fairy stories," old *piseogas* (superstitions), and homely, devout expressions ("May we meet again in heaven"; "I be pulling the divil [sic] by the tail, and yourself?"), and villagers go out of their way to be chatty, sociable, and far more robust in their manner than usual. When the tourists are English (as the majority are), the patriotic Kerryman finds himself in a double bind: to entertain the British is self-deprecatory; to *not* entertain them is poor business in a community largely sustained in the summer by tourism. The following vignette from my field notes illustrates the quandary felt by many:

Patsy is a Sinn Fein man, a "Provo" sympathizer whose patriotism has landed him in prison more than once, but has also made him something of a folk hero among parish adolescents. Every Sunday morning he stands at the gates selling An Phoblact, *the underground IRA newspaper. As we were chatting yesterday, a stranger walked up enquiring about the availability of village lots for sale. The man's bearing and accent betrayed him at once for a Londoner. To my surprise, Patsy cordially invites the fellow in from the rain, offers him a "sup" of tea, banters with him, and even walks him up the road to show him a vacant farm in Lis. The "stage Irishman" seems to have possessed even Patsy! Later that evening we meet on the main street and Patsy is "off form," irritated and gloomy. I made no comments, but hurried on. (July 16, 1974)*

▪ The Occupational Hierarchy Scale

In order to probe young villagers' appraisals of the relative value of current village trades, I asked a total of forty-eight secondary-school pupils to rank order twenty-one village occupations from the most to the least important within the community. The results (table 6) were somewhat surprising. The village doctor (a nonresident of the community) occupied the place of highest prestige, which I had been led to expect would be filled by the priest (see O'Súilleabháin 1963; John Murphy 1969; Sheehy 1968). Among village boys the priest was counted as less essential than the guard, another outsider (and one who frequently joked with one about his "high pressured" job keeping the peace within the "desperately peaceful" mountain community). The high regard for the doctor's role in the community was consistent with the secondary-school students' evaluation of "health" over "religious faith" in a Values Hierarchy Scale, administered separately (see table 14, p. 209). Eliminated from the scoring were the "write-in" ballots by several of the mischievous lads who listed "on the dole" or "Yankee emigrant" at the top of the list.

In a discussion following the results of the test, the pupils defended their choices and, among the boys especially, took pleasure in repeating anti-clerical proverbs, such as "priests are greedy for money" and "high

RANK ORDER	FEMALE SECONDARY STUDENTS (N = 32)	MALE SECONDARY STUDENTS (N = 16)
1	Doctor	Doctor
2	Priest	Guard
3	Primary teacher	Dairy farmer
4	Nurse/midwife	Priest
5	Secondary teacher	Primary teacher
6	Dairy farmer	Shopkeeper
7	Guard	Nurse/midwife
8	Shopkeeper	Secondary teacher
9	Postman	Carpenter/housebuilder
10	Carpenter/housebuilder	Fisherman
11	Fisherman	Postman
12	Bus driver	Publican
13	Shepherd	Bus driver
14	Tailor	Shepherd
15	Guesthouse operator	Tailor
16	Weaver	Creamery manager
17	Creamery manager	Guesthouse operator
18	Blacksmith/forge	Blacksmith/forge
19	Publican	Weaver
20	Water-bailiff	Water-bailiff
21	Tinker	Tinker

Note: Students were asked to rank order twenty-one village occupations from most to least important within the community.

money–high mass, low money–low mass, no money–no mass." However, this anticlerical sentiment was found to be directed at the conservative parish priest and not at his well-liked curate. The relatively high status accorded both primary- and secondary-school teachers (especially among the girls) is quite traditional, given the Irish countryman's proverbial love of learning.[8]

Curious to me, however, were the very low statuses given the village blacksmith and new guesthouse operators. In the not too distant past, the blacksmith (*an gabha*) was a central village figure, respected for his skill, strength, and magical powers of curing and cursing (see O'Súilleabháin n.d.; Power 1974: 28; Arensberg and Kimball 1968: 253). Such was certainly the case of the previous smith in Ballybran; the low status of his grandson is apparently a combined result of the decrease in the use of horses and iron utensils, and the fact that the newly apprenticed youth is largely sustained in his trade through parish and Gaeltacht subsidies. Village adolescents expressed some antagonism toward the guesthouse operators, who were accused of both bad taste (selling Irish charm) and greed. One lad volunteered during the discussion that "the money from the tourists only makes the individual richer; the community never sees any of it," to which the daughter of a guesthouse owner retaliated, " And whoever sees the farmer's money? It just gets holed up in a wall behind his bed." The water-bailiff, employed by an absentee English lord to keep salmon poachers from his river, and itinerant tinker-beggars are "polluted" roles in the community. The bailiff is characterized as an alcoholic buffoon, fair game for pranks, and the occasional tinker family that takes up temporary residence near the outskirts of the parish is used as a threat to scare children into good behavior.

Although it revealed adolescents' attitudes toward current work-slots in the village, the occupational hierarchy scale results did not parallel the youths' *own* occupational aspirations. This was supplied by a later exercise—a composition assigned on the topic of "my vocation." Of the thirty students who handed in the essay, over 85 percent of the girls and 60 percent of the boys hoped to leave the community to pursue higher education and occupations that would necessarily remove them from Ballybran. Among the girls, hospital nursing, secretarial/clerical work, and teaching were the preferred roles; among the boys, business, civil service, the guard, and teaching were most frequently listed. Not one of the students mentioned a religious vocation, either to the priesthood or sisterhood.

▪ Anomie, Alcoholism, and Mental Illness

I am anxious in my mind, turning it around and around, alone here
in my house two weeks since my wife is dead. Cait, my daughter, has
left me—gone aboard ship to America with a big crowd from Dingle.

I am troubled and fearful in my mind.

Tomorrow I will write her on a scrap of paper. She will send me help
and it will be bountiful. Flour, sugar, tobacco, tea I will have in the
larder. Maybe I will even live to see Cait return dressed in white silk,
with a purse of money and a yardful of cows.

Many a handsome well-built man will want to take her home, and
after I am dead and laid out in white sheets on the kitchen table, both
will "keen" me.

Cait! Cait! Come home to me! Don't lay me down to sleep in the
poorhouse of Dingle at the end of my days.

Would you send me out with a beggar's pack to wander the roads like
a tinker begging bread and tea from Castle to Dingle and kept in the
houses of strangers?

—Translation of a villager's "keen," or lament after the death of his wife

The combined effect of the steady erosion of the community through
childlessness and emigration, the disintegration of traditional values and
familism, the constriction of village social life and institutions, and the
national policy to retire even young and able-bodied farmers can be
observed in the contagious spread of a spirit of despair and anomie in Ballybran. This anomie is expressed in drinking patterns and alcoholism, in a
sexual devitalization, and most profoundly, perhaps, in the high incidence
of mental illness, especially schizophrenia, among middle-aged bachelors,
to be discussed in subsequent chapters.

I have chosen Durkheim's term *anomie* (1951: 241) to describe the emotional state of a majority of Ballybran villagers advisedly. It was first suggested within the context of rural Ireland by Robert Cresswell in his

detailed ethnography of a village in County Clare, although he devotes but a few lines to the subject. Cresswell concludes that the Irish countryside is suffering a social malaise, "l'anomie," which he contends is not a period of "transformation of the society, but one of great disintegration" (1969: 530; translation my own). Hugh Brody in his more recent and provocative book on the decline of western Irish society prefers the word *demoralization* to describe what he observed.

> *In Inishkillane people are demoralized: they feel outside their social system, and they have no faith in it continuing. They are lonely and withdrawn. . . . To be demoralized is, for such a people, to lose belief in the social advantage or moral worth of their own small society. The demoralization is aggravated by continuing to live in a milieu which, in the view of Inishkillane people, offers neither real advantage nor compensatory dignity. (1974: 16–17)*

While not wishing to quibble over words, I find Durkheim's original use of the word *anomie* with its reference to loss of meaningful work identity and its relationship to the proliferation of self-destructive tendencies—such as alcoholism—to be the more appropriate term. The concept of anomie focuses attention on the primary importance of men's and women's work to their sense of self-esteem. While bachelors are most prone to despondency drinking during the "idle" winter months, married men as well drink heavily during this time because, as one farmer confided, "I can't sit around in the kitchen all day where the missus can remind me that I have nothing to do." The pub provides a sense of solidarity and community as well as spirits for the dispirited. Among bachelors, isolated in their lonely stone cottages, heavy drinking is endemic, and these men are largely responsible for the alarming statistic that the Irish are hospitalized twelve times as often as the English for alcoholism (Cooney 1971: 51). Four of the six village pubs in Ballybran cater exclusively to single men, who gather in little "clubs" most evenings of the week, but in greatest number on weekends, fair days, and funeral days. Brody's poignant description of winter drinking patterns in a bilingual village of west Cork is reminiscent of pub behavior in Ballybran:

These men [village bachelors] do not stay [in winter] for the long hours
which characterize their summer drinking nor do they often consume the
sheer volume of alcohol drunk in summer. But when they do drink hard
and the effects of the drinking begin to appear, despondency becomes
more extreme and its behavioral indices more overt. A drunken man in
winter leans more heavily on the bar. He often seeks to draw another
drinker or two to his side. Such a group creates a tight circle of privacy
around itself—a privacy physically expressed by the arms they lay across
one another's shoulders. Then, with faces almost touching, they appear to
join closely in evident despair. This despair is not expressed in discussion
among the drinkers. Rather they exchange silence as if it were words, and
words in brief expressions of the lonesomeness. (1973: 32–33)

The majority of village bachelors are able to make an adequate adjustment
to the demands of their stoical existence through such strongly cathected
male-bonding patterns as evidenced in "round drinking" at the pub. For the
more psychologically vulnerable, however, a gradual withdrawal from peer
activities, such as sports events, Sunday dances, and cooperative turf-cutting
and haymaking, signals the onset of an engulfing spirit of depression and
despair—sometimes climaxing in fits of rage or violence directed against
neighbors or self.

A major theme in Thematic Apperception Test card 1 (a boy contemplating a violin on a table before him) told by both average and hospitalized
males, but not by girls, illustrates the Irish male's sense of anomie with
regard to his life and work. Half the village boys and a quarter of the male
mental patients told stories of despondency over a violin or fiddle that was
broken or sadly out of tune. Michael, a seventeen-year-old potential farm
heir of Ballybran, told this story:

He looks fed up, and his violin is broken. He doesn't know what to do.
He's looking at it disgustedly. It might have broken while he was playing
with it. Nothing to attract his attention to, only that. (NM8) *

* NM = Normal Male   HM = Hospitalized Male
  NF = Normal Female HF = Hospitalized Female

And, Seamas, a considerably older, Irish-speaking bachelor farmer and diagnosed schizophrenic, first imprisoned and then later hospitalized for violent and disorderly conduct at a dance hall, told this story:

He feels down and out. (Why?) It's broken, anyway. (What's the future?) He's thinking about his future as a fiddler. (What about it?) There is none. (HM1)

While to the psychoanalytically oriented the violin is a symbolically phallic instrument, and the broken violin image would be interpreted as an indication of severe castration anxiety among rural Irish males, I believe that the anthropologist can best contribute to the cultural interpretation of projective test material by examining first the manifest content of the images and placing them into the framework of the cultural or social meanings that these images might have on the conscious level. The violin or fiddle, for example, accompanied by the goatskin drum called the *bodhran* and by the melodeon and the tin whistle, is *the* music of the Irish countryside and conjures up strongly patriotic passions in the breasts of villagers at home and abroad. Irish music, like the Irish language itself, represents a way of life that the villagers sense is dying. Of their language the old storytellers are wont to say, "The words are broken in my mouth." Of their music, village musicians can be heard to comment, "My spirit is broken; how can I play when there are none to listen?" This malaise, this cultural demoralization, is expressed and felt most keenly by those young men who must sacrifice so much in remaining loyal to the village and the culture—and who intuitively sense that "things aren't working," that necessary relationships are "broken" and "out of tune."

By contrast, village girls responded to the violin image in an oddly characteristic fashion. More than half the girls in each sample (NF 55%; HF 55%) told stories that ignored or misidentified the violin. Some referred to it as a gun, a book, a painting, a plane, while others referred directly to the blank sheets of paper beneath the violin, ignoring the instrument itself. Since it has already been established that the fiddle is an important symbol of Irish culture, the failure to notice or recognize it on the part of the girls cannot originate in unfamiliarity. Rather, there seems to be an obstinate blocking, denial, or rejection of a possibly threatening instrument. The male phallus? Rural lifestyle? Probably both, I hypothesize.

While single girls, who rarely feel trapped by village life, evidence little of the winter depression suffered by village boys and men, married women are also prone to depression and despondency during this season. As a category, village women are more likely to be treated for the condition that they describe as "feeling run down" or "bad nerves." Between October and March the village dispensary, located in the back kitchen of the home of the village midwife, is filled with sighing, sad-faced middle-aged women of whom the dispensary doctor complained brusquely, "They are all nothing but a bunch of neurotic hypochondriacs. Not a thing wrong with them — just bored and feeling sorry for themselves." His blanket prescription: a mild tranquilizer and an admonition to get out and visit with the neighbors. The local folk remedy for winter despondency used by other women is prepackaged tonics and elixirs sold at village shops in large quantity. Alcohol is a refuge for many others.

The most depressed and dispirited group in the village, however, are the aged — many of them solitary widows, widowers, bachelors, and spinsters without family or friends to look after them. Within this group the desire for death can be strong, and I often heard the refrain "May God spare me the cold and loneliness of another winter." With one ninety-year-old bedridden woman I had a continuing dialogue about the morality of suicide, in which she debated her longing to die versus her fear of God's wrath at her lack of faith.

While the rate of reported suicide is lowest in Ireland of all Western nations — the Irish Catholic Church is particularly severe in its public censure of suicide[9] — the clinical experience of psychiatrists in the southwest indicates that attempted suicide is quite common (see Beckett 1972; also, David Dunne, personal communication). In addition, the incidence of other less severely sanctioned forms of self-destruction is high for the nation as a whole, and even higher for western coastal communities like Ballybran. In addition to alcoholism, endogenous depression, a severe damping down of all mental and bodily activities (interpreted psychoanalytically as self-directed rage), is an extremely common condition in the rural Irish population (see Beckett 1972: 8) and is almost endemic among middle-aged women in Ballybran, 15 percent of whom have at one time sought treatment for the problem. Other anomic or self-destructive tendencies can be noted in the remarkably high Irish rates for cigarette consumption, caloric intake, and deaths from hypertension, coronary disease, and gastric and duodenal ulcers. The dearth of marriages is possibly the most culturally suicidal aspect of rural Irish anomie. Deaths and emigrations without replacement through marriages and births can lead to no fortuitous demographic outcome. Table 7 lists international data on some of these phenomena. The composite picture for the Irish is one of tension, anxiety, and disequilibrium, and this profile is intensified for the western region, where the highest rates for hospitalized alcoholism and mental illness originate.

▪ Failure of the Gaelic Revival Movement

Although associated with industrialization and rapid change, the process of cultural disintegration accompanied by a general spirit of anomie is not a phenomenon unique to the twentieth century nor applicable only to the rapid transformation of rural agrarian societies into would-be modern industrial ones. A similar model has been used to describe the extreme "culture shock" experienced by tribal societies confronted, often violently, with Western culture (see Wallace 1956). A frequently successful defense against cultural disintegration or genocide has been noted in the pattern of so-called nativistic or revitalization movements. The Irish produced such a movement in the late nineteenth and early twentieth centuries, and its failure to revitalize the very communities of the west for which it was intended has increased villagers' sense of discouragement.

Anthony F.C. Wallace defined revitalization movements as "deliberate and conscious efforts by members of a society to construct a more satisfying culture during periods of heightened stress" (1956: 265). The orientation of such movements is relative to the kinds of cultural dominance and consequent stresses experienced, and may be millenarian in nature or messianic, revolutionary, acculturative, or revivalistic. The Irish (similar to the native Americans studied by Wallace) placed emphasis upon reviving or bringing

■TABLE 7: INTERNATIONAL DATA ON ANXIETY LEVELS, 1960

	HOSPITALIZED MENTAL ILLNESS (PER 1,000 POP.)	CORONARY HEART DISEASE DEATHS*	CALORIE INTAKE (PER PERSON PER DAY)	SUICIDES	CIGARETTE CONSUMPTION (PER ADULT PER YEAR)	GASTRIC AND DUODENAL ULCER DEATHS*	CELIBACY (% SINGLE MALES)	HYPER-TENSION DEATHS*
Australia	3.1	256.2	3,140	10.6	2,440	6.6	38.2	10.2
Austria	1.9	242.8	2,970	23.1	1,720	9.4	42.9	6.1
Belgium	3.1	142.3	3,040	14.6	1,570	5.7	34.4	25.8
Canada	3.9	237.0	3,020	7.5	2,910	5.1	37.8	5.5
Denmark	2.2	246.6	3,370	20.3	1,470	6.7	39.9	2.5
Finland	3.6	221.5	3,110	20.5	2,100	5.6	42.8	2.9
France	2.1	78.4	3,190	15.8	1,320	3.2	41.9	4.8
Germany	1.7	199.2	2,960	19.5	1,630	6.1	39.8	4.0
Ireland	7.3	313.5	3,490	3.0	2,560	7.4	60.9	12.4
Italy	2.2	188.4	2,720	6.3	1,300	6.3	49.9	7.6
Japan	1.1	50.1	2,260	21.6	1,880	11.9	45.5	9.2
Netherlands	2.3	168.2	3,030	6.6	1,700	4.9	40.9	4.4
New Zealand	3.5	243.7	3,490	9.7	1,930	6.7	35.8	4.6
Norway	2.9	210.0	2,930	6.5	550	3.0	41.2	4.4
Sweden	4.8	281.5	3,000	17.4	1,160	7.6	42.9	3.7
Switzerland	3.5	229.7	3,220	19.0	2,380	5.7	45.0	4.1
U.K.	4.5	314.6	3,280	10.6	2,760	10.2	36.2	13.7
U.S.A.	4.3	306.3	3,110	10.6	3,810	6.3	30.8	7.0

Source: Adapted from Richard Lynn (1971: 9).

*per 100,000 population

back selected traits of their indigenous culture, which was threatened first by British colonization and later by economic dependence and psychological identification with both England and the United States. The first effort, the Anglo-Irish literary revival, spearheaded by William Butler Yeats and assisted by a galaxy of literary genius in the persons of Lady Gregory, J. M. Synge, Douglas Hyde, George Moore, and James Stephens among others, hoped to cultivate a national literature of the highest aesthetic quality.[10] Lady Gregory and Synge took to the countryside and to the Aran Islands, Lady Gregory to record folklore and legends, Synge to capture the distinctively Celtic cadences of Irish peasant speech. This movement, however, was esoteric and lacked wide popular appeal. The latter was supplied by Conradh na Gaeilge, the Gaelic League, founded in 1893 by Douglas Hyde and Eoin McNeill, which gave birth to a truly national movement motivated by a single purpose: to maintain spoken Irish in the Gaeltacht, and to revive Irish as the national language in the rest of the Republic. The Gaelic League's "grass roots" approach of sponsoring language and history evening classes, music and dance festivals, Irish drama groups, and so forth, caught the popular imagination; it entertained as well as educated.

Leaders of the movement, then as today, concentrated on the symbolic importance of the Irish language as containing the very soul of the Irish people. Nationalists and nativists alike link the Irish speech with a kind of Jungian collective unconscious, and insist that the distinctive Celtic personality can only be expressed through the indigenous language (see, for example, P. L. Henry 1974). The revival of the language, it was hoped, would lead to the cherishing of other things Irish: the love of music and dance, sport and storytelling, homely peasant virtues of hospitality and warmth. A recent government pamphlet explained the rationale behind the policy of "compulsory" Irish in the national schools as follows:

The most powerful of all the emotional pistons known to man is a blazing love of place and a fond memory for the last generation of the tribe.
— SEAN O'FAOLAIN

The Irish language is the expression of our personality as a nation, of our identity, of our pride in being ourselves. The language has been associated throughout our history with the rights we demand as a nation, with the rights we were denied, with the rights we won, with the rights we hope to achieve. . . . Thomas Davis' statement is even more true now than . . . when he wrote it over a century ago: "A nation should guard its language more than its territories—'tis a surer barrier and more important than fortress or river." (O Tuama 1970: 37)

Among rural villagers the Gaelic revival is firmly wedded to their identity as Roman Catholics, another central symbol of Irish ethnicity and independence from Britain. Hence, it is no accident that the Cumann na Sagart, union of Irish-speaking priests, has been a most vigorous organizing force behind the Irish movement in the rural west. These nationalistic priests maintain that true Irish spirituality can only be expressed in the mother tongue. The decree of the Vatican Council in the early 1960s allowing Mass and the sacraments to be celebrated in the vernacular gave further fuel to the union of Irish-speaking priests, who revived the Gaelic Mass, suggested Irish baptismal names, encouraged parishioners to confess their sins in Irish, and revived the old folk-customs of blessing the ground, cattle, and houses on the Celtic quarterly feasts. In addition to Cumann na Sagart, a number of other religious organizations have worked to fuse the practice of Catholic folk piety with the revival of the language, among them An Realt, and two Irish-speaking sodalities, Cuallacht Mhuire gan Smal and Cuallacht an Scabaill. The ultimate goal of the supporters of the language-revival movement was that it might simultaneously stimulate a rebirth of national self-esteem, which had been severely damaged through English colonialism and American cultural dominance. Unfortunately, however, the Irish language was already moribund at the time the language movement began, and persistent efforts to preserve it in the isolated Blasket and Aran Islands or to revive it in semi-isolated coastal areas like Ballybran have been largely unsuccessful.

We were most fortunate to arrive in Ballybran during the week following a euphoric celebration of the community's official recognition as a Gaeltacht, or Irish-speaking community. In addition, the parish had won the national competition organized by Glor na nGael (Voice of Ireland) for having made the greatest progress in promoting the use of Irish within the community. The village had held Gaeltacht status in the past and lost it some ten years ago when the visiting inspectors had finally to admit that more English than Irish was spoken in the little community. The present Gaeltacht status was regained largely through the persistent efforts of Father Leary, an active member of the union of Irish-speaking priests and himself a Kerryman and son of a small farmer. Single-handedly and against the sentiments of his superior, the curate united schoolteachers, publicans, and shopkeepers in an effort to enforce the use of Irish in the classroom and in public places. The well-liked priest emphasized not only Irish pride and nationalism but also the very practical benefits that accrued to Gaeltachts in the form of grants and subsidies. Simultaneous with the language revival, the curate restored through subsidies the traditional occupational slots of blacksmith, weaver, and tailor in an attempt to keep a few dynamic young villagers from emigrating. The parish youth, however, accorded a particularly low status to these revived trades (see table 6).

During the first weeks of our stay in Ballybran, we heard a great deal of Irish spoken, and villagers hinted that we had better learn Irish ourselves if we intended to understand the community. Taking the villagers' word at face value that they were Irish-speaking (although clearly bilingual), I prefaced early interviews with apologies for speaking English, and my husband and I (he with far greater success) tried to twist our tongues around the complicated phrasing of greetings, salutations, blessings, and other ritual communications.

The euphoria generated by the curate's apparent success was short-lived, however, and as the more jovial and crowded summer months gave way to autumn and winter, not only villagers' spirits and optimism but also the use of Irish rapidly waned. Worse, perhaps, the early spirit of positivism was replaced with attitudes of cynicism and guilt. Villagers were particularly sensitive to criticism from the more solidly Irish-speaking communities west of Dingle that Ballybran had "pulled a fast one" or "codded" the government. "Do you know what they're saying about us?" offered one despondent villager. "They are pointing at Father Leary and saying, 'He's your Ballybran

Gaeltacht.'" Other villagers protested that the Irish revival movement and Gaeltacht status had made liars of the whole community, forcing villagers to pretend in the presence of outsiders (often suspected of being Gaeltacht inspectors in disguise) that Irish is their principal tongue. So fearful are parishioners of being caught speaking English by strangers that the visiting public health nurse reported considerable difficulty gaining entrance into the homes of new patients, who would often protest that they didn't understand her English. On one such occasion, after an old farmer had a chance to look at the nurse's official papers, he finally declared, "Glory be, mum, ye should have showed me these from the start."

Although the majority of Ballybran primary- and secondary-school teachers were active and committed members of the Comhar na Muinteoiri, the national organization of Irish-speaking teachers, a few have grave reservations about the "costs" of bilingualism, and point to the relatively low academic scores of Gaeltacht students on university qualifying examinations. They wondered whether their pupils weren't learning Irish at the expense of math, history, science, and English composition. But perhaps the most devastating criticism of the Irish revival movement came from the bachelor peer group of pub regulars who complained more than once of being "used" for display by the national government like museum relics. One bitter fisherman went so far as to describe Ballybran Gaeltacht as a "rare-bird sanctuary." Connotations of "stage Irishmen," performing in order to titillate condescending Dubliners and "Yankee" tourists, were intermixed with more positive sentiments expressed at other times.

A possibly insurmountable difficulty, however, in reviving the language is the absence of native-born Irish speakers. Only four households in the parish are Irish-speaking "from the cradle," and all of these comprise elderly bachelors or widows, none in any position to teach the language to a new generation. Village youngsters have had to learn Irish in the national school as a second language, and all speak (when they do at all) a version of what native speakers call "Christian Brothers Irish"—that is, book Irish after the teaching order. Finally, the very core group of the Irish revival in Ballybran, Father Leary's following of secondary-school adolescents, seemingly abandoned the movement about six months into our stay. The monthly Glor na nGael meetings dropped in attendance from fifty or sixty to a half-dozen members, and these appeared to attend reluctantly and out of loyalty to the curate. In midyear my husband assigned an exercise for his secondary-school pupils in which they were asked to assess the value of learning and speaking Irish. Over two-thirds (67%) of the forty students replied that they saw little or no value in perpetuating the language, and among the most frequently given explanations were that Irish is a dead language; Irish has no practical value—it can't help in commerce or business; Irish is useless for the emigrant—it won't get him any farther than Galway. A significant number added that their French lessons were far more valuable, preparing some for work on the continent.

The Irish village of the western coast is today the embodiment of a broken culture. As village social life and institutions have constricted, the lives of villagers have become more secretive, privatized, and isolated. The winter *ceilidhes*, friendly fireside chats with neighbor and spirited step-dancing in the kitchen, have been replaced by "telly" watching among the more prosperous and radio listening among the rest. Where parishioners once built their homes nestled closely against one another for comfort and support, today's villagers are abandoning ancestral shelters in order to build regulation stucco bungalows, appropriately modern, that remove the others from proximity and contact. Where once the villages and townlands were the center of activity, life, and meaning, today they are the centers of loneliness and despair. In the following chapter I shall focus on the most visible and outstanding effect of cultural decline and anomie as I analyze the statistical association between Irish culture and mental illness.

CHAPTER THREE

Saints, Scholars, and Schizophrenics

A ridiculous notion prevails
among the country people of Kerry
concerning a place they call
Glenagalt (Glen of the Madmen)
towards the eastern half of the
Dingle Peninsula, where they say
all the mad folk of Eire, if left to
their liberty, would flee. Indeed, for
the tremendous appearance of
these desolate glens and mountains at first sight, one might infer
that only madmen would enter.
— CHARLES SMITH, *The Ancient
and Present State of Kerry, 1756*

ON A GIVEN census day in 1971, two out of every hundred males in western Ireland were in a mental hospital. Nearly all of those hospitalized men (89%) were lifelong celibates, most were between the ages of thirty-five and fifty, and more than half were diagnosed as suffering from schizophrenia (O'Hare and Walsh 1974: 9–11; Kelleher and Copeland 1974).

On a given research day in 1975 in the tiny parish of Ballybran in southwest Kerry, almost 5 percent of the population of 461 people were receiving psychiatric care or medication as in-patients at the county mental hospital or as outpatients at the psychiatric clinic in nearby Dingle. Two-thirds of these patients were men, and all but one were single.

And on any given dark winter's night when the rest of the parish has long been asleep, one can pass by the ancient stone cow-house of Michael O'Brien and hear the old "saint" milking and talking to his cows, or merely "standing the night" with them while reciting several decades of the rosary. But, Misha M'god, what harm? Michael, the old recluse, is a saint and he serves his cows the way he once served his mother, God rest her soul.

Or, taking the rocky *boithrin* (little path) that separates the Finn pasture from the O'Neil's, one might encounter holy Maighread, dressed in vibrant reds and greens, on her way to a Mass long since over. She will stop you and hold you fast until she has been able to get it right—her loose, broken diffuse genealogy—counting the names and numbers of people long since dead or gone away, and groping for her place among the shadows, Maighread asks you again: "Has Jimmy Tuohy come home yet?"

Then, finally, as you turn up the winding mountain road to Ballybran you may run into Old Ned, who will startle at the still unfamiliar sound of a car motor and will stalk the machine as the proverbial angry bull stalks a red shirt. No, he will not let you pass the public road. Not today.

Mental illness, both treated and untreated, is uncommonly common in the land of saints and scholars, and is statistically associated with the western region, male status, peripheral agriculture, depopulation, isolation, and celibacy. In this chapter I shall sketch an epidemiological profile of mental illness in western Ireland, and I shall discuss the vulnerability of the rural Irish to psychiatric hospitalization in the light of what has been called "labeling theory" (see Scheff 1966)—that is, through an examination of community definitions of normal and abnormal behavior, variations in diagnostic usage, and cultural attitudes toward treatment and institutionalization.

Table 8 presents figures on psychiatric treatment rates from a broad cross-section of nations for 1955 and 1965—the most recent years for which such data are available (World Health Organization 1961; 1968).[1] These rates are even more disparate when the rural western and southern counties of Ireland are examined separately: 17.1 per thousand for Sligo and Leitram, and 13.5 for County Kerry, the locus of this study (Walsh and Walsh 1968: 15).

Reliance, however, upon such suspect measures as hospitalization rates to determine the prevalence or incidence of psychiatric disorders has been heavily criticized (see, especially, J. Kennedy 1973: 1121–1123). Treatment rates vary with the availability of psychiatric hospital beds to the extent that the two are roughly comparable.[2] Other methodological problems involve diagnostic usage and hospital admission criteria, which can vary not only from culture to culture, but between urban and rural regions. Finally, to the extent that factors such as family and community tolerance for deviant behavior affect diagnosis, treated cases may give a very misleading picture of the nature of the pathology (social or medical) that is

TABLE 8: PSYCHIATRIC HOSPITALIZATION, 1955 AND 1965, IN SELECTED COUNTRIES (RATES PER THOUSAND POPULATION)

COUNTRY	1955	COUNTRY	1965
Republic of Ireland	10.82	Republic of Ireland	7.37
Northern Ireland	7.43	Sweden	6.97
Sweden	6.70	Austria	5.29
Scotland	6.15	New Zealand	4.89
Canada	5.88	Israel	4.78
New Zealand	5.80	Scotland	4.74
United States	5.65	Northern Ireland	4.20
England and Wales	5.34	England and Wales	3.65
Italy	3.51	United States	2.93
Israel	2.52	Canada	2.59
Austria	2.96	Poland	2.58
Poland	2.01	Italy	2.06
Cyprus	1.71	Chile	1.62
Spain	1.67	Ceylon	1.42
Portugal	1.32	Spain	1.33
Ceylon	1.14	Japan	1.31
Brazil	0.65	Cyprus	1.09
Japan	0.64	Greece	1.06
Ghana	0.26	Portugal	1.01
Nigeria	0.02	Brazil	0.73
Chile	—	Ghana	0.52
Greece	—	Mexico	0.34
Kenya	—	Kenya	0.29
Mexico	—	Senegal	0.20
Senegal	—	Nigeria	0.02

Note: Mental patients in psychiatric hospitals on December 31, 1955, and December 31, 1965.
Source: Hospitalization Rates: WHO *Statistics Report*, vols. 14 and 21.
Population: UN Demographic Yearbook 1961, 1968

involved. Many of these problems will be dealt with in the following pages. Taking these shortcomings into account, the available epidemiological data are extremely valuable from a slightly different perspective. While they may not tell us the "true" prevalence rates of psychiatric disorder, they do tell us a great deal about a country's own assessment of its mental health and its sense of need or problem. One might expect West African nations such as Senegal and Nigeria (within which psychiatric nomenclature and hospitalization compete with folk classifications and shamanic healing) to report a low incidence of psychopathology. But what explains the propensity of the Irish to label, diagnose, and institutionalize so many of their population? What social processes or historical phenomena underlie the problem of Irish madness, as the Irish themselves see it? A breakdown of the most psychiatrically vulnerable segments of the Irish population offers some clues.

The Irish Psychiatric Hospital Census, 1971 (O'Hare and Walsh 1974), brings to light an epidemiological profile of the mentally ill population in the Republic that gives evidence of the role of sociocultural factors in either evoking or sustaining mental illness in the Republic. I shall summarize O'Hare and Walsh's findings (pp. 9–13) below.

Male patients outnumber female patients in Ireland for all age groups except seventy-five and over. The disparity is most remarkable for the age group twenty-five to forty-four, for which there are 2,432 male patients and only 1,414 female patients.

A most remarkable feature of the Irish mental hospital population is its celibacy (see table 9).[3] Eighty-two percent of all the patients are *unmarried*, with a higher proportion for the men (88.2%) than for the women (79.8%). Schizophrenics, in particular, tend to be unmarried: over 90 percent are single. While in any sample of schizophrenics one would expect a predominance of single persons (since the disease is usually recognized prior to marriage age and interferes with courtship and intimacy), available epidemiological data indicate that the celibacy of Irish schizophrenics far exceeds that of schizophrenics in America (see Jackson 1960; Bahn, et al. 1966), Canada (see H. B. M. Murphy 1967), and other western nations (see Lemkau and Crocetti 1958).

	SINGLE	MARRIED	WIDOWED	UNSPECIFIED	TOTAL
All diagnoses	13,703 (782.4)	1,961 (203.0)	964 (578.8)	33	16,661 (577.7)
Organic psychosis	1,136 (64.8)	298 (30.8)	378 (226.9)	5	1,817 (63.0)
Schizophrenia	7,414 (423.3)	722 (74.7)	201 (120.7)	16	8,353 (289.6)
Manic-depressive psychosis	1,388 (79.2)	459 (47.5)	198 (118.8)	6	2,051 (71.1)
Other and unspecified psychoses	215 (12.2)	82 (8.4)	48 (28.8)	0	345 (11.9)
Neurosis	367 (20.9)	125 (12.9)	61 (36.6)	2	555 (19.2)
Personality disorder	177 (10.1)	27 (2.7)	13 (7.8)	1	218 (7.6)
Alcoholism and alcoholic psychosis	173 (9.9)	180 (18.6)	36 (21.6)	3	392 (13.5)
Drug addiction	17 (0.9)	4 (0.4)	0 (0.0)	0	21 (0.7)
Mental handicap	2,626 (149.9)	40 (4.1)	14 (8.4)	0	2,680 (92.9)
Unspecified	190 (10.8)	24 (2.4)	15 (9.0)	0	229 (7.9)

Source: The Irish Psychiatric Hospital Census of 1971: 29.

Marital status has a significant effect upon length of hospitalization in Ireland, with prolonged stays (twenty-five years or more) associated with celibacy (90.3%), and short stays of less than one month associated with married status (60%). The overall pattern in Irish psychiatric hospitals, however, is one of long stays: 72.5 percent of all male patients and 68.5 percent of female patients had been in hospitals continuously for two years or more.

Age is another significant factor, as the census indicates that hospitalization rates increase with age up until age seventy and then decline. Overall, 30 percent of the hospital population was elderly—sixty-five and older. Children under fifteen are rarely interned in psychiatric hospitals. In 1971, only 209 children in this age bracket were psychiatric hospital residents, with more than three-quarters of these diagnosed as mentally handicapped.

In terms of diagnosis, schizophrenia is the illness of half (50.1%) the Irish psychiatric hospital population; it is a quarter of all diagnoses in United States hospitals (Jackson 1960: 3). The frequency of the disease (the prevalence of hospitalization) is 6.24 per thousand of total population for males and 4.57 per thousand for females. This is nearly *double* the prevalence rate of 2.90 suggested as a norm for Western societies by Lemkau and Crocetti (1958). The equivalent English rates are 1.85 for males and 1.70 for females (Beckett 1972: 7). Thus, per unit of population, the Republic of Ireland has about three times as many schizophrenic patients in hospitals as England. The incidence rates (i.e., new cases reported each year) tell a similar story: the Irish figures for both sexes of 10.1 per 10,000 of total population contrast markedly with the incidence rates from the United States of 2.47, England and Wales of 1.74 (World Health Organization 1973: 28), Northern Ireland of 3.5, and Canada of 3.8 (see table 10).

Sociocultural factors seem implicated in the differential distribution of schizophrenia by age and sex between nations. Where married women are most prone to the disease in the United States (see Bahn, et al. 1966; Bruhn, Brandt, and Shackelford 1966; Kraemer 1966), in Ireland schizophrenia is more frequently the disease of male bachelors (O'Hare and Walsh 1974: 26). In the United States and Canada the onset of the disease occurs early, often during the identity crisis period of late adolescence and early adulthood (Jackson 1960). In Ireland the first diagnosed episodes most commonly occur in the mid-twenties to the late thirties (O'Hare and Walsh 1970: 32, table 11). Interviews with Irish schizophrenics support the hypothesis that the later age of onset of the disease in rural Ireland is related to the postponed adulthood and hence later "identity crisis" of the Irish bachelor. It is normal in the countryside for young bachelors to be sheltered by their parents and free of decision

● TABLE 10: AGE STANDARDIZED RATES, PER 10,000 ADULTS, OF FIRST
ADMISSION TO MENTAL HOSPITALS BY RELIGION AND ETHNICITY

COUNTRY	SCHIZOPHRENIA		MANIC-DEPRESSIVE PSYCHOSIS		ALCOHOLISM AND ALCOHOLIC PSYCHOSIS	
	M	F	M	F	M	F
Republic of Ireland	11.1	9.0	6.7	8.6	6.8	0.9
Northern Ireland						
Roman Catholics	4.2	4.9	4.2	7.1	8.4	0.9
Others	2.3	2.6	4.2	5.7	3.6	0.4
Canada						
Roman Catholics,						
Irish origin	4.5	4.6	3.2	5.0	11.5	1.2
Others, British origin	3.2	3.0	4.0	5.1	4.4	0.6

Source: Murphy 1975: 118.

making and financial responsibilities until well into their thirties. Hence the state of perplexity and lack of competence associated with a diagnosis of schizophrenia might go unrecognized longer.

Mental handicap (including Down's Syndrome and phenylketonuria) is the next highest contributor to the Irish mental hospital population (16%) and may be related to the generally late age of marriage and consequently of childbearing in rural areas. Manic-depressive psychosis (12.3%) and in lesser numbers organic psychosis, alcoholism, personality disorders, and neurosis account for the remaining hospital diagnoses. Whereas Irish males evidence a greater tendency to schizophrenia and to alcoholism linked with immature and dependent personality characteristics, among women there is a higher percentage of endogenous depressions and psychosomatic disorders.

Regional variations affect not only the rates of hospitalization (with the lowest rates coming from the developed and industrialized east, and the highest rates from the underdeveloped and underpopulated west), but diagnoses as well. The highest rates for schizophrenia and affective psychosis (including endogenous depression) are from the west, while the highest rates for simple neurosis come from the east.

Social class and occupational status also affect vulnerability in the Republic, as they do elsewhere (see Hollingshead and Redlich 1958; Kohn 1968): disadvantaged farm laborers and fishermen have a hospitalization rate twice that of any other group in the society.

Irish Catholicism is another significant variable: psychiatric treatment rates in Northern Ireland are considerably higher for the Catholic minority than for the Protestant majority. Roman Catholics in Ulster, both male and female, are hospitalized twice as often as Protestants are for schizophrenia, and three times as often for alcoholism (H. B. M. Murphy 1975: 118). Similarly, Murphy's Canadian studies (1967, 1968a) indicate that Canadian Roman Catholics of Irish descent have schizophrenia rates significantly higher than do non-Catholics of British descent (table 10). However, whether these rates are a function of class discrimination and poverty experienced by the Catholic minorities in Ulster and Canada, or of guilt and stress generated by Irish Catholicism remains problematic.

▪ Mental Illness and Emigration

From the above data it is clear that the Irish are, in general, vulnerable to mental illness—particularly schizophrenia—and that within Ireland there exists a particularly high-risk population: the category of marginal bachelor farmers and fishermen from the isolated and depopulated bilingual villages of the western coast. These people represent what some social scientists refer to as a residual population—those left behind after generations of sifting out through marriage-out, internal migrations, and emigration abroad. This fact alone raises some important research issues. Are psychologically vulnerable people *less* likely to emigrate? Or have massive waves of emigration left behind a population more likely to develop illnesses such as schizophrenia and endogenous depression? If this is the case, can such group vulnerability be explained (as villagers and local doctors contend) in terms of heredity and the fairly common phenomenon in western Ireland of cousin marriage? While not attempting to deny the probable involvement of biogenetic factors in the transmission of some forms of schizophrenia, my own interest lies in analyzing the social conditions that either lessen or exacerbate what may be an initial vulnerability or tendency. In addition, the remarkable celibacy of Irish schizophrenic patients (90.3%), which is not only characteristic of the mental hospital population today, but was also the case in the eighteenth and nineteenth centuries (Anon. 1850; 1864: 299; O'Brien n.d.: 20–23), should certainly have impeded the transmission of defective genes. The rural Irish approach to marriage, as in other peasant societies, is eminently pragmatic and utilitarian (see chapter four), and no person with even a history of mental illness in his family stands a fair chance of marrying and having children — let alone the mentally ill person himself.

If I can eventually defend the contribution of sociocultural phenomena in the genesis of mental illness in western Ireland, I am still left with an additional problem (one to be handled by further research). Do the conclusions of Odegaard (1946, 1956) regarding psychiatric epidemiology still hold to the effect that it is *not* the populations left behind, but the migrants and immigrants of the world that have the greatest risk of mental illnesses? Do the Irish have it coming and going, or rather going and staying? In short, are the Irish susceptible to schizophrenia, depression, and alcoholism *wherever* they live? Available data indicate that the Irish vulnerability to mental illness has, in fact, crossed the Atlantic and that Irish immigrants and their descendants have psychiatric treatment rates far exceeding other ethnic groups in the United States (tables 11 and 12) and in Canada (H. B. M. Murphy 1967, 1968a). Interestingly, later statistics indicate that, while susceptibility to schizophrenia diminishes in each successive generation after emigration to the New World, the tendency to alcoholism increases. To a certain degree, mental health appears to be enhanced by distance from the pathogenic stresses of life in the old sod.

Before attempting to diagnose and interpret the Irish dilemma regarding mental illness, I shall comment further on some of the problems involved in the use of statistical data such as these.

■ TABLE 11: RATES OF FIRST ADMISSION TO MENTAL HOSPITALS
IN NEW YORK STATE, PER 100,000 TOTAL POPULATION, 1911

BIRTHPLACE	ALCOHOLIC DISORDERS	OTHER MENTAL DISORDERS
United States	5	30
Italy	2	45
Russia	1	66
Great Britain	18	50
Austria-Hungary	6	82
Scandinavia	16	89
Germany	11	87
Canada	22	90
France	16	111
Ireland	34	122

Source: Pollack (1913: 10–27), cited by H. B. M. Murphy 1975: 120.

■ TABLE 12: AVERAGE ANNUAL STANDARDIZED RATES OF WHITE FIRST
ADMISSIONS TO ALL HOSPITALS FOR MENTAL ILLNESS IN NEW YORK
STATE, 1949–1951, PER 100,000 POPULATION BY NATIVITY
AND PARENTAGE

	FOREIGN-BORN			NATIVE-BORN OF FOREIGN PARENTAGE		
	MALES	FEMALES	TOTAL	MALES	FEMALES	TOTAL
England	138.8	137.2	140.7	158.9	142.3	157.3
Ireland	240.7	216.9	231.7	228.4	194.3	220.2
Germany	157.3	175.5	169.4	144.2	147.2	152.4
Poland	167.3	207.6	191.3	151.9	146.1	155.5
Russia	169.8	153.0	164.1	160.2	146.9	157.1
Italy	146.2	130.4	141.3	139.2	102.8	114.6
All foreign-born	168.2	180.5	178.7	190.8	160.4	178.4

Source: Adapted from Malzberg (1969: 407).

▪ Variations in Diagnostic Usage

Schizophrenia constitutes the core problem of insanity in the Western world; it is also the largest unknown. Many psychiatrists concede that schizophrenia is, at best, a crude diagnostic label to describe a cluster of symptoms that, under further scrutiny and with greater refining of psychiatric nosology, may be found to represent more than one illness (see Jackson 1960; Fish 1969). The conditions subsumed under this label are among the most devastating to which humanity is heir: delusions, hallucinations, feelings of outside influence on bodily functions, interference and confusion with cognition, thought stealing, and loss of control over emotion, drive, and volition (see *The International Pilot Study of Schizophrenia*, World Health Organization 1973: 14–18). In short, the schizophrenic seems to have difficulty with the "osmosis" of experience. Perhaps the main characteristic of the schizophrenic is his fear of involvement with life and people, and his resulting withdrawal into childhood regressions where reality gives way to primitive fantasy and where self and others are not clearly distinguished. Thomas Szasz has called schizophrenia a "problem in living" (1960: 113).

Michel Foucault (1967) has traced Western society's altering perceptions of the schizophrenic from the concept of the "madman" as a moral renegade, to that of a criminal, to that of a romantic tragic hero, and finally to his confinement as a "diseased" member of a would-be healthy society. And so, in most quarters of the West during the past century, schizophrenia has come to be recognized as an illness analogous to other physical pathologies. However, in many non-Western and so-called primitive societies, the symptoms of life-crisis "reactive" schizophrenias are often identified with religious conversion or mystical experience, and the individual may be elevated to the role of prophet or shaman. (See, for example, the life history of the Seneca holy man Handsome Lake, in Wallace 1972: 339ff.) The fact that the hallucinations or "visions" of the shaman often provide a focus for the integration of a troubled community has resulted in a continuing scholarly dialogue regarding the "creative psychosis" and the "myth of mental illness" (see Laing 1965; Szasz 1961).

If there is such divergence of opinion concerning the very nature of the disease (if it can be called such at all), the question can also be raised whether clinicians from different cultural backgrounds are likely to use the label of schizophrenia in the same manner or with the same frequency. Is an Irish schizophrenic suffering from the same malady as an American or a Russian schizophrenic? And is it possible that discrepancies or merely preferences in diagnostic usage may account for the excessively high rates of schizophrenia in Ireland? A recent study (Kelleher and Copeland 1973) involving the use of videotapes of a variety of psychiatric "cases" demonstrated that psychiatrists trained in Dublin and Belfast generally agree on diagnostic labels with psychiatrists trained in England. The same research team also invited psychiatrists from the United States and from England, Scotland, and Wales to independently diagnose each of several cases presented for observation (see Copeland, et al. 1971). The results were surprising: American psychiatrists were far more likely to make a diagnosis of schizophrenia than were the psychiatrists from the British Isles. The latter more evenly distributed their diagnoses among affective disorders, personality disorders, and schizophrenia. It is unlikely, therefore, that the Republic's schizophrenia statistics have been inflated by misdiagnosis, or through the admission of mild cases (see D. Walsh n.d.), or through patients coming for treatment from Northern Ireland or abroad. In fact, the reverse is the case, for seasonal Irish migrants to London have a high treatment rate for both schizophrenia and alcoholism in that city (Bagley and Binitie 1970).

Although not professionally trained in psychiatric diagnosis, I am familiar with the usual checklist of symptoms in schizophrenia—withdrawal, flat affect, conceptual disorganization, perceptual disorder, deviant motor behavior, delusions, and hallucinations. While there may have been nothing to compel a diagnosis of "schizophrenia" (as opposed to shamanic hypersensitivity), the young men and women whom I met at the mental hospital were consciously suffering and in search of relief from their symptoms. Their perception of the "disorder" might differ markedly from that of the rational psychiatrist, but the patients usually intuitively grasped the breadth of the chasm separating themselves from others.

Twenty-eight-year-old Johnny ended the TAT storytelling task with his response to card 16 (blank card):

First impression: I'd like to be home with my family. Principally, I'd like to be cured of this disease that I suffer from. I don't want to be different. I was healthy up until two years ago. It just gets me down.

▪ Availability and Use of Hospital Beds

The social services in Ireland—including orphanages, old age homes, and hospitals—are exceptionally prolific, well staffed, and heavily endowed.

Church and state are nominally separate, but the Irish government recognizes the "special status" of the Catholic Church, and the two cooperate extensively in the fields of education and public welfare.[4] County hospitals are staffed, at least in part, by nursing Sisters, and are largely financed through Church donations and the Irish Sweepstakes, which in its forty-three-year history has contributed millions of pounds to the Irish Hospital Association. Either the clinics and hospitals are free or the charges are minimal and adjusted to income. A combined result of the availability of hospital beds, the highly esteemed care rendered by nursing Sisters, generally positive attitudes toward hospitalization, and the low cost of treatment results in exceptionally high usage of hospitals for both physical and psychological illnesses.

The villagers of Ballybran were often hospitalized for minor ailments (a bad flu, adult measles) and kept overnight for urine and blood tests and for routine bone-settings. Occasionally, women with unspecified complaints of tiredness and irritability were hospitalized in town for observation for a week or more before being sent home. The average maternity stay for a normal birth is three weeks in hospital, although one "modern" village woman returned to Ballybran after only a week, and another stayed for six. When my six-month-old son developed a skin rash that did not respond to changes in diet and clothing, the town doctor recommended hospitalization—a step I considered drastic given the mildness of his complaint. And the local curate was hospitalized two weeks for boils and would have stayed longer were he not finally driven to distraction by boredom. In all, there prevailed a general attitude of acceptance of hospitalization as a routine and not particularly traumatic event. The separation anxiety that surrounds periods of hospitalization in other rural and traditional societies of Europe and Latin America did not hold for Ballybran (see Friedl's description of village attitudes toward hospitalization in Greece, 1958). Several village children were hospitalized during our stay—the majority for appendectomies and tonsillectomies—and parents seemed, for the most part, blithely unconcerned about the two- and sometimes three-week separation from their toddlers and small children. The consensus was that the nursing Sisters would "pet" the children to the extent that the little ones would be "spoilt" [*sic*] and of "no use at home" once they returned.

▪ Warehousing of the Elderly

At the opposite end of the life-cycle spectrum, old people in the village were hospitalized and "put away" for minor physical and mental ailments in alarming numbers—that is, given the description of rural Ireland in the not so distant past as a "gerontocracy," a haven for the aged (see Streib 1968: 227). As a general axiom, the elderly villager of today can expect to spend his last months, weeks, or days not in a rocking chair by the fireplace, but in a hospital, old age home, or mental institution. Of the thirty-eight deaths in Ballybran during our stay, all but four occurred in an institution of some kind. From reports of villagers, as recently as the 1950s the only acceptable pattern of treatment for the elderly was a proper death at home followed by a kitchen wake.[5] While a few elderly women in Ballybran still keep a trunk with their home wake and funeral accouterments ready—white sheets, blessed candles, brown habit—the more pragmatic, like the self-sufficient widow Bridie, have prepared instead a traveling bag for the final trip over Connor Pass to Dingle Hospital where they can reasonably expect to die.

In the not so distant past, the old people were a natural extension of every farm family (see Arensberg and Kimball 1968: 76ff). Today when most old people in the village are isolated and unattached bachelors, spinsters, and widows, rather than grandparents, aunts, and uncles, the vast majority live alone in relative poverty and loneliness. Sickness and death at home pose an emotional and financial burden upon distant relatives who no longer feel a strong responsibility to care personally for their close, let alone their "far out," kin. The proliferation of old age pensions, Gaeltacht grants, free coal and electricity for the aged, and the presence of a visiting public health nurse has created among younger villagers a strong feeling that the government, rather than family and friends, has the primary responsibility to look after the aged. Today, villagers expect to be, and are, reimbursed by the County Welfare Services for their neighborly acts of visiting the sick and elderly. And institutionalization has become — even in rural Ireland — the main solution for dealing with the troublesome and ubiquitous old people. Since spaces are considerably more difficult to arrange in old-age and nursing homes, and since the rural aged are frequently driven to eccentricities by the isolation of their lives, the county mental hospital with its thousand-bed capacity in tiny, depopulated Kerry, has become the largest recipient of the unwanted elderly.

The director of the Kerry County mental hospital frequently addressed himself to this issue during our conversations. Although during his five years of directorship he reduced the resident population from its full thousand-bed capacity to seven hundred occupied beds, he expressed the desire for still further reduction. Of the seven hundred hospital residents, he said three hundred "could and should be returned to their communities this very day, except they are old and have no one who will take them in."

An assistant psychiatrist attached to the county medical hospital and administering a circuit of outpatient clinics in rural Kerry, confirmed that "psychogeriatrics" was his greatest problem as well. Many of the single,

Place of honor and privilege within the household belongs to the old couple. In their families they are objects of respect and a mild sort of veneration on the part of all younger members. This respect is as much folk custom as the norms of family life.
—ARENSBERG AND KIMBALL, *Family and Community in Ireland*

isolated old people referred to him at the Dingle clinic were in his estimation not mentally ill but *physically* ill—suffering from malnutrition and lack of human contact and care. "Many of these old people are weak and delusional from hunger and loneliness; if they seem 'paranoid' in their accusations against kin and neighbors, their accusations are often well founded. For every single old farmer there are a host of greedy neighbors waiting to pounce on his land and possessions."

While this same doctor was a psychiatric intern some years ago at a hospital in Donegal, he was asked by the director of the hospital to do a medical and psychiatric survey on 170 chronic and "questionable" mental patients. "Of all 170 I could positively diagnose only five patients as psychotic or severely mentally handicapped," the doctor said. "The remaining were somewhat senile, withdrawn, unattached old people with nowhere else to go."

The pathogenic loneliness of the village elderly is epitomized in the case history of David, a crusty old retired seaman under treatment for a rather eccentric disorder, which was diagnosed by the hospital psychiatrist as amnesia. David complained that he could not locate his image in the mirror. His eyes would search the glass over and again, but not a trace of "himself" could he find. To the best of his recollection he lost his image soon after the death of his best—indeed only—village friend, a fishing partner. With the death of his "soul mate," David's mirror image had disappeared.

Although the unwanted elderly swell, to a considerable extent, the mental hospital population in rural Ireland, they do not skew the rates for schizophrenia. The main diagnostic label used for the elderly psychiatric population is that of organic psychosis; schizophrenia is associated with the middle-aged mental hospital population (see O'Hare and Walsh 1974: 31, table 9).

▪ Hospital Admission

The laws governing temporary certification for psychiatric hospital admission in Ireland have changed in the last decade, but still appear to be in need of revision. Prior to 1945, most patients were admitted to mental hospitals by order of a judicial authority. Under the Mental Treatment Act (1945), hospitalization was effected upon medical certification only. The act provided for three main classes of patients: voluntary patients, who enter mental hospitals of their own accord; temporary patients, who may be committed for up to six months of treatment; and persons of unsound mind, those judged likely to require more than six months of treatment. This act has been amended, and although all commitments today are nominally "voluntary," upon entrance into a hospital the patient is still asked to sign away his freedom for a stipulated amount of time. In addition, referrals for commitment are still frequently made by family and community members working with the cooperation of the local dispensary doctor or visiting psychiatric nurse. The dissenting patient may be in a vulnerable position, unable to defend himself against "helpful" family and neighbors. The forms for temporary certification to the psychiatric hospital need only be signed by the district dispensary doctor, a general practitioner. The burden for proof is skewed—weighted toward proving sanity rather than the reverse, as the forms require the doctor to state reasons for refusing to certify an individual, while they do not require him to justify the institutionalization. This makes it difficult for the doctor to refuse certification in doubtful cases—especially under pressure from influential family and community members.

In familistic rural communities where bitter disputes, petty jealousies, and envies often divide social groups into factions, vindictiveness can and does sometimes result in psychiatric certification and commitment of rival family members and neighbors. The director of a psychiatric hospital in County Cork commented in his hospital's journal that there are often times when "the real reasons behind certification are ill will in the family, land disputes, desire to be rid of the elderly relatives once they have made deeds of assignment of their property in return for care, etc." (Dunne 1970: 33). Where some rural people are hospitalized without sufficient or proper cause, the following discussion deals with the reverse side of the coin: why are other village members, apparently suffering from some form of mental illness, never recognized as sick?

▪ Attitudes toward the Mentally Ill, Past and Present

A most striking fact about small villages in many parts of the world is the haunting presence of the "village idiot" or village "madman"—that one person, male or female, who is seemingly selected from an array of possible candidates to fill the sanctioned role of fool, entertainer, and clown. Ballybran was no exception; for while it was apparent that many eccentric, odd, and "crazy" people inhabited the village, only one was singled out for particular recognition as *the* village fool. The other recognizable eccentric villagers filled different roles and statuses and met a variety of different fates. Some were institutionalized and forgotten, others were secreted away in mountain farmsteads, living alone like isolated hermits. Still others were pampered and doted upon by family and neighbors as holy and harmless "saints." In this section I shall attempt to define the thin edge that separates normal from abnormal behavior in Ballybran. I shall outline the conditions that result in mental illness being ignored, "petted" and coddled, recognized and treated, or recognized and mistreated. I shall briefly review the beliefs of the ancient Irish toward the mentally ill and show how certain of these attitudes have persisted among the "folk" to this day and color the nature of village ambivalence toward the "insane."

The oldest recorded folk belief concerning mental illness in Ireland comes from the still surviving legend that the pre-Christian Druidic priests had the power to inflict madness by casting a "magic wisp of straw" (P. W. Joyce 1903, 1: 224). Once "touched" in this fashion, the mad man or woman was credited with certain magical properties—among these, weightlessness, or the ability to move from place to place with remarkable swiftness, merely touching the ground here and there. This belief persisted well into the Middle Ages in Ireland, and a description of such an experience ("Sweeney's Frenzy") during a famous battle is immortalized in the Celtic manuscript *Buile Shuibne* (ibid., 226).

The ancient laws of Ireland, called the Brehon Laws, which were codified about the time of Saint Patrick (A.D. 432) and which remained in effect until the fall of the Gaelic Order in 1603, placed great emphasis upon regulating the conduct of the mentally ill and incompetent (see vol. 1 of the *Senchus*

Mor, the "Law of Distress," 1865). The laws include many proscriptions against the insane copulating, marrying, or bearing children, and fear of the imputed violence of the mad was reflected in the necessity of "fettering those upon whom the magic wisp has been cast" (ibid., 143).

The Brehon Laws distinguished the madman ("lunatic") from the imbecile ("fool"). While the fool was considered capable of participation within the community, and was expected to work and earn his or her own keep (often as a minstrel), the "lunatic" was severed from the community and either imprisoned or set free to wander aimlessly about the country-side. If presumed violent or dangerous to the tribe, the madman was put to a swift death.

A vestige of the old dichotomy between "fool" and "lunatic" is very much apparent in the village today—as is the belief that madness is influenced by the phases of the moon. ("Maighread's been acting a bit queer, all right, lately," comments Aine, "but once the autumn tides are past she'll be bet-ter.") The harmless "fools" of the village of Ballybran are those referred to as "God's own"—the mentally retarded, the simple and withdrawn, the eccen-tric who—epitomized in Maighread—are childlike, innocent, presumably sexless, and clean of heart.

When Maighread bicycles ten miles over rough mountain paths to "show off" her new dress to the curate, villagers comment on her innocent and unconscious seductiveness: "God bless her, the critter, she hasn't the notion." It is the same Maighread, after all, who climbs Mount Brandon in pilgrimage each May, silent, barefoot, and fasting, and the same Maighread ("an example to us all") who fervently confesses her "sineens" (harmless venial sins) in Irish to Father Leary each Saturday night. And likewise, when the ageless bachelor Patsy sweats and stammers and hides his face in his jacket lapel when forced to speak with a member of the opposite sex, his buddies fondly and jokingly refer to him as "the woman hater," a common problem but nothing serious. And finally, when the retarded son of a village shopkeeper is taken to the altar to receive a wafer, the meaning of which he will never understand, the old women sigh and say, "Aye, the angel of God, who is more worthy than himself to receive the Blessed Sacrament?" For these villagers (as with Michael O'Brien who sits up with his cows in prayer each evening), there is a touch of blessing mixed in with the erratic (by village standards) behavior, and of these only Maighread is publicly regarded as being "mental" (although harmlessly so). When, however, the beleaguered Seamus, a hopeful suitor from west of Dingle, expresses his frustration and hostility at being shunned for every dance at a summer *ceilidhe* by partially exposing himself to a group of girls, the line has been crossed, and who was once a "fool" is converted into "lunatic" and his behavior must be censored.

▪ Labeling: Community Limits of Normal and Abnormal Behavior

George Devereux (1956) defined the "key problem" for psychiatric anthropologists as one of determining the exact locus of the culturally defined boundaries between "normal" and "abnormal" behavior. Early contributors to ethnopsychiatry concentrated on culturally relative definitions of "deviance" and abnormality (see Benedict 1935; Reider 1950). It was generally agreed that behavior that might be treated as a sickness in one society could be punished as a crime in another society, or considered a sin in yet another. Elsewhere, the very same behavior might be celebrated as a mark of holy or privileged status. Ozturk (1964), for example, points out that the designations *deli* (insane) and *veli* (saint) are closely related in Turkish society, paralleling the rural Irish definition of "saint," used in some contexts to describe an elderly and eccentric recluse. The culturally divergent interpretations of alcoholism, drug addiction, and transvestism are but a few other examples of the relativity of such terms as sick, sinful, deviant, and holy.

Later ethnopsychiatric studies have retreated, however, from an extremely relativistic stance (see Jane Murphy 1976), and there appears to be a growing consensus that certain near-universal categories of abnormal behavior do exist. Almost everywhere a pattern of afflictions bearing resemblance to the Western diagnosis of schizophrenia (including hallucinations, delusions, spatial and temporal disorientations, and behavioral aberrations) is at least recognized as deviant, if not labeled as "crazy." A Zulu informant described the characteristics by which an individual is recognized as a shaman or sorcerer as follows:

He is sturdy in appearance, but in time he becomes more and more deli-
cate . . . ; he is always complaining of being in pain. . . . He dreams
of all kinds of things and his body is muddy. . . . He has convulsions,
which cease for a time when water is sprinkled over him. As soon as he is
not shown respect, he bursts into tears and cries noisily. A man who is
about to become a wizard is a great source of trouble. (Cited by Fou-
cault 1976: 63)

Although madness exists throughout the world, its content and expression may be culturally specific. Such are the cases of the Native American *wittiko* psychosis in which the victim is seized by a cannibalistic panic, and the face-saving indiscriminate violent attacks by a man running amok in Southeast Asia. The underlying structure of the illnesses appear to be the same — paranoid schizophrenia — although its expression is patterned locally. A psychotic person must draw upon the imagery and symbolism of his own culture, whether Virgin and Savior motifs among the Irish, or monster myths among Cree and Ojibwa Indians. Certainly, the clinical histories of psychiatric patients from rural Kerry evidenced a greater tendency toward delusions of a religious nature than toward secular or electromagnetic persecution delusions, so common among American schizophrenics. In addition, societies will differ markedly in the attention they give to some symptoms and the disregard of others. Interviews and psychological tests of Irish schizophrenics demonstrated a tendency among them to withdraw into infantile fantasies and into delusions of grandeur (identification with local Irish saints and heroes, however, such as Saint Brendan and Sir Roger Casement took the place of the proverbial Napoleon). In addition, the Irish patients were frequently guilt-ridden and self-punishing — especially with regard to latent homosexuality and masturbation. Aggression was expressed through oral sadistic and cannibalistic fantasies as well as through morbid preoccupations with death, burial, and exhumation of the corpse. ("Last night I dreamed I killed a man," revealed a hospitalized young man, "but for the life of me I can't remember whether I buried him or I ate him.") Card 15 of the Thematic Apperception Test (a gaunt man with clenched hands standing among gravestones) elicited sadistic themes in half (seven of thirteen) the responses of psychiatric patients and in only 15 percent (two of thirteen) in the normal sample. The following response from a male schizophrenic is illustrative:

A graveyard. Somebody is rising from the dead. She's going to haunt someone. She's a vampire. . . . She's out to get people. She kills them with her teeth. Then she goes back into her coffin. (HM1)

Linked to the recognition or labeling of madness is the secondary issue of tolerance for deviant behavior. George DeVos (personal communication) estimated that in present-day Japan the proportion of mentally ill persons, recognized as such by those around them, is about the same as in the United States. In the West, however, there is a greater level of intolerance within the family and community, resulting in a higher rate of hospitalization. The Japanese family, by contrast, is more tolerant of mental illness and more duty-bound to family members, making hospitalization the exception rather than the rule.

Hospital psychiatrists who treated villagers from the Dingle Peninsula, but who were sometimes not familiar with the actualities of rural life, had a few erroneous stereotypes about inhabitants of the peninsula. One of the most persistent of these was the belief that although the mental hospital population for Kerry was very large, the villagers had endless tolerance for all kinds of bizarre behavior. "Why, a person who would be considered 'red mad' anywhere else in Ireland is simply taken in their stride as 'just old Jack' around Dingle," commented one clinic psychiatrist dryly.

In fact, conformity is very highly valued in Ballybran, reserved behavior is the expected norm, and notwithstanding their "fightin' Irish" reputation, all physical aggression is shunned. While the category of harmless "saints"—those eccentric but normally quiet and harmless people who keep to themselves—can live peaceable and integrated lives in the village despite certain eccentricities of behavior, tolerance is not to be extended to those persons (like Seamas, above) who violate the strong Irish sanctions against expressions of sexuality, aggression, and insubordination to parental and religious authority. Such nonconformists are prime candidates for the mental hospital.

In a society in which reserved behavior—especially among men—is the norm, uncontrolled excitability is noted as abnormal behavior, and "manic" persons are more likely to be recognized as mentally ill than are extremely depressed and quiet ones, who are more rarely hospitalized. The old maiden aunt Teresa, for example, spent the whole of the winter of 1974 indoors sitting passively and morosely in front of the turf range. Although normally a sociable woman, Teresa could not be coaxed into conversation with family members or neighbors. She was, in villagers' estimation, "very depressed." Although Teresa grew thin and haggard from her ordeal, the depression was interpreted within the realm of "normal" behavior given the long, uninterrupted, winter rains and the woman's advanced age.

Tolerance for, and definition of, normal and abnormal behavior is also influenced by the individual's integration, or lack of it, within a strong kinship network. A family "claim," so to speak, can protect and shield a villager from designation as insane. Although Auntie Peg is an aged, mentally handicapped, cantankerous old spinster given to episodes of rage followed by withdrawal and deep depression, she is considered "little bother" to her large extended family who owe her a lifetime of debts. Consequently, Peg will never see the dark walls of the county mental hospital. Over her lifetime, Auntie Peg had reared all of her sister's thirteen children, most of whom had emigrated and "made good" in America. The few nephews remaining feel a responsibility to dote on the "old one." Explained Brendan:

We leave her free-like. She raised us up and took care of us. She would never harm anyone, so why would we put her away now? We let her have her fags when she wants, buy her a pretty ring now and then, and we make sure she takes her tablets to keep away the gloom.

▪ Doublespeak, Doublethink: Communication Patterns and Schizophrenia

Village society places a high emphasis on sociable, although not intimate, behavior among peers. And a "normal" villager is one, above all, who can and does take part in the lively repartee of public places—be they shops for women or pubs for men. Communication patterns in these places are extremely formalized and intricate—relying on a skill with words, metaphor, veiled insult, and so forth, for which the Irish have achieved fame. The author Honor Tracy has described it as a "double-think and double-speak [requiring] a sharpness of ear, a feeling for half tones and shades and subtleties" (1953: 9). Group conversations in Ballybran are, indeed, laden with double-talk, obfuscations, interruptions, and non sequiturs, which make it difficult for the uninitiated outsider to follow and participate. No matter, the "Yank" is expected to be confused, for that is one intention of the interaction. But the native-born villager who cannot cope with such verbal intricacies, or who replies with inappropriate comment or affect, is regarded by his peers as "a queer kind of a man."

In his recent review of the literature on Irish alcoholism and schizophrenia, H. B. M. Murphy (1975) concludes that the so-called Irish doublespeak may create intolerable levels of ambiguity, which can provoke schizophrenia in vulnerable individuals. Elsewhere Murphy suggests that the characteristic Irish expressiveness was shaped by the nearly eight hundred years of English domination and colonialism. Verbal ambiguity is a common response of a defeated people toward their conquerors—that is, never giving the master a straight answer. Before I concede that the rich Irish oral tradition (which far precedes the period of English colonialism) is a breeder of madness, I shall offer an alternative explanation.

In my own observations of village (especially pub) repartee, I noticed a particularly low tolerance for the verbally inept; such men are excluded from conversations and round-drinking and are often made the butt of a joke, pun, or double-entendre. It appears to me not that the quick-wittedness and verbal acuity of the rural Irish would *cause* schizophrenia, but that schizoid or borderline schizophrenic persons, given their characteristic difficulties with language, would be quickly recognized and labeled as abnormal in such a community.

The tailor of Ballybran clarified the fine points of social philosophy with his (verbatim) interpretation of the unwritten code of normal and abnormal (or simply acceptable and unacceptable) behavior for men in the village. Most noticeable is the great emphasis placed upon communication.

> We like an honest man, a good living man. One who doesn't interfere in others' business. A man who mingles with all, enjoys life, and shares a pint with any decent fellow. We like a man who is calm, not excessive; a man neither idle nor a slave to his work. A reasonable man should have a rational approach to life. He must be a regular sort of person, eating his meals at the appointed hour, and sleeping at night and not during the day. We prefer a man who is dependable—on time for Mass, and not clattering in at the back of church like a foreigner. A regular sort of man should dress warm for the rain, and not walk about hatless. For that would be strange. He should be generous to a point, not mean and stingy, but neither should he be a fool, and fling his goods and money away so that his family will suffer. He should be a reasonable man in conversation, having things of interest to discuss, but not given to idle or meaningless words. For, it is written: "For every idle word a man shall speak, he will render an account on the day of judgment." We like a man who is at ease with other people, not an awkward kind of man who says nothing or who talks in a loud and gruff manner. We don't like nervous, excitable kind of men who rub and wave their arms about, not knowing the proper place to put them. We like a calm, placid, common sense kind of man.
> (Transcribed from a taped conversation, March 1975)

Indeed, the "straight and narrow," as Honor Tracy observed in her novelized account of Irish village life (1956), is a rigorous path of behavior for the parishioner to follow. Yet, exceptions are made. A certain amount of leeway, for example, is reserved for the erratic behavior of the "drinking man," and just as the old Brehon Laws distinguished between the "intoxication of drunkenness" (*Meisce Lenna*) and the "intoxication of madness" (*Meisce*

Merachta), so do villagers today make allowances for public displays under the influence of spirits, which they would never stand for in a sober man ("Pay Steve no mind; tis only the drink that's upon him"). A certain amount of mental illness and "abnormal" behavior (by village standards) is tolerated when disguised in the cloak of alcohol. In this regard, I might note that alcoholics find themselves far less often hospitalized than do schizophrenics in Ireland—alcoholism is, as such, a "safer" form of pathology. Since alcoholism is, to a degree, an accepted part of masculine role behavior (especially among bachelors), it is not recognized as "abnormal." The common Irish defenses of denial and "scapegoating" (see chapter six) also serve to protect village alcoholics from recognition and public shame. Just as what might be referred to as a "community myth" perpetuates within Ballybran the comfortable notion that only Maighread among us is really "crazy," so, too, the village at large attempted to deny alcoholism as a widespread mental and social problem by acknowledging the existence of only *one* village alcoholic—the despised water-bailiff.

▪ Attitude toward Treatment and Cure

The general methods of treatment for psychiatric illnesses in Ireland are strongly influenced (as they are elsewhere) by cultural factors, among them beliefs about the nature and cause of mental illness, moral and religious convictions, types and availability of treatment institutions, training and bias of medical and paramedical personnel, and community attitudes toward rehabilitation and acceptance of returned mental patients.

Although Ireland does not have the complete public availability of a national health care service and a social welfare system like Britain's, the model for care and treatment is based on that of England, and most Irish psychiatrists are trained in that country. There are in the Republic nineteen district hospitals (similar to American state mental hospitals) as well as fourteen private psychiatric hospitals run by nursing Sisters who care largely for the mentally handicapped. Each district hospital administers a number of psychiatric clinics in small towns within the catchment area of the hospital. There are virtually no halfway houses in the Republic. The vast majority of

Irish psychiatrists are attached to the district mental hospitals and clinics, and the few psychiatrists who do have private practices are clustered in the urban centers of Dublin and Cork. Hence, the villagers of the west have recourse to limited possibilities for treatment—the local dispensary general practitioner, who may or may not be responsive and sympathetic to mental and emotional problems; a visit to a psychiatric clinic in a neighboring town; hospitalization at the county mental hospital.

The identification of a complaint as a psychiatric problem is rarely made by the villager himself. The normal sequence of events in Ballybran leading to the identification and treatment of psychiatric problems is as follows. A woman villager would often instigate her own initial trip to the village dispensary doctor. Her complaints might be vague or psychosomatic in cast. She is run down and tired, but the doctor assures her that her color is good. He looks at the rims of her eyes and pinches her fingernails, and sends her off with what even he considers a worthless tonic. Or the woman complains of irritability and "nervousness" and asks that her blood pressure be checked. She is given a mild tranquilizer. Or still another woman—this one elderly—complains of a "burning inside her body" that she fears is entering her head. She calls it "neuralgia" and the doctor nods and gives her a placebo of candy "tablets." *These* women rarely get any further than the village dispensary, for the local "country doctor" is impatient with them. He complains that middle-aged women waste his time, which could be more usefully occupied with "real" problems—heart attacks, influenzas, bone-settings, dog bites. His rather unsympathetic and ill-informed interpretation of psychosomatic illnesses as "imaginary complaints made up by lonely old women" makes the doctor less than cooperative in making referrals to the psychiatric clinic in Dingle.

Village men are expected to shun the sick role, and must be coaxed and even fooled by womenfolk into seeing a doctor or a nurse for physical as well as psychiatric disorders. Hence, although theoretically the dispensary general practitioner is expected to make the necessary referrals to the psychiatric clinic, in fact the role is generally filled by a family member, by the public health nurse, and occasionally by the curate. However, by far the greatest number of referrals is made by the visiting psychiatric nurse, attached to the district mental hospital in Killarney and assigned to the isolated and mountainous regions of west Kerry.

Until recently, the nurse's role was largely that of dispensing weekly dosages of psychotropic drugs and checking up on newly discharged psychiatric patients. However, when in 1973 the power of the psychiatric nurse to dispense medicines was curtailed by law, the nurse redefined his role to include the early identification of psychiatric problems and mental health education. Today the psychiatric nurse in Ballybran sees himself largely as an educator, informing community and family members about the nature of mental illness so they will be more receptive to receiving home a former mental patient. The nurse attempts to gain a lively rapport with as many village families as possible in order to spot difficulties. Villagers, on their part, tend to give him wide berth in public and often evade him in the privacy of their homes as well. Although known and well liked for his personable nature, the psychiatric nurse is stigmatized in the village by his association with the "madhouse" of Killarney.

Once referred, a patient attends the outpatient clinic in Dingle — a twelve-mile drive over a mountain pass from Ballybran — which is held bimonthly in temporary and makeshift quarters: a dark and drafty back room of the town's geriatric hospital. Owing to inadequacy of staffing, as well as to attitudes toward the cause of psychopathology, the clinic functions largely as a drug dispensary. With its shelves crammed with medicine bottles, the clinic has more the appearance of a dusty village pharmacy than of a doctor's consulting room. The clinic psychiatrist once referred to himself with some chagrin as a "traveling chemist." The clinic is staffed by one psychiatrist with the help of the community psychiatric nurse. Together they are responsible for approximately three hundred outpatients. An appointment system is loosely adhered to, and between fifteen and twenty-five patients are scheduled on any one afternoon. Consequently, the average patient spends between one and two hours waiting for a fifteen-minute consultation.

The psychiatric model in use at the clinic is largely that of making a quick diagnosis and dispensing the appropriate pills. A patient's chart normally carries little more than a check mark next to the appropriate label — organic brain disease, schizophrenia, depression, mania, neurosis, psychopathy, or mental deficiency—and a note on medication. Follow-up clinic visits are oriented around physical exams and tests for toxicity and other side effects of prolonged medication. There is no provision at the clinic for counseling or psychotherapy, although the psychiatric nurse does attempt to gather a social, medical, and psychological life history from his patients during his round of house calls. However, he is very skeptical of his results: "One-third is lies, one-third is no-information, and one-third is half truths."

Despite the personalistic nature of social relations in western Ireland, where numbers are few and most families interrelated to a degree, the clinic is a cold, impersonal environment. Names are called out in public, often amidst flushed and embarrassed faces. Overcrowding results in a marked lack of privacy, and consultations sometimes spill out into the waiting room. One visit is sometimes more than any villager wishes to attempt. A frequent complaint about the clinic is its shared location in the public hospital, where psychiatric patients, who wish to maintain their anonymity, would occasionally be dismayed by running into a village neighbor in town for a sick call.

Treatment at the Kerry psychiatric hospital follows a model of care similar to that of the outpatient clinic, with the greatest reliance placed on chemotherapy. In addition to drug therapy, however, modified electroplexy is used for patients suffering from endogenous depression or from some forms of schizophrenia. Social rehabilitation is another important aspect of inpatient treatment, and the mental hospital has its own small factory and crafts shop where an average of seventy patients are employed in assembly-line fashion at minimum wage levels (about $15 per week in 1975). The director of the mental hospital places great emphasis on what he calls occupational therapy, and his belief is that learning to "clock in" at regular hours, to perform real tasks, and so forth, are the best methods for helping patients regain their lost or confused reality principle. For those patients successfully "graduated" from the hospital factory, the next step is placement into service jobs in the town community. Placement tends to be easier during the summer months when the influx of tourists to Killarney results in an inflated need for maids and waitresses in the town's many hotels and guesthouses.

In both clinic and hospital, a visiting American psychiatrist would be immediately struck by the lack of key supporting personnel—clinical psychologists and psychiatric social workers—and even more so by the virtual absence of psychotherapy, psychoanalysis, and group therapy. In large part this is a reflection of the emphasis placed throughout the British Isles on the hereditary, organic, chemical component to mental illness to the virtual exclusion of attention to social and environmental factors. It is also a function of the training of the Irish psychiatrist. A resident psychiatrist complained that in Irish medical schools psychiatry is still treated as a minor subject for the qualifying medical exams. As a specialization, it fares no better—accorded a low status on a par with dermatology and ears, nose, and throat. Undervalued within the Irish medical profession, psychiatry does not attract the numbers or perpetuate the quality of skilled analytical training that it does elsewhere. Those psychiatrists trained in England expressed the most sympathy for psychotherapy, but said that it was a luxury that could be ill afforded at the overcrowded and understaffed district mental hospitals.

An article in a British medical journal (Cooper and Brown 1967) in which the preferred treatment methods of American and British psychiatrists are compared concludes that the American emphasis on individual psychotherapy and analysis is a reflection of the capitalistic structure of American medicine and of the American ethos of rugged individualism and competitiveness. By contrast, the authors suggest that the British psychiatrists' emphasis on physical therapy and *social* rehabilitation is a function of England's system of socialized medicine and a reflection of cultural attitudes about the sick role—that is, the necessity of returning patients (treated at public expense) as speedily as possible to an active and responsibly productive role in society. Certainly, a similar attitude prevails among Irish psychiatrists, who place as *their* highest goal rehabilitating—rather than curing—mental patients. However, the resistance of Irish communities to accepting a rehabilitated mental patient thwarts the doctors' good intentions.

An even more culturally relative argument against the use of psychotherapy in Ireland was offered by a number of hospital and clinic psychiatrists as well as by the psychiatric nurse—a few of whom incorporate at least *some* aspects of psychotherapy into their work with patients. Widespread among them is the conviction that, given the Catholic scrupulosity of the rural Irish, it might be a violation of the bond of trust between doctor and patient to urge the latter to discuss repressed feelings and desires, for which the patient might later suffer pangs of guilt. As the psychiatric nurse phrased it: "What right do I have drawing a person out to the point where he may confess to me a horrible and unconfessed sin? I might leave the poor soul open to religious despair."

Interestingly, despite their biogenetic biases regarding psychogenesis, many Irish psychiatrists accept the role of sexual repression and religious guilt as contributory factors in the origin or perpetuation of mental illness among rural patients. One psychiatric hospital director spoke of guilt over latent or expressed homosexuality and, less frequently, over acts of bestiality as themes that occur in the case histories of his rural male patients from west Cork. Similarly, the psychiatric nurse spoke of the deep resentments expressed by his "west of Dingle" patients about the celibacy, isolation, and barrenness of their lives. Nonetheless, all the professionals expressed some belief that the confessional and not the "psychiatrist's couch" is the place where bachelor farmers feel most comfortable discussing the darkest secrets of their souls, many of which (they believed) deal with sexuality. In the opinion of one psychiatrist, it was not the place of the medical professional to attempt to undo a lifetime of sexual repression, which, for better or worse, is an integral part of these men's identities: "These men seek and need unmitigated forgiveness and not a hypothetical dispensation of guilt, which is all a psychiatrist can offer in psychotherapy."

▪ The Search for Asylum: Hospitalism, Rehabilitation, and Deterrents against a Return to Community Life

While the psychiatrists of Kerry are deeply committed to the task of rehabilitating patients in order to return them quickly to community life, the overall pattern at the county mental hospital is one of long stays. In 1971 the resident population of the hospital was 745. Of these, 179 had lengths of stay between one month and one year; 186 from one to ten years; and 380 from ten to thirty years (O'Hare and Walsh 1974: 44, table 9). According to the Ballybran parish death-register figures, sixteen villagers have died in the county mental hospital since 1928.

Secondary gain or voluntary dependency upon the total institution as an adaptive strategy is a characteristic of many mental patients (see Caudill 1958; Goffman 1961). In Ireland, this problem is especially acute and is a topic of great concern among psychiatric hospital directors. In this concluding section, I shall attempt a speculative analysis on the origin of Irish psychiatric "hospitalism" based on the interpretation of certain aspects of Irish ethos and world view, as well as on the passive "gestalt" of treatment methods, and the problems of reincorporating former psychiatric patients in the rural west.

It appears to me that the reliance on physical methods of cure (chemotherapy, shock treatments), grounded as they are in an interpretation of mental illness as an organic disorder, reduces the patient to a dependent and passive role in the sickness and the cure. The continually "shocked" patient perceives himself as a helpless and hapless victim of both his illness and the cure. Similarly, the fostering of a lifelong dependency upon psychotropic drugs imbues the mental patient with a view of himself as chronically sick beyond cure. With the best of intentions, and yet with detrimental consequences, the visiting psychiatric nurse in Ballybran informed worried parents and relatives of young schizophrenics that their "Sally" or "Jack" was suffering from a disease for which no one (least of all the patient) was responsible, and for which there was, like alcoholism, no cure. The nurse would clinch his argument with the statement that "schizophrenia is a disease that will never kill your son, but in order for him to live safely, he *must* take the tablets for the rest of his life." This negative and passive approach toward the cure of mental illness was often reiterated by the young patients I interviewed, and was a frequent theme on the Thematic Apperception Test, such as that of young Brenda, who, at age fifteen, saw herself as a "burnt-out case." The following is her reply to card 3GF, a sorrowful young woman with head bowed and arm stretched forward against a wooden door:

This woman reminds me of myself. She seems to be crying and she wants to get out, but she can't go because the door is locked and she haven't the key. (Where is she?) She could be in a mental hospital like me. She looks upset and lonely. Or, maybe her parents didn't come to see her. (Her future?) She'll be like this for the rest of her life.

A dispersal of a deterministic theory of pathogenesis and of the necessity for mechanistic control through mood drugs imbues villagers with a fear of the unpredictability of even "rehabilitated" returned patients. ("Finon tripped and fell on the way to the cemetery, and then he couldn't stop laughing yesterday," confided a shopkeeper. "I hope he's not forgetting to take his tablets.")

Once interned in a mental hospital, the patient finds that his family and the community at large tend to abrogate responsibility for his welfare. As Brenda expressed it above, family and community members rarely visit mental patients, and the occasional visit, when it does occur, tends to be strained and brief. If convincing villagers of the necessity for temporary hospitalization of a family member is sometimes a difficult chore for the psychiatric nurse, he admits that getting the same family to take *back* a patient after even a brief stint at the "asylum" is next to impossible. As thirty-four-year-old Patrick, a schizophrenic bachelor and farm heir, expressed his sense of abandonment by family and community, "I am their dead son."

Unfounded stereotypes of the uncontrollable violence and heightened sexuality of mentally ill people, which deviate from the clinical descriptions of schizophrenia (see Sullivan 1962), are propagated even by magazine articles supposedly informing and "enlightening" the layman about the nature of psychopathology. The *Saint Martin de Porres Magazine*, the most widely read Catholic monthly in Ballybran, carries a medical column that in one issue discussed the nature of schizophrenia, sections from which I quote below:

> *In some cases of schizophrenia the patient may show alternating moods of deep depression and normality and in severe cases they may be so unconsciously violent as to commit actual murder — often of a loved one — and when questioned about it afterwards, they may not recollect having done anything amiss. . . . Many schizophrenics need to be detained repeatedly or permanently in an institution for their own and other peoples' safety, but that is a decision for the doctor to make. . . .*

Treatment of the condition is difficult, but it is possible sometimes to keep the patient under control. Unfortunately, "flare ups" cannot be anticipated, and hence the tragedies that frequently occur. (1974, March: 36)

For the majority of villagers this was the only "authoritative" opinion on schizophrenia they had received all year. It is small wonder, then, at the resistance villagers expressed when faced with the request to take back into their homes a relative who might even attempt murder "of a loved one" — should he forget to take his tablets. Spending time in the "madhouse" was viewed by some young patients as a permanent "fall from grace" similar to a loss of virginity. "My good name is ruined," lamented Kitty, an adolescent hospitalized after she turned in rage and struck a nun at boarding school. Then she laughed a little deviously. "You know, since I've come here even my own parents are afraid of me. When they let me home for a visit last week the two of 'em watched my every move, waiting for me to do something 'crazy' like."

When the director of the county mental hospital attempted in 1974 to set up a halfway house for rehabilitated patients on a residential street in Killarney, the community reacted with panic. Residents reported in the weekly newspaper that they were opposed to the halfway house on the grounds of "safety to women and children living in the area" (*Kerryman*, October 14, 1974: 1). The statement alluded once again to the alleged sexual and violent tendencies of mental patients. In fact, schizophrenics — although they may become quite agitated at times — are, as a statistical group, less prone to acts of aggression or violence than are the "sane" members of society. Ironically, Irish schizophrenics, in particular, tend to be reserved, conforming to authority, guilt ridden, anxious about sexuality, and fearful of women. All but five of the twenty-two young patients tested from the county mental hospital were, by self report, virgins.

Even more serious, however, than the fear and rejection of mental patients by family and community members is the passive resignation of so many young men and women of County Kerry to long periods of institutionalization as a solution to their personal dilemmas. Faced with few and undesirable options — leaving home at a young age and unprepared for any but menial service jobs; or staying home "in service" to the old people and a future of almost certain celibacy and loneliness—the "total environment" of the mental hospital is truly an asylum for some from the "storms" of fate. As Denis, a twenty-four-year-old manic-depressive farm laborer and perennial patient explained it: "I feel quite useful here. What I would really like to do, once I'm cured of this sickness, is to get a job here at the hospital doing good for those people worse off than me. I can be more useful here than back in Innisdun."

As a purely speculative final analysis, I should like to suggest that the high rates for long-term occupancy of mental hospital beds might also be examined within the historical and cultural context of the retreat to isolation and confinement, particularly during periods of stress and cultural distortion. The "search for asylum" in County Kerry can be witnessed in the history of the primitive monk cells of Sceilig Mhichil and Mount Brandon, in the prolific convents and remains of poorhouses and workhouses in Dingle, in the presbyteries on every secluded hill, in the history of the Hedge Schools, and in the great stone monstrosity of the county mental hospital itself.

The search for asylum begins in Kerry with the introduction of Christianity through wandering bands of ascetic monks who, unlike the clerics on the continent, eschewed the relative comforts of communal monastic living and sought out and built individual stone cells on inaccessible rock promontories, deserted islands, and mountaintops—away from the wiles, pomps, and deceits of the world. Saint Brendan the Navigator, the patron saint of Ballybran, set an example in the fifth century that is still followed in the village today: celibacy, periodic peregrinations across the wild Atlantic, voluntary seclusion, and confinement. The ideology and ethos of the early Irish monks is perpetuated in small isolated hamlets like Ballybran, where often priest and schoolmaster, parent and publican alike, actively instill in the youth of the parish a disdain for sex, marriage, and family life and glorify the role of the social isolate (like Brendan and his heirs in the parish today—the foreign missionaries) over the group member. Celibacy is not only an unfortunate consequence of emigration and demographic imbalance—it is also a cherished ideal. It is, in the words of one village teacher, "the heroic sacrifice."

The search for asylum was brought to its fulfillment in the decades following the Great Famine of 1845–1849. For the peculiarly "Irish" resolution of the stresses of scarcity and overpopulation was not only in waves of forced emigrations to the safety of American cities but also in a massive exodus of boys and girls from the countryside into the solitary asylum offered by seminaries, convents, and monasteries. In 1844, just prior to the Great Famine, there were five thousand religious in the country to service a Catholic population of five million. By 1900 the number of *resident* religious had risen to fourteen thousand while the national population had dropped to only three million (John Murphy 1969: 238). Thousands more among the youth of the western villages left Ireland as missionaries throughout the world. Peasant parents had finally found a safe and secure outlet for their excess sons and undoweried daughters: permanent institutionalization.

In the years after World War II, a hundred years following the Great Famine, a new era of stress has spread through the western countryside—this time the result of scarcity and *underpopulation*. The dearth of eligible women left by emigration and marriage-out means that life on the land can no longer satisfy the needs of young farmers for love, attachment, and security. The casualties of *this* famine also find at least a temporary solution in institutionalization and confinement at the county mental hospital.

Each summer in Ballybran the population of the parish is doubled by the seasonal return of village-born emigrants. For the bright two weeks of August the strand sparkles with the flowing white robes of the emulated heros of Ballybran—the missionaries to Africa and Latin America, resplendent in the purity of their lonely sacrifice. The saints, scholars, and schizophrenics of Ireland—each in his own way—are culture bearers of the same tradition.

CHAPTER FOUR

Brothers, Sisters, and Other Lovers

MARRIAGE, CELIBACY,
AND RELATIONS
BETWEEN THE SEXES

The start of my story,
　　the source of my strain,
The reason I'm senseless
　　and almost insane . . .
Is the number of women,
　　old and young,
For whom no wedding bells
　　have rung . . .
O Aeval, you must find a way
To save our women without delay,
For if the men are allowed to shirk
We'll have to force them
　　to do their work.
By the time they're ready to take a wife
They're not worth taking
　　to save their life,
They're stiff and shrunken
　　and worn and weak
And when they mount you
　　they wheeze and creak.
—BRIAN MERRIMAN,
The Midnight Court, 1780

SEAMAS AND PADRAEC are native Irish speakers from an isolated hamlet west of Dingle.[1] Both are bachelors: Padraec, the elder, is fifty-one, Seamas a still "fresh" forty-three. Since the death of their widowed mother some ten years ago, the two brothers elected to stay at home and share the work of a small, unproductive mountain-end farm. Over their lifetime, the two have witnessed the fatal constriction of the once bustling household as death took the parents and emigration took each of their pretty and vivacious sisters and two older brothers. The brothers, although taciturn and withdrawn, were ever the dutiful sons and "had never harmed a soul," and were thus qualified for the status of village saints. Seamas, although the younger, by virtue of his more dominant personality is treated by villagers as the representative and spokesman for the household. It is Seamas who does the buying and selling, Seamas who mediates for the household in the public arenas of market, shop, pub, and church. And as it became increasingly impossible for the household to subsist on the proceeds of farm work and remittance money from the affluent relatives abroad, it was Seamas who took upon himself the dual lifestyle that carried him to Liverpool for part of every winter, where he worked at seasonal construction.

The older brother, Padraec, or Paudy, is considered a little simple ("not one hundred percent") and is known as a "woman hater." When it is Padraec's turn for a night out at the pub, he clings to the wall and rarely offers more than a timid affirmative "Ah, 'tis so, 'tis indeed" to the rounds of conversation. Paudy's fatal flaw and one with which he is teased unmercifully by his bachelor peer group is his terror of women. In the presence of the opposite sex Padraec blushes, stammers, perspires, and either resorts, ostrichlike, to hiding his head in his hands or even his jacket lapel or simply takes off in panicked flight. Knowing his weakness, which provides an occasion for cruel sport, Paudy's buddies will, during the tourist season, gently prod an unsuspecting stranger woman (like myself) to sit next to or strike up a conversation with the shy bachelor, who has even been known to cry with shame at such times.

Seamas, the younger, however, does not share his older brother's fear of women. On the contrary, for years he has actively (indeed aggressively) attempted to get a bride. Until finally accepting that his gray hair made him look ridiculously out of place, Seamas had attended every summer-night *ceilidhe* (traditional Irish dance) in the parish, where he would relentlessly compete with younger bachelors for the handful of remaining eligible women in the community. When attempts at romantic courtships failed, Seamas enlisted the aid of an intermediary who, according to the older traditions of the parish, made "accountings" of his land holdings, wealth, and willingness to eligible girls and women. Even visiting "Yanks" passing through the village on a summer holiday were sometimes the surprised recipients of one of Seamas's accountings. Or Seamas might see a pretty new face at Mass on a Sunday morning, would solicit from a parishioner her "history"—were her people from west Kerry, was she single, sound of body and mind, moral? And then he might muse aloud, "But yerra, would she suit?" Within a week, the woman would be approached and an offer made, and once again Seamas would be rebuffed. But Seamas did not resign himself to an easy or an early defeat, like the other confirmed bachelors of the parish. He *would* get a wife.

All agreed that the annual peregrinations to England represented as much a romantic as a financial quest. Rumor spread wildly during one spring that Seamas must finally have succeeded. On his return from England, he had determinedly, if silently, built an additional room to the family home, had bought a double bed, and had taken to whistling and wearing his peacap at a decidedly jaunty angle. Summer passed into winter and the wife failed to materialize. No questions were asked, but Seamas seemed to accept that his search was finished, and he withdrew more and more into the solace of alcohol and the companionship of his pub regulars.

Seamas might easily have slipped into the acceptable pattern—there is a definite role in Irish society for such men—but he was a rebel. And his rebellion finally took the form of sexual deviance—exposing himself to a dance-hall of sheltered village virgins, violating an ultimate taboo in rural Irish society. Next he turned on his neighbors and closest of kin, accusing them of poisoning his dogs, moving stone boundaries, and competing with him for eligible women.

By the time I met Seamas he was a fairly regular patient at the Dingle psychiatric clinic, where he was diagnosed as a paranoid schizophrenic given to periodic outbursts of irrational rage—rage that had been directed at his own livestock as well as at villagers whom he suspected of maliciousness. Seamas's treatment was limited to biweekly medication and physical examination. Some counseling was attempted, but Seamas was hostile and uncooperative. The clinic psychiatrist observed that even rudimentary attempts at psychotherapy would be counterindicated for people like Seamas, who come from a "primitively" Irish background where the covert rules of familism proscribe the discussion with strangers of "family" problems or difficulties. Seamas, he perceived, could be made to feel even more confused and conflicted after unburdening himself of problems that he had been taught to guard as family secrets. A native-born Irish speaker, Seamas's problem was compounded by his difficulty in finding the words to express his inner feelings. Words like "resentment" and "conflict," and words to express the various shades of human passions, of loves and hates and hurts, were unfamiliar ones to taciturn and inhibited farmers like Seamas. The bilingual psychiatrist observed that this difficulty was not only a reflection of Seamas's grasp of English, but also was reflected in his terse use of Irish.

Seamas agreed to take the Thematic Apperception Test, but was agitated and nervous throughout the storytelling task. His responses, however, are highly revelatory of his inner state and illustrate his preoccupation with loneliness and isolation, his fear of aging and death, his frustrated generativity, and his overwhelming sense of sadness, demoralization, and anomie:

Card 1 (boy and violin): It's in the mind of the brain he has it. He's asleep on the guitar.

Card 2 (farm scene): He's working hard with his horse plowing out grain for the farm. Another lady is looking on. They are setting rows, planning for the coming winter. Parsnips and turnips; he wants to feed his flock.

Card 3BM (boy huddled on the floor): He could be drunk, or he could be sick, or he could be affected in a mental way. It's the old age as it sets in. He might be sick in mind.

Card 5 (woman opening a door into a room): She's looking into the room and she expects to meet somebody, guests. But there's nobody there, they never come at all.

Card 6BM (elderly woman with her back turned to a younger man): They are looking disgusted out of the window. Mother and her son. (Why disgusted?) Because they are poor.

Card 7BM (older man looking down at a younger man): Two brothers thinking together. The one is getting old, he's gray. They have the same suggestion, thinking about the future. (What about it?) There is none.

Card 12 (young man lying on a couch with his eyes closed, another man bends down over him): He seems to be dead. Your man is praying over him. He might be the man's brother, you wouldn't know.

Card 13MF (young man with his head buried in his arm in front of a reclining half-nude woman): She could be his wife for all that. She might be dead anyway. She might have died sudden, and he's mourning.

Madness, I suggested earlier, could be seen as a projection of cultural themes. Nowhere is this more clear than in the dialogue between schizo-phrenia and celibacy in western Ireland, illustrated by the above case study. Both Seamas and Padraec are bachelors, both are awkward with women and troubled by sexuality, and both are perceived as "different" by their peers. But why is it that Seamas is recognized and labeled as "mad," while Paudy, his "woman-hating" brother, is considered only a bit "odd"? In terms of male roles and expected behavior, Paudy, too, is deviant by rural Irish stan-dards, but deviant only in his extreme exaggeration of the stereotypically reserved, sexually timid Irish male. Where Seamas blatantly rebels against the stereotype, Paudy is a caricature of it. The straight and narrow bound-aries separating normal from abnormal behavior are particularly prejudicial against the angry, unresigned celibate like Seamas.

Schizophrenia is clearly associated with male status and celibacy in rural Ireland; married men and single or married women rarely evidence symp-toms of the disorder. Among hospitalized males in County Kerry, the onset of schizophrenia occurs late[2]—in the late twenties to middle thirties—the age at which marriage, if it is to occur at all, is normally contracted. Para-noid delusions, like those of Seamas, often focus on competition for or rejection by potential marriage partners.

The psychological testing of normal and schizophrenic villagers, to be discussed at the end of this chapter, illustrates the preoccupation of the Irish "deviants" with "countercultural" themes of sexuality, intimacy, and gener-ativity, in contrast to the prudery and asceticism of the "normal" villagers. Before offering an interpretation of Irish celibacy and its implications for the mental health of villagers, I shall examine the background of the prob-lematic nature of relations between the sexes in the structure of rural Irish kinship, marriage, and family patterns as they have evolved in the forty years since the first edition of Arensberg and Kimball's definitive work, *Family and Community in Ireland* (1940).

▪ Family and Community in Ballybran

Most adults in Ballybran parish today are neither parents nor spouses, and "family life" as we know and define it—that core group of parents and children — is not the rule but the exception.[3] Only 41 of 138 households in the parish fall into the category of nuclear, stem, or extended families. Only one in three adult males is married. Yet, the concerns, conversations, and values of villagers are still oriented around "family" matters, although the families are but shadows of what they once were. Old widow women still sit around the glowing embers of turf fire tracing genealogies in space and time, but the names and relations are either dead or "gone foreign." And the bachelors and childless couples of the parish tend to feel cheated, unfulfilled, and envious of those villagers fortunate enough to have heirs carrying on their line.

Not so long ago it was difficult in small Irish communities like Ballybran to draw a line between family and community. Rural society was so permeated by familial connections that it was not easy to tell whether people thought of themselves as members of a community or as members of an overlapping network of extended families, which often spilled out into the towns and cities of Ireland. Today all that remains is the *ideal* of familism as described so vividly by Arensberg and Kimball (1968: 76–140).

The traditional Irish family in Ballybran until the early 1940s was the three-generational stem family, patrilocal and, to all appearances, patriarchal. Because of the decrease in marriage and the proliferation of solitary bachelors and brother-sister households, only 15 percent of all households today fit this description (see table 2). The independent nuclear family is a relatively new phenomenon in the parish and is associated with the nonagricultural sector — the shopkeepers, schoolteachers, carpenters, creamery workers, and publicans who reside on the single paved street of the central village.

Nonetheless, the adult population of Ballybran itself grew up in extended households overtly controlled by the fathers and subtly manipulated by the mothers. The father characteristically rose to power late in life after his own father loosened his reins and retired with his wife to the proverbial "west room" of the house (see Arensberg 1937).[4] Fathers passed on their names, lands, and household property to the favored (often firstborn) son, while the disinherited sons were prepared for village trades or town professions or were forced into emigration to England or America. Daughters were passed on like pawns in strategically arranged marriages with neighboring households. Although they were theoretically entitled to a dowry or "fortune" at marriage, this was nothing more than a circulating fund, which passed into the hands of the bride's father-in-law to be used as dowry money for his own daughters. Fathers delayed inheritance and dowry decisions for as long as possible in order to maintain control over their sons and daughters for as long as possible.

Among the teachers, shopkeepers, and tradespeople of the central village, occupations and businesses are still viewed as "family firms" to be passed on from one generation to the next, but with less sexual discrimination. Master Fenton, the autocratic primary-school teacher who drilled nearly every parish adult over fifty in his letters, sums, and paternosters, is himself the son of a teacher. Of his own children, however, it is the favored "pet" daughter, Maura, who remains on in Ballybran as village schoolmistress, while her brothers set out to make their fortunes in the New World. Likewise, the favorite publican of the bachelor farmers, Jim-O, passed on the pub to his lastborn daughter, Beit, who as a spinster has much in common with the solitary farmers who frequent the pub.

▪ Marriage

Because of the general mistrust of outsiders and the reluctance of village women to marry into the kitchen of a completely unknown mother-in-law, marriages have tended (until recently) to be parish endogamous. Within some isolated hamlets of Ballybran marriage options for generations have been limited to exchanges of women between the six or ten households that the townland comprises. "Marry on the dunghill and choose a sponsor from the mountain" is a local proverb meaning that it is wisest to "marry in."

A preferred form of marriage in past generations was the "double match" whereby a brother and sister married a brother and sister from a neighboring household. This arrangement was considered eminently fair, since neither household was deprived, even temporarily, of the labor of a woman and in such cases the dowry could be dispensed with. Unpopular marriages, which raise eyebrows and give scandal fall into several categories: a very old man taking a young bride; a widower with small children marrying any woman; a thrice-married widow or widower ("a first marriage is honorable, a second marriage is excusable, a third marriage is disgraceful"); a "mixed marriage" between a Protestant and a Catholic. All of these marriages are believed to produce bad *dutcas* (blood) in children born of the union.

Because of generations of endogamy most parishioners are related to one another through blood or marriage or both. There is a certain amount of guilt associated with the inbreeding of the community, and some villagers will go so far as to deny a relationship to distant kin where parish records indicate that such is the case. In one hillside hamlet where six of nine households share the same surname, the O'Carrolls disclaimed one another, saying, "We're all O'Carrolls all right, but not the same O'Carrolls."

The desire to keep relationships fuzzy is, in part, the result of an effort to conceal the number of cousin marriages in the parish. Despite the Roman Catholic Church's incest prohibitions,[5] second-degree-cousin marriages are not uncommon and are a favorite topic of malicious gossip. Although the parish priest or curate is responsible for searching the genealogies of prospective couples, and the publication of the banns of marriage is intended to uncover any impediments to a lawful Church marriage, the rural priest and his flock tend to be sympathetic to such dilemmas, and the details of kinship are often left hazy or ignored. In the rarer cases of first-cousin marriage, where the fear of God's wrath and His punishment in the form of insanity to the offspring is strong, couples customarily delay the marriage until they are well past the childbearing age.

As a consequence of parish endogamy, over 96 percent of all adult males are natives of the community, and 70 percent of the married women were born locally. Of the nonnative women the majority have been brought in from neighboring parishes in southwest Kerry and from the towns of Dingle and Tralee. The remaining few women are natives of distant counties to the north, or they are from the midlands and married into the parish following a period of emigration to England. In these cases the marriage was the result of a determined and aggressive move on the part of those bachelor farmers who make a practice of spending their winters as laborers in English cities where they seek out disillusioned and homesick Irish nurses, waitresses, and clerks, anxious to return to Ireland at any cost. Such courtships and marriages are hastily contracted—often during one three-month winter season—in order to allow the couple to return to Ireland in early spring for the start of the new agricultural cycle. Frequently, these marriages turn out unhappily for the bride,[6] who is not well received in the parish and who finds village life monotonous and boring. Such failures reinforce village beliefs about the benefits of marrying one's own kind.

In traditional extended farm households, the status of the in-marrying woman is low—even after giving birth to children—as long as the mother-in-law is alive. The newly married woman is made to feel like a stranger invading the cherished privacy of a tightly knit group. Kathleen recalls with chagrin the first month of her marriage some twenty-five years ago into the Donovan farm:

Well, I wouldn't will it on a person, the hell I lived through . . . no one ever knew the pain I suffered. I came in a shy, nervous, frightened bride into a house filled with silent strangers. At first, I thought they were queer-like because any of them didn't talk. They would sit around the fire and read. Sometimes a whole night would pass without a single word spoken. As the woman coming in I was the last one to speak, and the first one to serve on the old people. I sat in a corner, and I had to think about them all the time. I married into the whole lot of them! And with all the attention given the old woman, I forgot about my husband. Himself and I weren't given any privacy—we couldn't even whisper to each other in our room at night, for fear they might hear us. We began on the wrong foot—we had to talk distant to each other in front of the old people, and the habit grew on us, until even after they died, we spoke to each other in the same way.

The woman who marries in from a distant parish or county is subject to even greater coldness and reserve on the part of her in-laws and neighbors. The name for such women in Irish means "stranger-come-in," and many of these women said that even after ten or twenty years in the parish they are still viewed as strangers today. Catherine recalls that when her husband first brought her onto the farm the neighbors gathered around and discussed and criticized her roundly: "She's too tall and thin," said one. "She's town bred and can't milk a cow properly," said another. "She's far too tidy," said a third. As years went by, Catherine continued to be criticized, in particular for her unconventional child-rearing practices, one of which was the daily bath. A posse of neighbor women stopped by one afternoon to inform and warn Catherine that in Ballybran children should be bathed once a week, on Saturday night only.

In days past the in-marrying woman was the first person suspected of devious or mischievous behavior. Much of the surviving rural folklore links the power of curses, the evil eye, and other witchcraft with jealous and envious women. A favorite genre of folklore comprises tales of unsuspecting men who fall in love with a beautiful stranger, marry her, and have children, only to discover through some disaster or misfortune that they have married a witch or fairy woman. Occasionally such tales are translated into village vignettes. When Maggie, for example, married into the parish from the Magharee Peninsula, not only Tom's mother and unmarried brother but also the neighbors were distressed—could the stranger be trusted? That spring, cream production dropped in the parish. Rumor spread that Maggie was to blame. The old woman chuckled as she related the tale: "Erra, the fools said that I did be stealing the cream. They said that as they passed my window on the way to the creamery, that I did sweep my apron out and say, 'All to me Jimmy Tuohy's cream, all to me Ned Murphy's cream.'"

Similarly, when Kitty married into the prosperous O'Toole farm and inherited the use of her mother-in-law's fine china and silverware, the jealous sister-in-law, feeling cheated, began waging an unspoken war with her brother's new wife. Kitty brought home a little brood of chickens and one by one they died. Other household misfortune followed: dishes broke, silver disappeared, and a younger brother failed his graduation examinations. Each time, Kitty suspected her jealous sister-in-law of mischief, but the O'Tooles laid the blame on Kitty instead.

These stories dramatize a problem inherent in all kinship systems in which women occupy an interstitial position, standing halfway between two male lines—father's and husband's—and never fully incorporated into either.[7] In rural Kerry the problem is heightened by the generally late age at which women marry (twenty-seven to twenty-eight) and the fact that even after marriage the woman is referred to by her *maiden* name. Women's loyalties are suspect, particularly with regard to her husband's family. Hence, the suspicions in days past of evil eye, curses, and magical charms or incantations. These suspicions are grounded, to a certain extent, in fact: some women *are* uncommitted to the well-being and economics of a household in which they have so little at stake. Old Bridie, for example, balks at her seemingly endless chore of watching, driving, and feeding the cows and calves. "Bad *'cess* to them and to the rotten land, too," she grumbles to me, "they're none o' me own."

The only legitimate source of income for women of the older generation was their "butter and egg" money, which they often stashed away in secret hiding places. Until very recently, village women could not even claim welfare payments or the monthly Children's Allowance stipends without their husbands' signatures. The patriarchal nature of traditional family dynamics sometimes forced village women into devious, petty, and retaliatory behavior. Tom, an elderly farmer who suffers from rheumatism as well as car sickness, sends his wife to the Tralee market to sell their young calves. "Eileen is more bold than myself; she can strike a better bargain," he explains. Eileen, however, enjoys telling how she lies to Tom about the price she gets and keeps back "a lucky penny" to compensate herself for the bother of the journey. Such convoluted relations between the sexes contribute to villagers' reluctance toward matrimony.

Arranged marriages prevailed in the parish until the late 1950s, and some middle-aged men have not yet despaired of making a match through a traditional intermediary. There is no remembered tradition of courtship in the parish (which was replaced by arranged marriages after the Great Famine), and such innovative practices as dating or "doing a line," as the young people call it, are highly suspect, as immorality, by older villagers. Most elderly couples in the parish had never exchanged more than a few words with each other before their wedding day. Eugene tells of his match with Sarah:

Sarah first seen me at Castle fair. I went over selling a calf. We took a liking to each other and after I come home I asked my father would she suit. He said he knew the girl and that her "history" was good. So, come Shrovetide our hands were clasped [i.e., the match was made] and the next day, we had a fine Irish wedding. We killed two sheep and drank four barrels of porter. The match was a good one, and it "took."

Shrovetide, the weeks between Christmas and Ash Wednesday, was, by Irish Catholic peasant tradition, the only permissible time of the year for matches and weddings. Conveniently, this was also the time of heavy winter rains when farm work was minimal and leisure time could be devoted to sociability and celebrations.

Even in the "old days" marriages were never forced on unwilling parties, and potentially matched couples appraised each other from a safe distance on qualities such as physical attractiveness, strength, health, moral virtues, and skills at singing, dancing, fiddle playing, and sports. Lean and muscular men were preferred to heavier-set ones, and dark-haired, dark-eyed women to blondes or redheads. Redheaded women were believed to be unlucky, and fair skin, fair hair, and freckled faces were associated with the outcast "traveling people," better known as tinkers.

When Old More discovered that the girl to whom he was matched had her heart set on another man, he broke the match and married the more willing but less attractive Hannie, saying that he would never insist on a match that would break a poor girl's heart. Nonetheless, one could not be *too* choosy either, and any woman or man who refused year after year to accept a mate became sooner or later the object of a curious custom that prevailed in Ballybran (and throughout southwest Kerry) until the first few decades of this century.

Older villagers recall that on the night of Shrove Tuesday, the end of the marriage season, the young lads of the village, dressed in disguise as "Straw Boys," would travel in a pack and make mischief on the houses and farms of the resistant bachelors and spinsters of the parish, who had once again cheated them of the entertainment afforded by a wedding. They would splatter farmhouse walls with paint, turn over carts and wagons, let cows and horses out of their barns, stuff chimneys with rags, and so forth. Sawed-off bottles served as makeshift trumpets and with these the Straw Boys would summon the hardened celibates to take to the Skellig rocks off the coast of Kerry where the good monks of the monastery there could still marry them.[8] Ribald ballads were composed called "Skellig Lists" in which the most improbable and incongruous bachelors and spinsters would be suggested as suitable mates for each other. The mischief continued through the First Sunday of Lent when during Mass the Straw Boys would creep up behind the middle-aged bachelors and spinsters and draw a large X on each back. This custom clearly expressed the tensions in rural Irish society between men and women, married life and celibacy, and, as Nora added, "would be of great use today in getting all those great big lumps of men off to the altar rail."

Although love was not a necessary prerequisite to marriage, it was always hoped that the match would "take" and that the couple would develop affection, warmth, and eventually love for each other. Nonetheless, a marriage without these qualities could still be counted a success. Older villagers recall the day that the strikingly lovely Kate was brought over Connor Pass to marry skinny little Matty. After they were introduced, the girl was asked her feelings and whether she had any objection to the marriage. It is reputed that she replied, "Well, sure, he has the cows, doesn't he?"

In denying that love in the romantic sense is a necessary ingredient of marriage, villagers point to examples of marriages that "succeeded" in spite of years of mutual antagonism between the couples. The fulfillment of role expectations in terms of farm work, housework, childbearing and tending are all that is required, although more might be desired. Divorce, of course, does not exist in Ireland, and legal separations are unheard of in small villages like Ballybran.[9] Marriage is, indeed, for life, and this adds a heavy, cautionary note to the whole procedure. As Jimmy Tuohy put it: "I missed a lot in never marrying. But if, by mistake, I'd taken the wrong woman, I could have got stuck for good."

A remarkable division of labor and social activities between the sexes in rural Ireland functions on the one hand to make marriages difficult to contract, but serves on the other to remove unhappily matched couples from situations of prolonged, frequent, and intimate contact with each other.

▪ Division of the Sexes

Although all societies are characterized by sexual asymmetry to some extent, one would be hard put to find a society in which the sexes are as divided into opposing alien camps as they are in any small Irish village of the west. A general rule can be said to be observed: wherever men are, women will not be found, and vice versa. In the traditional Irish farmhouse, women's world is the kitchen and the haggard, while men keep to the barn and the fields. The kitchen is, however, the central living room of the house: it is the place where meals and teas are taken, where casual guests are entertained, where the family rosary is recited, and (in the home of the prosperous) where the television is located. Men are nervous and uncomfortable in the kitchen: they eat rapidly and either before or after the women and young children. If possible, they escape the family rosary, led by the mother or grandmother, and quickly flee to the pub, since men generally feel more comfortable socializing with one another outside the home.

Symbolically as well the sexes stand opposed. Estyn Evans observed (1957: 36) the segregation of men's and women's tools in the traditional Irish kitchen: men's tools to the right of the range or hearth; women's cooking utensils in a corner to the left. And he noted that in the most rustic of homes (those without plumbing or outhouse) men were expected to relieve themselves in the horse pasture, women within the confines of the cow stable.

Even in mythology, the sexes stand apart and opposed, as Ballybran claims two major origin myths: the first, the Giant Cow, a female-fertility motif; the second, Brendan's Bull, a male-castration motif. The Glas Gyneth (Glas Ghaibhneach) was a magical cow, who inhabited the parish and whose milk was ever plentiful. The animal was so large that she could walk between the two huge *galláns* (standing stones) near the bay. She left many permanent footprints in the vicinity of the village graveyard, and the pasture where she was believed to sleep at night is still called Mágha na Bó, Cow's Field, or the resting place of the Cow. The magical plenty of the Glas Gyneth was related to a stream in Ballydubh that never went dry, as well as to the original fertility of the land and women. However, this magical fertility of the cow (as well as of Ballybran) was destroyed by an evil maid who milked the poor creature into a sieve until the magic finally gave out. The story is used to explain the barrenness of the region—the difficulty with which animals are reared, the land is tilled, and babies are reared. The masculine counterpart is the tale (related in chapter one) of the taming and killing of the fierce bull belonging to the wanton pagan chieftain Crom Dubh by the ascetic and celibate Christian Brendan. Some villagers refer to this tale as the charter for their own tame and celibate lives.

Within the wider circles of village social life, the sexes congregate, each with its own kind. On Sunday mornings all the parish (except the agnostic tailor) turn out for Mass—the men coming earlier and in small groups, mostly walking although a few on bicycles; the women and small children coming later by car or hackney bus. Adolescent boys and girls come in their own groups. Seating is arranged within the chapel according to age, sex, and marriage status. In the very front rows sit the widow women, blessed and serene in their dark woolen shawls; behind them sit the married women of the parish in their hats and colored scarves; and in the balcony sit the adolescents—boys to one side, girls to the other, under the watchful eye of the village organist. Flanking the walls of the church below and to the rear by the door, stand or kneel the married men of the parish, some with their transitional seven- and eight-year-old sons, too old to sit with "Mummy" and too young for the balcony. In the church vestibule and on the front steps of the church are the bachelors, caps and rosaries in hand, who stand silent and at attention at a religious rite they can neither see nor hear. "Why don't you go inside, up to the altar, and receive Communion like the women?" I ask, to which the men reply, "Women 'have right' to receive; men have 'shame,'" an allusion to the curious inversion in rural Ireland of the Mediterranean and Latin American phenomenon of feminine *verguenza* (shame) and masculine honor.[10] Throughout rural Ireland men are the bearers of sexual pollution and shame and women the bearers of ritual honor and purity, another barrier that divides the sexes. The belief is strongly held in Ballybran that men are more prone than women to mortal or serious sin. The little "sineens" (venial sins) of women, such as lying, gossip, impatience, and cursing, do not disqualify them from the state of grace. The more serious masculine sins. however, such as "bad thoughts," masturbation, drunkenness, idleness, and irresponsibility, disqualify men from receiving Holy Communion save on Easter Sunday, Christmas Eve, and at the "station" masses. A man who receives the Blessed Sacrament more frequently is categorized by his male peers either as simple, effeminate, putting on airs, or as castrated by his wife or mother. Women of the parish, however, consider such men progressive and educated.

As the congregation files out of the church after Mass the sexes again separate, women to Maggie's shop to pick up a can of peas and the local gossip before returning home to cook Sunday dinner, and the men to the traditional (if illegal) "jar or two" at the pub.

In all the months I spent in Ballybran I never saw a married couple walk together down the main street of the central village, and rarely did I see a couple appear together at one of the few public social functions. Even at wakes, when all adult parishioners are expected to pay their respects, married couples came at separate hours. And, following the church funeral and burial, men took once again to the pub, and women to one another's homes for a "supeen" of sherry and biscuits. Before I realized the extent and rigidity of the sexual segregation, I had sent out numerous invitations to couples in the parish to come to our home for an evening tea or supper. Either husband or wife came, never both. Similarly, when we invited the whole community to a Christmas party, only village women and none of the men (with the exception of the curate and the schoolmaster) attended. At the biannual custom of house masses, followed by a party, called "stations,"[11] I enjoyed hearing the excuses husbands and wives made for their better and missing halves: "Himself had to stay home, Father, and watch the thieving cow." When Eugene and Sarah, however, came to their station mass together, everyone was surprised: "Together?" they asked incredulously. "The divil a bit," complained Sarah, "what with me in front and himself pulling up the rear grumbling a hundred yards behind!"

Body comportment and styles of communication between the sexes add a further component to the symbolic separation of women and men in rural Ireland. Whereas in the company of the same sex adult villagers can relax to the point of touching each other, and can be intimate, suggestive, and earthy in their speech, once in the company of the opposite sex, their body posture is rigid and conversations distant, often sardonic, and elusive. Although I never saw even a husband and wife so much as hold hands or bring home a point by touching each other, older women—especially widows—will grab at each other when laughing, and even occasionally bury their head into another woman's shoulder when terribly amused. (This behavior is not characteristic, however, of younger married women.) Similarly, there is affectionate touching between unmarried males at the pub. Custom demands that, when asked, each man at the pub will sing in turn in order to entertain his friends. Some bachelors are extremely shy and have difficulty performing even in this small a group. On these occasions a great tenderness and sympathy seemed to flow among the men, and they would help the backward fellow out by forming a tight circle, lacing their arms around one another's shoulders, and singing with him. No sexual embarrassment or inhibition prevented men from urinating together in a back yard of the pub; and young girls would similarly relieve themselves in each other's company at summer dances.

Because of the routine of their separate work and leisure activities, husbands and wives were spared frequent contact with each other, and some women admitted that when forced to spend time alone with their husbands they felt uncomfortable. The widow Cait told me the following story:

Mickey was a hackney driver for the village, and the times I dreaded the most were when I had to go along with him to pick up a customer in Tralee. We'd get in the car together and it was like we'd be strangers, trying hard to think of what in the world to say to each other. Finally, I would give up and turn on the radio, and we'd both be relieved.

When Jerry died I was damned lonesome after him and I am yet. . . . I remember how lonesome it was sitting there with my hand on his coffin and thinking that he would not be there in the spring for the planting of the spuds or the cutting of the turf, and he would not eat the goose with me and drink the punch at Christmas.
—ERIC CROSS,
The Tailor and Ansty

Older couples rarely refer to each other by their first names, but use the indirect "himself," "herself," and "they" when referring to each other ("if it's *herself* you're wanting, she's in the back kitchen"). Mat, for example, was critical of his wife's baking. As we all sat around the table for tea, I complimented his wife: "Siobhan, your bread is delicious, not at all heavy." Slipping in a final complaint, Mat retaliated: "But *they* do waste the flour."

Jack and Nora were married for over thirty years and had five children. "Not once in his whole life did that *man,* may he rest in peace, call me by my Christian name," said Nora of her recently deceased husband. "He couldn't bring himself to do it. He would come in from work and yell up the stairs, 'Hey, you, I'm home.' And I'd be up there gritting my teeth, saying, 'Nora, Nora.'" "Did you ever tell him how you felt?" I asked, and Nora replied, "I did, yes, finally. It was on his deathbed and I held him cradled in my arms and for the first time in my life I said, 'Jack, I love you. You were an honest, upright, good living man, but like all the Nelligans before you, you were a cold man, Jack, and I wish it could have been different between us.'"

The following description from my field notes demonstrates the qualities of indirectness and passive aggression that characterize the relationship between a tired old couple in Ballybran who, despite it all, realize that they would be lost without each other.

This ancient couple has been married for over forty years and they have never forgiven each other for it. A conversation with the two is impossible—they talk at each other through Mike and me, simultaneously and usually inaudibly. It is a running diatribe of abuses which they fling at each other, yet it has the quality of a polished ballet, an act they have perfected. Finon yells commands at Maura; they slide off

My nerves are bad tonight. Yes, bad. Speak to me. Why do you never speak? Speak. What are you thinking of? What thinking? What? I never know what you are thinking. Think.
—T. S. ELIOT

her back. He prods Maura to be the gracious hostess: "Get the sherry, woman, get the sweets for the babas." Maura doesn't move, pretends not to hear, mumbles to herself. Finon gets up to find the sherry. "Where did she hide it?" he yells into us. "In the bottom of the bzzz," Maura answers, and then adds in an aside to us, "so ignorant, that man." Later we hay in the fields, and every two hours old Maura comes sweating and swearing with a pail of lukewarm tea and very hard soda bread. She always forgets to serve one person, usually it is Finon.

Younger couples in the parish do not follow the extreme patterns of distance and separation characteristic of older couples, but it was Father Leary's observation that with the passage of each year young couples tend to grow apart and to develop closer ties with their own sex. The priest told how Katie and Denis, now married three years, were at first fiercely private and defensive of their relationship. Their courtship was a secret in order to keep the prying eyes and wagging tongues of the village at bay, and their wedding ceremony was performed without announcement and behind the locked doors of the chapel early one Saturday morning. Following the marriage, the couple moved into a new home, which Denis had built, rather than move in with the in-laws. When Denis demonstrated his intent to sit next to Katie during Sunday Mass, rather than stand up with his cronies, word spread that he was putting on city airs and "acting queer." After the birth of a child and Denis took to promenading on the strand with the baby buggy, criticism turned to vicious ridicule. By the third year of their marriage, however—the year of our stay—the couple was indistinguishable from any other in the parish: Katie and Denis were never seen together in public.

▪ Irish Patriarchy and Female Desertion

Over the past forty years, the structure of Irish familism and rural patriarchy has been rapidly crumbling, as options for women outside the countryside have increased. Where women of the older generation expressed their lack of commitment to the "system" symbolically, women of the younger generation are simply walking out on it. Over the past two decades, an average of twelve young women of marriageable age have left the village each year, contrasted to an average of four young men. The privilege of male inheritance carries a weighty responsibility, as boys are less free to leave their homes. The girls leave with the blessing and encouragement of their mothers: "Do I want Aine to lead the life I had, stuck up here in the back of beyond with only the cows and the teakettle for company?" asks Aine's mother rhetorically. And those young women, like Marion the weaver and Joan the schoolteacher, who do decide to stay in the village express little interest in marriage. "Oh, I'm far too young for that," says twenty-seven-year-old Joan.

The result is that women in Ballybran, by virtue of their scarcity, have achieved new independence and authority. When Kitty's father died and left the farm to her in the absence of any male heirs, she decided to stay in Ballybran and manage the farm herself. She was approached by several suitors, anxious to annex the farm to their holdings, but Kitty stood firm in her resolve: any man wanting to marry her would have to move into her household and the farm would remain in her name. Although it occasionally happens, few men are willing to take on the stigmatized role and title of *clann isteach*, literally "into the family," but implying a kind of Irish gigolo.

In previous generations village men were delayed in marrying and setting up a household because of the greed of their fathers and the jealous possessiveness of their mothers. The young men of the present generation are more often thwarted by the indifference of village women toward courtship and marriage under the patriarchal conditions that exploited their mothers and grandmothers in the past. Some men, caught in the transition from arranged marriages to romantic courtship, have been shortchanged by both. Bally-

I have no luck with women . . . [but] I am not alone. The countryside is tainted by slowly withering blossoms like me. At the creamery in the mornings I see them with their black overcoats and unwashed faces, many of them smelling of the very milk which they have come to deliver, except that, like themselves, the milk has gone sour. They have missed out in the game of love.
—JOHN B. KEANE,
Letters of a Love-Hungry Farmer

bran today is filled with the casualties of crumbling familism — those forty- and fifty-year-old bachelors who patiently stayed at home waiting for the farm inheritance from the father and approval from the mother to bring in a woman. In most cases both came too late to be of any use.

Brendan is a forty-six-year-old bachelor from a mountain hamlet living with his elderly parents and maternal aunt. Last year the farm was finally signed over in his name, and Brendan has become the center of a cruel form of joking behavior among his peers in the village. Now that he is finally a landowner, his colleagues tease him that he must find a wife. The following dialogue took place on the main street of the central village as Brendan sat on his motorbike surrounded by a group of both younger and older village bachelors:

"Brendan, have ye found a woman for that farm of yours, yet?"

"Aye, not yet. I'm too choosy."

"Brendan, you be like a man looking for a job and hoping to God he won't find one."

"I'm plenty fresh yet, and I have lots of time."

"Wisha, man, your day has come and gone, but they say there's good women to be had for the likes of us in the want ads of the Kerryman."

"None o' that, none o' that. Now that we're in the EEC [i.e., Common Market] I couldn't take my pick. I might have to take a bid from Brussels. And they say Brussels women are very fat."

As Brendan drives away on his motor scooter, the heckling voices follow him with a final rejoinder, "Don't worry, Brendan. Ye'll have a good night up in Ballybee yet."

The truth is, however, that Brendan's day, as his friends suggest, has come and gone. He has never had a girlfriend and he does not know how to go about the business of finding one. The Saturday night dances in the village are dominated by the adolescent crowd, who can legitimately "make themselves bold" on the few single women. The older bachelors hang along the edges of the hall socializing with each other. When a middle-aged man can and does gather up the courage to ask a girl or a woman for a dance, courtesy demands that she accept the first invitation. But thinly disguised glances and raised eyebrows are exchanged between girlfriends during the painful exercise. Rarely does the older man attempt a second invitation.

A more socially acceptable approach to marriage for the older set is through the sending of an "account," the modern-day version of the match. Farmer Murphy, for example, has his eye on Cait Dowd, the twenty-eight-year-old daughter of a village fisherman. Murphy asks his sister to write a letter or drop by Cait's house to outline the terms of the proposal (farmer, thirty-eight years old, grass of ten cows, fifty sheep, has old mother living in). Rarely are such attempts successful, however, as village and town women consider such a formal bid absurdly old-fashioned. Meg, it is said, can dance the number of accountings she has received off the end of each finger, and yet she remains determinedly single.

Given the scarcity of eligible women and the gratitude of those few farmers who have succeeded in finding wives, those women who marry into the village today clearly have the upper hand. They are treated with kid gloves. When shy, balding James Moriarty announced to his neighbor that a Tralee woman had agreed to marry him and move onto his farm, he was overwhelmed with both joy and insecurity. "I have her now, but, by God above, will I be able to keep her?" he asked.

Increasingly today, interested women make the first move in a courtship, given the reticence of bachelors who fear rejection and hurt. Jean, for example, was a nurse at the county hospital in Dingle. She dated her pick of the more prosperous farmers of the Dingle Peninsula until her eye fell upon Joseph, a village schoolteacher, and his small family business: a dry-goods shop. It was Jean who telephoned Joseph, asking him to a hospital dance. The couple dated for five years until the disapproving and domineering old mother died. A few months after the death, Jean entered the family business and the village "wearing the trousers," as the villagers perceive it.

Irish Celibacy and Sexuality: An Interpretation

The apparent reluctance of the Irish villager to court and marry, and his inclination to marry late and intermarry with cousins, if and when he marries at all, has fascinated social scientists for a generation (see Connell 1962, 1968; R. Kennedy 1973; Messenger 1969; Opler 1967; B. Walsh 1970). Many levels of explanation have been offered: historical, sociocultural, and psychological.

Economic historians and demographers (Connell 1962, 1968; R. Kennedy 1973) have singled out the years and traumatic experience of the Great Famine (1845–1849) as the turning point in the trend to later and fewer marriages. They suggest that celibacy should be seen as a socially adaptive response to control the once excessively high rural birth rate.

Sociocultural explanations have concentrated on the unique patterns of land tenure and inheritance in Ireland (Arensberg 1937) whereby only one son stands to inherit the farm and the privilege of marrying. John Messenger (1969) emphasizes the role of Irish Catholicism—a tradition steeped in sexual repression, mistrust of the flesh, and the glorification of the ascetic virtues of temperance, continence, and self-mortification.

Psychosocial analyses suggest that the "basic personality structure" of the Irish male pivots around feelings of masculine inadequacy and ambivalent hostility and dependency feelings toward women, originating in strong mother-son Oedipal conflicts (Opler and Singer 1956).

The interpretation I shall give to this many-faceted problem concentrates on still other psychosocial and cultural phenomena that have not received as much attention by social scientists. Marriage in rural Ireland is, I suggest, inhibited by anomie, expressed in a lack of sexual vitality; familistic loyalties that exaggerate latent brother-sister incestuous inclinations; an emotional climate fearful of intimacy and mistrustful of love; and an excessive preoccupation with sexual purity and pollution, fostered by an ascetic Catholic tradition. That these impediments to marriage and to an uninhibited expression of sexuality also contribute to the high rates of mental illness among middle-aged bachelor farmers is implicit in the following interpretations and verified in the life history materials and psychological tests of these men.

Maguire was faithful to death;
He stayed with his mother til she died
At the age of ninety-one.
She stayed too long,
Wife and mother in one.
When she died
The knuckle-bones were cutting
  the skin of her son's backside
And he was sixty-five.
— PATRICK KAVANAGH,
The Great Hunger

The reluctance of mothers to relinquish their "pet" sons, and the reluctance of fathers to relinquish their land and authority to the up-and-coming generation, have inhibited marriage in rural Ireland for generations. A backfiring aspect of familism can be observed in the spirit of competition among extended families, which makes the necessary circulation of women among them difficult. Village mothers bristle at the notion of bringing a Fitzmorris woman into a Shea household and defensively rear their stay-at-home farm heirs as shy, women-fearing bachelors. But from bachelor sons will come no grandchildren and no continuity for the self-contained unit, and such short-sighted, selfish familism results in the constriction and death of households.

Responses of average villagers to the Thematic Apperception Test illustrate the remarkable tendency of the rural Irish to define "family" in terms of blood rather than marriage ties. Village stories, like the parish of Ballybran, are peopled with unmarried characters, overly preoccupied with the relationships of childhood. Forty-three percent of the males and 36 percent of the females (some of whom were as old as twenty and twenty-one) described the farm scene of card 2 as a sibling set (two sisters and a brother, or brother, sister, and mother) rather than as the usual conjugal or sexual rivalry themes given by most people in other cultures. When sexual rivalry was discussed it was in the context of *mother* and son or *sister* and brother versus a female rival (table 13).

The following response by an eighteen-year-old boy, middle child in a

	VILLAGE GIRLS (N = 22)	VILLAGE BOYS (N = 14)
1. Total conjugal themes	14 (64%)	8 (57%)
2. Total consanguineal themes	8 (36%)	6 (43%)
a. Sibling solidarity	5 (23%)	6 (43%)
b. Sexual rivalry: mother-son vs. girlfriend intruder	3 (14%)	0
c. Sexual rivalry: brother-sister vs. girlfriend intruder (double-scored with sibling solidarity)	2 (9%)	1 (7%)

family of six children, to card 2 demonstrates the intensity of cross-sex sibling solidarity in some Irish households:

> Brother and a sister, right? The girl is thinking about what is going to happen in the future, that when her mother will die, she will really have to get down to work. . . . The boy, well, the mother seems to have gotten the upper hand of him. She has beaten him, not walloped him, but gotten the better of him. The boy is thinking that when his mother will die, he and his sister can live happily together for the rest of their lives without any bossing around. (NM9)

Familism, interpreted as sibling sets struggling against parents, is probably a healthy defense against the authoritarianism of Irish family life, where bonds of duty unite children to their parents, but where even stronger bonds of affection unite siblings to one another. However, it is just this same bond of familism that contributes to the ethic of celibacy and has such an adverse effect on the marriage and birth rates in Ballybran. In reply to the question "How large is your family?" villagers—even those long since married and with children of their own—will invariably reply: "We are six (or four or seven) in family," referring to their brothers and sisters.

Marriage, even at a late age, is hardest for the first and eldest sibling—

for it is he or she who breaks the initial link in the chain of family loyalties. "I cried on the morning of my wedding" said the thirty-four-year-old Teresa of her marriage three years ago, "and I couldn't look my younger sisters and brothers in the eye—it was me they always counted on for support, and here I was deserting them."

A similar theme of inhibiting family loyalties and guilt comes through the following response to card 2 by a young village girl, who is herself contemplating a move from the parish to a nursing school in England:

This is worse than the first one. Brother, sister, and a mother. It hasn't been too bad for her up until now and now she's at an age where she must decide what to do. The brother seems content enough working at home. I think she can get on [i.e., succeed] if she wants to, but because of him staying at home—their farm doesn't seem to be a very big one, from what I see here—there's little hope for him. If she would leave, I think she can get a good job, a teacher or a nurse, something like that. I think he'll just stay on at home and maybe get married, but probably not. (And her?) She hates to leave him, but I think she will. (NF3)

When village women were asked why they married so late (in several cases past the childbearing age) they frequently replied in terms of love or attachment to siblings. Nora said that she had to be "talked into" marrying handsome Joseph Rourke. "What did I want to marry for? I was happy enough let alone at home with my brothers and sisters," she offered. In similar spirit a widow woman explained that after the drowning of her favorite brother, Morris, she "lost interest in marrying altogether."

Marriage is perceived by many village women as an interruption in their normal life cycle and an intrusion into their primary relationships and responsibilities. Since the death of her mother and the emigration of her three older sisters, Peggy serves as dedicated sister/wife/mother to a large extended household comprising three generations of unmarried and widowed relatives. Besides Peggy, there are her widowed grandmother of ninety-four years, her spinster aunt, her bachelor uncle, her widowed father, and her two unmarried adult brothers. Peggy speaks with nothing if not a note of awe and respect for the men of the household. She is a traditionalist in her relationships with them and cooks separate meals to accommodate the different tastes and work schedules of the men, and each morning she washes their clothing by hand. As the men come home from work, one by one, they drop their clothes in a heap by the door and each is handed a new set of clean and pressed clothes. Because of her sweet disposition and her much-noted devotion to her male relatives, Peggy has received more marriage proposals than any eligible woman in the parish. When questioned about her insistence upon remaining single, Peggy replies with a twinkle in her eye, "What! Exchange a household of four healthy, strong men—God bless them—for a household with only one?"

Perhaps the most surprising data emerged from taking the life histories of village widows. These lonely women, who were quite amenable to long interview sessions on tape, gave in the course of their stories very little attention to their married lives. Many had married late in life and were matched to men they barely knew and who were often many years their senior, with the result that the husband died after only a decade or two of marriage. Following the death of their husbands, widows try to return to their native homes and farms, or as close to them as possible. In the telling of their life histories, the period of marriage often shrank in significance and was only alluded to in passing. Some widows actually left out this era in their life cycles entirely. On one such occasion I finally asked a woman pointedly, "Hannah, you *did* marry, didn't you?" to which she replied:

> When I was ready for marriage at home—they were match-making for me with a young farmer—I knew I had to escape from it. So I took the tea out to my brother Pat in the fields and I said, "Pat-O, I have written to Margaret [a sister] for the fare to America! I want to see the world, and that's that." "Oh, you will not go, girleen," says Pat; "stay at home with me." Says I, "They have a farmer picked out for me, Pat-O, so it's not with you I'd be staying." So it happened that I went to America, and I would never be here telling you the story of my life if I hadn't traveled—it gives you courage so you can make yourself bold with strangers like ye are.

"But you did finally come home and marry, didn't you?" I asked again, and Hannah finally answered, "Yes, I married Tim two years after I got back from America. But I only married him so I could be near my sister who was a neighbor to him."

Another widow woman during her life history addressed herself from time to time to an enlarged and yellowed photo of a young man over her fireplace. "Is that your husband?" I finally asked, and the old woman laughed incredulously. "My husband! No, dearie, my husband was never so fine and handsome a man as that. Up there is my brother, Brendan Fitz, God rest his soul, he died a policeman on duty in New York."

Michael's fantasy in his TAT response above, of his mother dying and he and his sister living happily ever after together "without any bossing around," represents a real alternative to marriage in Ballybran, where 14 percent of the households are composed of middle-aged or elderly siblings living together. In the cases of brother-sister households, clear advantages emerge for the woman. These homes tend to be equalitarian to a degree rarely achieved in conjugal households. In the O'Mara farm owned and worked by two brothers and a sister, I noted the siblings taking turns at cooking and housework. When I asked who owned the farm, one of the brothers replied, "We all do," and when I inquired further how decisions were made, the sister said, "All of us together like."

The threat of marriage, however, can be used as a powerful weapon in the family dynamics of sibling households, and in the few instances where one member eventually takes a spouse, bitter enmities often result. In one such case when a villager successfully proposed marriage, his bachelor brother protested the union by going to live with his sheep in a crude mountain hut made of stones and inadequately roofed. He created a scandal, and many villagers took the shepherd's side, saying that a woman should never come between two brothers. The shepherd's protest continued until his remaining spinster sister coaxed him down with the suggestion that the two of them set up their own household apart from the newly married brother. Conflicting loyalties between blood and marriage ties is a recurring theme in Irish literature as well. The heroine of Patrick Kavanaugh's *The Great Hunger* (1964) is reluctant to marry and leave her brother. And in Sam Hannah Bell's novel

December Bride (1951) a live-in female housekeeper initially brings division between the two bachelor brothers, who both fall in love with her. The woman resolves the problem by living with both brothers in a polyandrous triad with incestuous overtones.[12]

While I have no evidence to suggest that there are consciously incestuous overtones to any of the brother-sister households of Ballybran, subconscious incest fantasies were expressed in a number of the TAT responses. One village woman told the following story to the sexually suggestive card 13MF—a young man standing with downcast head in front of a partially nude woman in bed:

> *The room is dark. He seems to be in remorse for something he has done. He has injured the girl, but she is not dead. Her breasts are exposed . . . it looks like he has wronged her sexually. (Who is he?) Not a stranger, someone close to her. It's not a love scene. He seems like a brother, he's so close to her. Something in the family has gone amiss. (NF 7)*

In all, 17 percent of the villagers tested described a blood rather than a conjugal or lover relationship in the bedroom-scene card (see table 15). Among these responses were a number of death and mourning motifs, of a father for his favorite daughter, or of a brother for his beloved sister, as in the following example:

> *The woman in the picture seems to have just died, and the man is crying. He has his hand to his head. She seems young, too young to have been married. He is young, too. Perhaps then are a brother and a sister, and he is crying because his dear sister has died suddenly. He calls for the priest and she is given last rites. (NM 13)*

Another villager told of a man weeping over his brother's body at a home wake, an odd response given the prominent breasts on the reclining figure. Among male psychiatric patients latent and overt incest themes were particularly strong, both in the test responses and in their life history material. One patient told of his terrible guilt over a vaguely sexual incident with a younger brother, with whom he shared a bed at home. Another said that his sexual experience was limited to intercourse with his mother. Although I doubted the authenticity of his tale, the sentiments behind the elaborate fantasy were real enough.

Closeness between siblings in Ballybran originates in the relative isolation of farm households and the strict segregation of the sexes outside the home, as well as in early socialization practices. It is common among farm families for older sisters to rear younger siblings, leaving mother free for more strenuous household chores. Sisters are expected to be particularly doting and protective of their younger brothers. Tomás O'Crohan, a native of the Blasket Islands, just off the coast from Ballybran, included in his autobiography numerous allusions to the devotion with which his older sisters cared for him: "Four sisters I had, everyone putting her own tidbit into my mouth. They treated me like a little bird in the nest" (1951: 1). It seems likely that unresolved conflicts related to these early experiences, reinforced in adulthood by the ethic of familism, contribute to the inhibited low-energy sexual system of the rural Irish and have resulted in the relative infrequency of marriage and of premarital and extramarital relationships.

FEAR OF INTIMACY

By the way we're ignored you'd
think we were wrecks
Possessed of gender, but not of sex;
At night with longing I'm lacerated,
Alone in bed I lie frustrated
And damned with dreams of desire denied
My hunger goes unsatisfied. — BRYAN MERRIMAN, *The Midnight Court,* (1780)

An Irish psychiatrist and director of a district mental hospital in County Cork summed up the basic psychological problems he encountered in his clinical practice as follows:

Emotions which seem to me, and indeed to others, to cause particular
problems to many persons presenting as patients in this region are greed,

envy, bitterness, frustration (sexual and otherwise), guilt, hatred, anger, a general feeling of lack of love, often associated with a fear of love, a fear of loss, indeed a very high expectancy of and resignation to loss, with consequent fear and avoidance of tenderness and intimacy (Dunne 1970: 23).

Certainly both a fear of and a longing for intimacy was a central theme on the TAT records of males and females, hospitalized and normal villagers (see Appendix D, table D-6). My own feelings are that this apparent state of lovelessness, lack of tenderness, and consequent feelings of psychological abandonment and loss are part of the basic emotional cast of the "Irish personality." These predispositions are, I believe, learned early through the experience of a less than satisfactory relationship to the first love object, the mother, to be discussed in the following chapter. The learning continues, however, as the early orientation toward emotional distance and sexual "flatness" is reinforced by religious ideology and social patterns, which separate the sexes and likewise keep the generations apart. Above all, it is in the home that the child learns to withdraw from touch and to respond to hurt or disappointment with silent resentment (see chapter five), a pattern that later interferes with marital and sexual intimacy.

Communication failures, or simply absence of communication, between family members appear to be largely responsible for the sense of personal alienation, loss, and isolation that permeate the TAT responses in each of the four samples.* In the domestic scene of card 2, for example, half the males (NM 50%; HM 45%) and more than a third of the females (NF 41%; HF 27%) told stories in which one or more of the characters feels isolated from or unloved and scapegoated by the rest of the family (Appendix D, table D-6), as in Maura's poignant response:

A girl going away to school. Her mother doesn't say goodbye. Her father is too busy working to look up. They work hard and want their daughter to

---

* NM = Normal Male   HM = Hospitalized Male
   NF = Normal Female   HF = Hospitalized Female

help out, too, but she feels like a stranger to them. She doesn't fit in at all, and her parents outcast her and reject her. (NF 22)

In general the story characters tend to be walled off, locked within themselves: sulking, hurting, longing, crying *internally*, while externally expressing nothing. In response to card 3BM (figure huddled on floor), young Peter says, "The boy feels so hurt and angry he wants to cry" (but he doesn't); and Grainne, a seriously depressed eighteen-year-old from an isolated mountain farm, says:

This poor creature, she have nobody to talk to. She wants to tell her problems to somebody, but she can't. (Why can't she?) She's the type that keeps to herself. (HF3)

In those TAT cards particularly evocative of dynamic family interactions — 4, 6BM, 7BM (see Appendix A) — it was characteristic of the style of Irish response to tell a good deal about what the characters were thinking and somewhat less of what they were feeling, but to create little dialogue between the figures, even when the card clearly suggests conversation. Frequently, one or more characters was described as "a silent type," "the kind that doesn't say much," "a dreamer," "lost in thought," "in a world of her own," or (among schizophrenics) the people were described as lifeless statues or paintings.

In actual village society, a lack of communication is characteristic not only of the parent-child dyad, but also of relationships between adult peers: friends, neighbors, men and women, husbands and wives. Long-standing feuds between villagers no longer erupt into the famous "faction fights" of the past (see Fox 1962); rather, anger and disapproval are expressed in silence — "not giving them the time of day." Although same-sex peers fare considerably better in the TAT responses, there is a definite preference for the diluted group camaraderie of card 9BM over the threatening intimacy suggested by the one-to-one relationship in card 7BM. In a third of all responses to card 7BM there intruded a fear of betrayal or treachery on the part of the older man, who was portrayed more often as a friend than as a father figure. This strikes me as a reflection of village friendship patterns in which both young and old of both sexes avoid the intimacy of particular relationships in preference for undifferentiated "pals in groups." In the small, crowded pubs of the village, for example, there is an effort to keep conversation "general" and superficial and to break up private dialogues. A village artisan and raconteur articulated village etiquette to me on one occasion. Noteworthy is the wariness of human nature and lack of what Erik Erikson might call "basic trust":

> *I do find that in Ballybran there's more of a general conversation between people. If you or I went to Tom's [the pub] we couldn't just chat it up, you and I. No, not at all. Because if I say something to you, and you say something to me, well, the other man will think we have a secret and he'll want to hear it, too. So, he'll come over to us and say, "Hello, dearies, give me a fag, and how's the races?" To my own ideas, it does great harm, great harm, indeed, to become too intimate with a person. When people become too intimate, they have too much knowledge of each other, and that is very detrimental. You confide in them, and they "soft" it out, and "soft" it out, and you say this and that, and later on you live to regret it. (Transcription of taped conversation, November 1974)*

In a similar vein a well-liked villager once told me his formula for successful human relationships: "Be courteous to all, have few friends, and trust no one." In such an emotional climate it is little wonder that attempts at courtship and romantic love are so often unsuccessful. When one seemingly happy village couple stopped seeing each other I inquired why, and the young girl replied, "It was all right at first, but then we couldn't think of anything more to say to each other. I guess we just talked ourselves out." Related to the fear of intimacy and difficulties with communicating feelings is the quintessentially Irish suspiciousness of the flesh and sexuality.

IRISH BODY IMAGE: "PURITY AND DANGER"

But it was to the mortification of touch that he brought the most assiduous ingenuity of inventiveness. He never consciously changed his position

in bed, sat in the most uncomfortable positions, suffered patiently every
itch and pain, . . . [and] carried his arms stiffly at his side like a runner
and never in his pockets or clasped behind him. . . . [But] to merge his life
in the common tide of other lives was harder for him than any fasting or
prayer . . . [and] caused in his soul at last a sensation of spiritual dryness.
— JAMES JOYCE, A *Portrait of the Artist as a Young Man*

According to Irish folk belief, there are two ways of achieving certain salvation. The first is through a red martyrdom, or dying for one's faith in the
tradition of the early Christians and the great missionary saints. The second
path to sainthood, and the one chosen by most ordinary people, is the white
martyrdom (ban-martra), a slow "death to self" through acts of self-denial —
fasting, penance — and, above all, a life characterized by sexual purity. The
lives of numerous "little" saints such as the Black Saint Martin and Saint
Teresa the Little Flower are held up to villagers by the clergy as role models.
However, no one better illustrates the virtues of Irish asceticism and scorn
for the body than the modern-day Catholic hero Mat Talbot, a reformed
alcoholic and laborer who died in 1925. The Irish clergy have succeeded in
bringing Talbot's case to the attention of Rome, and he is presently being
considered for canonization. Mat's main attribute is that following a youthful period of drinking and dissipation, he converted to a life of rigorous and
unremitting penance. According to his biographer, Albert Dolan, Talbot's
normal day consisted of equal parts of prayer and work, followed by three
hours of sleep and a single scant meal. When Mat finally dropped dead on
a Dublin street, heavy chains were found wrapped around his body and legs
underneath his clothing, presumably to prevent any temptation to sexual
sin. Father Dolan said of him, "There was packed into Mat Talbot everything that is *best* in Irish character" (cited by Blanshard 1953: 176).

So much has been written in recent decades about the puritanical
nature of Irish Catholicism and its eroding effect on Irish marriage and
freedom of sexual expression (see John O'Brien 1954; O'Faolain 1949; Messenger 1969; Sheehy 1968; Fennell 1974; Rohan 1969), that I shall add only
my scattered observations on the ways in which Irish body image unconsciously reflects and reinforces sexual repression.

The Irish Catholic Church has been accused of being antilife, bitter, gloomy, and sexist.[13] Several years ago, Oliver Gogarty protested to the Irish Senate that "it is high time the people of this country found some other way of loving God other than by hating women" (cited by Sheehy 1968: 203). As late as the 1940s and 1950s, the "peasant priests" of Maynooth seminary were trained in a moral theology so repressive that the sacrament of marriage was seen as an occasion of sin that necessitated constant supervision on the part of Mother Church. The affectionately termed "penny catechism" on which most Ballybran villagers were raised taught that celibacy is the highest status in life, and that the married state is a problematic union of two concupiscent natures. Sexual intercourse in marriage was lawful but only when indulged in modestly and for the purposes of procreation. The sexual sins of marriage included intercourse for pleasure alone (or "lust," as the Irish clergy referred to it), deviations from the approved coital position, and contraception. Irish women were prohibited from cooperating in sexual intercourse if the husband used a condom. The clergy counseled such women to resist their husbands as a "virgin threatened with rape" (Blanshard 1953: 156). In addition, sexual intercourse was forbidden on the eve of reception of Holy Communion and on high holy days. The rural clergy, armed with the ability to forgive and retain sins as well as with the authority to withhold Holy Communion at the altar rail as a sign of public censure (a form of social control still effectively used in the Irish countryside), maintained a firm control over the bodies as well as the souls of their notoriously obedient parishioners.

Such restrictions on sexual expression have been found to be implicated in a number of prevalent social problems in the Republic, among them alcoholism ("the good man's vice"; see Bales 1962); marital desertion and wife beating (O'Higgins 1974); hypochondria, depression, and masochism (Messenger 1969: 107); and female ignorance of orgasm (Rohan 1969: 67–70). Although newly ordained post–Vatican II clergy have attempted to correct the Augustinian excesses of past ideology (in the interests of preserving their dwindling flocks),[14] most adult villagers, permeated with years of prior indoctrination, still tend to view sex as dirty and shameful and still refer modestly to the "decent" and "indecent" parts of the body. When

Father Leary reinstituted the tradition of Sunday night dances for parish youth (after years of their suppression by his predecessors), village parents insisted upon the curate's presence as a chaperon and limited the dancing to daylight hours. Some parents were alarmed to learn that the priest had approved slow, close dancing between the couples as well as traditional Irish step-dancing with its minimum of and highly formalized body contact. In response to a village schoolteacher who protested the slow dancing as "sinful," the good priest retaliated that the problem with village youth was not too much caressing between the sexes but too little of it. Parental resistance was also strong with regard to sex education for their adolescent children. At a parish meeting on the topic headed by a representative of the Catholic Marriage Advisory Council, several parents expressed their fear that frank discussions of sexuality might awaken the dormant "appetites" of their naive adolescents. As one mother put it, " 'Tis better to let sleeping dogs lie."

That adult attitudes toward the "wicked flesh" have already been transmitted to the younger generation was demonstrated through a Values Hierarchy Scale (table 14) that I administered to sixty-seven primary- and secondary-school children. The students were asked to rank order the following values from most to least important: knowledge, career success, health, honor, economic security, freedom, friendship, respect, character, love, religious faith, good disposition, humor, wealth, and power.[15] The reactions of the youth to the test itself were quite revelatory: they protested that certain of the values were either irrelevant or repetitious (didn't respect include a notion of honor, and wasn't good disposition the same as humor?), while other very essential values were left out, among them self-discipline and happy death. In the subsequently modified test, self-discipline occupied a middle rank in

> *The sight of that medley of wet nakedness chilled him to the bone. Their bodies corpsewhite . . . gleamed with the wet of the sea. . . . It was a swordlike pain to see the signs of adolescence which made repellent their pitiable nakedness.*
> —JAMES JOYCE,
> A Portrait of the Artist as a Young Man

■ TABLE 14: VALUES HIERARCHY SCALE

A. BALLYBRAN NATIONAL SCHOOL (6TH FORM), AGES 10–12

Rank Order	Boys (10)	Girls (11)
1	Religious faith	Religious faith
2	Health	Health
3	Friendship	Respect
4	Respect	Happy death
5	Freedom	Friendship
6	Love	Love
7	Economic security	Knowledge
8	Self-discipline	Economic security
9	Happy death	Self-discipline
10	Career success	Freedom
11	Power	Humor
12	Knowledge	Power
13	Wealth	Wealth
14	Humor	Career Success

B. BALLYBRAN SECONDARY-SCHOOL
(4TH- AND 5TH-YEAR CLASSES), AGES 15–19

Rank Order	Boys (12)	Girls (31)
1	Health	Health
2	Freedom	Religious faith
3	Friendship	Love
4	Love	Friendship
5	Religious faith	Freedom
6	Respect	Respect
7	Career success	Humor
8	Self-discipline	Self-discipline
9	Happy death	Happy death
10	Economic security	Career success
11	Humor	Knowledge-learning
12	Knowledge-learning	Economic security
13	Wealth	Wealth
14	Power	Power

the students' evaluations. "Mind the body and you will lose the soul," explained one adolescent.

Mary Douglas has suggested (1966, 1970) that all societies might be classified along what she called "group-grid" lines according to body symbolization and concern with ritual pollution. She would see the body as a natural and primary symbol for the social order such that peoples' attitudes toward the governing of their bodies would reflect their ideas about the ways in which social relations (especially between the sexes) should be ordered. Certainly, the rural Irish share with Orthodox Jews, Hindus, and the Yurok Indians of California, among others, a rather strong preoccupation with matters of ritual and sexual purity, which is often expressed through a rigid vigilance over bodily boundaries. Ballybran villagers, for example, evidenced a high degree of anxiety over both what goes in and what comes out of the body. Ambivalence toward "giving out" or "letting go" was reflected in women's beliefs that breast-feeding is "too draining" an experience, in men's fears of wasting seed, in older villagers' attitudes toward guarding gossip and secrets ("I have a prayer," confided old Maggie, "and nobody else have it, and if you think you can get it from me, just see if I don't die with me lips sealed").

The "giving out" of sins in confession was particularly anxiety-provoking for many villagers, and their scrupulosity was expressed in an agonizing regard for the proper religious fulfillment of the sacrament: Had they confessed the exact number of omissions and commissions? Were there any extenuating circumstances that might increase or mitigate blame? Had they recited their penance adequately? Shouldn't they perhaps repeat it, just to be sure? One elderly villager expressed her state of confusion, impatience, and ambivalence about the sacrament as we were standing together on a particularly slow-moving confessional line. She volunteered, "Yerra, we do make mountains out of nothing. And I think we do be wasting the priest's time in the box. But we never know for sure what is a sin, and so we do confess it all."

A kind of ornery retentiveness was suspected of sick children who did not respond well to medication—they were said to be "holding in" the bug, fever, or infection. One distraught village mother asked me to have a look at her three-year-old, who she was sure might succumb to a severe strain of the measles that was spreading through the village during the spring of our stay. The child had a high fever but not a sign of the characteristic rash. "That's just the trouble," said the mother; "the girl is too stubborn to put out the spots and be done with it." Similar sentiments were expressed about cancer: the bad kind, said villagers, was not the visible growths, but rather the kind people held inside them, the dreaded "inwardly disease" referred to so frequently in the Ballybran death register.

The concern with bodily exits, entrances, and boundaries, and the fear of violation and penetration extend as well to those convenient symbols of the body—the home with its doors, gates, fences, and (in Ireland) stone boundaries (see Bachelard 1969; Jung 1964). The same Irish defensiveness and guardedness is projected into the numerous allusions in Irish folklore to the proper way to enter or leave a home, the magical marking of the four corners of a new house site, and in the protective precaution of a Saint Bridget's cross over every door lintel. Before going to bed at night, the old grandmother blesses each of the four bedposts and asks that a holy sentinel stand guard at each one:

Matthew, Mark, Luke and John
Bless the bed that I lie on.
One to guide me, one to guard me,
And two to carry my soul to heaven.

In "smooring" the fire for the night it was customary to pray:

I save this fire as noble Christ saves.
Mary on the top of the house,
Bridget in its center,
The eight strongest angels in heaven
Preserving this home and keeping its people safe.

In terms of Irish body image, folk beliefs about the soul are revelatory of Irish anxieties about penetration, loss, retentiveness, and vigilance. The soul, traditionally believed to be a slippery bit of muscle located under the arm in the form of a fish (hence called *iasc na beathadh*, the fish of life), is not to be entirely trusted. According to folklore from the Blasket Islands (and still recited by older parishioners of Ballybran), the soul can escape from the body in the form of a butterfly should the unwary person fall asleep with his mouth open.[16] Similarly, mothers are relieved when the vulnerable fontanel (*loigín na baithise*) closes in their infants—another port of exit for the wily soul. Current wake rituals are oriented around the precaution that friends and kin sit with the body for a few days to be sure that the unpredictable soul has left the body. As one young farmer explained, "We don't like to bring the body into church while it's still 'fresh-like.' You'd want to be good and sure the soul isn't still hovering about." Finally, I am reminded of the tradition in west Kerry of annually checking the heavy stone boundaries that separate one small, rocky field from the next in order to be certain of no "tinkering" on the part of a mischievous neighbor—a common source, I might add, of paranoid delusion among schizophrenic patients in Kerry. A violation of the land (symbolic of family integrity and pride) is tantamount to a violation of the body.

On the other hand, villagers are equally guarded both about what they take into the body (as in sex and food) and about being "taken in" (as with "codding," flattery, or blarney). Hence, one finds a receptivity to fasting and abstinence, a concern with eating only "plain and simple" food, and a preference for liquids over solids. Many village women rejected tampons as "dirty things," and the few women who would discuss it thought that protective sheaths and condoms (i.e., sex-once-removed) would be preferable to either intrusive diaphragms or the pill. There is a tendency among country people to use clothing defensively as well. Although adult villagers demonstrated the characteristic Irish "scorn for the body" in wearing the same woolen sweaters, heavy boots, and pants or skirts both indoors and out, in summer and in winter, in wet weather and in dry, the clothing tended to be layered, long and loose, both concealing and protecting the body. Long black shawls wrapped across part of the face served as a disguise for older women, and waistcoats and sweaters, often pulled tightly across the chest in a defensive gesture, served as armor. Legs crossed, arms folded, head slightly bowed, the typical Ballybran pub stance is a posture of caution and guardedness. The country man (and woman) is equally reserved and dignified in his walk, and when working in the field he anchors his feet with his legs stiffly and firmly together. He makes no idle or random gestures with his hands while talking, and a subtle snap of the neck or a raised index finger is his greeting. In all, the body image of the Kerryman is a study in control, understatement, and tenseness.

The traditional Irish reticence regarding the reception of Holy Communion also fits into the general pattern I am describing. Even many years after the late Pope John relaxed fasting and confessional regulations prior to Communion, older villagers will not take anything into their mouths after midnight on the eve of receiving the Blessed Sacrament, nor will the majority receive without prior confession of their faults. The public act of receiving the wafer on the tongue is embarrassing for some, and criticism is reserved for those who "snap up the Host" too quickly or those who extend their tongue too far or too early. Stories about the "improper" reception of the Eucharist are a common genre of folklore. In analyzing numerous Communion motifs, which I collected in the village as well as through the courtesy of Professor Seán O'Súilleabháin, the tension between "taking in" and "putting out" is particularly marked. Two tales will serve to illustrate this prominent theme: "The Woman Who Could Not Die" and "The Fairy Rider." In the first, a priest encounters a woman over a hundred years old, infirm and suffering terribly, but apparently unable to die. The priest acts as her confessor, and the old woman reveals a terrible secret that she had kept back all her life. Once when she was a child and was returning from the altar rail after receiving Holy Communion, the wafer slipped from her mouth and fell to the floor. Shyness and shame prevented her from bending down to pick it up, so she left it there and went back to her pew. She carried this grave sacrilege unconfessed all her lifetime and had finally come to realize that her punishment was a curse that she would never die until the Sacred Host was recovered and placed back in the ciborium on the altar or else received properly. The priest, filled with sorrow and compassion at the old woman's tale, gallops to the site of the church, which had been destroyed, and finds a beautiful bush flowering among the ruins. He finds the Sacred Host at the roots of the bush, and he carefully carries it to the ancient woman, who receives it as Holy Viaticum (Communion at death), at which point her tortured soul is released from captivity in the decrepit body and flies up to eternity (Seán O'Súilleabháin, personal communication).

The second tale is of an old woman who dies and is waked but who is visited every night by a mysterious horse and rider who commands her to sit up in her wake bed. The people are terrified and run away to find a priest, who reluctantly agrees to sit watch on the third night and confront the horse and rider. The rider appears and explains to the priest that the old woman had taken Holy Communion with an unconfessed mortal sin on her soul, and hence the devil was coming to claim her soul. The priest commands the dead woman to sit up and surrender the Host, which had been received unworthily. The woman obediently complies, and once the priest has the wafer in his consecrated fingers he announces loudly, "Be gone, Satan. Now that I have her soul safely, you can have her worthless body" (field notes, November 1974). This message is reinforced at Mass where one missionary, a frequent visitor of the parish, would remind the congregation immediately *after* the Communion ceremony that "whosoever receives unworthily, he is guilty of the Body and Blood of Christ."

If I am correct in my speculation, these oppositional themes of flesh/spirit, purity/pollution, guilt/shame, taking in/giving out, so basic to rural Irish personality modalities, and expressed through body image as well as reinforced by folklore, inhibit the expression of physical sexuality and make celibacy a natural way of life for the great number. Some years ago the Irish Catholic Church called for a national movement of "moral rearmament" to combat the twin evils of materialism and secularization. To the social critic, even more serious, perhaps, are the twin evils of sexual devitalization and cultural demoralization, and these might be countered through a call for "physical disarmament"—a surrender of those heavily guarded body boundaries and the fears of penetration, loss, giving up, and taking in that are preventative of the expression of conjugal love.

A ROMANCE WITH LOVE OR DEATH

An Irish deviant (or "queer," as the story goes) is described as a man who prefers women to drink. That there is a morsel of truth in this witticism is demonstrated in the fact that the young psychiatric patients of Kerry were ostensibly disturbed by their single status and frequently discussed their fear of loneliness and desire for sexual relationships. By contrast, normal young villagers were often resigned to future celibacy and seemingly disinterested in or scornful of (as one adolescent phrased it) "mere" sexuality.[17]

Throughout the TAT responses of normal adolescents of both sexes (most noticeable in card 4—a woman clutching the shoulders of a man, and in card 13MF—a man turned away from a partially nude woman in bed), there is an absence of sexual love or intimacy themes, a dearth of romance or marriage stories, and a consistent attempt to defuse or desexualize situations in which the sexes are in proximate contact.

Familism functions as a defense against perceptions of sexual intimacy, and frequently a young man and woman together are described as a brother and sister, or a large age gap is perceived between the two, again removing the threat of sexuality. A few adolescents toy with the idea of a romance or marriage theme in card 13MF, but then reject it by pronouncing the characters "too young for that sort of thing." and the oft-noted Irish fascination with death takes the place of sexuality insofar as almost half of the normal adolescent villagers described card 13MF as a scene of suffering, illness, or death, as contrasted to a fifth of the hospitalized patients (table 15).

Indeed, if American youth can be described as "in love with love," then the Irish TAT responses might lead one to characterize the Kerry youth as in love with death. It would appear that the preoccupation and fascination with death (found in responses to cards 3BM, 8BM, 12M, 15, and 13MF) functions—like the American preoccupation with sex—as a romantic fantasy. It is in the act of death (rather than in the passion of sex) that the Irish youth imagines his or her moment of final triumph, glory, or fullest appreciation. The following is the response of a sixteen-year-old village lad to card 16 (the blank card):

John was a little boy whom everyone loved. He was well mannered, good at everything he wanted to be good at, and he got good grades at school. One day his young life was taken when he was knocked down by a motor car. Because everyone liked him, they took this as a great loss to the community, and it was the biggest funeral that there ever was in the parish. As his expensive coffin was lowered into the ground, a great moment of silence came over everyone. Even the dogs seemed to realize that something was wrong and they whined or barked pitifully; even they realized the loss. (NM11)

Whereas little physical contact is described between the living, village adolescents tell six stories in which a character wants to hold, for one last time (or perhaps for the only time), the body of a dead loved one (wife, husband, lover, mother, or father) as in the following examples:

■ TABLE 15: SELECTED THEMES ON TAT CARD 13MF
(MAN WITH PARTIALLY NUDE WOMAN)

	FEMALES			MALES		
THEMES	Normal (n = 22)	Hospital (n = 11)	Total (n = 33)	Normal (n = 14)	Hospital (n = 10)	Total (n = 24)
1. Guilt, shame, or fear regarding sexuality	9 41%	3 27%	12 36%	5 36%	7 70%	12 50%
2. Man forces or beats wife/ sweetheart who refuses sex*	1 5%	2 18%	3 9%	3 21%	1 10%	4 17%
3. Sickness or death theme	10 45%	3 27%	13 39%	6 43%	1 10%	7 29%
4. Romance/fascination with death theme†	3 14%	1 9%	4 12%	1 7%	0 —	1 4%
5. Birth scene	0 —	2 18%	2 6%	0 —	2 20%	2 8%
6. Familistic or latent incest theme (couple perceived as brother-sister, father-daughter, mother-son)‡	4 18%	0 —	4 12%	2 14%	0 —	2 8%

* Double-scored with 1   † Double-scored with 3   ‡ Double-scored with 1, 3, or 5

Card 18GF: This man has fallen down the stairs and he is probably dead. The woman doesn't know what to do with him. I'd say she loves him and wants to keep him forever, not bury him at all. She brings along the priest and explains it to him. Maybe she's a dear friend to the priest, and she asks his advice about what to do with the man. I'd say the priest tells her to bury him. (NF4)

Card 3BM: This is a woman trying to open the coffin of a loved one. (HM7)

Card 3BM: A young man has lost his father who was killed in a battle. He kneels beside the grave now, crying and mourning for the father he never realized how much he loved. . . . He feels sad and empty as he kneels beside the concrete tomb in which his father lies. He wishes he could open the tomb and take his father's body out and hold it to his breast, just once, as he's always wished he could. (NM9)

Card 15: In a graveyard. An old man with rheumatism is praying over his wife's grave. He looks as if he's come back from a long journey. He's old and worn away, and he's reading the inscription on his wife's tomb. It's taking place at about 10 P.M. and he goes away, and tells somebody to return and close up the grave again. (NM8; emphasis my own)

The young peoples' "romance with death" also surfaced in the Values Hierarchy Scale (table 14). Love—at the students' request expanded to include love of God and love of country—only narrowly outranked happy death, while the latter was considered more important than knowledge, success, power, respect, wealth, and economic security. ("And what doth it profit a man if he gain the whole world and suffer the loss of his eternal soul?")

In contrast to normal village adolescents, the young psychiatric patients of both sexes told a high proportion of romantic love, sex, and marriage stories on the TAT (table 16). Male psychiatric patients were, for example, especially inclined to interpret the man-woman scene in card 4 positively (45% of their themes), and their descriptions include the following: "two lovers who are very sad at parting for a while"; "I suppose these two are in love at any rate";

■ TABLE 16: SELECTED THEMES ON TAT CARD 4
(WOMAN CLUTCHING SHOULDERS OF MAN)

THEMES	FEMALES			MALES		
	Normal (n = 22)	Hospit. (n = 10)	Total (n = 32)	Normal (n = 14)	Hospit. (n = 11)	Total (n = 25)
Love, affiliation between the sexes	3 14%	2 20%	5 16%	0 —	5 45%	5 20%
Isolation, alienation, indifference between the sexes	8 36%	4 40%	12 38%	4 29%	1 9%	5 20%
Conflict between the sexes	7 32%	4 40%	11 14%	5 36%	4 36%	9 36%

"they appear to be married, I believe, and quite happy." Village adolescents, however, gave twice as many themes as the hospitalized sample in which either the man or woman is seen as indifferent or lacking in love or warmth, as in the following examples:

> She's in love with him. But he doesn't take much notice of her. She's saying, "I'm in love with you," and he says, "I don't want to hear about it." (NM1)

> A husband and a wife. I'd say that he's disinterested in her, and he's determined that his job comes first. . . . The outcome is that he'll go abroad and she'll just get used to being at home alone. (NW3)

A fear of celibacy, isolation, and childlessness pervades the stories of psychiatric patients, the majority of whom were adults in their late twenties or early thirties and still single. While village girls tended to tell "grandmother" stories to card 12F (young woman in front of an old woman in a shawl; see sample picture, Appendix A), I received the following two stories from hospitalized girls:

> I think that this is a lady when she . . . that's what she'll look like when she gets old. She's thinking about that, displeased with being an old maid. (HF1)

I'd say that's a kind of gypsy woman telling her the future, and she finds out that she won't marry the man she's in love with, and that she won't marry at all. And now she's just dreading what will happen. I bet she's sorry for going to that gypsy. (HF4)

And Padraec, a malcontent bachelor farmer and hospitalized schizophrenic, told this story to card 3BM:

He seems to be down and out crying. (Why?) Because he's lonely; he can't get a wife. (Why is that?) He isn't very attractive. (Future?) He haven't much of a future. (HM10)

While themes of guilt, shame, fear, and rejection of sexuality were high for each of the four samples in response to card 13MF (table 15), hospitalized males were the most troubled by and concerned with sexuality. Where normal villagers were defensively evasive in their handling of the sexually suggestive card, both male and female patients tended to confront the issue at hand directly, as in the following two examples:

The girl seems to be dead. He's weeping. He reads a lot of books. He's no one to go to, so he buries her himself. (How did she die?) He killed her. (Why?) Because she wouldn't have the sexual intercourse. (Why not?) She don't like it. (HM 3)

This is a bedroom scene between a husband and wife. The gentleman is just after making love to his wife. This is his first time, and he turns away in disgust, having changed his clothes first, of course. (Why is he disgusted?) He has some kind of guilt complex due to his religion. (HM2)

Such explicitly sexual stories were absent among normal village adolescents who, when they did not immediately identify the card as a sickness or death scene, created farfetched explanations for the compromising situation—for example, that of a poor damsel in distress. The nudity of the woman was particularly disturbing to village boys, who in four stories attempted to clothe her or modestly turned away from the sight. Brendan's story below contains elements of both:

This woman went swimming in a mountain river where she almost drowns. She gets out of the water alive and then tries to find help. The woman falls unconscious on the doorstep of your man's house. Then, while he waits for the doctor to arrive he takes off her wet clothes, with his eyes closed, and turning away so as not to get bad thoughts, he goes over to the dresser to get her dry ones. (NM14)

Where average village adolescents unquestioningly accepted sexual repression as right and necessary in their stories, the more rebellious and "deviant" hospitalized group occasionally ended their stories to card 13MF with an affirmation of the need for more sexual freedom or understanding, as in the following examples:

I'd say they probably come to the conclusion that sex is a fact of life, and millions do it. If they're in love, what shame? (HM4)

He has had sexual intercourse and now he is bitten with pangs of remorse, a thing which shouldn't happen if only we were educated properly to the normality of sexual behavior. (HM9)

But certainly the most touching theme of a sexual nature was told in the form of a parable by a sixteen-year-old girl, hospitalized for a personality disorder:

Card 16 (blank card): One day in summer there was a boy out walking near a road and by and by he came across two oak trees. He walked between them and he had a magnificent view. A lovely girl came out to him and she offered him a sweet. But he was very shy. She joined him in walking, and they decided to go home. He took her into his house and his mother was angry. So the girl went home in bad form. The boy forgot to ask her name or address, so he ran back to the same place, but he found the two oak trees glued together and no opening to them. And that's the end. He couldn't get through. (HF2)

A theme of generativity also distinguished the average village adolescents from young psychiatric patients, as the latter frequently made allusions to their largely frustrated urge to nurture, to see living things—crops, animals, and babies—grow, survive, and outlive themselves. Seamas's replies to card 2: "They are setting rows, planning for the coming winter. Parsnips and turnips. He wants to feed his flock." And Paddy says, on the same card, "He's being very patient with his horse." The devotion of bachelors to their farm animals is viewed by married villagers as a somewhat humorous eccentricity of these lonely men.

While hospitalized villagers of both sexes somewhat shyly and tentatively alluded to the pregnancy of the older woman suggested in card 2, as "she's that way" or "she could be expecting," not one average villager mentioned or presumably noticed the pregnancy at all. And card 13MF was described as a birth scene by four "disturbed" young people, and not by any in the "normal" sample. Peter, a twenty-two-year-old tradesman and hospitalized alcoholic given to fits of violence and aggression, told this rather gentle story:

This is a young girl and she seems to be in great pain, and your man can't bear to look at her. She could be in labor and having difficulties. You want an ending? O.K. The girl dies, but the baby lives, and the father takes care of it. (HM7)

Following the TAT, I would at times ask the more outgoing mental patients to consent to the Draw-a-Person test. Denis, a thirty-year-old attempted rapist (who never succeeded in losing his virginity), drew within a very few minutes a comical but sorry caricature of a man with a huge phallus, which, on second thought, he exed from the self-portrait (see Appendix B). A heavy burden for Denis, and perhaps for others like him, this seemingly enormous, bothersome, and unused organ. And Seamas, the reluctant celibate with whom I began this chapter, summed up in his picture all the longing in lonely souls like himself for growth, creativity, and intimacy. For Seamas Danaher, the bachelor, drew the portrait of a very pregnant woman.

CHAPTER FIVE

Problems in Rural
Irish Socialization

Even after a lad takes a few wild turns in life—drinking, joining the army— he's always got an eye on home and the mother. The maternal instinct is supernatural, and that kitchen floor has great bearing in the child for good or evil ever after.

—THE TAILOR OF BALLYBRAN

ON FIRST impression Ballybran strikes the outsider not only as an ancient village, but as a village of ancients as well. The single winding road, alongside which a row of stone houses lean tiredly against one another, is empty. A donkey cart jangling its milk jugs on its timeless way to the creamery stops briefly at the post office, and suddenly, unexpectedly, there is excitement and commotion as two and then three and then more children seemingly scamper out of cracks in the walls to greet and taunt their favorite bachelor, Pat-O, to pet his donkey, and to pester him for a free ride to the creamery. The middle-aged spinster Kitty darts her graying head out the pub door and warns the children to stay clear of the road, and muttering to herself, "The road will be the death of them yet," returns to her solitary morning customer. "Cheeky little divils," calls out Pat-O with false gruffness; "stay back or I'll carry ye up to Ballybee and tie ye to a haycock!" Although both Kitty and Pat-O are childless, village children are common property to the extent that they may be alternately scolded and shamed, petted and pitied, or, more often than not, blithely ignored in their capers by all.

In this first of two chapters on rural Irish socialization, I shall describe and interpret the norms of infant and toddler tending in Ballybran in terms of its possible consequences for the mental health of child and adult. I shall probe the meaning of the many observable expressions of ambivalence toward the infant and baby in the village. Why are children seemingly greatly desired—the source of envy and jealousy among adult villagers who have none—and yet often resented by those who do? Why are small children both "spoilt" and "slashed," overprotected and yet frequently ignored? And, most germane to this study, what if any is the relationship between rural Irish socialization and the high rates of mental illness—especially schizophrenia—in the west?

The following analysis will suggest that Irish ambivalence toward the child is grounded in conflicts regarding generativity, nurturance, physicality, and sexuality, which are themselves products of the ascetic Jansenist tradition of Irish Catholicism. There is a strong tendency among Irish mothers and fathers to repress, deny, and ignore babies' demands for physical gratification and stimulation (including sucking, rocking, and holding) to the extent that Irish toddlers are remarkably undemanding and frequently shy and withdrawn. To a large degree, this is an essay on the dangers and consequences of being alone—for rural infants and toddlers spend an inordinate amount of time by themselves, unrocked, unheld, and unreassured.

▪ Socialization, Personality Development, and Human Needs

"Ah," said the Cat, listening, "but what is the Baby fond of?" "He is fond of things that are soft and tickle," said the Bat. "He is fond of warm things to hold in his arms when he goes to sleep. He is fond of being played with. He is fond of all these things."
—RUDYARD KIPLING, *Just So Stories*

The relationship between child rearing and adult personality has been a central concern of psychological anthropologists since the earliest "culture and personality" studies (see Margaret Mead 1928; Benedict 1934; DuBois 1944). In these first studies the focus was on discovering the processes through which children are taught their respective cultures and ultimately come to adopt the appropriate values, cognitive orientations, and covert rules of behavior. The orientation of early culture and personality studies was Freudian, best exemplified perhaps in Abram Kardiner's formulation of the Basic Personality Structure, which he defined as "that group of psychic and behavioral characteristics derived from contact with the same cultural institutions" (1939: 12). Like breeds like, and it was assumed that exposure to similar institutions would produce similar personality types. And so it could be concluded that the orally indulged French were, by and large, very different from the bound and swaddled Russians, and that the orally deprived Alorese were very unlike the gratified Balinese. Kardiner's model has since been greatly modified and expanded by Whiting and Child (1953) and by Whiting, et al. (1966).

Nonetheless, anthropologists have come to discard this static and deterministic model, which perceives personality as molded in early childhood and then passed on from generation to generation through standardized child-rearing practices. Through the influence of developmental and ego psychiatrists such as Erik Erikson (1963) and Jean Piaget (1954), and role theorists such as George H. Mead (1934), Charles Cooley (1956), and Erving Goffman (1959), psychological anthropologists have come to see the individual as subject to continual biological and environmental changes and hence to subsequent personality adjustments and to external adaptations to new roles. The experience of early childhood is now generally accepted as *one* important and fundamental stage among *many* stages of personality development and growth.

As the earlier theories of personality acquisition and development have been discarded for newer and more dynamic paradigms, so too have psychiatrists begun to revise their classical notion that psychiatric disorder is an interpersonal problem which *always* has its origins within the first decade of life. In part, the reformulations have been the product of increased communication between analysts and social scientists. As the latter laid the foundations for a consideration of man as a social being, the former began to notice the role of cultural determinants and social stresses (e.g., poverty, occupational hazards, migration, rapid change) in psychological disorders.

Thus far, I have examined mental illness in western Ireland within the context of the social stresses caused by cultural disintegration, economic decline, depopulation, and social isolation. In the following two chapters I shall look at the contributing role of child rearing and family dynamics in the genesis of mental illness—bearing in mind the relationship between current socialization practices and the drastic changes in the composition and *meaning* of the rural farm family over the past fifty years.

In the following analysis of the consequences of rural Irish parenting on the mental health of young villagers I shall be guided by a number of assumptions or biases regarding basic human needs and their frustration, which might best be made explicit from the onset. I share, for example, with John Bowlby (1969, 1973) the conviction that the nature and origin of the infant's attachment to the mother is based on the innate need of all young primates to be in touch with and to cling to another being. It has been demonstrated in the early experiments of Harlow and Harlow (1958, 1965) that the instinctual need in young primates to cling exists apart from and independent of the more readily recognizable needs for food and warmth. The mother (unless taught or conditioned otherwise) shares this necessary attachment behavior with her young baby and seeks to keep the newborn close and "in touch." Whiting and Child's comparative socialization studies (1953) indicate that most tribal people throughout the world are particularly sensitive to their infant's need to be held close, rocked, stroked, and carried next to the body. The following account, for example, comes from Levine and Levine's observation of infant care in a Bantu-speaking community of East Africa.

Mothers recognize a kind of crying during the first three months that cannot be satisfied by nursing. . . . Most often at night . . . the mother puts on a light, binds the infant to her back and walks about the house, shaking him up and down. With the side of his face pressed tightly against her back, the infant is frequently silenced by jostling in this position. In the daytime, child nurses also use shaking, either on the back or in the arms, as a means of calming a small infant who cries but refuses food (1966: 121).

The powerfully instinctual need of infants and small children for clinging and rocking was dramatically brought home to me during the two years I spent as a health and community-development worker in a squatter settlement of northeast Brazil. The most pressing problem of the *favela* (hillside squatter settlement) was its infantile mortality rate—more than half of the babies born each year died before reaching their first birthday, through the combined effect of prenatal malnutrition, insufficient breast milk, infant diarrheas, and parasitic infections. I worked daily in a crowded, makeshift childcare center for working mothers, which also contained a "clinic" for the treatment of dehydrated babies. Many of those children brought to us were unable to walk, stand up, or talk, although they were as old as two and three years. Severe malnutrition had made them disinterested in food and retarded in social development. One human need or "instinct" remained fully intact, however—the desire to hold on and cling to a mother or mother substitute. One frail toddler, in particular, would often startle me by leaping from his crib onto my back from behind. He would cling around my neck with all his might, while wrapping his spindly legs around my waist. His outrage at being loosed from this position was formidable.[1] The impression has never left me and no doubt influences the interpretation of Irish infant care given below.[2]

▪ Desire for Children: Envy versus Resentment

The dearth of children and new births in Ballybran is aired by the community as its greatest continuing tragedy, and village folklore and proverbs are mighty in their condemnation of sterility and barrenness. "Children," villagers agree, "are a gift of God." " A person with one child has no child at all," states the widow woman Bridie who never had any of her own. "Aye, a poor man can't have too many," offers Augusta whose own babies were miscarried or died in infancy. Old people say that to mock a woman with many children carries a curse: her face will turn into that of a pig. "Dry marriages" (sterile unions) are viewed as a punishment from Jesus or the Virgin, and it is almost always believed to be the wife's fault. "Women are like that, sometimes," says Martin philosophically, of his wife's infertility. "She looked fine and strong enough on the outside, how was I to know she was no good inside." Folk remedies (now only a part of memory culture) for barrenness are plentiful—visits to holy wells, rounds at the graveyard, the kissing of a holy stone near Dingle—whereas I could record no *piseogas* (superstitions) regarding contraception.

Envy of married couples with children is a strong, overtly expressed theme by the many bachelors, spinsters, and childless couples of the parish, who lavish attention upon, "borrow," and fill with sweets the available village children. An underlying motif of unconscious maliciousness, however, pervades some of this behavior—most demonstrably in the teasing games of old bachelors (less often spinsters) who threaten to "steal" or carry a baby away with them. A standard greeting between Peadar, Pat-O, or Jack and any village child is "Will you come up with me, or shall I carry you away?" It is a continuous game played with deep enjoyment by the aging men, despite the oft-expressed protests on the part of the children involved. The invitation to "kidnap" is sometimes followed by a thinly disguised wish-fulfillment as the lonely bachelor farmer adds, "Come with me, laddie, and I'll teach you how to farm."

Among childless women (spinsters as well as barren wives and widows) their misfortune is explained and their envy expressed in a different manner. Although the words "evil eye" are obsolete in Ballybran, the sentiment behind them is still apparent. Some village women are believed to have bad luck at whatever womanly task they touch—particularly concerning the conception and nurturance of babies. Old Ellen is a good case in point. Ellen has a reputation in the village for, among other things, her "bad" bread: she cannot, for the life of her, make a loaf of soda bread rise properly. This she associates symbolically with her other feminine failures, specifically her inability to produce living children—each of her five having been stillbirths. Her notorious bad luck has fallen upon other village children with whom she has come into contact over the years. She recalls that one day, some years ago, she gave a sourball sweet to the only baby of a village shopkeeper. The child choked and very nearly died on it. This was followed by a neighbor's toddler being seriously bitten by Ellen's mangy sheepdog. When Ellen "fumbled" our five-month-old son and his eye was scratched on a bramble, Ellen's husband roared at her from a distance, "Get away from the baba, woman, do you want to kill him?" As an aside to us, Matty added, " 'Tis best all our children died; she could never have been a good mother; she has no sense for it." Yet, both Ellen and Matty are fixated on their longing for children even though both are now in their seventies.

While village bachelors and spinsters are generally envious of those in the parish who are fortunate enough to have children, village parents (particularly mothers) often express resentment at having had more children than they want or need. "I am a prisoner in my house and my children are the jailers," said Deirdre with poetic grace, about her life on an isolated mountain farm with seven children.

What is so unique about Irish fertility patterns, exemplified in Ballybran, is that the Republic claims two seemingly contradictory distinctions: it has the greatest amount of postponed marriage and permanent celibacy (see Appendix D, tables D-7 and D-8) as well as the highest marital fertility rate (table D-9) in the world. It appears to me that the former can be explained, in part, by the latter. Villagers are reluctant to marry early when they can reasonably expect to have a child each year or every other year of their fertile married lives. The extraordinary marital fertility rate is the result of Irish Catholic strictures against artificial birth control and of the idealization of large families by the rural clergy and the older generation. Not only are contraceptives morally censored, they are banned by law in the Republic.[3] A bill in early 1975 to amend this law by allowing for the distribution of contraceptives at nationally controlled clinics was vetoed by the Irish prime minister and to date the sale and distribution of birth control pills or devices remains a criminal offense, although the *use* of them by individuals is not.[4]

While the urban middle classes in the Republic have access to contraceptives through sophisticated doctors and by purchase from Northern Ireland, devout and conservative rural couples like those in Ballybran remain unable to control their fertility by any other than heroic means. The average-sized family in the parish in 1974, however, was 4.1 children — considerably below the norm in 1924 of 6.1 children. Table 17 shows the breakdown of those households in the parish with children twenty-one years of age and under.

What this table does not demonstrate, however, is that those families in the upper half of the spectrum represent the older and completed families of the parish, whereas those with two and three children are the younger and presumably still fertile couples. A second major determinant of family

ONE	TWO	THREE	FOUR	FIVE	SIX	SEVEN	EIGHT	NINE	TEN
1	7	11	4	5	3	3	0	1	1

Note: Total households = 36.

size in Ballybran is the sexual composition of offspring, and those families with six or more children tend to have a predominance of one sex over the other—usually of girls. In farm households, where sons are needed well into adulthood as unpaid farm laborers and where the selection of an heir among sons is an important aspect of family dynamics (see chapter six), parents hope to have a minimum of two sons to assure continuity of the farm, and they will keep trying until they reach this goal.

In their public presentation of self as Irish Catholics, villagers staunchly defend the Holy Father's condemnation of artificial contraception in his encyclical *Humanae Vitae*. "Birth control is murder plain and simple," volunteered the outspoken shopkeeper, Sheila. Privately, however, villagers question the prudence of those couples like the Maguires and O'Carrolls who multiply beyond their means. And I overheard a harried father, tired and depressed after a bad day at the Dingle sheep fair, comment wryly, "Yerra, what does the Holy Father know about bringing babies into the world?"

While a tiny percentage of married women in the parish have made furtive contacts with "liberal" doctors and family-planning clinics in Cork and Dublin, the vast majority of young couples rely upon religiously sanctioned methods of partial or total sexual abstinence. The temperature and newer Billings (mucous) methods of natural birth control are taught to interested couples by a visiting representative of the Catholic Marriage Advisory Council (CMAC). When followed rigorously and with "large doses of self-discipline," as the CMAC representative advises, these methods are fairly reliable. However, as both allow a "safe" period of only seven to ten days immediately prior to the menses, it was considered normal for a couple practicing natural birth control to have intercourse as infrequently as once or twice a month. And at least three young couples of the parish (in their late thirties or early forties) had decided that nothing other than total sexual abstinence could give them the peace of mind and security they wanted. In reverting to what the Irish clergy condone as a "brother-sister" marriage, the couples believe they are aided by a shower of heavenly graces to withstand their "heroic sacrifice."

Traditional Catholic values in rural Ireland concerning the desirability of large families and the folk practice of "offering up to God" the trials, disappointments, and constraints on personal liberties which a large family entails are, however, under siege in the urban centers of the Republic today (see Rohan 1969; Fennell 1974). And even in relatively isolated and tradition-bound communities like Ballybran, villagers are exposed to urban ideas and trends. The rapid spread of what the rural Church calls the "twin evils of materialism and secularism" into the rural west has resulted in a clash of values and ideologies and has contributed, I am certain, to the ambivalence and resentment expressed by Irish parents toward procreation and child rearing, which I shall describe at length below.

▪ Pregnancy and Birth: Conflicts Regarding Nurturance

Pregnancy, like the birth that follows, is a private matter in Ballybran and is kept a secret by women from their relatives, neighbors, and children for as long as possible. Even a husband may learn quite belatedly of a pregnancy, as intimate conversations (particularly those bearing on sexuality) are handled with great difficulty between married couples. In a village the size of Ballybran, where gossip is a major form of entertainment as well as an aspect of social control, the ability to conceal information as vital to the community as a pregnancy is a powerful controlling device for the woman. Only the most rude and bold villager would question a woman directly about her condition, and it is considered the prerogative of the mother to deny any such accusations. Elderly women, however, tend to be skilled observers, and most women will be found out, much to their own chagrin, by their third or fourth month.

Although married couples are expected to be sexually innocent on the night of their wedding, it is hoped by extended family members waiting in the wings that a pregnancy will occur immediately. If the desired pregnancy is not forthcoming, disapproval will be indirectly expressed. A village woman who married into her husband's farm from a distant parish told of her excruciating embarrassment at her in-laws' scrutiny: "The worst part of living with the old people that first year was their watching me to see if I were pregnant. The old couple feared the worst and kept asking friends of mine if I were pregnant yet. It was humiliating." It is also customary to keep the news of an anticipated birth from children, in part because parents wish to keep their children innocent of sexual matters. "It doesn't do to have them curious about things like that," offered one mother. "They might get bad thoughts."

If the birth occurs at home (which is customary today only in the most traditional farm households), the children are sent away to spend the day with relatives. If the mother delivers at a hospital or maternity home in town, young children are often told that mother has gone shopping. Even children as old as ten and eleven are told that babies are ordered through Penney's Department Store, while younger children are told that the new "baba" was found on the beach, washed up with the tide, or that it was carried to the home in Dr. Finley's black bag. It is a common assumption of urban dwellers that rural children learn about the facts of life naturally by watching the "bulling" of cows and the birth of farm animals and pets, but in Ballybran children and adolescents are carefully sheltered from such earthy scenes and tend to accept miraculous-birth myths, often well into adolescence.

Until very recently, pregnancy was shrouded in the rural west with an aura of danger and fears of magical and supernatural influences over or through the mother and fetus. Older villagers still hold some of these beliefs today. The "dangerous period" lasted from the moment of conception until the mother was "churched" (ritually purified), about forty days following the birth.[5] Pregnant women had to follow many ritual proscriptions in order to avoid harming or "marking" their unborn child: they were not allowed to witness the birth of farm animals or to see animals slaughtered; they were prohibited from remaining in a house while a corpse was being placed in or taken out of a coffin; they could not act as sponsors for a wedding or a baptism (Seán O'Súilleabháin, personal communication). In addition, pregnant women were cautioned against entering a graveyard lest they twist their foot on a grave and their child be born with a club foot. Above all, however, the pregnant woman was admonished to be gay, for depression was believed to cause mental retardation or insanity in an infant.

A folk belief that survives among some villagers today is that a pregnant woman's cravings must always be satisfied lest harm come to the mother, her unborn child, or the person who refuses her. "It is said," offered Nora, with some embarrassment at appearing foolish or old-fashioned, "that if a woman's cravings aren't satisfied, her baby will be born with its tongue hanging out." Still told on the Dingle Peninsula is the tale of a husband and his wife taking a stroll near the cliffs of the Blasket Islands. The woman suddenly craved a piece of her husband's flesh. Reluctantly, he obliged her. They walked on a bit further and she asked for a second bite. Again the husband gave in to the bizarre craving. When the woman asked for a third bite, however, her husband pushed her over the cliffs into Dingle Bay. When she was washed ashore, three infants were found in her womb. The folktale metaphorically states a strong theme regarding child rearing in Ballybran — that the fetus and later the infant can make extraordinary and unfair demands on the mother and those around her. As such, the tale is revelatory of the conflicts and negative attitudes regarding nurturance and oral gratification in Irish culture.

While it is generally accepted in Ballybran that pregnancy is a dangerous hour in the life cycle, that it is a somewhat debilitating state for the mother, and a critical one for the infant that she carries, there is also a parallel and conflicting belief that women will use pregnancy to escape their household and farm responsibilities. Nothing but scorn is reserved for the pregnant woman who "coddles" or "pampers" herself, including the very few who actually remain in bed to avoid a threatened miscarriage. Village women try to conform to the model expectant mother: the strong, self-possessed woman who is ignoring of her condition, matter-of-fact, hardworking, and, above all, mobile up until the time of confinement. Maureen, village mother of four children, told of the strict regime she had to follow while pregnant—particularly before the death of her mother-in-law.

My troubles really began when I became pregnant. I think the old woman was jealous of me for it. She never helped me at my chores, and there were days I would be carrying four buckets of milk on my arm and she would just let me struggle. If I complained and said I was tired and wanted to sleep a bit during the day, she wouldn't say anything to me, but I would overhear her telling a neighbor that I thought I was a "pet," that I needed to rest where no Boyle woman had ever needed to rest when they were pregnant. So, I kept on working even though my feet and legs were swollen and my blood pressure was high. I had to sneak out to see the doctor because the old people thought a woman was "soft" who went to a doctor just for pregnancy.

The emphasis on stoicism is reflected as well by the rural medical profession's attitude toward pregnancy and birth. Dr. Finley, for example, does not like to be bothered by "well" people. He considers his job to be one of crisis intervention, and he is most attentive to and competent with villagers suffering from broken bones, farm injuries, heart attacks, dog bites, and so forth. As a result of his attitude, most village women do not bother about prenatal examinations, and although I could not obtain any official statistical data on miscarriages, from the self-reportage of village mothers both toxemia and spontaneous abortion are not infrequent occurrences.

During labor the rural woman is expected to be equally self-possessed and stoical. The model of behavior was offered to me in the story of the Tralee midwife who delivered a village woman of a seven-pound boy, only to withdraw into an anteroom of the maternity home some minutes later to deliver herself of a little girl. Those few mothers who still give birth at home liked to boast that their little children sleep through or are otherwise oblivious to the events in the master bedroom. And village women who deliver in the county hospital often complained of the scandalous behavior of lower-class tinker women who "carry on and fuss" during delivery. Although anesthesia is taken for the final stage of delivery by village women in hospitals, women who give birth at home rely on a "sup" of sherry, brandy, or porter and the comfort of religious medals, holy water, and traditional birthing prayers, recited by the nurse/midwife, such as the following: "Woman bear your child as Anne bore Mary, as Mary bore Jesus, without disfigurement or blindness or lack of a foot or hand."[6] The stoicism of the Irish country-woman in labor has a long history and has been commented on by travelers, such as in the following description from the seventeenth-century *Dunton Letters* (cited by Fleming 1953: 56):

> *And surely if the curse laid upon Eve to bring forth her children in sor-row has missed any of her posterity, it must be here, many of the poorer sort of women bearing their children without any long labour or extreme pains . . . nay even without the assistance of other women, often proving their own midwives. Tho when they fall into any greate distresse as they sometimes do, the barbarities . . . often used . . . by those who call them-selves their assistants are such as would make a reasonable man believe they were used to frustrate the verie intentions of nature, such as plung-ing the woman when her labour is long into a pitt of cold waters, or layeing her upon the cold earthen floor . . . or tak[ing] a rope and fasten-ing it about the infant's neck they pull and hale it until they deliver the woman or pull off the child's head.*

Until the turn of the century husbands played an important role in childbirth. It was said that midwives had the power of transferring the woman's pains onto her husband, and Seán O'Súilleabháin (n.d.) records from elsewhere in County Kerry the couvade-like custom of the laboring woman wearing some piece of her husband's clothing, often his vest. The expectant father in Ballybran today is characterized by villagers as nerv-ously occupying himself with some repetitive and monotonous task, such as turf stacking, until the birth is over. "First I listen for the baby's whine, and then I hold my breath until I hear Peg's deep voice. And if it sounds like herself, then I go out and fetch the children," said Declan of his wife's births at home.

Once the infant is born, whether in the hospital or at home, he or she is carefully scrutinized from head to toe by the mother, the doctor, or the mid-wife. Among rural people the sex of the child is of primary importance. Sons are still generally preferred over daughters, and in those farms where a son has been particularly long in forthcoming, the word is spread on foot from house to house in the townland that the O'Malleys or the McCabes at last have an heir. In the most traditional homes the question is raised: "Is it a boy or a child?"

Of equal importance, however, is the general health and appearance of the child. Some village grandmothers still examine the baby for the presence of bad omens — if the index finger is longer than the middle finger, the child might turn out a thief; or, if the baby has a crooked finger, he might grow into a liar. The rural Irish, above all a deeply pragmatic people, have a low tolerance for physical deformity, mongolism, or other signs of weakness. Such infants are usually put away in special institutions to remove them from public view.

Until the mid-nineteenth century, it was popularly believed in the west of Ireland that infant illnesses and deformity were the handiwork of the fairies, the devil, or the bad wishes of jealous neighbors. Deformed, mentally handicapped, or sickly infants were sometimes viewed as "changelings" rather than as human infants, and until the practice was brought to the attention of the Irish courts, such babies were abandoned, tortured, or burned by their parents.[7] Fairy stories still abound in the parish about beautiful, healthy newborns who were whisked away overnight only to be replaced by a sickly and demonic fairy child, but where they were once believed, today they are stories told to "cod" or entertain the children. In the old days one sure protection against the fairies or the evil eye of an envious neighbor was for the parents to out-trick them. Hence, pregnancy was not discussed, baptisms were unannounced, births went uncelebrated, the name of the newborn was withheld, and the infant itself was hidden from view — customs which have survived, but for different motivations, to this day in Ballybran.

I may risk injuring the sensitivities of many villagers by interjecting vestiges of old *piseogas* into my interpretation of the routines of infant tending in the parish today; however, it appears to me that unconscious defenses against the envy of ill-intentioned neighbors or against nameless supernatural influences, in addition to strong conflicts regarding nurturance, are plausible explanations for the relative isolation and lack of attention given the infant and small child, which I am about to describe below. Although intuitively designed to protect the infant, who is perceived as extremely vulnerable and fragile, such practices have been linked by psychiatrists and psychologists to the emotional wounding of young children (see Spitz 1946; Bowlby 1973).

▪ Infant Tending: Isolation and Invisibility

Sing a song at a wake, and shed a tear when a baby is born.
— Irish Proverb

A most remarkable aspect of infant tending in Ballybran today is the low profile of the infant and toddler, in both the public and private spheres of village life. Small children, it appeared, were neither to be heard *nor* seen.

While pregnancy, because classified as "secret," generated some amount of gossip, the arrival of a new infant was anticlimactic, greeted by villagers with an air of studied indifference — an attitude that may perhaps indicate suppressed envy. When Peadar, the first child born into the central village for two years, and his mother returned from the hospital, the pair remained sequestered for several weeks. No friendly flow of well-wishers, presents, congratulations, or offers of assistance ensued. When I asked the generally nosey widow woman Catherine why she hadn't run in to see the new village "baba" (in whom she had expressed so much interest prior to his birth) the old woman snapped at me, "Yerra, we take no interest in babies." Other village women, in reply to my inquiries, were evasive, saying, "Sure, 'tis true, it would be friendly-like for us to drop in." However, I remained the only nonrelative to visit the infant prior to his baptism some two months following the birth.

Subsequent observations and interviews with village mothers revealed that babies, although briefly brought out for baptism, are not made public in the village until the "coming out" in street play at about age two and a half or three years. Until that time "babies" are kept indoors in a carry-cot (portable crib), pram, and later playpen, "safely out of harm's way," as their mothers explained.

A baby born in the autumn or winter would often not get his first whiff of fresh air in the backyard until summertime. Although the pram or baby carriage is an essential mark of middle-class status among the upwardly mobile residents of the central village, there is no custom of promenading the baby down the village street as there is in the towns and cities of Ireland. The pram, like the baby, is kept indoors, often in the upstairs bedroom out of public view. Beliefs in the vulnerability of young children to changes in air, temperature, lights, and noise were offered by parents as reasons for keeping them quietly indoors.

Unbaptized infants are viewed as particularly vulnerable to ills (both physical and spiritual), and a mother who unduly postpones her child's baptism is criticized for risking the well-being of the baby. Frances, for example, had a difficult labor and birth with her fourth child and decided to wait for both her own and the baby's sake until the third month for his christening. When the child broke out with an extensive case of hives, the country doctor was called in for consultation. He looked over the child and commented gravely to the mother, "Well, and what do you expect with an unbaptized child?"

Village infants who die unbaptized are not recorded in the parish death register, since as "little pagans" they are viewed as somewhat less than fully human. In past generations such babies were buried, not in the consecrated ground of the village cemetery, but rather beyond the walls of the graveyard in the space also reserved for the bodies of strangers, such as those reclaimed from shipwrecks off the coast of Ballybran Bay. In village folklore the souls of baptized children are represented as clear, bright lights pointing the way to heaven, whereas the souls of unbaptized infants appear as dim, flickering lights.

Despite Vatican II guidelines, which have revised the sacrament of baptism and integrated it into the general celebration of the Mass, village parents have adamantly refused to comply with such public christenings, and Father Leary has reluctantly reverted to the traditional secretive "back of the church" afternoon ceremony. "Isn't baptism a very backward sacrament after all?" mused an old woman. When I asked what she meant, the grandmother replied, "I always felt like it was a 'hush-hush-pushed-away-into-the-sacristy' affair. No one is supposed to know when it happens, and not even the mother and father attend."

Inside village homes I was able to decipher a pattern of infant tending based on the rather curious premise that babies prefer to be left quietly alone. The fact that most babies are kept isolated from the hub of household activity required an effort to observe mother-infant interactions. When visiting a home with a small member, I normally asked that the baby or toddler be brought down during the chat or interview, but mothers tended to dismiss my request, saying the baby would only get in our way, or (of a toddler) "little pitchers have big ears." Upon repeated requests I might be taken upstairs or into a back bedroom where the infant lay, tightly wrapped in many layers of blankets. If toddler age, the child might be sitting in a playpen with a stuffed animal or toy car. I encountered a few large farm households in which the current "baby"—sometimes as old as two years—was brought down into the central kitchen/living room only once a week for the ritual Sunday dinner. Otherwise the child was kept upstairs in the children's bedroom. When the baby cried, an older sibling would be sent upstairs or "behind" with a bottle or pacifier. For the very young baby, the bottle would be propped up on a blanket or a rolled diaper so that he could feed himself. In village homes I most noticed the absence of the rocking chair (so widespread in the rest of western Europe), for rural babies are rarely held and rocked as they were (according to village grandmothers) but a few generations ago.

▪ Social Change, Rural Decline, and Modern Childcare

With the gradual demise and transformation of the extended farm-family household (discussed in chapters two and four), the traditional infant caretaker has also disappeared: the live-in grandmother or elderly maiden aunt. As village households become increasingly nuclear in orientation, the "excess" relatives—grandparents, in-laws, aunts, and uncles—are expected to set up their own small households or, if still young, to emigrate. Of necessity, patterns of child rearing have changed radically. "My grandmother said 'twas she who reared me, carding wool or knitting and rocking the cradle with her foot," said Mame, herself the mother of three little girls none of whom was rocked. "My mother died, God rest her soul, before she laid eyes on any of her grandchildren, and I'm always too busy with the chores to give time to petting the babas."

The division of labor in today's understaffed farm households requires that the young mother be engaged in many agricultural tasks. She is entrusted with the care of baby livestock and the vegetable garden, and is sometimes responsible for driving and watching the cows. In summer she must cooperate with the "hay saving," turf stacking, and potato planting. In addition, she must attend to her household activities of cleaning, cooking, sewing, and washing. These tasks are valued and the rural woman takes pride in her active lifestyle. Although young children are also a great source of pride for rural women, child rearing is regarded as low-status work, suitable for the less vital old women who were responsible for it in the past. The low regard for childcare is revealed, for example, in Kathleen's statement that all eight of her children (now fully grown) were raised by her retarded younger sister, Sarah. "Poor creature," says Kathleen, "she was never suited to any 'real' work."

Among the current generation, Grandma and Aunt Sarah have been largely replaced by the confinement of babies to crib and playpen. Grainne, the semi-retired village midwife, is well versed in the radical changes in rural child rearing, which she attributes to villagers' emulation of the "cold" English:

> It was so very wrong, but no woman in my generation ever knew the pleasure and warmth of cuddling a baby. We never thought we had time for that. Most women were needed on the farm, and me, I was needed by the whole community. There were times when I would be called out for a birth and Conn would have to drive me. I'd sprinkle the babies with holy water and leave them alone in the care of the Sacred Heart.

Farm and household activities were offered by village mothers as reasons for the disappearance of two other traditional child-rearing practices—the lullaby and breast-feeding. Whereas the rich store of hauntingly beautiful Irish lullabies has gone the way of the Irish language itself, as villagers first forget the words and then even the melodies of the traditional airs, breast-feeding appears to have disappeared in the first decades of this century with the introduction of the bottle (if the midwife is correct) by the English. Nursing is described by village mothers today as "vulgar and common," "cow-like," and as "an old slobbery habit of our grandmothers." While not a single mother of the current generation has successfully breast-fed her child (although two or three made a brief attempt), Tomás O'Crohan could write of his childhood on the Blasket Islands off the coast of Ballybran during the late nineteenth century (1951: 1), "I can recall being at my mother's breast for I was four years old before I was weaned." Expressions of revulsion toward the physical closeness necessary between nursing mother and infant in addition to sexual shame ("How could I ever give the 'didi' in this house never knowing when 'the boss' [her husband] might come bursting in?") were bolstered by negative beliefs about the value of breast milk. It is popularly held, for example, that breast milk is too thin and weak to sustain an infant, let alone a toddler, and that nursing is a draining and exhausting experience for the mother. Beliefs that breast-fed children become "soft" and overly dependent upon the mother are also expressed.

A perusal of Seán O'Súilleabháin's (1963) and Patrick Logan's (1972) collections in Irish folklore and folk medicine revealed that, even in the past, mother's milk was not credited with the curative powers attached to other bodily emissions, including spittle, urine, feces, and blood. Interestingly, there is an abundance of folklore on the magical and curative powers of cow's and goat's milk, which are recorded as cures for babies suffering from diarrhea, tuberculosis, bronchitis, whooping cough, and jaundice (Logan 1972: 23, 32, 44). Seán O'Súilleabháin (personal communication) remarked that the early Irish poet Carroll O'Daley is said to have received his gift for words from taking his first nourishment from the milk of a cow inseminated by a magical bull, rather than from his mother's breast. Certainly, the goat's milk cure is still recommended by villagers for any number of human maladies. At one point I was persuaded by villagers into switching my ailing six-month-old son from the breast to the milk of the postman's famed goat. Although I could see no great improvement and eventually returned to nursing, villagers spread the myth that Peter Tuohy's goat had cured Nathanael.

The persistence of folk beliefs regarding the exceptional value of animal milk explains, in part, the preference of Irish mothers for the bottle over the breast, despite the problems that sometimes resulted. Patricia, now the middle-aged mother of three children, recalled that when she returned home from the maternity hospital with her first child she hadn't really understood the ratio of cow's milk, water, and sugar to go in the formula that she had been advised to use. Patricia's elderly mother, having breast-fed her own children, couldn't help her. The pair experimented with various combinations of formula while the infant became fretful and each day grew more weak and listless. "I was nearly demented with anxiety," said Patricia. "My first baby was dying and we were too ashamed to let anyone in the village know what fools we were." It was only when "Jimmy-Post," Patricia's first cousin, came by with a letter that she could bring herself to make the plea for help which eventually saved her child's life.

Most village mothers insist that they have or had quiet babies who were good sleepers. In fact, parents demonstrated a very low tolerance for crying in infants and toddlers. A toddler will be slapped and then given a teaspoon of sugar to quiet him. One mother explained that newborns should be allowed to "cry it out" at first until they finally learn that crying will get them nowhere. Then she added, "Sometimes you must be cruel in order to be kind." Highly recommended to soothe colicky or teething infants were two folk remedies: a "supeen" of brandy in the baby bottle or a few drops of a commercial preparation of phenobarbital. The regime of enforced quietude for babies normally begins in the town maternity hospital where the under-staffed nurses are said to tranquilize difficult babies and who recommend the practice to young and inexperienced mothers. Even village women who are themselves "tee-totaling" members of the Pioneers for Total Abstinence Society did not perceive any contradiction in giving a spot of alcohol to their children as a "medication." Above all, the "good" baby is described as one who is quiet, passive, and undemanding. Kattie once lamented to me, "How was I to know that my Eddie was a sickly child when he was such a good baby—all he did was drink bottles and sleep?"

▪ The Father in Early Child Tending

In Ballybran I recorded a folktale in which a mother's negligence of her infant's thirst results in tragedy. In brief the story tells of a couple who were wakened by their wailing infant. The husband asks his wife, "What ails the baba?" The wife replies, "'Tis nothing but the thirst that's upon him." "Well, and would you ever get up and give him something to drink?" asks the husband. The wife silences her spouse, telling him that the baby will soon cry himself to sleep. The husband is angered and retorts, "How is it you think I can sleep with my baby so unhappy?" The wife ignores him, and the husband gets up only to find that there is no milk in the house and the water jug is empty. He goes outside to the well, but falls down dead upon his return. The moral lesson is, "A woman must always have water in the house." What is curious about the tale, however, is the portrayal of the mother as less nurturant and "maternal" than the father—a theme that occurs with patterned regularity in the TAT responses of young villagers (see Appendix D, table D-5) as well as in the life histories of villagers. "Papa" is often characterized by his adult daughters as having been the "soft" member of the family. In one elderly villager's life history it was her "Da" who got on his horse in the middle of a storm to ride over to her Auntie's house, where she was spending the night, in order to sing her to sleep amidst the howling winds. Many a village woman recalls with fondness working with her Papa in the bog or fixing the thatch roof or walking over Connor's Pass with him to sell the young calves, or even sharing with him her first "sup" of wine punch to celebrate the sale.

The role of the father in *early* child rearing, however, is quite minimal. Until the age of four or five, children are very much the property and concern of their mothers. "The farm and the land and the house down to the last teacup belong to Christy, I suppose," said Valery; "but I *own* the children." The result of this attitude is that men are socialized into feeling extremely inadequate and clumsy around babies. Helen, for example, attended a community social, and her husband volunteered to watch their three-month-old son. When she returned, the mother found her infant howling on the edge of a straight-backed chair, with his worried father sitting next to him. Hugh explained that he was afraid to pick up the infant for fear of hurting him.

▪ The Learning of "Irish" Attitudes toward Food

At about the time rural babies are weaned from the bottle—between ten and eighteen months—they receive their first semisolid foods: cereals, mashed biscuits, potatoes, soups, and tea. A few mothers postpone the giving of solids for as long as two years because of the widespread belief in the value of fresh cow's milk as the "perfect food" for babies.

Training in proper food habits is an important first lesson for the Irish toddler, as eating (like sexuality) is an aspect of physicality that carries connotations of anxiety, guilt, and shame in rural areas. Even small children soon learn to share in the adult's depreciatory regard of food and eating. A social historian's description (M. J. F. McCarthy 1911: 28) of rural Irish attitudes toward food at the turn of the century is still applicable in some village households today.

> Allowing for exceptions, the Irish . . . have what the English would call very unpractical notions about food. If a stranger, even of their own class, discovers them eating, they are quite confused, especially the women, and hurry through the meal, or finish before they have taken as much as they had intended to take; while the children retire into the dark corners of the cottage. . . . The sensation of shame at being found eating . . . is partly due to a suspicion that the food and its mode of service are not good enough to do them credit; and partly to a feeling of pain that they cannot ask the visitor to join them; and also because the self-sacrificing Celtic spirit thinks it is a weakness to be obliged to eat at all. Most Irishmen and Irish women are proud of being able to fast, and would be ashamed to complain to a stranger about shortness of food, or to admit they were hungry.

The rural Irish are perhaps the only European "peasant" people who do not equate fatness with health in babies. Fatness is abhorred in all age groups, for it is associated with the "deadly sins" of sloth, gluttony, and idleness. The "fleshy" baby is believed to be particularly prone to respiratory ailments, influenzas, and colds. He or she is thought to be slower at walking and not as mentally alert as the thin baby or child.

The small child soon learns not to cry for or demand food, for he or she might be punished by being sent away from the table without anything. Like his adult models, the small child is expected to eat quickly, without comment on the quantity or quality of what is before him. And it is not considered odd for children to develop strong aversions to certain categories of food, this within an already restricted diet. There are village children, for example, who will not touch soda bread, a staple food; others abhor sausages, another staple; and a few children would not drink milk or eat butter. While parents tolerate such food aversions, they have little patience with children playing with their food, and it is not uncommon for a mother to spoon-feed even a four-year-old while explaining "I can do it so much quicker than she can."

Because very little ceremony surrounds eating, the village school does not have a lunchroom, although all but the pupils from the nearby central village bring a bag lunch. School children (including the four-year-old "infant" class) are expected to eat their lunches "on the run" while playing in the school yard. When it rains, the children huddle in the partially open corridor between classrooms, where they eat sitting on the floor. Sometimes children forget their lunches, as school children will, but the village child will not admit to being hungry nor ask a friend to share his or her lunch. Teachers pointed this out to me on a few occasions, since they were generally proud when their pupils demonstrated early the ascetic traits of a stalwart Kerryman.

Data collected by other ethnographers (Bales 1962; Messenger 1969) suggest that psychological strictures on eating may be the result of the irregular and inadequate food supply in Ireland throughout its past. Severe famines may have had an effect on national food habits, including the Irish proclivity toward fasting, abstaining from meat (even following changes in Roman Catholic dietary rules), and participating in hunger strikes for political as well as personal reasons. I might note here, as an aside, that nearly half of the twenty-two young mental patients interviewed reported serious eating disturbances, manifested in an inability or a refusal to eat. Bales (1962: 159) noted the Irish tendency to substitute drinking for eating in social situations, and my data indicate that this pattern is learned very early as mothers tend to withhold solid foods in preference for milk during the first two years of life, soothe babies with teaspoons of alcohol, and deprive naughty children of dinner or sweets.

▪ Potty Training

Of all aspects of early child rearing, the mothers of Ballybran are most relaxed about "potty training." Children are kept in cloth "nappies" until age three and sometimes even four. The only expectation mothers have is that their sons and daughters be fully trained by the time they begin school at age four. A few children were kept away from school beyond their fourth birthdays specifically because mothers feared the little ones might accidentally wet or soil their pants and hence humiliate not only themselves but their parents. And one "crabbit" (wise) little four-and-a-half-year-old confided in me that the only reason he was still in "nappies" was so his "Mummy" couldn't possibly send him off to "that mean old Mrs. Houlihan," the village schoolteacher. Chamber pots are a common sight in farm households, as potty training is a very gradual process, which begins at a year and a half but is rarely completed for another two or three years. Both boys and girls tend to be modest about relieving themselves, but this seems to have more reference to the display of partial nudity required than to any embarrassment about urination or defecation per se.

▪ Safety and Danger

I left my baba lying here,
A-lying here, a-lying here,
I left my darling lying here
To go and gather blackberries.

I found the wee brown otter's track,
The otter's track, the otter's track,
I found the wee brown otter's track,
But ne'er a trace of the baby-o.
—Traditional, from the Gaelic

Conflicts and vacillations between under- and overprotectiveness toward infants and small children result in anomalous and inconsistent practices with regard to what John Whiting refers to as self-reliance training (Whiting, et al. 1966: 91). Overprotectiveness results in the virtual sequestering of small children as well as in early inhibitions of physical mobility. Village babies, confined for long periods in cot, crib, and playpen, tend to include a high proportion of noncrawlers, late walkers, and self-rockers. Crawling is not encouraged, because rural mothers feel that their farmhouse floors are too difficult to keep clean and the open fireplace is a continual hazard. A few village mothers were quite proud that their toddlers had "skipped a stage" in going directly from sitting and standing to walking. One farm mother who disapproved of playpens resorted instead to tethering her toddlers to a long rope attached to the kitchen table legs while she was out of the house on necessary errands.

Despite such solicitous overprotection, accidents and near fatalities to young children are not uncommon in the tiny parish. During the year of our stay, a number of village toddlers were treated for poison ingestion, dog bites, and falls. Accidents were the main cause of childhood deaths in the parish, according to the death register kept sporadically between 1923 and 1969. One-third of the seventeen childhood deaths recorded fall into accident categories (burned, drowned, "caught-in-throat," etc.) and another three childhood deaths fall into the inscrutable category of "sudden" (see chapter six, table 20, p. 274).

It occurred to me that such accidents as well as the frequent accounts of lost or wandering toddlers are the result of the radical transition for children in the parish from overprotected baby to independent "lad" or "lass," which occurs as early as age three and almost always by age four. Maureen, the "invisible" baby of the McKennas', made her public debut on the village street just following her third birthday. Seemingly bursting with pride, the little girl was taken in hand by her older brothers and brought from house to house and backyard to backyard, where she was initiated into the small "crowd" of village youngsters with whom she would now spend most of her waking hours. It was not a month later that I encountered Maureen's mother tensely pacing the main street of the central village in search of her daughter who had wandered off with a five-year-old playmate some time before. To both her relief and her horror, the mother eventually found her little girl and the neighbor's boy sitting behind an ancient stone in the village graveyard "having a picnic."

The transition from private "baby" to public "child" is ritually formalized in the ominous event of the "first day of school," an event recalled with remarkable clarity by elderly villagers, even as their private "babyhood" was muddled or utterly forgotten. For the older generation, the start of school meant the boy's first pair of pants and the girl's first dress, as up until this time both sexes wore the shapeless asexual *baneen* (woolen sack dress) of infancy. Today, initiation to school and into the stage of independent childhood is signaled by the trip into town (often the child's first) for the purchase of shoulder-strap school bag, pencils, and notebook. Both mother and child recognize the significance of the event; from the first day of school onward the mother has limited authority and control over her child's life.

Although four is the normal age for the start of school, in some cases the day of separation from the mother comes even earlier. The village school is lacking pupils, and teachers welcome any child who is sent. Bernadette, for example, was the last child at home in an isolated mountain farm, and although only three years old, cried bitterly each morning as her six brothers and sisters set out on the two-mile trek to the village schoolhouse. On the day her child turned three and a half, Therese declared that she could keep Bernadette home with her no longer:

> On that morning I packed her lunch along with the others, put a miraculous medal around her neck, offered her up to the Holy Virgin, and sent her out the door with the rest of them. I had a lump in my throat the size of a hen's egg—she was all I had left at home—but it doesn't do to keep 'em back when they're straining at the bit.

▪ The Folklore of Infancy and Irish Catholic Beliefs about Human Nature

The apparent conflicts regarding mother-infant nurturance, and the "liberal" use of caning and other forms of corporal punishment for the older child (to be described below), are strongly reinforced by village folklore and moral code. Child tending in Ballybran can be seen as a reflection of Irish Catholic attitudes toward human nature in general.

Although the Irish countryman holds many doctrinal beliefs in common with other Catholics throughout the world, the particular school of thought that dominates the rural Irish church has been called monastic, ascetic, Augustinian, Jansenist, and puritanical (see Sheehy 1968; Hughes 1966; Messenger 1971; Humphreys 1966; Ussher 1949). Clearly the terms simply represent, through various historical phases, the continuity of a penitential version of Christianity—a tradition emphasizing sin, guilt, the innate weakness of human nature, the need for purification and rituals of self-mortification, a distrust of reason, a fear of sex, and a high regard for fasting and sexual abstinence.

The moral education of the infant—born into the disgrace of original sin and believed to possess an innate proclivity toward evil—begins early. A village schoolmaster commented in this regard that even during their first years of life children must learn to control both the senses of the body and the "senses" of the soul. Master Courtney explained that the senses of the soul comprised those "light" or natural passions of the interior: greed, sloth, gluttony, anger, jealousy, and hate. These "fleshy" passions, the sacrament of baptism reduces but does not obliterate. Insofar as the infant symbolizes unmodified impulse, or human nature as yet unrestrained by societal mores, the devoutly religious Irish mother acts as though she were obligated to ignore her baby's wants for sucking, stroking, and rocking and to view these human *needs* as unnecessary *demands*.

The affectionate holding and cuddling of infants is believed by some mothers to contribute to an attitude of self-indulgence in the child, which must be curtailed ("petting *do* ruin the little divils"). Kissing children is considered a "slobbery" Yankee habit. Irish folklore and proverbs criticize the mother who showers too much *toir* (attention, devotion) on her baby. A fear of stimulating or exciting babies is another related theme, and noise, bright lights, loud talk, and bustling activity is interpreted by some as bad for baby's nervous system, and justifies the monotony and inactivity of confinement to pram or crib. One young mother was convinced that her small child did not like to be picked up, and replied with amused surprise when her baby responded with a smile to being stroked, "Why, you'd almost think the little creature likes it."

"Poor critter," said a woman, "to make a little one carry such a load." "What harm?" replied another, "little creatures don't think."
—Overheard at a Tinker Fair

Any suggestion of the possibly detrimental effects of a harsh rearing is quickly dispensed with through recourse to the folk belief that "children have no sense." Toddlers, for example, are believed to have extremely short memories. It is also said that small children are fickle in their affections and attachments. During their three- to four-week confinement in the county hospital for delivery, village mothers sometimes leave their older children in the care of a relative, often without preparing them for the separation. Upon her return with a "surprise package," the mother will often be greeted with either shyness or rejection or both on the part of her older children. On one such occasion I heard a mother comment on her four-year-old's "strange" behavior: "Sure, I'm gone for only a few weeks, and the 'critter' doesn't even remember who I am!" Another mother insisted that her three-year-old daughter never even realized she was gone for the month of confinement because the mother's greatly resembling sister came up from Cork to manage the household during her absence. The mother was certain that a three-year-old hadn't "sense" enough to distinguish between her mother and a strongly resembling aunt. "Children's minds are like jelly," the mother concluded; "they will take to whoever can bribe them with sweets."

Because little sense or reason are attributed to children, deception ("codding the children") is widely used as a means of discipline and control. If she is a "bold" child, the little one is warned that she will be given away to the tinkers, the fairies or to the "boody-man." A little boy begging for a sweet at Nelligan's shop will be told by his mother, "It's against the law to sell sweets on Tuesdays," and Nelligan will nod her head gravely in agreement. A tearful child sitting in the waiting room of Dr. Finley's dispensary is told that "the nice old gent will give you a surprise," when more than likely the surprise is an injection. Finally, Tim Dempsey tells his four young girls that he is only going into town for the day, when in fact he is leaving them for a season of migrant work in Scotland. Parents *do* recognize that such deceptions gradually nibble away at the fragile bond of trust between adult and child, but they try to interpret the consequences positively. One village mother, for example, after being discovered in an extravagant lie to her five-year-old, commented: "Himself and I aren't on very good terms now. I don't suppose he'll get over it for a good long while. But it will toughen him up all right."

If young children are perceived as having no sense and short memories, they are also said to be somewhat impervious to pain. A toddler who falls from a stone boundary is immediately silenced of crying and then praised with a brisk "There's a brave lad (or girl)," and the mother may then comment to an onlooker, "Thank God, they're like rubber; they bounce and feel nothing." In the same spirit, the dispensary doctor does not believe in administering anesthetics before stitching a wound for children under the "age of reason" (about age seven) on the grounds that little children don't feel pain to the same degree as an older child or adult.

▪ Corporal Punishment: The Irish Home as a "Novitiate for Violence"

Off we went, slowly and reluctantly, til we strolled in through the door. I was seized at once by the hair and Mikil the same. The clothes were stripped off us. Blow after blow fell til they had us half dead, and then not a bite nor a sup, but threw us into bed. There was no sleep for us that night for the aches and pains darting through us.
—MAURICE O'SULLIVAN, *Twenty Years A-Growing*

Village parents have been conditioned to expect both immediate obedience and unconditional respect from their children. If either of these parental "rights" is violated, canings or beatings with a strap may follow to enforce the "natural order" of parental dominance. The cardinal sin of early childhood is "boldness," and a *bold* child is, by definition, one who questions the orders that come down to him, who does not do as he or she is told, or who does not demonstrate proper shy and deferential comportment before the elders. One of the few practicing child-psychiatrists in Ireland described the situation as follows:

What ye gonna do wi'
  the baby-o?
What ye gonna do wi'
  the baby-o?
What ye gonna do wi'
  the baby-o?
Wup him good and let
  him go.
—Traditional

> *The family home in Ireland is a novitiate for violence. Even from the cradle the child is made to feel rejection, hostility and open physical pain. The infant is left to cry in his cot because his mother does not want to "give in to him." Later he is smacked with the hand or a stick. He is made to go to bed early. He is not allowed to have his tea. He is put into a room by himself. . . . In order to invite this morale-breaking treatment from his parents all the Irish child has to do is be normal. It's the normality of childhood which sets parents' teeth on edge. They take no joy in childishness. (Daly 1976: 15)*

Beatings are used for both sexes and for all age groups, but the Irish violate a near-universal canon regarding the application of physical punishment. In most societies severe spankings are not considered appropriate for very young children. In Ballybran, however, I was told by the more traditionalist parents that beatings were *most* effective during the supposed pre-reason and pre-memory period of toddlerhood. As one mother of three young boys put it: "You've got to slash them while they're still too young to remember it and hold it against you." In questioning mothers about the age at which physical punishment is first administered, I was given answers spanning a range from as early as six months to as late as a year. One particularly sensitive mother shed tears of remorse as she recalled impulsively striking her six-month-old baby girl who had spit out some oatmeal.

Ironically, few village parents, when questioned, could volunteer any recollections or feelings about their own treatment as very young children, while bachelors and spinsters frequently lashed out with angry words upon recalling old hurts and physical or psychological bruises suffered at the hands of parents and later of teachers. "They broke our spirits, and now look at us — old, timid, and afraid to try anything new. Fear — that's the Golden Rule we were reared by," commented one lonely old bachelor shepherd.

What do I remember about school? Now that's a good one. What I remember is Master O'Grady strutting around the classroom waving his cane, and the rest of us stunned into silence like so many stupid donkeys or thieving cows. Guilty? We were always guilty!
— Villager's Recollection

If the home is a novitiate for violence — the place where children learn, as their parents did before them, to deal harshly with those weaker and more vulnerable than themselves — then the schoolroom is the place where the final lessons are perfected. Corporal punishment is not only allowed in the classroom, it is condoned and *encouraged* in the Church-controlled public schools of the Republic as the very *essence* of an Irish Catholic education. The following defense of corporal punishment in the schools as an inalienable "right" of teachers was made in a recent speech to the Irish Parliament by Richard Burke, then minister of education:

> *If we are to begin to prohibit the use of corporal punishment in the schoolroom, are we then to forbide parents to use corporal punishment in their own homes? That would be absurd and ridiculous, as well as being an indefensible invasion of individual and family privacy (cited by J. Daly in the Irish Times, June 6, 1976: 2).*

The curate of Ballybran, who manages the village school (and himself a gentle and mild-mannered man), has often supported local teachers against those few "bold" parents who have complained of unjust punishment to their children. When questioned, Father Leary replied that teachers have a higher obligation to instill in small children a sense of justice. He concluded:

> Children must be made aware of the presence of some larger force in the world. Call it fear, if you like. But without this fear of punishment, a child will grow up with a sense of being an island and a law unto himself.

The fact that fear is, indeed, a strong sentiment among young children with regard to their elders—schoolteachers in particular—is expressed in the high incidence of school phobias among first-grade children, to be discussed below.

▪ Consequences and Interpretations

Travelers and casual reporters on the Irish country scene frequently wax poetic on the beautiful, shy, and unspoiled Irish children who scatter into bushes and hide behind hayricks at first sighting of a stranger (see Böll 1967). Romantic to the tourist, perhaps, but a perennial problem to the village schoolteachers who must coax at least half a dozen new children at the start of each year into learning to speak above a whisper, if they will speak at all, and somehow less than quaint once it is known that a few of these same children will similarly duck behind a hedgerow with "shyness" at the appearance of their father coming home from the fields or the pub.

Indeed, by the age of two or three, most village children are bashful, obedient, and well-behaved in the presence of adults. They are, by Irish standards, good children. This limited definition of goodness, however, is dependent upon the early repression of many life-sustaining needs and desires. For the most part, Irish toddlers do not seek to be kissed, held, or "petted." They shy away from the physical (for touch is all too often associated with pain) and seek appreciation through words of endearment and, symbolically, from rewards of sweets. The bold or sassy child exists, of course, and although often privately admired for his or her "spunk," his parents are publicly criticized for having been "too soft." The bold child is a deviation from the established norm.

By age four, most village children have learned to be concealing and evasive in their speech. Temper tantrums and "back chat" are severely punished, and angry children soon learn to handle their outrage by withdrawing into what parents refer to as "the sulk." Hiding in the cow-house, locking themselves in the bathroom, or simply refusing to speak to their parents are characteristic childhood responses to hurt and anger in Ballybran, and are a reflection of adult interactional patterns.

In the more remote farm households, where children cannot mix freely with other children because of distance, overprotectiveness, or long-standing feuds between neighboring households, young children spend long hours in private, imaginative play: quietly building stone "cow-houses," fortresses, and even graveyards from pebbles; or wielding a stick while driving imaginary cows home from pasture. Although much lip service is given by parents to the values of "friendliness" and sociability ("we like a child who is a 'good mixer'"), the bonds of familism impose many restraints on childhood friendships, particularly among traditional farm households beyond the central village.

The radical transition from private to public sphere, when the four-year-old enters the village school, often results for the more fragile in emotional trauma. School phobia, for example, is not uncommon in Ballybran, and several parents reported delaying the start, or removing a young child from school because of the occurrence of vomiting, bedwetting, or general nervousness related to separation from home. Recent studies of separation anxieties in schoolchildren have indicated that the difficulty is often related to a lack of basic trust in the parent (see Bowlby 1973: 258–289). If the child's dependency (and "clinging" needs) were not satisfied earlier, the child remains unable to "leave" his mother; his needs for her remain primitive and infantile. However, in the case of young Irish pupils, fear of the teacher (who is often used as a threat at home) is at least as germane to the phobia as separation anxiety. Finally, the necessity of communicating for the first time with strangers and non-kin was clearly a focus of the school fear for some village children. Within this context, it was not altogether surprising that the anxiety is commonly expressed in stuttering, facial tics, or "elective mutism"—simply refusing to speak at all.

In interviewing the parents of children with school phobias, I found that the mothers themselves were often anxious about and suspicious of school in general and teachers in particular. A few mothers suspected teachers of playing favorites with the children from more affluent households; others feared that teachers might try to pry "family secrets" from unsuspecting children. When parents warn their small children not to reveal or discuss any personal or family matters at school, it is little wonder that a few obedient and frightened children should react by refusing to speak at all. Mutism in young children can be seen as yet another example of the socialization of children into characteristically Irish interactional patterns of suspiciousness, evasion, and withdrawal.

▪ Parenting and Schizophrenia

The psychoanalytic literature on the etiology of schizophrenia (Sullivan 1962; Haley 1959; Hill 1955; Jackson 1960) indicates that, in many cases, the disease (although undetected) begins early, possibly within the first six months of life, and that a serious disturbance in the mother-infant relationship is often implicated. It is generally accepted that schizophrenia is a condition in which the person alters his representation of reality in order to escape and withdraw from seemingly unresolvable conflicts and from social interactions that are painful or are reminiscent of earlier painful experiences. The symptoms of schizophrenia include ideas of immaturity, fixation, regression, and of consequent impoverishment of the ego, resulting in failure to live in present reality (Hill 1955: 68–83).

Because the mother-child relationship is suspect in the etiology of the disease, a rather ugly and disparaging term has crept into clinical usage for the mothers of schizophrenics. These women are called "schizophrenogenic mothers" (Lidz, et al. 1958; Eisenberg 1968). The unfortunate term conjures up the image of hysterical, possessed women imbued with discriminating pathogenic powers that destroy the lives of one or more of their children, leaving the others unscathed. "Schizophrenogenic mothers" are described in the literature as obsessive, sexually and emotionally immature, repressed, and guilt ridden. In relationship to their children they are seen as overly protective and extremely possessive and at the same time unconscious and ignoring of their children's expressed needs and demands. They are, in addition, described as excessively preoccupied with controlling their children's sexuality. Interpersonally, schizophrenogenic mothers are seen as mistrusting and fearful of outsiders and secretive. Little attention is given in the psychoanalytic literature to the fathers of schizophrenics, and they are certainly never referred to as "schizophrenogenic." When they are described at all, the fathers are characterized as merely "inadequate," or as weak, ineffectual, passive, dominated by their wives, and often alcoholic.

It has been suggested that the child liable to develop schizophrenia in adulthood would have been conditioned early in life to react to dangers—either real or imaged—by flight. And the particular flight of the schizophrenic takes its form in quiet, passive, somnolent withdrawal into infantile regression and fantasy. Given the self-centered nature of the schizophrenogenic mother (who is also described as a poor reader of nonverbal cues and basic body language), the passive withdrawal of her baby or young child is mistakenly interpreted as a sign of relaxation and contentment, rather than as a signal of distress. Hence, the flight reaction goes unrecognized as a symptom and becomes instead a life-sustaining pattern under the painful circumstances of unresponsive parenting.

This psychoanalytic model, however, is rife with difficulties. The traits ascribed to the "schizophrenogenic" mother are not only sexist with witch-hunting connotations (i.e., "everyone" hates the selfish, domineering, jealously possessive woman—she is "everyone's" negative mother archetype), but many of the same traits can be found in other mothers, who have no schizophrenic children, as well as in a great many men. And it must further be explained why usually only one of the schizophrenogenic mother's children falls prey to the illness, while the others grow up to lead normal, productive adult lives.

Although I am concerned in this and the following chapter with the contributing role of family dynamics in Irish schizophrenia—that is, with the unintentional and "hidden injuries" of parenting—it is not my intention to assign blame for psychosis on the individual "mistakes" of particular parents. For this reason I did not single out the parents of hospitalized adolescents and young adults for study. In addition, the patients selected did *not* reside in Ballybran, but in neighboring parishes of the Dingle Peninsula and elsewhere in southwest Kerry. As an anthropologist, my primary interest is not so much in the individual parent or child as in the *norms* of parenting shared by a culture. I wish, therefore, only to raise the issue of the apparent parallels between the stereotypic "schizophrenogenic" mother and the stereotypic rural Irish mother. I am dealing, obviously, with ideal types, and I realize that there is no more such a person as the "schizophrenogenic" mother than there is the "Irish mother" or the proverbial "Jewish mother." Even in the tiny parish of Ballybran there are *many* ways of being a mother. Some rural mothers are warm, nurturant, and "soft," just as some village children are bold, willful, and spoiled. Nonetheless, the "soft" mother and the "bold" child are viewed and labeled as deviant, and mothers who are *not* hard taskmasters, repressive and denying, feel guilty and worry whether they are hurting their children in the long run. There is, in short, a public village consensus regarding "proper" child rearing against which parents measure their own performance. And it is *this* set of cultural guidelines for parenting (rigidly adhered to by some, in modified form by most, and not at all by a "progressive" minority) that I perceive as possibly laying the foundations for the psychotic episodes of the more psychologically vulnerable children.

Certainly, my psychological testing of both hospitalized and village adolescents indicated that the mother-child relationship tends to be problematic. A mother figure appears on cards, 2, 5, 6BM, 18GF, and one is often written into the script of cards 1 and 3BM (see Appendix A). Village boys were most prone to viewing the mother negatively or ambivalently. In cards 1 and 3BM she is characterized by them as punishing and overly controlling (see Appendix D, table D-3). Card 2, the farm scene, elicited maternal-deprivation themes for village males (tables D-5 and D-6), who described the mother as "selfish," "proud and domineering," "depriving," and "doesn't really care about those around her." Sixteen-year-old Patrick, for example, compared the mother figure in card 2 with the harsh, inhospitable Dingle landscape.

> *This picture reminds me of Ballybran. . . . There are parallels here between the older woman and the scenery. The scene is brutal and stony, with a kind of distant noble approach, very much like the mother. (NM 5)**

Another village boy volunteered the following story:

> *This woman looks bossy and lazy. . . . The mother seems to deprive her [the girl with books] of reading, of her education. They live in the country-side, near the sea. The house seems to deprive them of the view of the sea. Her husband seems to be dead and she is taking a view of all the land she now owns. . . . The mother is very lazy. She tells the son that he's spoiled, that he doesn't work hard enough. She tells the daughter that she's too pampered. The mother doesn't really regard them as a family at all, the way she's looking over them into the distance. (NM8)*

Village girls were more ambivalent in their descriptions of mother figures, and they consistently tried to overcome intruding negative archetypes with positive outcomes. In card 2 the responses were equally divided (5 to 5) between a perception of the mother as hardworking, self-denying, and saintly ("the mother is the soul of fortitude"; "she sacrifices everything to educate her child"; "her worn hands are folded humbly in prayer") and a description of her as depriving, mean, selfish, and rejecting ("the girl has just gotten slaps from the mother"; "the mother takes away the books from her daughter and forces her to work in the fields"; "her parents outcast and reject her"; "the mother is bitter and resentful"). Female responses to card 18GF (older woman apparently strangling a younger woman) were also divided, with the

---

* NM = Normal Male   HM = Hospitalized Male
    NF = Normal Female   HF = Hospitalized Female

mother figure oddly seen as nurturant in six stories ("a picture of Our Lady of Sorrows"), as violent to a child in two stories, and as cruelly indifferent to a sick or injured child in three themes. (The remaining stories were described as husband-wife motifs.)

Among hospitalized youth, schizophrenics were most blocked and unintelligible when responding to cards with a mother figure. There was a definite tendency to distance themselves from the family characters in card 2 by perceiving the figures as unreal: "This is a period painting"; "just a bunch of farmer statues"; "saints in a church"; "she could be a statue of St. Teresa." Far less troubling to look beyond the human figures altogether, as in Peter's response:

> This is a period painting of an agricultural scene. There are a lady and her daughter and a gentleman, not counting the horse, which is an animal. The horse is working very hard. (HM2)

Finally, males and females in all samples portrayed the mother figure in card 6BM as manipulative and guilt-inducing (Appendix D, table D-4), a topic I shall discuss in the following chapter. These test responses correspond with earlier studies of Irish and Irish-American personality. In Bales's survey (1962), 60 percent of his sample of Irish alcoholics viewed their mothers as excessively domineering. And Opler and Singer (1956) found a tendency among Irish-American schizophrenics to react both fearfully and hostilely to mother figures, to attribute little importance to their fathers, and to suffer from feelings of inadequacy, maternal deprivation, and oral fixations. The origin of such negative maternal stereotypes among Irish and Irish Americans may be found in the patterns of child rearing I have just described.

It would seem, for example, that the absence of breast-feeding, the strictures against cuddling and fondling infants, and conflicts surrounding infant feedings might result in a lack of oral and dependency gratification in infancy. The relative isolation of the infant and small child, followed by the traumatic weaning into public life, might result in a predisposition to resolve conflict and handle painful interactions by "flight" (into withdrawal and fantasy) rather than "fight." And the regime of forced quietude, the low tolerance for crying, and the "rewarding" of passivity in small children may result in a predisposition to deny and repress life-sustaining loves, angers, desires, and passions.

That the majority of rural villagers are *invulnerables*—healthy, sane, well-adjusted individuals—despite exposure to a problematic early socialization experience, does not invalidate my discussion. It remains that the rural Irish are inordinately prone to mental illness, especially schizophrenia in adulthood. It is also recognized that not one but many pathogenic factors (biochemical as well as environmental) are necessary for psychosis to erupt. In the next chapter I shall examine socialization at a later age, the period during which the first psychotic episodes may occur: late adolescence and early adulthood. At this point I shall narrow the focus and attempt to answer this difficult question: What differentiates the vulnerable from the invulnerable, not only within the same culture and society, but within the same families?

CHAPTER SIX

"Breeding Breaks Out in the Eye of the Cat"

SEX ROLES, BIRTH ORDER,
AND THE IRISH DOUBLE BIND

I was born on St. Thomas Day in the year 1856. . . . I am the "scraping of the pot," the "last of the litter.". . . I was a spoilt child too . . . and besides that I was an "old cow's calf," not easy to rear. . . . I wore a petticoat of undressed wool . . . until the woman from across the way used to say to my mother every Sunday: "You'll leave the gray petticoat on him till you're looking for a wife for him."
—TOMÁS O'CROHAN,
The Islandman

J I M M Y   H E N N E S Y is a twenty-six-year-old sometime fisherman, butcher's apprentice, and pub entertainer.[1] He is the younger son in a family including two married sisters and a brother who emigrated to America. When he is not in treatment at the county mental hospital, Jimmy lives at home on the outskirts of Dingle with his aged mother and his now retired father, once a migrant construction worker. He both looks after, and is looked after in turn, by the old couple. Jimmy's diagnosis: "psychoneurosis and alcoholism in an immature, dependent personality."

Pacing the corridor of the dreary hospital is a rather boyishly handsome young man who extends a shaky, moist palm in greeting. Yes, he is anxious to talk with me and to take the Thematic Apperception Test. He wants to do *anything*, he says, that might help him. After I correct his impression of me as a clinician, Jimmy launches into a lengthy discussion of himself. He is in the mental hospital ("the madhouse," he calls it wryly) because he suffers from phobias: he is afraid of crowds, water, open spaces, closed spaces, wind and rain storms, and knives. Because of these fears, he cannot hold down a job, and when he is out of work he gets depressed and drinks heavily. His first job at age fourteen was as a butcher's apprentice in Dingle. He was quite successful until he developed a fear of handling the tools of the trade. While hacking away at the carcass of a cow or a sheep, he would at times be haunted by the image of a customer, a friend, or a relative stretched out on the chopping block. When such an uncomfortable thought possessed him, Jimmy would feel faint and sick to his stomach, often having to leave the shop in the midst of waiting on a customer. Finally, he was fired.

Sure, we're crucified by the weather. I trust Him all right with the lightning; I don't think He'd harm us with that. But with the wind . . . who knows what He'd do?
—Village Widow Woman

Jimmy turned next to fishing, a lucrative trade in Dingle, and for a while all went well. He could go out with a small crew all night and even manage to sleep on deck intermittently during North Atlantic storms. Gradually, however, he came to dread the storms and to contemplate the risk involved at sea. As is characteristic for the west of Ireland, neither Jimmy nor any other crew members could swim, but his suggestions that the boat be equipped with life jackets, flares, and a radio were met with scorn and ridicule by the fishermen, who pride themselves on their reliance upon luck, their skill at wind and storm prediction, and Divine Providence. Before long, Jimmy developed a fear of water and a vertigo around boats and piers, which resulted in a second failure.

After a long period of unemployment and bouts with alcoholism, Jimmy took up his childhood skill at fiddle playing and gradually established a reputation for himself, playing in pubs and dancehalls throughout southwest Kerry. However, a fear of crowds soon developed—Jimmy imagined the amiable groups turning violent and ganging up on him—which resulted in yet a third failure. A severe depression followed and Jimmy went to see his local doctor, who dismissed the symptoms as a "case of bad nerves" and prescribed a year's supply of Valium. Jimmy soon discovered that he was becoming addicted to the drug, taking increased amounts by day, and continuing to drink heavily at night. Finally, he went to the Dingle psychiatric clinic where, after a period of unsuccessful treatment, he asked if he could be taken into the mental hospital. Jimmy considers his plea for asylum the most courageous and independent step he has ever taken: his mother did not approve.

Concerning his home life, Jimmy is less communicative. He volunteers that he was reared almost exclusively by his domineering mother with some help from an older sister. His father, a "quiet and solitary man," spent half of every year working abroad. The father was a distant, shadowy figure, and Jimmy attributes his own "weak character" to his having been reared by women. In addition to scorn for his personality, Jimmy expresses contempt for his "pudgy, fleshy" physique, and feels that if his body were more lean and muscular he could better withstand his illness. In fact, Jimmy, although not tall and lean in the characteristic Kerryman fashion, is sturdy and quite muscular.

In his relationships with women Jimmy follows a familiar pattern: initial success followed by a failure to carry through. He has had sexual relations with a woman several years his senior, but each time he found sex unsatisfying, and he suffered from religious scruples afterwards. Jimmy's mother is an overly protective woman who has resisted her son's attempts to work, on the grounds that he is physically frail (which he clearly is not), and has interfered with his attempts at courting local women, on the grounds that they are his social inferiors (which they clearly are not). The fact that Jimmy gives credence to these "myths" about himself is symptomatic of his illness.

Jimmy's responses to the Thematic Apperception Test (see Appendix C) illustrate the conflicts and anxieties of a young man who perceives himself as a child (3BM; 6BM); as a helpless, disinterested pawn who is passed among the significant women in his life (2); as a weak innocent who is easily corrupted by shady, male characters (7BM; 9BM); as a person who naturally expects help and consolation from women (4), while resenting the influence they wield over his life (6BM); and as a repressed person who cannot quite convince himself that sex isn't shameful (5; 13MF).

Although I never had occasion to meet him, Jimmy's older brother, Robert, is the success story of the family and one of several in the locality. According to Jimmy, Robert is his parents' pride and joy, a successful New York City construction worker, married to a Yankee woman, and the father of four children. Remittance money comes home faithfully each month from America, and the brother's enlarged photo is enshrined over the mantelpiece in the front kitchen—a constant reminder to Jimmy of his own inadequacy. For while Robert's is a success story, Jimmy's is one of humiliation and repeated failure. And where Robert is "the pet," Jimmy is the family's *aindeiseoir*, their awkward, miserable, incompetent "leftover" son—one of many like him in the community. Yet, both Robert and Jimmy were born into the same household and parish, and both were reared by the same overbearing mother and absentee father. During adolescence each had to confront the same set of limited alternatives: whether to emigrate and try to "make good" elsewhere, or whether to stay behind and prove "loyal" to mother and motherland.

There are many "Jimmys" in Ballybran among the more than thirty still young, often lastborn sons, bachelors who stayed home to inherit the farm or take care of a widowed mother or complete a village fishing crew. And there are many firstborn "Roberts" who write home flamboyant letters of financial and amorous successes gained in America, Canada, or England. Obviously, not all the stay-at-home bachelors and farm heirs are as unhappy or neurotic as Jimmy Hennesy, but many share with him the perception of themselves as leftovers and incompetents, at best good enough for Ballybran—a place generally thought of today as not very good at all.

In this chapter I shall describe differences in the socialization experiences of the "Jimmys" and "Roberts" and their sisters in terms of the basic economic and psychological strategies of today's farm families, themselves caught in a terrific bind. The economic strategy revolves around the selection of a male heir, while the related psychological strategy concerns the apparent need of many rural families to create a scapegoat, a vulnerable member—be he the alcoholic black sheep or the painfully shy, frightened, and sometimes mentally ill bachelor son.

The process I am about to describe—through which parents' professed beliefs in the innate strengths or weaknesses, superiority or inferiority, of one child over another become accepted by the child himself and then by the community at large—has reference to "labeling theory" (see Becker 1973; Scheff 1966; Goffman 1963) and to what Antonio Ferreira calls the dynamics of "family myths" (1963, 1965, 1966, 1967). In addition, that aspect of the same process whereby the rural male adolescent is offered a choice between two equally unsatisfactory alternatives (indeed, at times two conflicting role demands) is reminiscent of the type of human dilemma that Bateson, et al. (1956) coined the "double bind."

Where in the previous chapter I suggested that the cultural norms of early child rearing in Ballybran may contain some psychologically harmful elements in general, here I shall demonstrate the particular effect of *sex* and *birth order* on the quality of the child's socialization experiences—especially during the critical period of decision making and identity formation in late adolescence and early adulthood. The dynamics of rural Irish socialization, I conclude, is weighted in favor of the mental health of daughters and earlier-born sons, and against the chances of healthy ego integration of later-born sons in large and traditional farm families. The data on sex and mental illness in the Republic strongly support this hypothesis, as there are nearly twice as many male as female psychiatric patients for the age group twenty-five to forty-four (O'Hare and Walsh 1974: 27). Unfortunately, there are no official statistics on mental illness and birth order in the Irish Psychiatric Hospital Censuses. However, of the twenty-two young psychiatric patients I interviewed, the majority fell, like Jimmy, at the latter end of the birth-order spectrum (tables 18, 19).

The question of the relationship between birth order and mental illness (especially schizophrenia) has been controversial. Data on the subject have been so mixed that some social scientists (Altus 1966; Erlenmeyer-Kimbling, et al. 1969) have dismissed the evidence as contradictory. Samples conducted in the United States (Schooler 1961; Farina, Barry, and Garmezy 1963), Canada (Smith and McIntyre 1963; Gregory 1959), and England (Granville-Grossman 1966) demonstrated a tendency for schizophrenic patients to be overly represented in last or later birth-order positions. By contrast, samples drawn from India (Sundararaj and Rao 1966), China (H. B. M. Murphy 1959), and Japan (Caudill 1964) evidenced a majority of firstborn or earlier-born schizophrenic patients. From a cultural perspective, it appears likely that what is being dramatized is the impact of differential social and environmental stresses on family members. Barry and Barry (1967), for

AGE	OCCUPATION	PERIOD OF EMIGRATION	DIAGNOSIS	BIRTH ORDER	MARITAL STATUS
20	Farming	No	Schizophrenia	Youngest in family of five	S
24	Farm labor	No data	Paranoid psychosis	No data	S
34	Farmer	No data	Schizophrenia	Third in family of four; youngest emigrated	S
26	Construction	No data	Hypomania in dependent personality	No data	S
29	Farming	No	Alcoholism in immature personality	Youngest; two older sisters	S
25	Farm labor	No	Schizo-affective	Fifth in family of six	S
36	Farmer	Yes	Schizophrenia	Youngest of two sons	S
23	Construction	Yes	Psychopath with possible schizophrenia	Orphan, raised with older cousins	S
28	Fisherman	No	Psychoneurosis/ dependent personality	Youngest son; two older sisters, one older brother	S
21	Labor	No	Alcoholism/ personality disorder	Middle child in large family	S
35	Farmer	No	Schizophrenia	Fourth in family of seven, but youngest son	S

AGE	OCCUPATION	PERIOD OF EMIGRATION	DIAGNOSIS	BIRTH ORDER	MARITAL STATUS
17	Student	No data	Personality disorder	No data	S
27	Housewife	No data	Puerperal paranoid psychosis	No data	M
27	Domestic	Yes	Endogenous depression	Second eldest in family of six	S
18	At home	No	Schizophrenia	Youngest, family of three	S
19	At home	No data	Reactive depression	No data	S
25	Domestic	Yes	Endogenous depression	Middle child	S
16	Student	No	Personality disorder	Orphan, no data	S
15	Student	No	Alcoholism/ personality disorder	Sixth child in family of nine	S
19	Worked in pub	Yes	Schizophrenia	Second youngest in large family	S
32	Farmer's wife	Yes	Reactive depression	No data	M
16	Student	No	Paranoid psychosis	Youngest child	S

example, suggest that later-born members of American families may be suffering from parental rejection and powerful competitive pressures. Caudill (1964) concludes that the unusually burdensome responsibilities of being a firstborn son in Japanese families may account for the vulnerability of this group. In the following discussion, I shall add another cultural case study to the literature on birth order and mental illness.

▪ *Naduir* and *Dutcas:*
A Folk Taxonomy of Personality Development

Although village parents strive to correct their children and instill in them proper comportment ("beware of the habit you give them"), the "characters" of individual children—their personalities, talents, abilities, and natures—are held to be largely predetermined by birth and inheritance. *Briseann an dutcas tri shuilibh an chait*—breeding breaks out in the eye of the cat—is a common proverbial explanation of good or bad character in a village child. Another proverb, *Is treise dutcas na oileamaint*—what a child inherits is stronger than how he is raised—releases parents from some of the responsibility for the ways in which their children develop. Hence, when villagers comment on how clever the engineer son of "Timmy-Post" turned out, they attribute little to the son's enlightened home environment and literally think of the adult as "turning out" in much the same way a loaf of bread rises, given its innate proportions and quality of yeast, flour, milk, and salt. And when Ellen, the mother of two particularly unruly little boys, throws her hands up in despair and says, " 'Tis no use, the more I kill them, the worse they be. They're too full of their father's *dutcas*," she expresses the belief that nature holds sway over nurture. Parental influence is seen largely in the negative, as it is believed that *too much* love, freedom, and indulgence can spoil a child with perfectly good *dutcas*.

Dutcas, translated as blood, "history," stock, or breeding, is the sum total of the physical and moral attributes an individual inherits from his paternal ancestors. It is associated with the family name, and whole family trees often become characterized by a single *dutcas*, which can be for good or ill. So it is said, for example, that "the O'Connors are a family of saints," "those Doyles are worldly," "there was never a Moriarty didn't have the heart of a mouse." Similarly, every trade, skill, or talent has its unparalleled master in the village, and these supposedly inherited traits are passed down from father to son, such that the Sheas are the village storytellers, the O'Malleys the village poets; from the Murphys have come a line of priests and nuns, from the O'Reillys a line of poachers and publicans; the Kanes are noted at wind prediction, and the O'Keefes are best for calling sheep. It's in their *dutcas*.

Like genes, *dutcas* can lie dormant for many generations, but will eventually (like the breeding of the cat) "break out" in progeny. Hence, a thieving child does not stand alone in his shame; the sin casts a pall over his whole "history," and it is said that he is surely a throwback to a semimythological ancestor with the same bad blood. It sometimes happens that siblings inherit their *dutcas* from different paternal ancestors, with Sean taking after thrifty grandfather Euge, and Paddy taking after idle Uncle Morris. Used in this sense, *dutcas* can be called upon to explain the apparent success of one child (like Robert) in contrast to the hopelessness of another (like Jimmy). There can be a damningly deterministic quality to *dutcas*, and just as it is said to be a cat's instinct to kill a mouse (*Is e dutcas an cait a luc do masbugad*), it is said of some children that they are fundamentally bad: "*Tá an droch-dutcas ann*," a bad seed. Hence, a shopkeeper disciplines a bold McCarthy child and comments, "It will do no good; his whole history is bad, his people from way back were ever the same." Although fathers are normally held responsible for passing on the blood of their ancestors, bad blood can also result from a particularly infelicitous marriage. Most villagers agree that bad *dutcas* can be predicted in at least some of the children born of a first-cousin marriage; a Protestant-Catholic union; an old mother (i.e., "the old cow's calf"); an unmarried mother; a mentally ill parent on either side.

A second quality of inherited personality, *naduir*, or nature, comes to the child through the matriline. It was translated to mean kindness, *naturalness*, warmth, sensitivity, and above all, strong feelings for, or attachment to, one's own kindred (as in the saying *Bi an naduir riam ann*—he was always loving to his own people). Children are believed to be born with a fixed capacity for *naduir*, which (in the days when breast-feeding was still common) was believed to be transmitted through the mother's milk. Like equals like, and mother's milk produced in the suckling "the milk of human kindness," *naduir*. Today, it is said that *naduir*, or "softness," in an individual is the result of an overly protecting, doting mother. The association between *naduir* and "womanly" traits is underscored by the secondary meaning of the word: the generative organs of women.

Interestingly, boys are believed to inherit more *naduir* than girls—a result of the greater attention and devotion that mothers are expected to lavish on their infant sons, including (in past generations) a generally longer nursing period. The presumed "softness" of their sons is a quality that many rural mothers play upon in order to bind at least one son to themselves and to the land. However, the term can also carry connotations of pity or scorn, as when it is used to describe an overly obedient or good-natured son (or, less frequently, daughter), as in these expressions: "He's a *natural*, good-hearted slob of a boy," or *"Is nadurta an ruidin i"* — "What a pitiful, affectionate poor creature she is." The frequently diagnosed "immature" or "dependent" personality traits among young male psychiatric patients in Kerry are, I am convinced, a result of the overprotection of sons, justified by the concept of *naduir*, which I am about to describe.

▪ Differential Treatment of the Sexes

Traditionally, and to this day, boys are more valued than girls in rural Irish society. Daughters, after all, would grow up into the "traitors" who would marry into an enemy camp, and whose children would carry the *dutcas* of a different patriline. Sons assure the continuity of family name, lands, and ancestral stock.

In the days when villagers still gave credence to such "old *piseogas*," infant sons were believed to be greatly desired by the fairies as well as envied by neighbors, whereas girl babies were seen as having little fascination for either. Therefore, great precautions were taken to protect male infants: bits of coal or iron (invested with magical properties in Eire from pre-Christian times), or tongs opened in the sign of the cross, were kept in the boy's cradle; red ribbons were tied across his bed; or red thread was sewn covertly into the infant's underwear. Holy water was (and still is) sprinkled over the child liberally. To assure that the boy baby would not be abducted by the "little people," a mother was cautioned never to leave her son alone prior to his baptism — a bit of folk wisdom that would be of great service today.

Girl babies, however, received no such attention. In fact, the greatest protection against harm to an infant son was for the parents to trick the fairies into believing that their newborn was a girl. Even as late as the 1940s it was customary in Ballybran for boys and girls to be dressed alike until school age in the gray woolen petticoat called the "baneen." Séan O'Súilleabháin (personal communication) remembers meeting adolescent boys on the Dingle Peninsula as old as fourteen and fifteen and still dressed like girls. And village grandmothers told me that girls' pseudonyms were sometimes given to boy infants until their baptism.

By virtue of their *naduir*, boy babies are considered more delicate and less "thriving" than little girls. Mothers unselfconsciously defend their preferential treatment of sons (i.e., allowing them more sweets, punishing them less harshly, demanding less cooperation and fewer chores), saying that little boys *need* more attention and comforts than little girls do, that they are hurt more easily and are more prone to illness. In addition, boys are said to be, by nature, more demanding of their mothers—cravings during pregnancy, for example, come more often from boy than from girl babies. The folk belief in the innate physical stamina of girl over boy babies is even reflected in the medical practice of Dr. Finley, for the old doctor will inoculate little girls, but has refused at times to "take such a risk" where the child was an only son.

One result of the overprotection of sons—or rather of the underprotection of daughters—is the differential childhood mortality rate for the sexes as recorded in the parish death registry. Of the seventeen childhood deaths (one month to ten years) recorded for the years 1928–1969, ten of the deaths were of girls, and these fall heavily into the accident over illness categories.[2] The fact that only boy children were listed as having died of "ill health" or were recorded under the folk category "delicate" implies a willingness to impute physical fragility to the male sex in childhood.

Village parents also distinguish gross personality differences between boys and girls. Whereas girls are perceived as "catty, sharp, and underhanded," little boys are often described as helpless, innocent, and guileless ("like jelly," one mother offered).

Daughters are said to be more resistant to and questioning of parental authority than boys are, and overall, girls are said to be "harder to raise." When I asked Kate how she would characterize the personality differences between her school-aged son and daughter, born one year apart, she replied, "Sheila could take Timmy to Dingle Fair and sell him without the poor 'boyeen' being any the wiser."

CAUSE OF DEATH	SEX	AGE
Accident (unspecified)	F	4 years
	F	2 years
Burst appendix	F	2 years
	M	3 years
Burned	F	18 months
"Chin cough" (whooping cough)	M	4 months
	F	6 months
"Delicate"/ill health	M	1 month
	M	2 years
	M	5 years
	M	6 months
Drowned	F	4 years
Hit by horse/hit by car	F	3 years
	F	6 years
"Sudden"	F	1 month
	M	3 months
	F	2 years

Source: St. Brendan Church, Parish Death Registry

Because sisters are believed to be more *crabbit* (bold) and "cute" (sly), they are expected to watch over their brothers and take care of their wants and needs. And where little girls as young as five and six are expected to take responsibility for real chores around the house and garden and are frequently sent out to run errands and gather gossip for their mothers, little boys of the same age are assigned only make-believe tasks. The whole family smiles indulgently as little Rory, for example, pretends to drive the cows home with a tiny stick behind Daddy, who wields the real switch. "Isn't he ever the little man?" a mother will ask in mocking jest. On one such occasion the five-year-old, realizing he was being ridiculed, flew into a rage at his mother, directing at her decidedly adult abusive language. All to no avail, however, as the mother laughed at his "innocent roguery."

By the age of puberty, village girls have learned the womanly arts of child tending, housekeeping, and bread making as well as the social graces necessary for mixing with strangers: neighbors, clergy, and shopkeepers. By contrast, adolescent boys have had only sporadic contact with the agricultural and herding work of their fathers, and little introduction to the wider adult male social spheres of pub, cattle market, and fireside visits. The farmer's workday is usually over by the time his sons come home from school. And even during summertime, when agricultural activity is at its peak, discouraged and dispirited farmers will often allow their sons to idle away hours at the shops or crossroads, rather than let the young "scholars" dirty their hands at the lowly chores of turf collecting and haymaking. While some village fathers complain that the new secondary-school in the parish has turned their sons away from traditional work and values, others are all too ready to concede: "But sure, 'tis better after all; this is no life for them."

With the demise of traditional family farming and its values, the rural Irish father is no longer the regal paterfamilias once described in the literature (see Arensberg 1937; Humphreys 1966). Today he is, like the patriarchal culture he represents, a broken figure. At best, he is humanely tolerated; at worst, he is openly ridiculed by his wife and adult children. The shadowy, invisible presence of the rural father was brought home to me during an evening visit with Teresa, Brian, and their teenaged son and daughter. While the adolescents and their mother conversed animatedly with my husband and me, old Brian stood off alone in a corner of the kitchen. It grew dark, and as the evening shadows began to cast themselves on the walls, my four-year-old was startled to see

My father, after a few kingly turns back and forth the floor, to show everybody that he was lord and master in his own home, left, as was usual with him, the tinker to my mother's care, and . . . stepped out and glanced hastily up and down the road, looking for new worlds to conquer. I, a boy of ten, stood by the wall, admiring his greatness.
—PAT MULLEN,
Come Another Day

the dark, nearly motionless figure of Brian. She hadn't noticed him earlier. "Mummy, who *is* that man?" asked Jenny fearfully. This was met with a long pause, followed by a stifled giggle from Teresa and her daughter. It was left for me to say, with great embarrassment, "That's Kathleen's Papa." Later in the evening, when Teresa began to belittle her husband for his careless dress and appearance, the old man responded by picking up his goatskin drum and beating out a tune—at first melancholy and then fierce and warlike. Such was his release. But never a word spoken.

Divested of his authority and without compensatory dignity through wealth or education, the rural father no longer presents himself as a strong and adequate role-model for his adolescent and young adult sons—that is, once he can no longer beat them into at least the semblance of compliance. Such is not the case for daughters; they, for the most part, perceive their mothers as either strong-willed and depriving or alternatively as saintly and long-suffering, but always as adequate figures (see contrasting images of the mother and father in TAT responses: appendix D, table D-5).

In short, it would be accurate to say that girls grow up in Ballybran with a greater sense of responsibility, competence, and independence and, correspondingly, with a greater sense of self-esteem than their brothers. Their greater sense of autonomy prepares village girls for early emigration from the village and allows them to feel less guilty about severing ties with the old people. By contrast, young boys are socialized into feelings of personal inadequacy and hostile dependency upon the parents. Such differences are again reflected in the marked contrast of attitude between the sexes toward achievement, competence, and responsibility in the TAT responses.

ACHIEVEMENT

Card 1 (boy and violin) generally elicits achievement and competence themes in most cultures. In the Irish sample, more than half of the twenty-two village girls (all but three of whom were contemplating emigration) told positive achievement stories to this card—themes in which they set out, often in the path of difficult obstacles, to accomplish set goals. By contrast, eight of the fourteen village boys (two-thirds of whom were potential farm heirs) and five of the eleven male psychiatric patients told stories with themes of negative achievement in which they withdrew from social goals, felt bored, sleepy, or otherwise disinterested in the task before them (see Appendix D, table D-1). Eighteen-year-old Peig says, "The boy is thinking, I'll be rich and popular, and the greatest violinist in the world" (NF7), while sixteen-year-old Paddy volunteers, "This one is either bored at his work, or he doesn't understand the lesson he has gotten, or he might be giving himself a little rest" (NM4). Disinterest, sleepiness, and boredom were also frequently referred to by adolescent males in other of the TAT cards: 2, 3BM, and 9BM. The man in the sexually suggestive bedroom scene of card 13MF is described as yawning or "feeling sleepy" in 10 percent of village boys' responses and in none of the girls' stories. It is possible that sleep and boredom may function as defenses against Irish males' repressed and threatening drives for achievement as well as sexuality. Subsequent TAT themes indicate at least two underlying psychological explanations for the low achievement motivation of rural boys: inhibiting and selective guilt, from which rural girls are largely exempt, and feelings of personal inadequacy.

COMPETENCE/INADEQUACY
Village lads are doubtful of themselves to the extent that thirteen of the fourteen told stories to card 1 expressing failure, feelings of incompetence or inadequacy, mediated or resolved by dependency (sometimes hostile) on parents or other authority figures (see Appendix D, table D-2). Not only are fiddles broken and out of tune in the male themes, but in a quarter of their responses the protagonist cannot fix the instrument without looking or crying for help. Although village girls are also concerned about their abilities (55% of their stories to card 1 raised the issue of competence), they are almost twice as likely (64% to 36%) as village boys to have the youth resolve his self-doubts and go on to succeed.

Sexual differences regarding competence also emerged in responses to cards 2 and 6BM. Card 2 (farm family scene) evoked emigration themes for all four samples, but where half the average and hospitalized girls told stories in which the girl or boy in the picture decides to "give it a try" beyond the village, males more often (24%) expressed the conviction that fate or low aptitude had destined the youth to life on the farm. Example:

This family has a small farm. The girl wants to escape this life through education. The mother is proud and domineering. The father is simple and hardworking. The son is like the father. He would like to escape, but from the looks of the picture he's not a very brainy lad. So, he has no choice. He'll just be a farmer for the rest of his days. (NM 13)

The low self-esteem characteristic of young Irish males is related to the pattern of vicious ridicule and "cutting down to size" of their sons by rural mothers, which I shall discuss at length further on. Card 6BM, for example (mother-son scene), evoked a number of stories from both male samples (36% normals; 20% disturbed) in which a mother chastizes her son for turning out a failure, or alternatively in which the son apologizes to the mother for being a hopeless incompetent in school, in business, or during a brief period of attempted emigration. The first extract is from a hospitalized male, the second from a village lad:

He's just after coming home from someplace. He's just told his mother that he's had bad luck in a job; he's been fired again. She is very disappointed in him. . . . Now he has to come home to live again. She is saying that he is a failure. (How old is he?) Forty-one. (His future?) Not much. (HM4)

This lady looks like his mother. He's after confessing some tragedy, and he's worried all right. She looks out the window into nothingness. Is there any hope left? She thinks that this is the end—if he failed once, he will always fail in life. (NM2)

Such incompetence themes were noticeably absent in the stories of village girls, who were more concerned with rebelling against the parental control implicit in this and other TAT cards.

CONTROL: AUTONOMY VERSUS DEPENDENCY

Parental coercion emerged as a dominant theme for the Irish youth in responding to cards 1, 3BM, and 6BM; but where village girls told stories in which the young protagonist questions or confronts authority, village boys were more externally conforming in their themes while often locked into silent and seething resentment (Appendix D, table D-3). The passivity and conformity of the males' responses to card 1 can be contrasted with the rebelliousness of the girls, five of whom told stories in which they actively threw the violin down or broke it in anger or walked out on the tedious lesson. There is a vitality to the girls' stories almost totally lacking in the boys'. Contrast Anna's story:

> *He's fed up and feels like breaking the old fiddle now. He's gotten no good out of it, and he throws it down and says, "the hell with it." Then he goes out to have a "craic" with the other lads (NF8)*

with Peter's story:

> *It seems to me that this boy was sent to do his violin practice which he doesn't like. . . . I don't think he likes music much and he's in a sulk. (Outcome?) He'll get bored and then fall asleep on the violin. (NM3)*

Physical punishment themes were equally high in the responses of village boys and girls to card 3BM (boy huddled against a couch). But where the latter resolve the physical or psychological abuse within the home through running away (41% of their themes), or in a verbal outlash against the punishing parent (9%), male adolescents resolved the conflict by having the youthful protagonist sulk in his room (28%). Themes of self-pity and threatened suicide were also more prevalent in male than in female responses to this card (20%, 6%).

The differential responses of the sexes to parental control is nowhere more dramatic, however, than in the mother-son card, 6BM. Roughly, 70 percent of *all* the stories collected for this card concern a conflict of interest between the generations regarding the son's intended emigration or his choice of a profession or marriage partner. But where village girls tell stories in which the son asserts himself against the mother (36% girls, 14% village boys), both village and hospitalized males tended to tell stories in which the son ultimately bends to the mother's wishes (64% NM; 30% HM; *no* such stories for either female sample). The following are illustrative:

> Village girl: *This is a widow woman and her son. She had many fine plans for him when he finished school: he would be a doctor. How can he tell his mother? He wants to be a priest and not a doctor. She is taking the news very bad. She refuses . . . but the boy insists, and in the end he becomes a priest, and the mother learns to accept it. (NF20)*

> Village male: *Mother and child problem. He's obviously told her something that upset her. Maybe he wants to marry somebody not to her liking. . . . He doesn't seem to be rather determined. He's rather shy. . . . It could be that his mother could easily influence him, domineering. . . . So she could decide the whole factor. She could really make up his mind for him. (HM4)*

However passive and conforming to authority figures adolescent male stories are on the surface, a certain amount of suppressed rage and rebelliousness does break through in antiauthoritarian fantasies. Prison breaks and mental hospital escapes are a favorite theme on card 17BM for males (but not for females), and "accidental" patricide is the subject of seven of thirteen male responses to card 8BM (surgical scene).

RESPONSIBILITY/GUILT THEMES

If physical punishment were the only form of social control used within the Irish home, one might be led to expect a rather superficial internalization of social responsibility and moral standards among the Irish youth. But such is not the case, for Irish children are not only physically beaten, they are also psychologically "walloped" by the continual reminder of sin and eternal damnation as well as through the equation of human motherhood with the divine motherhood of Mary. As a toddler, the Irish child is cautioned, "Don't do that; it will make Holy Mary cry." As an adolescent, the child is told, "Don't do that; it will break your poor mother's heart." The powers of folk Catholicism and Irish motherhood reinforce each other to the extent that one village mother complained that when Pope John "dethroned" Mary he had abandoned the Irish mother as well. With the Immaculate (and bleeding) Heart of Mary as their role model, Irish mothers are artists in the guilt-inducing techniques of moral masochism, and the old woman wields control over the lives of her children (especially her sons) long after they can be effectively beaten with a cane. The results of this influence can be witnessed in the Irish youths' overly developed sense of conscience (Appendix D, table D-4).

Although the tendency to guilt feelings is free floating and runs through all the TAT responses, three situations seem to be particularly guilt-provoking: all aspects of sexual behavior; failure to live up to mother's expectations (i.e., the failure and incompetency themes); and, to be discussed here, negligence with regard to the "old people." A double-binding quality to Irish guilt can be seen in the emigration stories given to cards 2 and 6BM in which the protagonist is frequently pictured as agonizing over his desire to leave home versus his obligations to care for his aged parents. Parental expectations differ for girls and boys, and although village girls are susceptible to some of the same guilt feelings, it is the village boys who accept the brunt of the burden, and who suffer most under the impossible task of reconciling conflicting role demands. This can be seen in comparing the attitudes of the sexes to the frequently perceived "parting scene" in card 6BM. That this scene is interpreted as melodramatic by village girls as well as by boys is revealed in the stock response of the mother to the news of her son's intended emigration: shocked silence, as in the following examples from each group:

The old woman turns pale and stares out the window, speechless. (NM10)

She doesn't cry or say anything. (NF13)

. . . and as he tells her, she looks out the window and tries not to listen to the words. (NM14)

The woman looks out the window to her environment for comfort. (HF5)

His poor mother is heartbroken and turns away to hide her grief. (HM9)

When she is not totally silent, the mother threatens to withhold love, her blessing, or, ultimately, communication:

The mother refuses to say goodbye or to give her blessing to her son, who feels very sad. (NF 16)

His mother is so angry and disappointed in him, that when he goes away, he never hears from her again. (NM19)

Yet, despite these sentiments, village girls are less in conflict about choosing between what they want to do (leave home) and what they feel they *ought* to do (take care of parents) than are village boys. The girls can imaginatively enact the final parting scene with all its conflicting emotions and still accept the parting as inevitable:

This man and his mother must part. . . . She is sad but she accepts her son as a man, free of her. She doesn't cry or say anything because that would only stop him from going, and she knows that what he is doing is only right. (NF13)

And whereas the village girls' emigration themes all conclude with the son leaving home, half the male emigration stories have outcomes in which the mother's grief or disapproval deters the son from leaving (Appendix D, tables D-3, D-4). A common sequence in the male stories is that of a son who leaves home only to learn that a parent had fallen sick or died during his absence. The guilt-stricken son invariably returns to look after the remaining parent and vows never to leave home again.

Village girls tend to justify emigration from home on the basis of imputed social or economic deprivations suffered (Appendix D, table D-5). Fourteen of twenty-two village girls and four of the eleven female psychiatric patients told deprivation stories to card 2 (family farm scene), which are resolved through escape from the countryside. Whereas both the average and the "disturbed" girls described the rural scene in card 2 as "a small bit of mountain end," "a poor farm in the outback," or a "miserable piece of rocky land" (realistic assessments of farming in economically depressed County Kerry), village boys were given to romanticizing the rural scene, calling the farmers "rich and prosperous" or saying they are "doing all they can to make their farm a civilized environment." The eleven male psychiatric patients, however, sided with the women, and none of these told stories on card 2 with "pastoral ideal" motifs; five told social or economic deprivation stories, which were resolved, however, in *resignation* rather than *emigration*. In all, what is being illustrated is the end result of the differential socialization experience for rural male farm heirs and their upwardly and outwardly mobile sisters. Not all the sons in the rural family, however, are reared in the same fashion, and an equally important distinction as that between sons and daughters separates the treatment of the family's "whiteheaded boy," their pet son, from the scapegoated *iarlais* and *aindeiseoir*—the hopelessly incompetent, "leftover" son.

▪ Pets, Black Sheep, and Leftovers: The Socialization of Family Myths

And why shouldn't I make a difference? Is there anyone living who'd stand up on the floor and say that Denis isn't smarter and cleverer than his two younger brothers—or his sisters either—or the whole menagerie of the Geoghegans lumped together? From the day he was born I knew he was different. . . . 'Twas like a miracle, a boy to come after those two lumps of girls. He was a lovely child.
—LENOX ROBINSON, *The Whiteheaded Boy*

If Gregory Bateson (1956, 1963) and his student R. D. Laing have made one great contribution to psychiatry, it is in their shared perception that madness is often not only the condition of an individual but that of a whole family. Laing suggests, for example (1969), that the more he is involved with the families of identified psychotics, the more hard pressed he is to say exactly who is sick.

Laing, Bateson, and their followers have moved the focus of psychiatry away from a consideration of the *intrapsychic* to a consideration of the interpersonal; away from the individual to a diagnosis of the family. In this context, madness is seen as the product of a skewed communication system shared by all members of a disturbed family (see Jules Henry 1965; Mishler and Waxler 1968).

Elaborating on this theme, Antonio Ferreira has suggested a particular model for studying the interpersonal nature of psychotic behavior, which he calls "family myths." It is a model that has particular applicability to rural Irish family dynamics. Ferreira refers to family myths as

> *a series of well-integrated beliefs shared by all family members concerning each other and their mutual position in the family life, beliefs that go unchallenged by everyone involved in spite of the reality distortions which they may conspicuously imply. . . . In terms of the family's "inner image," the family myth refers to the identified roles of its members. (1963: 475)*

Family myths, then, refer to the "inner image" of the group (to be distinguished from the social façade, or "front," that families try to present to outsiders) and are represented in the covert rules of relationship between members that establish patterns of dominance, subordination, equality, and inequality. Ferreira is particularly concerned, however, with the psychotic content that such myths can have, and in his case studies he concentrates on disturbed families in which the homeostasis of the group seems to hinge upon shared, often fictional, beliefs in the sickness or psychosis of one family member. Within this paradigm, schizophrenia is seen, not as a disease, but rather as a desperate strategy adopted by a family in trouble. The complex web of emotional transactions and communications between family members is a self-regulating system; when the internal pressures mount and threaten to blow the family apart, one member (usually a child) tacitly agrees to become "mentally ill." He is the family scapegoat, and by locating the disorder in him, the other members can preserve the illusion of normalcy for themselves. By taking on the sins of the family, so to speak, he releases them from guilt.

Family dynamics in Ballybran fairly reek with "family myths," for labeling, scapegoating, and blaming appear to be an integral part of Irish personality structure. What most differentiates the "normal" from the "disturbed" young villager, I contend, is the ability of the former to project evil and blame outwards, and the tendency of the latter toward self-blame and paralyzing guilt. In my observations of Irish family dynamics I became interested not only in the apparent labeling of psychotic family members, but also in the broader pattern of mythmaking whereby each family in the village seemed to have its successful, high achieving (usually firstborn) "pet son" as well as its black sheep alcoholic, or its shy, incompetent (often lastborn) bachelor son. That these statuses occur with almost patterned regularity and have reference to birth order leads me to believe that the underlying dynamic is one of social role allocation, given the scarce resources of the rural west. The creation of fixed statuses from the cradle allows for the fulfillment of village parents' conflicting aspirations for achievement in, as well as for service from, their children.

Irish mothers are divided, like Gaul, into three parts. One group want their sons to be "lovely priests"; the second want them to be a comfort and support to them in their old age; and the third want their sons to get cracking about the business of turning them into grandmothers.
The Saint Crohane's Letters, Irish Times, February 7, 1974

The main problem faced by the parents of Ballybran today is one of social and cultural continuity—how to deter at least one son from leaving the village so that the name and the lands of the Murphys or the Fitzgeralds will not be wiped from the Dingle Peninsula. In the days when farming was still a valued lifestyle, Arensberg (1937) described a lively family life in which the patriarchal father delayed retirement and set son against son in competition for his favor and eventual inheritance of the land. The intervening years have given way to a new system of land transfer governed by the principle of elimination—that is, last one to escape (usually the youngest son) gets stuck by default with the land and saddled with a life of almost certain celibacy and self-negating service to the old people. The transfer of obligation for aged parents from married to permanently single children is demonstrated in the Macra na Feirme survey (Commins and Kelleher 1973), which indicates that 40 percent of Ireland's bachelor farmers and only 20 percent of married farmers are currently caring for one or more dependent parents. Obviously, parents today may have some stake in seeing that at least one child remains single.

I have used the word *escape* advisedly, since in order for a potential chosen heir to leave his parents and the farm he must symbolically enact a jailbreak. He is considered by others and so considers himself a deserter. Old Maggie, for example, was near to dying, and her last son, Paddy, saw the writing on the wall. He would bury his mother, inherit the sixteen-acre mountain-end farm, and consequently bury himself as well. In characteristic Kerryman fashion, Paddy could not bring himself to confess to his mother that he wanted no part of the farm, that he wanted to leave and join his brothers in Worcester, Massachusetts. So, when his mother sent Paddy into Tralee one Saturday to make the spring purchases, he simply never returned. Shame and guilt prevented him from writing home, but the remittance checks arrived faithfully each month.

Paddy is, perhaps, more lucky than those whose consciences and self-esteem will not allow them the liberty of such an escape. For the potential farm heirs of today are prepared from early childhood for their destined role by a subtle but persistent process of victimization and scapegoating on the part of parents, siblings, and the community at large. It is this ego-deflating process, I hypothesize, that contributes to the high rate of psychosis (especially schizophrenia) among young, male, bachelor farmers.

In interviewing the parents of each of the nuclear households in Ballybran, I discovered a pattern of fixed statuses for children, ordained by sex, birth order, physical and mental aptitude, and supposedly inborn qualities of *dutcas* and *naduir*. There was hardly a farm family that could not boast of its "pet child," its "whiteheaded boy" whose given name was frequently affixed with the nickname *ban* (meaning white, pure, and chaste—*mo buacaill ban*, my beloved boy), as in the rhyme one jealous sister had composed: "Here's our Paddy-Ban, mother's pet who can do no wrong." A mother will also refer to her favorite child as her *plúr*, the whitest, purest flour and the "flower" of her children. Parents are unselfconscious about such preferences, considering them natural, despite the jealousy they produce. One pair of younger siblings once referred to their older brother as "Mummy's *only* child" within earshot of the mother, who then defended her preference.

Although no farm owners today would ever admit to having been reared a pet, it appears from the life histories of older villagers that, in former generations, the family pet was often the firstborn son, traditionally named after his paternal grandfather and reared in order to fill his projected role of farm heir. Today the pattern has been reversed, for the greatest aspirations of village parents no longer rest in agriculture or farm ownership. The firstborn "Paddy-Bans" of today are reared for export—for the occupations of schoolteacher, civil servant, successful emigrant, possibly the priesthood. Daughters may be called "pets," but being Daddy's pet daughter carries far fewer implications than being Papa's or Mummy's pet son.

Parents usually defend the special treatment of a pet son on the grounds of his supposed inherited superiority. Yet the criteria for, or the attributes of, a pet son differ from family to family. The firstborn Paddy-Ban of one household may be praised for his drive—"guts and ambition," as one mother put it. The pet son in another family, however, may be cherished for his "masculine decorum"—for being a quiet, decent, self-contained kind of boy. In another family, academic achievement is held to be the criterion for "petting," where in another it is the son's skill at music or dance, and in yet another his achievement in sports. One mother even defended her preference for her firstborn and notorious "Peck's bad boy" on the grounds of an Irish proverb: *An te na fuil laidir, ni folair do bheith glic* (the boy who is not strong *has* to be cunning). The lack of community consensus regarding the characteristics of a pet make it all the easier for parents to cherish *whatever* strengths or talents the firstborn son may possess.

Children born with physical handicaps have traditionally been and still are to some extent prepared for the town and village trades. But the greatly disvalued role and status of farm heir is reserved today for the family's lastborn son, their so-called runt, *cul* (backward, shy, spiritless child), *iarlais* (changeling, leftover, last of the litter), "bottom of the barrel," "scraping of the pot," or *aindeiseoir* (awkward, ungainly, wretched youth) — the hopeless child who everyone believes will never amount to anything.

"Tadgh is perfect for the farm," said one mother within the presence of her adolescent son. "From the time he could understand, we've called him Farmer Tadgh. He's desperate . . . hopeless in school, the one child I could never get any good out of." In an almost exact paraphrase of his mother's sentiment, Tadgh, when tested on the TAT, identified strongly with the somewhat downcast-looking young man in card 6BM (an elderly woman standing with her back turned to a tall young man) and told the following story:

> *The mother is telling the son that she is disappointed in him because he failed his exams. She is saying, "Nick, from the day you were born I could see that you would never amount to anything but a stay-at-home. The boy is thinking that he stayed at home too long, that he should leave. But he realizes that the time is past, it is already too late. (Outcome?) He does the best he can and hopes that his mother will come to accept him for what he is.*

The folk belief that the moral attributes of a *cul* or a *iarlais* are determined by birth (i.e., blood, or *dutcas*) even creeps into the writings of a distinguished research professor of the Economic and Social Research Institute in Dublin.

> *In many families it is common for one member to do rather particularly well; most will have competent but unspectacular careers; and there is also the occasional black sheep who fails to make a go of anything and winds up in debt or bohemia. . . . All members of a family are brought up in roughly the same way, exposed to pretty well the same standards of conversation, books, discipline, education and so forth. Since the environment is much of a muchness for all, we can best account for the differences in intelligence and personality by heredity. (Lynn 1968: 5)*

It occurred to me that the negative associations of "leftover" and "unwanted" status often attached to the lastborn son might even be subliminally sustained by the old Irish folk beliefs that tend to attribute good luck, prosperity, and special powers to the *first* person, animal, or crop in a series, and bad luck and evil omens to the *last* in a series. The great summer festival of Lughnasa, for example, celebrated the eating of the first potatoes and the picking of the first wild berries. In Ballybran today there is still much fortuitous folklore surrounding the birth of the first spring lamb or foal. Seán O'Súilleabháin (1963: 364–371) records many other "first in a series" beliefs, these among them: that the first person to take the water from a well on New Year's Day would have the luck and prosperity of the year; that the first milk given by a certain cow would give the gift of song or poetry to the person who drinks it; that it is propitious to get the first kiss of a new bride or the first blessing of a newly ordained priest. Conversely, the folklore associated with the *last* in any series

The other night I dreamed I was up at the old graveyard and there was a funeral going on. I was dressed in black but I didn't know who belonging to me had died. They brought me over to the open grave and as I looked down I saw it was my son's shiny, black suitcase they were lowering into the ground. Do you think it could be God's way of telling me that Mick will be leaving for America soon?
— *Village Mother*

tends to be negative. The last person buried in a graveyard is destined to wait on those who arrived before him; and bad luck or ill forebodings are associated with the digging of the last potatoes; the birth of the last in a litter of pigs, dogs, or cats; the cutting of the last sheaf of the harvest; the stacking of the last sod of turf; and the taking of the last bit of food on a platter. Reminiscent of these beliefs is the observation that the lastborn son, the so-called "scraping of the pot," is all too often expected (like the last one buried) to wait on those who had the good fortune to arrive in the family before him.

While everything is sacrificed in order to educate the family's "pet" at a town boarding school, the runt will often be encouraged by parents, and sometimes by teachers who accept the family's definition, to end his education with primary-school. Or, if the *aindeiseoir* is allowed to continue, he will be sent to the local secondary-school, often with a warning attached to his record: "Don't expect much from Johnny." Thus, the unfortunate "leftovers" of the village are reared according to the covert rules of self-fulfilling prophecy. Parents seem to realize that the more emotionally delicate and dependent the child, the less talented and self-confident, the more bashful and socially awkward, the greater their ability to bind this one son to themselves and the land. Like "Nick" in Tadgh's TAT story, the potential heir of the family is often told to his face and even in the presence of outsiders such as myself, that he is "hopeless," the family's n'er-do-well and "slob" — a person who could never make it beyond the pale of Ballybran, and a lad no girl would ever care to marry.

A few weeks ago I took the bull by the horns and asked her would she like to come out with me some night to the singing pub. The answer was no. I asked her if she had anything personal against me. "Nothing," she said; "it's just that you're such a manky little runt."
—JOHN B. KEANE, *Letters of a Love-Hungry Farmer*

I am immediately reminded of Ned, the thirtyish son of a village publican, who watched his two sisters emigrate while he was burdened with the thankless task of running the pub for the elderly parents. The parents, although retired, maintained ownership of the business, and as if adding insult to injury, the pub still went under the banner of "Christy's pub," after Ned's father. Fanny, Ned's bedridden mother, would entertain favored guests (I was often so honored) in her upstairs room. On such occasions, Fanny would call down orders for Ned to bring up tea and cakes, porter, sherry, or whatever the guest desired. When Ned would appear at the door with the tray, Fanny would begin her tirade of abuses against the devoted son: "Look after yourself better, Ned. You haven't even combed your hair today." As an aside to me Fanny once added in a stage whisper, "Isn't he a great slob of a man? What woman will ever have him?" Without a word, Ned would turn on his heels and leave, while Fanny elaborated yet again on the many successes of her daughters and their fine husbands, in contrast to "poor Ned."

While village schoolteachers, themselves natives of the parish, often share parents' assessments of a child's *dutcas*, they will on occasion take exception. Mistress Maloney, for example, raved about Barry Shea: "There was never a Shea could add one and one and have it come up two, but Barry has a way with numbers that makes me sit up and take notice." And it happens that teachers sometimes interfere with parental aspirations, if they feel that a potential "genius" may be wasted on the farm. However, when one such adolescent was "rescued" by the secondary-school teacher who found the boy to be particularly talented in music and drama, his parents refused to be convinced. Diarmuid was given a leading role in the school's Christmas play, which the whole parish attended, save the boy's own father, who protested that he didn't want to be publicly shamed by his foolish son.

The status of leftover and farm heir was not always rigidly affixed to the youngest son, but as the first one chosen might eventually prove himself too "bright" or ambitious for the role, it would be passed on down the line. Sometimes a middle child or an older child seemed naturally suited to the task. Jack, for example, now a bachelor in his late thirties, living with his mother, invalid father, and spinster aunt, is the middle child in a family of five boys, all considered handsome and bright. However, Jack was seen as ever the most timid of the "crowd" and stayed behind when the others left. Patrick, the "baby," left home with the greatest sense of guilt, and during the first few years, returned each summer in an attempt to lure Jack away with him. But Jack stood firm, feeling that the role of farm heir and parent caretaker rightfully belonged to him by virtue of his "soft" temperament. Jack described himself to me as a shy, retiring, "traditional kind of man," who loves his parents and the peace and quiet of country living. Villagers refer to Jack as a "corner boy," and when not working, he could often be found sitting on a stone wall with several buddies, or lying by the side of the road "chatting it up" with a male

Often and often afterwards, the beloved Aunt would ask me why I had never told anyone how I was being treated. Children tell little more than animals, for what comes to them they accept as eternally established.
— RUDYARD KIPLING,
Something of Myself

cousin. When I would encounter him like this, Jack would adjust his cap and comment with pleasure, "Now where in New York or Cincinnati do you think I could find friends like these who have no airs and like to have a good 'craic?'" The fact that the "craics" were often on him (allusions to his failures in comparison with the other brothers, jokes about his sexuality—a preference for sheep over women, or boys over girls, etc.) and were but a thinly disguised form of hostile ridicule, seemed to escape Jack, and he always accepted the banter in great good humor. "It's all friendly-like," he always assured me, although not always convincingly. And the fact that his seventy-two-year-old mother still commanded the farm, handled the money, and did not so much as allow Jack to buy a pair of shoes without her consent hardly seemed on the surface to bother him. Jack's mother, like his friends, tended to "cod" and patronize him. Often she alluded to the fact that "poor Jack" had no bed to sleep on, but used a pallet on the kitchen floor, like a child. And with a wink and a condescending pat on Jack's shoulder, she would add, "But, sure, he's the man of the house now, and we'd be in a sorry state without him."

▪ Ridicule, "the Craic," and the Ballybran Double Bind

> —*Tell us, Daedalus, do you kiss your mother before going to bed?*
> *Stephen answered:—I do. Wells turned to the other fellows and*
> *said:—O, I say, here's a fellow says he kisses his mother every night*
> *before he goes to bed. The other fellows stopped in their games and*
> *turned around laughing. Stephen blushed under their eyes and*
> *said:—I do not. Wells said:—O, I say, here's a fellow says he doesn't*
> *kiss his mother before he goes to bed. They all laughed again. Stephen*
> *tried to laugh with them. He felt his whole body hot and confused. . . .*
> *What was the right answer to the question? He had given two and*
> *Wells still laughed.*
> —JAMES JOYCE, *A Portrait of the Artist as a Young Man*

A practicing psychotherapist in the west of Ireland (Dunne 1970: 24–27) has discussed the tendency among rural Irish males to "cut each other down" through those interactional patterns called, in the vernacular, "taking the mickey" and "having a craic." Supposedly good-humored ridicule of this nature is used to censure those young men who try to "shake off village apathy" by trying to get ahead or who demonstrate feelings for others. If I may draw a parallel, similar to Black urban culture in America, it is considered a sign of weakness for Irish males to reveal tenderness, love, and affection—a loss of the cool, distant, ironical reserve characteristic of male comportment. Dunne refers to the craic as a

> *form of psychological castration or mutilation, and is probably the most damaging single factor in Mayo life, acting as it often does as a cloak for envy, bitterness, hatred and fear, thus reducing the humanity of the ridiculer and the ridiculed. (p. 25)*

He goes on to describe a particularly vicious form of ridicule, very common in the west, in which the "victim" is kept in suspense, never knowing for sure whether the interaction is serious or not. Like Jack, he wants to believe that it's all friendly, but fears the true barb underneath. And there is implicit a kind of "double bind"—if he treats the seemingly hostile ridicule as a joke, he is lacking in masculine decorum; if he takes the ridicule seriously, he is branded as lacking in humor, that all-important Irish trait. That such forms of psychological castration are used not only between peers, but by parents in relation to their children, especially the vulnerable *aindeiseoir*, is the most seriously pathogenic factor in Irish family dynamics. Called to his face a wretched, unfortunate, ungainly soul, a leftover, miserable remnant of flesh, the "old cow's calf" is caught in a classical double bind in which he is damned if he does and damned if he doesn't.[3] The parent can be observed belittling the runt for trying to put himself ahead, and then with the same breath chiding him for not being more aggressive and achievement oriented like his older brothers. A double-binding predicament is also implicit in the lastborn son's limited choice of alternatives, neither of which is satisfactory. The boy can leave home and "abandon" his parents, but terrible guilt and possibly his mother's curse will follow him ever after ("Johnny, you're the last one we have left!"). Or he can gracefully

accept the assigned role of stay-at-home bachelor farmer and parent caretaker, but in this case he will have to face the cruel ridicule and mocking
pity of parents and neighbors, who will remind him ever after that he is an
inadequate adult, forever a "boy-o," and never a man. The only defenses
against such hurtful and harmful interactions are passive strategies: among
children and adolescents, sulking and gradually withdrawing from intimate
contacts. Among adults, there is always recourse to that widespread blend
of self-pity and fatalism which the Irish call "the poor-mouth" — that is, it
isn't my fault that I am (an alcoholic, unemployed, a bachelor, a stay-at-
home, etc.), followed by a tragic tale to elicit sighs, nods, and sympathy.

Gregory Bateson's insight regarding the harmful effects of continually
skewed communications between family members, and Antonio Ferreira's
model of the "family myth," can be applied to whole communities, as in
Ballybran. Not only individual families, but also social situations can be
double binding. And an entire little community can come to accept and
reinforce the distorted perceptions and beliefs which were originally only
"all in the family" myths. The ambiguous and contradictory role options
that are communicated to the Irish lad during late adolescence — the period
in the life cycle during which the individual is attempting to solidify his
identity and sort out his relationships to others (see Erikson 1963: 190) —
must perforce have tragic consequences, even resulting for some in that
state of perplexity known as schizophrenia.

Toward a Responsive
Human Community

Blessed are the meek,
for they shall inherit the earth.
—Matthew 5:5

IN THE PRECEDING pages I have drawn a rather grim portrait of Irish country life, one that differs markedly from previous ethnographies. Village social life and institutions are, I contend, in a state of disintegration, and villagers are suffering from anomie, of which the most visible sign is the spiraling rates for schizophrenia. Traditional culture has become unadaptive, and the newly emerging cultural forms as yet lack integration. The sexes are locked into isolation and mutual hostility. Deaths and emigrations surpass marriages and births. Socialization is harsh, particularly for the youngest or the weakest child. These are, I am aware, brutal observations representing one outsider's eyewitness account. In these concluding pages I shall link what might seem to be the "exceptional" case study of the Irish with other epidemiological studies in order to pull together the various strands representing a sociocultural perspective on schizophrenia.

▪ Schizophrenia as a Social Dis-ease

Schizophrenia has been regarded from two basic perspectives: the medical and the sociological. The first has examined schizophrenia as a disease based on a personal inner disturbance, either organic in nature, as in biogenetic theories (see Rosenthal 1970), or intrapsychic, as in psychoanalytic theory (see Sullivan 1962). The second, or interactionist, perspective has tended to see schizophrenia as a social process, as a manifestation of dis-ease between an individual and his milieu (see Foucault 1967; Scheff 1966). Whereas the former locates the disorder within the individual, the latter focuses on the pathogenic disorder within *society*. I have tried to integrate both approaches insofar as historical, interpersonal, and intrapsychic processes can be seen in dialogue with one another. The history and cultural patterns provide the context and often the content of Irish madness, the quality of village and family dynamics evoke peculiarly Irish conflicts, and the personal history of the schizophrenic reveals the individual's unique interpretation of his dis-ease and his lonely resolution through descent into psychosis.

Twenty-year-old Kitty, for example, explains that her first episode occurred during a brief period of emigration to London, where she worked in a sleazy pub in the Soho district. She was revolted to the point of hysterical paralysis at her assigned task of pouring leftover beer "slops" into the fresh glasses of unsuspecting clients. This she unconsciously equated with the sexual "slops" of her "Black Protestant" English clients who, she observed, poured themselves from dirty, used whores into the fresh containers of their unsuspecting wives. Later her story evokes previous conflicts in Kitty's background within a rural Kerry family torn asunder between the disorderly drinking patterns of an occasionally brutal father and the compulsive attention to Catholic ritual of a sexually repressed mother. Order/disorder, female/male, pure/impure, Catholic/Protestant, Celt/Anglo are the symbolic axes upon which hovers her paralyzing ambivalence.

Thirty-four-year-old Patrick, a farm heir, rarely speaks and prefers to remain quite still. In the few responses he musters to the Thematic Apperception Test the story figures are described as statues, or, even further removed, as "pictures of a picture." In commenting on his relationship to his parents, Patrick says: "I am their dead son." Patrick is an *aindeiseoir*, one of the many lastborn sons in County Kerry crippled by his parents' double-binding attempts to keep him safely at home, reserved and eternally postponed for their old age. And Patrick's living-in-death must also be seen as set within the background of a demoralized, dying, western village. It is possible that case histories similar to these can be found elsewhere in the world, but the power upon which they draw is based on cultural images, symbols, and conflicts.

The tentative diagnosis of the schizophrenia-evoking factors in rural Irish society has focused on the breakdown of traditional patterns of Irish familism, its symptoms: the steady decline in marriage and birth rates and the proliferation of consanguineal and independent nuclear households; its causes: the spread of a secular worldview and an individualistic ethos of rural capitalism; and its consequences: a demoralizing spirit of anomie. The emotional isolation, loss of self-esteem, and uncertainty and confusion about roles expressed by villagers—both young and old—has reference to several related sociocultural interpretations of mental illness, which I shall discuss below.

Some years ago, E. G. Jaco (1954) suggested that communities having high rates of schizophrenia would also evidence a high degree of social isolation: poor communication networks, few organizations and voluntary associations, little recreational activity, and so forth. Jaco speculated that without such incentives to active participation in community life, borderline and otherwise psychiatrically vulnerable individuals would be even more inclined to withdraw and regress. Although his "schizophrenia and social isolation hypothesis" never received much serious attention, the sparsely settled, devitalized, and schizophrenia-prone villages of western Ireland are reminiscent of his description—as are the marginal rural communities of Nova Scotia studied by Leighton (1959), and the island of Martha's Vineyard (Mazer 1976), all of which have a high incidence of mental disorder and a correspondingly high degree of social isolation.

More *au courant*, perhaps, are those epidemiological studies that have linked high rates of mental illness with intolerable levels of stress generated by rapid social change (see Carothers 1953; Tooth 1950; Field 1960, Leighton, et al. 1963; Lin, et al. 1969). Most frequently cited is Anthony F. C. Wallace's theory (1961) of "mazeway" disintegration—the collapse of a cultural gestalt or worldview—by which he explained the prevalence of mental pathologies among the colonialized Iroquois Indians. Alexander Leighton's research among rural Canadians (1959, 1961) and later among detribalized Yoruba (Leighton, et al. 1963) lead him to conclude that social disintegration generates personality disintegration. The former he measured by indices such as low and unstable income, conflicting and confusing cultural values, secularization, broken homes, weak associations and few leaders, few recreational outlets, and fragmented networks of communication.

Social disintegration and rapid change have likewise been studied from the microlevel of individual family history. In Israel, as Antonovsky (1972) demonstrated, a high "life crisis" score—including such factors as moves, death in the family, divorce, loss of work, and so forth—often creates stress leading to either physical or mental "breakdown." Still other studies have associated vulnerability to mental illness with a disintegration of social networks (Holmes and Rahe 1967), migration and social mobility (Dunham 1965; Stein 1957; Odegaard 1946), lower socioeconomic status (Hollingshead and Redlich 1968; Strole, et al. 1962), and individuals without affinal or consanguineal ties—that is, the familistically disenfranchised (Kraemer 1970; Norris 1956; O'Hare and Walsh 1974; Brooke 1967). Epidemiological studies such as these indicate that, while mental illness is found throughout the world, its prevalence in particular communities is dependent on the degree or lack of social cohesion. Above all, what such diverse groups as the Nesilik Eskimo, Midtown Manhattanites, urbanizing Yoruba, Ojibwa Indians, migrants and immigrants throughout the world, and the rural Irish of County Kerry have in common is an acute experience of social disorganization accompanied by a state of normlessness.

The death of a culture begins when its evaluative institutions—the source of all moral energy—falter, when they fail to provide a compelling sense of pride and dignity in the ways of the group. In the words immortalized by Yeats, this occurs when "things fall apart; the center cannot hold; mere anarchy is loosed upon the world. . . . [When] the best lack all conviction, while the worst are full of passionate intensity." [1]

In the sixteenth and seventeenth centuries, Western colonizing nations spread a pestilence of smallpox, venereal disease, and fatal influenzas to the simpler peoples of the new worlds with whom they came into contact (see William H. McNeill 1976). In the twentieth century, a plague of mental disorders—especially anomic schizophrenias—are spreading to the transitional peasant and tribal backwater areas of the world (see World Health Organization 1973), a possible consequence of exposure to the increasing complexities of modern life, and the ebbing away of those integrative values and "folkways" of traditional society. It is not my intention to wax romantic or poetic about the healthier lives of unspoiled peoples; mental illness is to be found throughout the world and over all historical periods. However, where schizophrenia was once considered largely the disease of Western industrialized nations—as a metaphor, perhaps, for the perplexity of the divided, alienated modern man—recent epidemiological surveys are plotting its spread and increase in those areas once characterized by more culture-specific syndromes. The Transcultural Psychiatric Research Group at McGill University distributed a questionnaire (H. B. M. Murphy 1963) to psychiatrists in many nations concerning the prevalence and characteristics of various mental disorders, and schizophrenic types of symptoms were reported everywhere as "frequent," but most especially in rapidly modernizing and industrializing areas.

The process of culture change over human history has been relatively slow until this century. Anthropologists have often emphasized that human communities tend to be traditional, conservative, and ethnocentric (see Margaret Mead 1961; Foster 1973). This stubborn conservatism, resistance to new ideas and techniques, and suspiciousness of outsiders (which is so discouraging to agents of social change such as agricultural innovators and regional planners) may also be interpreted for its psychologically adaptive advantages. As the evidence demonstrates, change—even change for the better (see Antonovsky 1972)—can generate breakdown, and the worldview of the proverbially closed-minded, plodding, foot-dragging "sack of potatoes" peasant (as Marx described him) is apparently rooted in common sense and with self-preservation in mind.

During periods of rapid change and cultural distortion, many individuals will tend to become disorganized internally and will manifest such symptoms as anxiety, depression, guilt, nihilism, and so forth. Other individuals (those perhaps who have a genetic predisposition to react in stress in this way) will manifest the more dramatic symptoms of schizophrenia: hearing voices, hallucinations, feelings of influence, delusions, and so forth. The fact that persons experiencing similar symptoms in non-Western societies often become elevated to the status of prophet, shaman, or medicine man, and have been known to organize and reintegrate a troubled society around the cultural symbols expressed by the psychosis has led some psychiatric anthropologists (see Foulks 1975) to see schizophrenia as having once had adaptive advantages for the social group.[2] Such was certainly the case with the Seneca prophet Handsome Lake, and a similar interpretation could be made of the lives of several outstanding Catholic saints in European history, among them Joan of Arc, Francis of Assisi, and Ireland's Saint Brendan. If the hallucinating or delusional person is given credibility, his psychosis may serve to pinpoint the trouble areas in a given community. If she is treated as a gifted healer or visionary rather than locked up as a lunatic or witch, she can often serve a valuable role in society (see the life history of the urban *curandera* Nora, in Day and Davidson 1976). The successful completion of the role can itself result in a natural remission of symptoms (as Joan of Arc reputedly complained at the end of her short life: "The work is over; my voices have left me"). In the midst of interviewing and testing young Irish schizophrenics I often caught the flashes of brilliant insight that many who have worked with such people have commented on. These critics and non-conformers of rural society were often all too keenly aware of the problems within their families and villages: the guilt and oppression caused by sexual repression; the harmful effects of canings, ridicule, and scapegoating of children; the distracting boredom of daily life within a community in which traditional work has lost its meaning; the fear of forced retirement and growing old in a society of lonely and dependent old people. Unfortunately, rural Irish society offers no sanctioned role for the prophetic "visions" of these troubled and overly sensitive individuals.

In these concluding pages I do not wish to imply a denial of the probable involvement of genetics in the etiology of mental illness; recent studies indicate that something is transmitted genetically to at least some of those persons diagnosed as schizophrenic (see Rosenthal 1970). However, I do wish to suggest that a more tenable theory of pathogenesis should take into account not only the biogenetic and the psychodynamic, but also the sociocultural. Concerning the latter, I have in mind a theory that could deal not only with an identification of individual family situations and patterns that seemingly evoke mental illness, but also with some definition of social and economic institutions that may define and limit the quality of interpersonal relations in a given society.

In virtually all studies of the etiology and chronicity of schizophrenia the role of the family—whether in terms of physiological or psychodynamic transmission—is a central issue. With this very much in mind, I wrote the last chapters of the book as an essay on the rural Irish family: its current state of change and disorganization; relations between the sexes, husbands and wives, and parents and children. I concluded that the economic changes of the past fifty years have radically altered traditional patterns of parenting. Before the demise of the extended farm family, children were numerous, and child tending was evenly divided among the mother, her unmarried sister or sister-in-law, and the elderly paternal grandmother. Babies were nursed until two or three years old, were kept warm and rocked in a cradle in front of the kitchen hearth in the central room of the small cottage. With the spread of the nuclear family and modern conveniences such as bottles, cribs, and central heating, infants and toddlers have lost their central position in the household. In addition to "modernization," I suggest that the Jansenist version of Irish Catholicism with its accompanying ethic of sexual repression interferes with warm maternal behavior in Ballybran and has a detrimental effect on the mental health of Irish children.

Beginning in the late fifties, a number of social scientists (see Bateson, et al. 1956; Lidz, et al. 1958; Mishler and Waxler 1968; Singer 1963) initiated studies of family interactions and communication patterns and have concluded that at least some of these (i.e., "the double bind," "family myths") seem to sustain—if not to cause—mental illness in children. In chapter six I attempted to take these valuable insights one step further by suggesting that certain social or economic conditions may influence the structure of family life so as to encourage or perpetuate schizophrenia-provoking situations. Such appeared to me to be the case of lastborn, farm-inheriting sons, who of necessity were scapegoated and victimized by their role in the declining community. Not only individually disturbed parents, but also unfortunate social situations can "double bind" innocent victims—as is the case with the Kerry youth who perceives all possible role options as limiting and unsatisfactory.

A coherent and responsive human community is one in which its members are not subjected to intolerable levels of stress from its economic and social institutions or from its values and belief system. Although a certain degree of stress is inevitable in all communities in which people grow, develop, change, and strive for things that subsequently alter their lives, an examination of village life in Ballybran seems to indicate that the levels of stress have surpassed the ability of existing social institutions and of individuals to handle them. The fact that Ballybran parish has been reduced to a dependency upon the summer tourist industry and winter "doles" has had a devastating effect on the self-esteem of villagers. The forced retirement of able-bodied, middle-aged farmers, and the intended restructuring of Kerry farming away from the family model to the large-scale productive pattern of industrialized agriculture, undercuts the basic value system of the region. The family farm has traditionally served two distinct functions—the one, economic; the other, psychological. The farm work or "business" can be judged, perhaps, as hopelessly dated and unproductive, but the farm "household" remains the affective and spiritual core of rural Irish society, and cannot be dispensed with so easily. The farm household confers on each member a sense of identity, community, and history, linking the individual with an immortal chain of ancestors. The villagers' ambivalent attachment to the land—that "worthless bit of turf," that "miserable piece of rocky land"; that "pitiful grass of three sheep and a tubercular cow"—for all its local depreciation, should not be underestimated for the wealth of color, warmth, and sense of belonging that it likewise conveys.

Any attempt to reduce the serious stresses caused by feelings of relative deprivation and the conflict between secular and traditional values depends largely on the ability of village leaders to stimulate a viable rural economy—one based on cottage industries and innovative and cooperative farming, such as the thriving Comharchumann Forbartha with its eight hundred farmer-shareholders near "Ballydavid." Since 1967 the cooperative has rejuvenated the ancient fishing villages across the mountain pass from Ballybran through the building of community halls, by creating pastureland from useless bog, and in setting up Irish-language courses for summer students. Through these efforts the older villagers are coming again to appreciate who they are and what they have and do, and younger villagers may yet desist in their single-minded exodus from the peninsula.

On a less grand scale but equally praiseworthy is the dynamic program of community development begun by the curate of Ballybran. His tireless efforts at reviving the old trades of blacksmith, weaver, and potter among the youth (largely ignored by the government until now) should be fully supported by the Office of the Gaeltacht. In addition to community development, it seems to me that the parish could also benefit from a program of mental health education and marital and premarital counseling: a program affiliated, perhaps, with the local secondary school—an institution, like the Church, in which villagers invest both pride and trust.

In the final analysis, the cost of inheriting the land and perpetuating the presently demoralized rural culture, with its demands of an austere and stressful lifestyle, leaves the young adult few choices. Without a coherent and responsive plan of community revitalization, the majority of youth will continue to opt for escape through emigration. For those who remain, the solution will continue to be a stoical acceptance through repression and denial. And for the more delicate and psychologically vulnerable, one can predict increasing periods of maladjustment during which time the delicate balance tips and the normally repressed individual is flooded with uncontrollable angers, resentments, and more important, with felt needs for attachment and intimacy with the absent or nonexistent significant others in his life. Schizophrenia is one of the many expressions of the human condition. Writ large, it is the translation of social ills into private troubles, to paraphrase C. Wright Mills (1959: 60).

Whatever happens or fails to happen, it is clear that in the next fifteen or twenty years the future viability of the ancient village of Ballybran (and of hundreds of other tiny crossroads just like it along the western coast) will be decided once and for all. If the national government remains determined to seduce strong young farmers into an early retirement on the "dole," then widespread demoralization (and its consequent mental illnesses) is inevitable. And if the rural Catholic Church continues to decry sexuality as the main evil of modern life, then the already dispirited God- and woman-fearing young bachelors will remain unmarried and childless. And as the population decreases, and as boarded-up farms and caved-in stone barns become more numerous than those with a tuft of smoke circling comfortably around the roof, some progressive Dublin legislators may live to see their vision of the Dingle Peninsula preserved as the first (but surely not the last) uninhabited National Park of Ireland. Then the legacy of one of the earliest and oldest sites of Celtic civilization will belong to backpacking German, English, and Norwegian tourists. They will, no doubt, appreciate the rugged beauty of the Dingle landscape. But the mountains, glens, and strands will be forever silenced of the far more beautiful poetry of the present-day Peig Sayerses, Tomás O'Crohans, and Maurice O'Sullivans, who, like their recent ancestors on Great Blasket, are predicting and very much feeling the demise of a way of life, as old Bridie says, "the likes of which will never be seen again."

I am thankful to those who opened their doors and lent their thoughts to me, and I end with the words of "Big Peig" Sayers herself, who at the close of her autobiography (1973: 212) set everything into its proper perspective:

Old as I am, there's a great deal more in my head that I can't write down here. I did my best to give an accurate account of the people I knew so that they'd be remembered when we all moved on to eternity. People will yet walk above our heads; it could even happen that they'd walk into the graveyard where I'll be lying, but people like us will never again be there. We will be stretched out quietly—and the old world will have vanished.

Crediting
An Clochán

Fulingeann fuil fuil I ngorta
ach Ni fhuilingeann
fuil fuil a dortadh.

*A man can tolerate his own blood
starving to death, but he won't tolerate
his blood attacked by a stranger.*
—*Local Proverb*

"*A Hundred Thousand Welcomes*"
—*Board Failte (Irish Tourist Board)*

JUNE 1999

"WELL, I am sorry to tell you, Nancy, but you are not welcome. No you are not. Have they let you a place to stay down in the village?" I was standing awkwardly in the once familiar doorway of "Martin's" sturdy country house in a ruggedly beautiful mountain hamlet of An Clochán, a bachelor's outpost of some nine or ten vestigial farm households. Once, we had been good neighbors. During the summer of 1974 Martin had warded off the suspicions and dire warnings of his wary older sisters and had befriended us so far as to feel out my political sympathies toward various activities of the local IRA in which he and his extended family were involved. "Ah, I should have listened to Aine," Martin said.

Over the past quarter of a century, some memories in An Clochán were engraved in stone like the family names of the Moriaritys and the O'Neills carved over the smallest village shops in West Kerry signifying that this public house, *this* name, *this* family are forever. And what was remembered in this instance was a slight (in village terms, a slander) committed by me against the good name of the community. Ever the proud nationalist and aligned with the real or breakaway IRA, which is still holding out against the

Peace Accords, Martin warned me to stay clear of village institutions: "You'll not be expecting any mail while you are here," he said ominously.

Martin still cut a dashing, if compact, figure, now sporting a pair of gold wire-rimmed designer eyeglasses and dressed on that afternoon in an impeccably starched white shirt. A shiny new sedan was parked outside his door. Martin's bachelor household, shared on the odd weekend with an older sister who works in the city, had clearly prospered over the past two decades. But all traces of active engagement with the land are gone. There was no sign of the haying that should have been going on during those precious few warm and sunny days in mid June. No symmetrical mound of soft, boggy turf stood in front of the farm house. A quick sidelong glance to the right showed the barn standing empty and swept clean. Above all, the neat row of newly laundered clothing strung across the outdoor line included no workaday overalls or denim shirts. What was once an active and viable farm had become a gentlemanly country home, a far cry from the days of Martin's youth when his beloved Da, the patriarch of a large household, rose early on winter mornings and, half-freezing in his shirttails and warming himself by beating his sturdy arms across his chest, went down to the sea to gather crannach, *duileask*, carageen and other native edible seaweeds. This, mind you, accomplished before the *real* work day of the farm had begun.

When Martin was still a very young man an older and more robust brother was sent off to America to make room for Martin, one of the younger and more vulnerable sons, to take up the family farm. Although primogeniture was then still customary, the father-patriarch had the freedom to chose his primary heir among his sons, according to his perceptions of his sons' skills, personalities, aptitudes, and needs, as well as his and his wife's needs as they grew older. And the Da had settled upon Martin. But during the man's lifetime, farming ceased being an enviable way of life and sibling jealousy had turned to sympathy toward those who were left behind to till the small "rock farms" of An Clochán. Martin's diasporic siblings had fared exceedingly well, numbering among them college teachers and clergy.[1]

Aine, the older sister, scowling while drying a plate and peering over Martin's shoulder, came out of the back of the house to give me a scolding:

"Who made *you* such an authority? You weren't such a grand person when you and your family came to live in our bungalow. You could hardly control your own children. Why don't you go home and write about your own troubles. God knows, you've got plenty of them, with school children shooting each other and U.S. planes bombing hospitals in Kosovo. Why pick on us?"

Martin interjected: "Admit it. You wrote a book to please yourself at our expense. *You ran us down, girl, you ran us down.* You call what you do a science?" And before I could deny that I did, he continued, "A science, to be sure, the science of scandals. We warn our village children before they go off to the university in Cork or Dublin to beware books about Ireland written by strangers." Seeing that his words had found their mark and tears were coursing freely down my cheeks, Martin softened his stance a bit. But his sister roundly rejected my apologies: "You say you are sorry, but we don't believe it. Those are crocodile tears! You are just crying for yourself."

Breaking the mood, Martin turned to my adult son, Nate, who was busy trying to hide himself in a thick hedge near the barn. Martin's words were soft and courtly: "You are a fine looking lad to be sure, Nate, and I'm sorry to be talking to your mother like this in your presence." Then, he returned his gaze to me: "Sure, nobody's perfect, nobody's a saint. We all have our weaknesses. But you never wrote about our strengths. You never said what a beautiful and a safe place our village is. You never wrote about the vast sweep of the eye that the village offers over the sea and up to Connor Pass. You said nothing about our fine musicians and poets, and our step dancers who move through the air with the grace of a silk thread. And we are not such a backwater today. There are many educated people among us. You wrote about our troubles, all right, but not about our strengths. What about the friendliness of neighbors? What about our love for Mother Ireland and our proud work of defending it." When I protested that I could not have written about those radical activities for fear of reprisals against the village, Martin replied: "Ah, you were only protecting yourself." "Is there *anything* I can do?" I asked. "You should have thought about that before. Look, girl, the fact is that ya *just didn't give us credit.*"

▪ Crediting An Clochán

Well, let me give it a try. What I might have said about An Clochán in the mid-1970s (and did not say) was that the village offered an extraordinary glimpse of a closed corporate rural community in which social hierarchy and social difference were successfully curtailed, where "putting on airs" was spurned in the interests of *communitas*, and where, despite the general rule of farm family patriarchy, *girls* were reared to be high achievers, women did *not* have to marry, and single women could raise sheep, drive cows, manage a village pub, run a primary or secondary-school, scold the local gombeen man, or boss the local curate till he "cried uncle" and gave in on a particular theological or political point. Rural women could choose to marry young or they could wait and marry late in life and then marry men much younger than themselves. Alternatively, especially in a family of daughters, they could refuse several marriage proposals in order to remain at home and inherit their father's fields and their favorite pipe or her father's pub and his celebrated goatskin drum. Moreover, married women kept their maiden names *and* their premarital social and self identities.

Perhaps nowhere else in the world were women so free to walk country roads at night without fear of either physical assault or malicious gossip. Nowhere else have I seen women and men banter with one another in public without every source of humor being reduced to a double entendre. And nowhere else were bachelors and spinsters accepted as normal and unremarkable members of society, able to lead autonomous, if lonely, lives. No eyebrows were raised at the bachelor who not only planted and harvested but also cooked his own spuds, who not only raised his own sheep but also was quite capable of knitting his own socks and sweaters. How distant this was from Ivan Illich's description (1982: 67) of the woeful state of bachelors in those parts of traditional Europe more characterized by gender complementarity: "You could recognize the bachelor from afar by his stench and gloomy looks. . . . Solitary men left no sheets or shirts when they died. . . . A man without a wife, sister, mother, or daughter had no way to make, wash, and mend his clothes; it was impossible for him to keep chickens or to milk a goat."

In An Clochán at the time of my study social life was not confined to couples. Dress for both sexes was casual and the sturdy figure ahead of you on the road wrapped in layers of trousers, woolen vests, and long coat, shod in muddy green Wellington boots, and waving a stick was just as likely to be that of a woman driving her small herd of cows. I may have misread important aspects of social life in a community where gender and sibling bonding was as or more important than the sexual or the erotic bond. If marital relations were problematic, it was in part because marriage interrupted and intruded upon other competing and equally valued affections and loyalties. Surely any anthropologist practicing today would not wish to suggest a hierarchy of appropriate affections such that lifelong friendships, brotherly and sisterly in nature, would somehow count for less than conjugal relations.

If psychiatric hospitalization rates were high, rape and sexual assault were unknown at that same time. Theft was so rare that one definition of an eccentric was a person who was overly preoccupied about the safety of his property; a case of paranoid schizophrenia could be diagnosed on the grounds of one's having accused the neighbors of wanting to steal one's sheep or cows or having shifted the stone boundaries that mark off one field from another. And "Brendan the rapist," who I interviewed at the county mental hospital in Killarney, had sinned only in his thoughts and was by his own account a virgin, unlucky in sex. So, as a young married woman in An Clochán, I could hail a ride on the back of Morris's motorbike without any hint of scandal, just as I could sit and talk with the local curate over a mid-morning cup of tea in his living room with the priest still in his pajamas.

Housekeeping, gardening, and meal preparation were kept to a minimum thus freeing both women and men for other voluntary activities and a good deal of leisure time that was spent in fostering friendship and conviviality — for men in one of several village pubs, at local sheep fairs and regional markets and, for women in shops, church, and school-related activities and, for older women and widows, in house calls to friends and distant kin. There was time out for storytelling and time out for play. There was time to gather around deaths, wakes, and funerals — a full day was given over to the funerals of each of the thirty-eight villagers who died during 1974–1975.

Everyone had radios and some owned televisions, but most people still preferred live entertainment and gathered frequently, especially during the

winter, at pubs, church halls, and in one another's homes to entertain themselves with their own music, singing, step dancing, and poetry recitation.
Both young and old, male and female, were encouraged to develop their
own repertoire of songs, recitations, or steps, which they could be called on
to perform at the drop of a hat. Though the shyness and modesty of bachelors could be heart breaking, the institutionalized pattern of coaxing could
bring even the most reluctant fisherman or shepherd to perform his party
piece and shine before his peers. How often I had seen and been moved by
something like the following sequence between a bachelor and his small
circle of drinking partners at Peig's pub:

> "How about a song, Paddy?"
> "I'm no good."
> "Come on, you are a great singer."
> "Why, he's the best in the village."
> "Now you are putting me on lads."
> "No, you're great, really you are."
> "The voice box is all dry and raspy, like."
> "Give the man another drink, then."
> "How about Croppy Boys? Give it a try."
> "I don't know it. I don't have it."
> "You do. We've heard you sing it."
> "I hate singing. I'm no good at it."
> "You're among friends. We'll help you along, right lads?"
> [a chorus of "Good man," "good man"]

And at last, a nervous, lip-wetting Paddy sings "Croppy Boys" surrounded
by his friends interjecting a chorus of "take your time," "good man, good
man," "that's right" to help him through.

The ethic of modesty and deference assured that no one singer ever stood
out or sought undue attention (see also Steiner n.d.) Meanwhile, the recip-
rocal call and response mode — "sing us a song, Paddy"; "Oh, I couldn't," and
so on — allowed for the limited expression of praise and appreciation, which
could always destabilize into "codding" — "Sure, he's the best singer in the
village." Together these promoted a strong sense of community solidarity at

the expense of the individual, aimed as they were at suppressing any hint of unseemly arrogance or self-importance. In other words, social equality was fostered through the very same witty games of "codding," "giving the mickey," and "having the craic," that I described in chapter six as having a decidedly adverse effect on the more psychologically vulnerable individuals who were less able to evaluate and respond appropriately to the double-binding messages they carried. To wit: Refuse the praise and you are putting a damper on the high spirits of your companions; accept the praise and you appear the fool for taking it seriously.

Gregory Bateson, who had developed the double-bind theory of schizophrenia that I used in this volume, understood that human communication patterns were extremely complex and that some double-binding injunctions were damaging to certain individuals while some were beneficial, even therapeutic to others. The verbal duels and interactional challenges so characteristic of rural Irish wit may have contributed to the cognitive dissonance suffered by Irish schizophrenics unable to differentiate literal from metaphorical truth. But just as surely these communication patterns contributed to the development of Ireland's long tradition of saints, poets, and scholars as well.

An equally strong village code censored those who appeared too avaricious or materialist. Estate auctions, which were held occasionally following the death of a bachelor or spinster, could provoke rounds of barbed joking that made these events seem like sociological primal scenes. In the winter of 1975 the pub house and worldly belongings of an old widow were auctioned off three years after her demise. I recorded the event in my field notes:

Villagers began to congregate in front of the old stone house an hour before the auction. A few women walked gingerly through the narrow rooms of the house, furtively casting an eye on a water pitcher here and a bedspread there. The mood alternated between embarrassed humor and tense disapproval. The whole event struck villagers as unseemly. It was wrong to break up the poor woman's home like this, taking possession of her glasses and chairs and religious relics. One commented: 'Poor woman! Her things should be respected, left untouched.' Another woman said: 'Spare me, I myself want none of this.'

Later, after a painfully slow beginning, the auctioneer, an outsider from Tralee—a Protestant, to boot, some whispered—balancing himself on a hastily constructed platform, eventually got the bidding going by working the small crowd, comfortably resting his arm on one or another of the men, and picking up their names very quickly. 'Well, what am I bid, Freddie boy?' Disparaging comments from those standing around would turn to joking until the auctioneer would intervene: 'Now, lads, we have some serious business to attend to.' Each time a religious object, a statue or a painting, went up for sale, it was greeted with silence later punctuated by irreverent stage whispers. There was discomfort at the public display of local faith, and anxiety about taking possession of another person's blessed icons. The auctioneer tried to gloss over the embarrassment by pretending that the villagers were really bidding for the frames and not for the holy images they contained. 'Good for the frames, Good for the frames,' he said, while waving the Sacred Heart of Jesus or the Immaculate Heart of Mary over the heads of the small crowd, to which one cheeky young man countered: 'Good for the flames! Good for the flames!' (which could be taken either as a sacrilegious remark or as a warning of hell's fire awaiting those willing to participate in the unholy bidding). A few men tried to coax Pat to purchase the images to decorate his newly renovated singing pub. He replied, "Our Holy Mother would hardly be wanting a pint of Guinness."

Finally, the nervous joking turned to grumbling about one villager who had been bidding quite seriously and had bought up more than his share. 'Whatever is eating at Dermot?' 'What could he possibly want with all that?' 'Sure, it's very unfriendly behavior,' at which point, his wife, who overheard the remarks, and several other women left the vexing and anxiety provoking scene.

It was in small dramas like these that the nature of community life was continually addressed and reinforced. It was a sure sign that, amidst the transition to a more secular and materialist society, the older and communal values that resisted "the commodification of everything" were still firmly in place.

And while I told the anecdote about the cruel codding in the pub of a shy bachelor who was teased unmercifully about his inability to speak to me without stammering, I failed to tell the anecdote about the day of our leave-taking from the village when I saw through my front window the very same painfully shy man standing under a tree at the bottom of the little path that led up to our cottage. I wondered what he was doing there, "loitering" for such a long time. I went about my packing and housecleaning, but each time I passed the window I saw him standing there, so still, hardly changing his posture. Eventually, after a few hours, it occurred to me that perhaps he was waiting for me to come down the path on my way to the village on an errand. So, I packed up the babies into strollers and backpacks and we made our way down the path as if on our way to the village post office. As I came close to Padraec, I shyly lifted a finger and crooked my neck at him in the traditional, understated Kerryman greeting at which he came forward and put out his hand, which I clasped in both of mine as he said: "You're leaving us. I just wished . . . I wanted . . . well . . . God bless you, Mum. And God bless Michael and the wee ones, too." In all my many comings and goings as an anthropologist, there was no good-bye that I have held as dear over the years as this one, which had been wrested from the giver with so much difficulty.

The supreme irony is that the anthropologist who has always been in search of a relatively classless, genderless, egalitarian society, had stumbled onto one early in her career without ever recognizing it as such or singing its praises in this regard. This village egalitarianism was expressed as well in the painful decisions that had to be made about inheritance, the argument that was so central to my thesis. While these decisions never came easily to either generation, parents or children, in the end they were decided with a strong commitment to fairness and with attention to correcting the unwitting losses experienced by one sibling at the hands of the other. Unlike rural English patterns of primogeniture based on a "winner takes all" model, Irish farm families always strived to settle each of their "disinherited" sons and daughters with some kind of life security—whether through carefully sought-after connections with potential patrons in commerce and the trades in the next town (see Arensberg 1937) or through the Catholic

Church and its extensive web of educational and social welfare institutions, or through helpful relatives and former neighbors abroad. Consequently, virtually no "disinherited" Irish child was sent out into the world to "seek their fortune" utterly alone as had so many generations of "disinherited" rural English children (see Birdwell-Pheasant 1998). Consequently, the traveling and diasporic Irish, including over the generations a great many from the little parish of An Clochán, have contributed, disproportionately, to the culture and civilization of the larger English-speaking world (see Hout 1989, chapter 5; Keneally 1998). For all these reasons and for whatever it could possibly matter now—all credit to An Clochán!

▪ Crediting Ethnography

To begin with, I wanted that truth to life to possess a concrete reliability, and I rejoiced most when the poem seemed most direct, an upfront representation of the world it stood in for or stood up for or stood its ground against. — SEAMUS HEANEY, *Crediting Poetry*, 1995

At the heart of the anthropological method is the practice of witnessing, which requires an engaged immersion over time in the lived worlds of our anthropological subjects. Like poetry, ethnography is an act of translation and the kind of "truth" that it produces is necessarily deeply subjective, resulting from the collision between two worlds and two cultures. And so, the question often posed to anthropologist-ethnographers about the dangers of "losing one's objectivity" in the field is really quite beside the point. Our task requires of us only a highly disciplined subjectivity. There are scientific methods and models appropriate to other ways of doing anthropological research, but ethnography, as I understand it, is not a science.

A local friend and I stopped to admire an impressionist painting of the main street of An Clochán hanging in the window of a local artist's studio. We both agreed that the work was extraordinary, but I noted the odd color of the bay in the painting and asked my friend, "Have you ever seen the water here take on that shade?" "No," he replied, "but surely your man has his right to paint it the way he sees it." "Indeed," I replied pointedly and my friend nodded with a smile, putting to rest the discussion we had just been having about a particular shade of ethnographic understanding as depicted in this book.

Very much like the poet who decides to enter another oeuvre for the purpose of translation—Seamus Heaney, for example, describing his entering the poetry of Dante[2]—the anthropologist sees something in another world that intrigues them. It can be as simple as "Oh, I like that! Let me see if I can't understand how that particular mode of being and thinking and feeling and sensing the world works, the sense it makes, the logic and the illogic of it, the pragmatics and the poetics of that other way of life." And so we think, "Yes, I'll go there for a while and see if I can't come back with a narrative, a natural history, a thick description— call it what you will—that will enrich our ways of understanding the world." Like any other form of "translation," ethnography has a predatory and a writerly motive to it. It is not done "for nothing" in an entirely disinterested way. It is *for* something; often it is to help us understand something—whether it is about schizophrenia as a projection of cultural themes or about ways of solving perennial human problems involving the reproduction of bodies and families and homes and farms.

In referring to his own long-term project of translating the Beowulf, Seamus Heaney (2000) drew on a generative metaphor based on the Viking relationship between England and Ireland, distinguishing between the historical period known as the Viking raids and the period known as the Settlement. The raid, he said, is a very good motive for poetic translation. The poet can raid Italian or German poetry and come back with a kind of booty called imitations of Homer or imitations of Virgil, for example. Or, alternatively—as Heaney did with his *Beowulf* translation—the poet can approach the translation through "settlement"—that is, entering the oeuvre, colonizing it, taking it over for one's own artistic purposes. Heaney took more than twenty years, for example, to translate the Beowulf into a modern English idiom that captured both the coarse and spiky consonants of Anglo-Saxon speech *and* the soft and beguiling Irish-English of his own Ulster kin and forefathers. In settling in with the work, Heaney advises, you stay with it a long time, identify with it in an imaginative way: you change it and it changes you.

Tailor Dean of An Clochán

Then there are ethnography and *participant observation*, the settlement metaphor par excellence. Here we enter, settle down, and try to stay for as long as people will tolerate our presence, as I tried to do in Ballybran. As archetypal traveling people, anthropologists are at the mercy of those who agree to take us in as much as they are at our mercy in the ways we represent them after the living in and living with period is over. Anthropologists are a restless and nomadic tribe, hunters and gatherers of human values. Often we are motivated by our own sense of estrangement from the natal society and culture into which we were existentially thrown. I went to rural Ireland, in no small part, in search of better ways to live and I found them, especially among the old ones like Tailor Dean of An Clochán with whom I spent the greater part of my days and long winter evenings and who, no doubt, biased me toward an overly critical view of village life in the mid-1970s.

▪ Rabbit Run: Taking Leave

Between my finger and my thumb
The squat pen rests; snug as a gun.
—SEAMUS HEANEY, *"Digging,"* 1968

You don't take up a dangerous trade like literature in Ireland
without developing the hide of a rhinoceros and renting a
house in a strategic spot with direct access to the sea.
—FRANK O'CONNOR, 1964

The fateful visit with Martin spelled the beginning of the end of my return to An Clochán. By the next day I was beginning to feel the weight of social censure closing in, not so much on me personally, as on those in the village who had taken me in—those who, in the village vernacular, had "fed me and kept me"—or had taken me under their wing. When S., for example, arrived to meet me for breakfast the next morning, she was in a state of considerable agitation. She had not slept well the previous night. "I was awakened," she said, "by a terrible nightmare. Oh, it was an awful sensation, as if my house was being invaded by a dark force, an ill wind, or an alien invader." She looked hesitantly to me for a clue to her ominous dream. I replied only that houses were often symbols of the body and of the self and left it at that.

But that night it was my turn to be awakened by a ghostly visitation, a hooded creature who pointed a long skinny finger over and beyond my head and toward the sea. Like Scrooge, I was happy to find myself unchanged in the morning and I suppressed the urge to hug the wooden bedstead, promising, "I am *not* the woman I was, I am not the woman I was." But I knew this to be untrue in certain fundamental ways. And I took out my little notebook—the one that would prove to be my undoing—and jotted down a few ragged thoughts.

Shaken, I continued my daily rounds of the village, by now heavy of heart and uncertain of step. I waved to a solitary haymaker, the first one I'd seen in several days. He did not recognize me and he stopped to take a break.

Ballynalacken,
Cloghane.
Jan 3 1975

My Dear friend, Nancy & Mike and children
I lost track of ye I was expecting a
letter the time back Euge was posting me
to write to Mike and Nancy but you said
not to write untill ye would remove,
but all is well that ends well, I was so last
Oct, and I was not well this year as I met
with an accident and had 14 stiches but on
my leg the Docter is visiting me all the
year and nurses life is all suffering, Euge is
padling away all the time, I had no card made
to send you so I said the children would enjoy
this donkey, I received your five dollars Nan
and we said you wanted it for your children
                bought a publick House
in Cloghane and paid 11 thousand for it
its near his own house.   was in
Hospital well be back soon, Bridge Moarty
is fine. and Euge sends his best love
so for this time, I will say Happy New year
        Nora & Euge God bless

Euge Moriarty bounces our youngest 'baba', Nate, in Ballynalacken during a break in
the haying in June 1974. Matched and married off late in life and consequently childless, Euge and his wife, Nora, helped co-parent our children during the year of our stay
with great pleasure and much bickering between them over what the "'strange little
critters needed." ["Yerra, get that old woman away from the baba—she'll kill him yet!"
Euge would often bellow with reference to Nora, who would just laugh and shrug him
off.] Like the Tailor and Ansty, Euge and Nora were 'old style' country people who dis-
dained those villagers who 'put on airs'. This letter was one of the last ones exchanged
before both died—no doubt bickering up to the end—within months of each other.
Nora refused to be photographed and always covered her face with her ample apron
whenever I tried, and always failed, to catch her unawares. Euge, however, enjoyed
having his picture taken.

Making small talk, I asked the man why he took such care in making several small haycocks rather than larger haystacks. "Because the hay is much sweeter this way and it pleases the animals more," he replied, tipping his cap as I walked on. After the visit with Martin I began to walk the country roads with my head bowed, practicing a government of my eyes so as not to elicit an automatic greeting from those who might later regret it. And I took to announcing myself at the open door of older friends and acquaintances: "It's Crom Dubh, the crooked one, come back to An Clochán." Indeed, I *was* beginning to feel very much like Crom Dubh, the pagan force and alter ego of the village, who epitomized everything dark, hidden, secret, and overgrown, tangled among the brambles of the old graveyard — everything that needed to be resisted. My presence was a daily reminder — "salt in the wound" said one villager — of everything they would like to hide, deny, and secret away.

In fact, however, most villagers did not avoid me. Many fell back into the old habit of telling me poignant stories and catching me up on people, events, and changes in the parish. At times there seemed to be a pressure, even a hunger to speak. Kathleen shook her head one evening, "You are like the village analyst and we are all on the couch. We can't seem to stop ourselves from talking." It made no difference that I was not back looking for secrets; there was simply no way of escaping them. Since I had no other reason for being in the village except to visit with people, my presence became something of an obstacle, even to myself. In this small world, words were as dangerous as hand grenades or bullets, as much for those who gave as for those who received them.

A distinguished older couple took to going about with me in public at considerable social risk to themselves. It was, they said, the Christian thing to do, and never mind what others thought or said. Aiden even appointed himself my colleague in arms and after an afternoon of making house calls together, he commented wearily, "Ah, but this fieldwork is tiring." But as the situation grew more prickly I asked the new priest of An Clochán to help me call a parish meeting so that I could apologize in general terms for any pain I caused the community and so that villagers who wished could collectively express their anger. I hoped, naively perhaps, that we could clear the air and move forward. I explained how difficult it was to try to do this work of apology and explanation door to door. The priest was unsure. "Will you be up for it?" he mused. "Will *they* be up for it? *Should* you apologize? Would this be drawing too much attention to an old hurt? Better to let sleeping dogs lie, perhaps?" The good priest promised to mull it over for a few days and to get back in touch with me. "But come to Mass this Sunday," he urged. When, a few days later, I approached the Communion line, Father M. held the Host up high and looked about him reciting my name very loudly indeed: "*Nancy*, receive the body and blood of Christ." After Mass Father said that a parish meeting would be too risky and that I should just continue as I was doing, making my rounds, door to door, as best I could. As I walked home alone from the old stone chapel I wondered how much longer I should stay.

"It's beginning to feel desperately lonely here," I wrote in my notebook during the last week in An Clochán. I was staying at the lovely guesthouse of old acquaintances. The new home had replaced the original white caravan that had shook and rattled so with the fierce winter storms in the 1970s that B. and her then-small children often sat huddled together fearing that they might all be blown out into the sea. As the days wore on, I tried to stay out of harm's way and in my atticlike room reading and writing. By midday I might take a walk to a part of the parish where I was less notorious and order a pint of ale and some pub food. Nibbling around a plate of sodden and grayish fish and chips, I could spend up to an hour staring forlornly at the water lapping against the old quay at Brandon. From there I could spot the shapes of a few sightseers on Ballyguin strand huddling around the remains of a beached killer whale.

The drumming out of the village, when it came, was swift. There were warning signs a few days before that trouble was brewing. Conversation would suddenly stop when I entered a pub; I would smile weakly and turn on my heel. During an afternoon drive I was taken past a few sites that had been subject to local harassment, including car and house bombings. No one had ever been hurt in these attacks, but the damage to property was considerable and the message conveyed was clear. The parish was controlled, in part, by threats and intimidation from a small but active group of local cultural nationalists. Among the kinds of people evidently "unwanted" in the village were British landowners, suspected homosexuals, purported drug dealers, "gombeen men" (local petty capitalists who bought up old farms) and me, that new species of traitor and friend, the anthropologist.

Luckily, I was no novice in the fine art of quick getaways. Following the military coup in Brazil I was detained and held for questioning in 1965 by members of the Fifth Army at an old military base near the airport in Recife. I was accused of subversive activities among the sugarcane cutters and their families in "Bom Jesus da Mata." After a period of "house arrest" when I was made to check in daily with the judge in Bom Jesus, I made a quick exit to Rio and from there to Manaus for several weeks before returning to rural Pernambuco to complete the work I had started—a "subversive" children's daycare center and a project to provide clean drinking water. Later, in southwest Alabama as a civil rights worker affiliated with SNCC (the Student Non-Violent Coordinating Commiteee) during a period of transition to Black power, I had to elude at various times both radical militants *and* Selma's finest police, once taking refuge in a Catholic priest's rectory for a few weeks until the local bishop found out and identified a more appropriate safe house. But each time in the past my leave-takings had been cushioned by local supporters and, once the tricky period had passed, I would be helped back into the community to occupy one of those many spaces of solidarity that give life meaning, whether one is a refugee, a political activist, or an anthropologist.

In this instance, my local friends were shaken by the tide of rejection and were understandably torn by divided loyalties. On the last evening of my stay in An Clochán I returned to my B & B filled with stories to share. It had been a good day and I had managed to make contact with some dear old acquaintances. My flagging spirits were on the rebound. As I popped my head into the kitchen to tell B. that I'd be down for tea in a few minutes, she turned from the stove with a face that was flushed by more than the gas burners. "I have some terrible news," she blurted. "Is something wrong at home?" I asked, clutching at my throat. "Did something happen to Michael or one of the children?" "No, no, not that. But, Nancy, you have to leave. Right now. This evening. You can't eat here. You can't sleep here anymore."

I became stupid, unable to think quickly or clearly. "Did I do something wrong?" I asked. "Did I offend someone in the village today?" It was evening, I was dog tired, and my feet were sore. I had no transportation. Was it even possible to call up a taxi from distant Tralee at this hour? "Is there anyone else who can put you up tonight?" B. asked. "Let me think," I said, "while I go upstairs to pack." In the little attic room I moved slowly as in a dream, folding my few things into the suitcase pulled out from under the bed. I hadn't eaten since morning and I had missed dinner the evening before. So I was terribly hungry as well as tired. But where could I go? Who would be safe from whatever intimidation B. had gotten? And what was she told? "Get that woman out of here immediately before someone gets hurt."? I sat on the edge of the narrow bed and jotted down a few thoughts to clear my head. But they were so scrambled I tore out the page, crumpled it into a small wad, and tossed it carelessly into the wastepaper basket.

Outside night was falling. The closest home where I thought I might be able to stay was a mile away and I walked there quickly. My reception was kind but wary, and my friend let me know, at last, that indeed the community as a whole had closed down where I was concerned. "It's not fair," he said, "but I can't tell you that it hasn't happened. It's really not very good right now for *anyone* to be seen with you." Nonetheless, he kindly insisted that I spend the night, or even the week, if I wished. He refused, he said, to be intimidated. "Well, I'll go back and get my bags, but I will only stay until morning. And I'm so sorry for putting you in this situation." "It's only a book," he said. "And people here will tell you on the side that it has made them re-think a thing or two, for example, about how to raise and treat one's children." He laughed, "The young mothers, here, they now go all out of the way to nurse their babies, and they are forever hugging them. Just to show you, I sometimes think."

By the time I walked back to my original guesthouse to pick up my bags, an older village friend was waiting for me in the parlor. "Where have you been? We've been worried. We've worked out a solution," he said glumly. "You can spend your last night here—I'll see to it that no one blames B.— and I'll be back to fetch you first thing in the morning. Be completely ready. I'll carry you as far as Limerick and from there you'll take the bus to Dublin.

No, don't argue; I insist. We can at least see you off to the next county. And we can use the extra time to talk."

The next morning, after having crept quietly down the creaking stairs, I found a good strong bowl of tea and a plate of toast waiting for me in the "guest room." Ah, I thought, it's the *Lon na Bais*, the custom of the last meal that was left out just before an old one dies.[3] The family of the house had gathered around the long table in the kitchen for a breakfast that was taken in almost monastic silence. I tried to be equally silent in the next room. In taking my leave at last from B., I was confronted with my crime: "All that time you spent in your room upstairs. You weren't just reading— you were writing![4] You left a trail in the wastepaper basket. People *said* you were writing. They saw you scribbling into your notebook outside the pub in Brandon." "I won't deny it," I said. "But was it such a grave sin? I needed to write my way through my own confusion and loneliness." Then B. gave me a quick hug and whispered in my ear, "I'm so sorry for this. Ignore them. Keep up the good work."

The *Lon na Bais* ritual continued as my village mentor took me on our final rounds together of the village, this time for me to feast my eyes for the last time. Like a local funeral procession, he drove me slowly past all the sites that were dearest to me. "Take a good look," he said. "There's your Brandon Head. And there's your creamery, what's left of it. And here is your primary-school. In a few hours the children will be lining up to march inside. And here's your Peig's pub, your Tailor Dean's house, and your old widow Bridget's cottage overgrown with brambles." Then, as we turned the last curve past the abandoned little hamlet of Ballydubh, with the village almost out of sight, he forced me to turn around and take in the full sweep of the mountains and the sea. "And there," he said, "is your An Clochán. You had best say good-bye now."

In the end perhaps we deserve each other—well matched and well met, tougher than nails, both of us. Proud and stubborn, too. *Unrepentant* meets *Unforgiving*. And in a way villagers were right to say, "We don't believe you are *really* sorry." For in their view this would mean nothing less than a renunciation of self and of my vexed profession, a move I could not make.

Nancy Scheper-Hughes

But time, as they say, is a great healer. There is no such thing as everlasting ire any more than there is undying love. Anything can change. A sense of proportion and a sense of humor may eventually replace injured pride.[5]

In the meantime, as the Tailor of Ballybran would have said, "just leave that there." The next twenty-five years may pass even more swiftly than the last. And, God willing, by then *both* Crom Dubh and I will have found a way to return to "our" village.

The following TAT pictures that were used and referred to in the text:

1. A young boy is contemplating a violin, which rests on a table in front of him.

2. Country scene: in the foreground is a young woman with books in her hand; in the background a man is working in the fields and an older woman is looking on.

3BM. On the floor against a couch is the huddled form of a boy with his head bowed on his right arm. Beside him on the floor is a revolver.

3GF. A young woman is standing with downcast head, her face covered with her right hand. Her left arm is stretched forward against a wooden door.

4. A woman is clutching the shoulders of a man whose face and body are averted as if he were trying to pull away from her.

Note: The descriptions of the pictures are taken from the Thematic Apperception Test Manual by Henry Alexander Murray and the Staff of the Harvard Psychological Clinic (Harvard University Press 1971), pp. 18–20.

5.   A middle-aged woman is standing on the threshold of a half-opened door looking into a room.

6BM.   A short elderly woman stands with her back turned to a tall young man. The latter is looking downward with a perplexed expression.

7BM.   A gray-haired man is looking at a younger man who is sullenly staring into space.

8BM.   An adolescent boy looks straight out of the picture. The barrel of a rifle is visible at one side, and in the background is the dim scene of a surgical operation, like a reverie-image.

9BM.   Four men in overalls are lying on the grass taking it easy.

12M.   A young man is lying on a couch with his eyes closed. Leaning over him is the gaunt form of an elderly man, his hand stretched out above the face of the reclining figure.

12F.   The portrait of a young woman. A weird old woman with a shawl over her head is grimacing in the background.

13MF.   A young man is standing with downcast head buried in his arm. Behind him is the figure of a woman lying in bed.

15.   A gaunt man with clenched hands is standing among gravestones.

16.   Blank card.

17BM.   A naked man is clinging to a rope. He is in the act of climbing up or down.

18GF.   A woman has her hands squeezed around the throat of another woman whom she appears to be pushing backward across the banister of a stairway.

Seamus, "A Pregnant Lady"

Denis, "Self-Portrait"

AGE 26; PSYCHIATRIC PATIENT

Card 1. This one is inclined . . . either he's bored at his work, or he don't understand the particular lesson he's got in music. Or he might be giving himself a rest. (Outcome?) Well, it all depends. He might not like music. He might be forced into it.

Card 2. What particular era is this? (You can make it be any era you wish.) It could be rivalry between two women over this particular man at work in the fields. One seems to be more of the peasant type, the other more of the educated class. There is a class difference between them. He doesn't seem to be taking much notice of the two ladies. The work he is doing might be more important to him. This lady at first seems to be pregnant. And, then again, this particular lady [the student] might be thinking of the comfortable life that these people are living and that she hasn't got. (Which story do you want?) If it was a rivalry between the two women, then the two of them will have to battle it out between them. (Conclusion?) If the farm lady was in the same category as the other lady [the student], she might have a better chance.

Card 3BM. Do I have to distinguish whether he's a child or a man? (As you wish.) Ummmm . . . [a long pause]. First impression, he's young, boyish . . . twentyish. This here appears to be something like a gun on the floor. Has the boy contemplated suicide? Has he actually done it? I'd say contemplated. You want me to sum up? Maybe he's just thought things over, his present position, and he decides life is worth living after all. Probably he thought of better things in life worth living for: family, hobbies, something that appeals to him.

Card 4. He's in trouble. Naturally, she's trying to help him or console him. He's not inclined to listen to her. That's my first impression.

Card 5. Well, my first impression is of a lady who has just opened a door suddenly and possibly finds her daughter making love with someone. Either she looks horrified at the fact . . . no, no, her expression don't seem to show . . . actually her expression looks beyond the scope of this picture. Second impression: she's opening the door of a sitting room and asking her husband would he like some tea. (You have two stories here. Give me a conclusion for each.) In the first instance, the mother would throw whoever it was out, and the daughter would be in for a bundle of trouble. But I prefer the second. She'll just bring in a tray of tea.

Card 6BM. Mother and child problem. He's obviously told her something that upset her. Maybe he wants to marry someone not to her liking. Or, join the army. (Try to stick to one story.) The first then. Well, it might be a difference in the mother's view. Maybe the girl is not good enough socially or financially. Maybe the mother has a plan for him to marry somebody else. He seems to be fed up now, by the expression on his face. He doesn't seem to be rather determined. He's rather shy. The picture I can see . . . is of a boy . . . it could be that his mother could easily influence him, domineering. He's inclined to feel guilty about whatever he's told her. So, she could decide the whole factor. She could really make up his mind for him.

Card 7BM. First impression, it's a sinister looking photograph. Either a business plot or a shady deal of some kind. I should think the older man would be the more intelligent of the two. The boy seems to be dead eagle [*sic*] to do the older man's bidding to the last. (What's the deal about?) Business, competition, acquiring some contract or another . . . some form of blackmail maybe. (Outcome?) I suppose you could contribute that to Providence, luck over whether he's caught or not. But that one [the younger] is quite determined to do whatever this other man asks him.

Card 9BM. Winos. No reason to live, just to die. And, I find this younger one, strangely odd, that he should be with a bunch that are older, dirtier. He's younger, cleaner. He might be addicted. He could be sleeping, or maybe he's thinking out his problems. I should say that he's strong enough . . . from the picture he's well built. I'd say he gets out of it.

Card 12M. A man and a wife, say. She seems to be ill. He's afraid of the thought that she's dead. Afraid to touch her. First impression, he might run for help: doctor, priest, neighbors next door. Conclusion? (Yes.) All depends. If she's dead, she's dead. If she's ill, she could be made better.

Card 13MF. He hasn't raped her. She looks to be dead. Maybe she is someone special to him. They just had intercourse for the first time. He's ashamed, sorry that he did this. He's a student due to the books on the table. Either she's asleep, happy with herself, or she's dead . . . no. I'd say he had a very special respect for her which was broken after the intercourse. (Outcome?) I'd say that she tries to convince him that this is a fact of life, that millions and millions do it. If they are in love, what shame? He might marry her.

■ TABLE D–1: ACHIEVEMENT–ANOMIE THEMES

THEMES/CARDS	FEMALES			MALES		
	Normal	Hospitalized	Total	Normal	Hospitalized	Total
Card 1 (boy and violin)	(n = 22)	(n = 11)	(n = 33)	(n = 14)	(n = 11)	(n = 25)
Positive achievement	14	7	21	6	2	8
	64%	63%	64%	43%	18%	32%
Negative achievement	5	0	5	8	5	13
	23%	—	15%	57%	45%	52%
Violin broken or out of tune	1	1	2	7	3	10
	5%	9%	6%	50%	27%	40%
Violin not seen, or misidentified	12	6	18	3	4	7
	55%	55%	55%	21%	36%	28%
Card 2 (farm scene)	(n = 22)	(n = 11)	(n = 33)	(n = 14)	(n = 11)	(n = 25)
Positive achievement (re schooling, emigration)	12	5	17	5	3	8
	55%	45%	52%	36%	27%	32%
Negative achievement (withdrawal from school, work; daydreaming)	3	1	4	5	2	7
	14%	9%	12%	36%	18%	28%
Card 3BM (boy huddled on floor)	(n = 22)	(n = 11)	(n = 33)	(n = 14)	(n = 11)	(n = 25)
Boredom themes	2	1	3	3	2	5
	9%	9%	9%	21%	18%	20%

Note: Most of the stories told are characterized by one dominant theme, but often contain from two to four additional subthemes, and these are, at times, double-scored.

■ TABLE D—2: COMPETENCE—INADEQUACY THEMES

THEMES/CARDS	FEMALES			MALES		
	Normal	Hospitalized	Total	Normal	Hospitalized	Total
Card 1 (boy and violin)	(n=22)	(n=11)	(n=33)	(n=14)	(n=11)	(n=25)
Positive competence; avowal of capacity	5	2	7	1	0	1
	23%	18%	21%	7%	—	4%
Negative competence; failure or doubt about capacity	12	3	15	13	4	17
	55%	27%	45%	93%	36%	68%
Positive outcome: success theme	14	4	18	5	1	6
	64%	36%	55%	36%	9%	24%
Card 2 (farm scene)	(n=22)	(n=11)	(n=33)	(n=14)	(n=11)	(n=25)
Avowal of capacity regarding emigration	14	4	18	1	5	6
	64%	36%	55%	7%	45%	24%
Sense of fate or destiny deciding one's success or failure	0	0	0	4	2	6
	—	—	—	29%	18%	24%
Card 6BM (mother-son)	(n=14)	(n=6)	(n=20)	(n=14)	(n=10)	(n=24)
Failure; incompetence of son motif	4	2	6	5	2	7
	29%	33%	30%	36%	20%	29%
Son defends his abilities or asserts himself against his mother	5	1	6	2	1	3
	36%	17%	30%	14%	10%	13%

▪ TABLE D-3: CONTROL THEMES

THEMES/CARDS	FEMALES			MALES		
	Normal	*Hospitalized*	*Total*	*Normal*	*Hospitalized*	*Total*
Card 1 (boy and violin)	(n = 22)	(n = 11)	(n = 33)	(n = 14)	(n = 11)	(n = 25)
Coercion themes	6	1	7	4	2	6
	27%	9%	21%	29%	18%	24%
Child rebels against authority figure	5	0	5	0	0	0
	23%	—	15%	—	—	—
Card 3BM (boy huddled against couch)	(n = 22)	(n = 11)	(n = 33)	(n = 14)	(n = 11)	(n = 25)
Punishment themes	10	4	14	7	1	8
	45%	36%	42%	50%	9%	32%
Escape from punishment themes	9	0	9	0	0	0
	41%	—	27%	—	—	—
Verbal or physical attack against punishing parent	2	0	2	0	0	0
	9%	—	6%	—	—	—
Sulking as response to hurt or anger	0	0	0	4	1	5
	—	—	—	29%	9%	20%
Self-pity; suicide preoccupation	1	1	2	2	3	5
	5%	9%	6%	14%	27%	20%
Card 6BM (Mother-son)	(n = 14)	(n = 6)	(n = 20)	(n = 14)	(n = 10)	(n = 24)
Maternal control themes	9	4	13	11	7	18
	64%	67%	65%	78%	70%	75%
Son asserts himself against mother	5	1	6	2	1	3
	36%	17%	30%	14%	10%	13%
Son lacks autonomy; gives in to mother	0	0	0	9	3	12
	—	—	—	64%	30%	50%
Card 8BM (Surgical scene)	(n = 7)	(n = 3)	(n = 10)	(n = 8)	(n = 5)	(n = 13)
Accidental patricide; death of father	0	0	0	4	3	7
	—	—	—	50%	60%	54%

THEMES/CARDS	FEMALES			MALES		
	Normal	Hospitalized	Total	Normal	Hospitalized	Total
Card 12M (man on couch)	(n = 22)	(n = 12)	(n = 34)	(n = 14)	(n = 10)	(n = 24)
Confession/sin motifs	10	5	15	10	2	12
	45%	42%	44%	71%	20%	50%
Card 2 (farm scene)	(n = 22)	(n = 11)	(n = 33)	(n = 14)	(n = 11)	(n = 25)
Positive responsibility (toward work, parents, farm)	7	1	8	7	1	8
	32%	9%	24%	50%	9%	32%
Negative responsibility (escape themes)	9	3	12	3	2	5
	41%	27%	36%	21%	18%	20%
Guilt (about escape, parents, or an implied sexual sin)	6	2	8	3	1	4
	27%	18%	24%	21%	9%	16%
Card 6BM (Mother-son)	(n = 14)	(n = 6)	(n = 20)	(n = 14)	(n = 10)	(n = 24)
Son feels guilty about leaving home	4	0	4	6	3	9
	29%	—	20%	43%	30%	38%
Son leaves home: death strikes aged parent, son blames himself	1	0	1	6	1	7
	7%	—	5%	43%	10%	29%
Card 5 (woman opening door)	(n = 12)	(n = 6)	(n = 18)	(n = 10)	(n = 6)	(n = 16)
Mother seen as "snooping," eavesdropping	8	6	14	9	5	14
	67%	100%	78%	90%	83%	88%
Mother discovers child in sex play	2	2	4	0	3	3
	17%	33%	22%	—	50%	18%
Card 13MF (man with partially nude woman in bed)	(n = 22)	(n = 11)	(n = 33)	(n = 14)	(n = 10)	(n = 24)
Guilt, shame regarding sexuality	9	3	12	5	7	12
	41%	27%	36%	36%	70%	50%

▪ TABLE D—5: NURTURANCE—DEPRIVATION THEMES

THEMES/CARDS	FEMALES			MALES		
	Normal	Hospitalized	Total	Normal	Hospitalized	Total
Card 2 (farm scene)	(n=22)	(n=11)	(n=33)	(n=14)	(n=11)	(n=25)
Sense of social or economic deprivation expressed	14 64%	4 36%	18 55%	1 7%	5 45%	6 24%
Mother figure seen as mean, cruel, or depriving	5 23%	0 —	5 15%	7 50%	0 —	7 28%
Mother figure seen as kind, holy, or saintly	5 23%	5 45%	10 30%	0 —	2 18%	2 8%
Father figure seen as passive, distant, or uninvolved	2 9%	0 —	2 6%	1 7%	0 —	1 4%
Father figure seen as kind and hardworking	2 9%	2 18%	4 12%	6 43%	2 18%	8 32%
Card 3BM (huddled figure)	(n=22)	(n=11)	(n=33)	(n=14)	(n=11)	(n=25)
Father figure perceived as profligate, irresponsible, drunk	4 18%	1 9%	5 15%	4 29%	3 27%	7 28%
Card 7BM (father-son)	(n=14)	(n=5)	(n=19)	(n=14)	(n=10)	(n=24)
Father counsels son	2 14%	2 40%	4 21%	7 50%	5 50%	12 50%
Father corrupts or betrays son	3 21%	0 —	3 16%	4 29%	2 20%	6 25%
Card 18GF (woman squeezing throat of another woman)	(n=22)	(n=10)	(n=32)	(n=8)	(n=5)	(n=13)
Mother-child nurturance	6 27%	6 60%	12 38%	3 38%	2 40%	5 38%
Mother-child conflict with violence	2 9%	0 —	2 6%	5 63%	3 60%	8 62%
Mother indifferent to child's suffering*	3 14%	2 20%	5 16%	2 25%	2 40%	4 31%

*Double-scored with mother-child conflict.

THEMES/CARDS	FEMALES			MALES		
	Normal	Hospitalized	Total	Normal	Hospitalized	Total
Card 2 (farm scene)	(n=22)	(n=11)	(n=33)	(n=14)	(n=11)	(n=25)
Affiliation, love between family members	3	0	3	5	0	5
	14%	—	9%	36%	—	20%
Isolation, alienation between family members	9	3	12	7	5	12
	41%	27%	36%	50%	45%	48%
Affiliation between the sexes	5	5	10	0	3	3
	23%	45%	30%	—	27%	12%
Theme of sibling solidarity	5	0	5	6	0	6
	23%	—	15%	43%	—	24%
Card 4 (man and woman)	(n=22)	(n=10)	(n=32)	(n=14)	(n=11)	(n=25)
Love, affiliation between the sexes	3	2	5	0	5	5
	14%	20%	16%	—	45%	20%
Isolation, alienation, indifference between the sexes	8	4	12	4	1	5
	36%	40%	38%	29%	9%	20%
Conflict between the sexes	7	4	11	5	4	9
	32%	40%	34%	36%	36%	36%
Card 9BM (men on grass)	(n=5)	(n=3)	(n=8)	(n=8)	(n=6)	(n=14)
Male solidarity theme	2	1	3	6	5	11
	40%	33%	38%	75%	83%	79%
Idleness; sleeping theme	3	2	5	2	1	3
	60%	66%	62%	25%	17%	21%

THEMES/CARDS	FEMALES			MALES		
	Normal	*Hospitalized*	*Total*	*Normal*	*Hospitalized*	*Total*
Card 13MF (man with partially nude woman)	(n = 22)	(n = 11)	(n = 33)	(n = 14)	(n = 10)	(n = 24)
Guilt, shame, fear, or disgust regarding sexuality	9 41%	3 27%	12 36%	5 36%	7 70%	12 50%
Man forces or beats wife or sweetheart because she refuses sex	1 5%	2 18%	3 9%	3 21%	1 10%	4 17%
Familistic or latent incest theme: perception of couple as brother-sister, father-daughter, or mother-son	4 18%	0 —	4 12%	2 14%	0 —	2 8%
Sickness-death scene	10 45%	3 27%	13 39%	6 43%	1 10%	7 29%
Romance with death; desire to keep dead body	3 14%	1 9%	4 12%	1 7%	0 —	1 4%

COUNTRY AND EXACT YEARS	PERCENTAGE SINGLE AMONG PERSONS AGED 25–34 YEARS			
	FEMALES		MALES	
	1930s	1960s	1930s	1960s
Ireland (1936, 1966)	55	31	74	50
Northern Ireland (1937, 1966)	47	20	55	29
Finland (1930, 1965)	44	19	50	28
Sweden (1930, 1958)	43	16	54	30
Norway (1930, 1960)	43	15	51	32
Scotland (1931, 1966)	41	13	44	21
Austria (1934, 1967)	41	19	53	30
Iceland (1940, 1966)	40	14	55	26
Switzerland (1930, 1960)	39	23	46	35
Spain (1940, 1960)	35	28	46	39
England, Wales (1931, 1966)	33	12	35	21
Italy (1936, 1966)	32	21	41	38
Netherlands (1930, 1967)	30	12	36	22
Belgium (1930, 1961)	22	12	29	20
U.S.A. (1930, 1967)	18	7	29	14
France (1936, 1967)	15	14	17	27

Source: Robert Kennedy 1973: 141.

■ TABLE D–8: PERMANENT CELIBACY BY SEX IN SELECTED COUNTRIES, 1930S AND 1960S

| | PERCENTAGE SINGLE AMONG PERSONS AGED 45 YEARS AND OVER | | | |
| | FEMALES | | MALES | |
COUNTRY AND EXACT YEARS	1930s	1960s	1930s	1960s
Northern Ireland (1937, 1966)	25	21	22	18
Ireland (1936, 1966)	24	23	29	28
Iceland (1940, 1966)	24	20	17	20
Finland (1930, 1965)	21	16	22	9
Sweden (1930, 1965)	21	15	14	14
Scotland (1931, 1965)	21	18	15	12
Norway (1930, 1960)	20	18	12	13
Switzerland (1930, 1960)	18	17	13	12
Austria (1934, 1967)	16	13	11	7
England, Wales (1931, 1966)	16	12	10	8
Belgium (1930, 1961)	14	10	11	8
Netherlands (1930, 1967)	14	11	10	7
Italy (1936, 1966)	12	13	9	8
Spain (1940, 1960)	12	14	8	7
France (1936, 1967)	10	10	8	8
U.S.A. (1930, 1967)	9	6	10	6

Source: Robert Kennedy 1973: 142.

COUNTRY AND EXACT YEAR OF MARITAL FERTILITY RATE	NO. OF LEGITIMATE BIRTHS PER 1,000 MARRIED WOMEN AGED 10-49 YEARS
Ireland (1961)	195.5
New Zealand (1961)	154.6
Canada (1961)	152.9
Portugal (1960)	148.9
Spain (1960)	142.1
Netherlands (1963)	138.4
United States (1960)	132.7
Australia (1961)	131.9
Poland (1960)	130.1
Scotland (1964)	124.5
Finland (1963)	119.8
France (1963)	118.5
Switzerland (1960)	117.2
Austria (1961)	116.4
Norway (1960)	109.8
England and Wales (1964)	108.3
Belgium (1961)	106.3
Denmark (1963)	103.2
Sweden (1963)	86.9

Source: Adapted from Robert Kennedy 1973: 175.

NOTES

PREFACE TO THE 1982 PAPERBACK EDITION

1. One notable exception is the volume edited by Jay Ruby, *A Crack in the Mirror: Reflexive Perspectives in Anthropology* (Philadelphia: University of Pennsylvania Press, 1982); see especially Eric Michael's contribution pp. 133–148, "How To Look at Us Looking at the Yanomami."

2. See, for example, John Messenger's biting reply to his Irish critics, in his paper "When the 'Natives' Can Read and Respond: A New Projective Test," paper read at the American Anthropological Association Meetings, Los Angeles, December 5, 1981.

3. In chronological order: David Nowland, "Death by Suppression," *Irish Times*, August 4, 1979; Eileen Kane, "Is Rural Ireland Blighted?," *Irish Press*, December 13, 1979: 1; Michael Viney, "Geared For a Gale," *Viney's Irish Journey*, Irish Times, September 24, 1980, p. 12; Nancy Scheper-Hughes, "Reply to Ballybran," *Irish Times* (*Weekend* supplement) February 21, 1981, pp. 9–10.

4. Sir Raymond Firth, 1981, "Engagement and Detachment: Reflections on Applying Social Anthropology to Public Affairs," *Human Organization* 40 (3): 193–201. Originally presented as the Malinowski Award address at the 41st Annual Meeting of the Society for Applied Anthropology, Edinburgh, Scotland.

PROLOGUE: WRITING IRELAND

1. Among Edna O'Brien's many novels are *The Country Girls, The Lonely Girl, The Girl with the Green Eyes, August Is a Wicked Month, Casualties of a Peace, The Love Object, A Pagan Place,* and *Night.* Some of her best short stories are collected in *A Scandalous Woman and Other Stories.* A memoir, *Mother Ireland* (with photos by Fergus Bourke), was published in 1976.

2. I was the product of what was known in Brooklyn Irish Catholic circles as a "mixed marriage." My mother was, at the time, a somewhat lapsed Czech Catholic, my father a more resolute, though nonpracticing, German Lutheran. Catholic Church rules forced my father to sign an agreement,

before the marriage, that any children born of the union would be raised Catholic. The decision, however, to attend Catholic school was mine alone.

3. Drawing on her own fieldwork experiences in Lesu, Mississippi, Hollywood, and in the Rhodesian Copperbelt, Powdermaker noted that anthropological insight is often derived directly from self-understanding. In studying southern Blacks — especially the channeling of anger and aggression toward dominant Whites — Powdermaker said that she drew on her own experiences as a disenfranchised "minority" in her own family, (she saw herself as the least-favored child) and to her later experiences as a marginalized Jewish undergraduate student at the predominantly WASP Goucher College in Baltimore. Later, she used her own narcissistic tendencies — her passion for clothing and her attention to physical appearance — to identify with the psychological drives and infantile needs of Hollywood directors and stars. Mary Douglas had also drawn on her own experience of Anglo-Catholicism to understand the power and force of "natural symbols" among the Bog Irish. Powdermaker's reflections on anthropology as the practice of a disciplined subjectivity is treated throughout, but especially in the conclusions of, *Stranger and Friend: The Way of an Anthropologist* (1968).

4. There were also the ethnographies of that other Ireland, Northern Ireland, including Elliott Leyton's *The One Blood* (1975) and Rosemary Harris's *Prejudice and Tolerance in Ulster* (1972). Robin Fox's *The Tory Islanders: A People of the Celtic Fringe* (1978) which appeared almost simultaneously with *Saints, Scholars, and Schizophrenics*.

5. The sexual frankness found in the Irish prose epic, *Tain Bo Cuailnge*, The Cattle Raid of Cooley, set in the eighth century, comes first to mind. Medb, the Celtic queen, offers "her own friendly thighs" to seal a pact with the warrior Daire; Cuchulainn, still a young and green lad, wooes Emer, while peering down her dress, with the earthly taunt: "I see a sweet country. I could rest my weapon there!" (cited by Cahill 1995: 76-77). This robust Celtic tradition has been continued in the verses of the Northern Irish poet, Maeve McGillicuddy, and in poetry of Maire Mhac an tSaoi and that of her protégée, Nuala Ni Dhomhnaill, both writing in the searing and translucent "language of the tribe." Two verses plucked from Nuala Ni Dhomhnaill's *Taimid Damanta, A Dheirfearacha*, are exemplary:

We are damned, my sisters
we who accepted the priests' challenge
our kindred's challenge: who ate from destiny's dish
who have knowledge of good and evil
who are no longer concerned.

We spent nights in Eden's fields
eating apples, gooseberries; roses
behind our ears, singing songs
around the gypsy bon-fires
drinking and romping with sailors and robbers:
and so damned, my sisters

Our eyes will go to the worms
our lips to the clawed crabs
and our livers will be given as food to the parish dogs.
The hair will be torn from our heads
the flesh flayed from our bones.
They'll find apple seeds and gooseberry skins
in the remains of our vomit
when we are damned, my sisters.
— NUALA NI DHOMHNAILL (translated by Michael Harnett)

6. In addition to the more obvious issues related to land tenure, Irish workers suffered under British rule (and later under British economic hegemony) because Ireland, still agrarian, could not compete with British industry and factory products. The increased demand for beef shifted Irish agriculture from subsistence-based family farming to pasture conducive to neither employment nor population growth.

7. Ireland, thick with writers and poets but short on interpretive or reflexive social scientists, has left American and British anthropology to dominate the field, as it were. Today, this vacuum is being addressed by a fledgling graduate degree program in cultural anthropology at St. Patrick's College in Maynooth. In Ireland today (north and south) one can choose between two anthropology programs, one in Belfast at Queen's University, the bastion of Anglo-Irish Protestantism, the other at Maynooth, where anthropology is destined to exist, for better or worse, cheek by jowl with Ireland's National Catholic seminary.

8. Crom Dubh's head was the only Celtic stone carving to be found in the southwest of Ireland. The traditional pilgrimage to the top of Mount Brandon, which took place in July on Crom Dubh Sunday, was a local celebration associated with the ancient Festival of Lughnasa, which marked the beginning of the summer harvest. For some, the pilgrimage would begin with "rounds" at the stone head. Older people would kiss the stone as a cure for toothache.

9. The Celtic Tiger label referred to Ireland's impressive economic growth

throughout the decade of the 1990s, which approximated those of the four Asian tigers, South Korea, Hong Kong, Taiwan, and Singapore, whose rates of growth have averaged 8 percent a year over the past three decades.

10. See, for example, Peter Ward, *Divorce in Ireland* (Cork University Press, 1993); Carol Coulter, *The Hidden Tradition: Feminism, Women, and Nationalism in Ireland* (Cork University Press); Kieran Rose, *Diverse Communities: the Evolution of Lesbian and Gay Politics in Ireland* (Cork University Press).

11. I was introduced in the early 1980s by a Brazilian psychiatrist, Naomar Almeida Filho, to Franco Basaglia's seminal article, *"Silence in the Dialogue with the Psychotic"* (1964), which I read with a rush of recognition and fellow feeling, nodding in agreement. Basaglia described so exactly the difficulty of trying to communicate with people suffering from an uncanny fear of engulfment and annihilation by others.

12. Today, all the district mental hospitals, including St. Finan's, have already been or are scheduled for closure. The remaining patients — elderly, intractable, incontinent, senile, or simply abandoned — will be transferred to the psychiatric wards of general hospitals or released to nursing homes. Two decades of deinstitutionalization policy in Ireland have left behind an elderly, debilitated, and socially abandoned population. Today, St. Finan's Psychiatric Hospital is more old folks home than mental asylum, and it too has been scheduled for closure in the next year or two.

13. In 1903 Irish emigrants made up 16 percent of the foreign-born white population of the United States and 29 percent of those institutionalized in U.S. mental asylums. Young Irish women emigrants were particularly prone to mental hospitalization in New York City and Boston. The Irish also crowded the pauper houses. Between 1849 and 1891 60 percent of the population of the New York City almshouse were native-born Irish. Joseph Robins (1986: 125) notes that "in the nineteenth century Irish immigrants acquired a name for being madder, drunker, and less respectful of the law" than those of other origins, but that the Irish "had come from a life of hardship to one of far greater deprivation . . . and that their shortcomings were aggravated and exaggerated by Anglo-American prejudices against the Catholic Irish in general" (ibid).

14. The history of Irish mental and other "total" institutions begins with British colonial medical and psychiatric experiments in Ireland followed by the ravages of the Great Famine, which produced a system of workhouses and poor houses where surplus rural populations — unattached elderly, single women, disinherited sons — were unloaded. The overproduction of mental hospitals continued through the early twentieth century as the new government of the

Irish Republic mindlessly followed the policies of the former British rulers in building and maintaining an excessive number of psychiatric hospital beds (see Robins 1986; Saris 1996; Healy, n.d).

15. The situation I described here (see especially chapters four and six) also bears resemblance to one described by Jeanne Favret-Saada (1981, 1989) in a rural area in western France. In the Bocage the political economy of small farms requires, as in rural western Ireland, that the head of the farm and the stem family exploit the free labor (and the goodwill) of a great many kin. Consequently, when new male heads of household first accede to ownership and control of the family farm they often fall prey to chaotic forms of illness and paralysis that they understand within the local idiom of witchcraft. Favret-Saada, a psychoanalyst as well as an ethnographer, understood "bewitchment" as a projection of the farmer's guilt about his culturally sanctioned acts of violence toward those closest and dearest to him, who would now be making considerable sacrifices in his name. Techniques of unbewitching served to divert and redirect the accumulated hostile tensions within the farm family and free the farmer from his own guilt so that he could resume the necessary work and direction of the small farm.

16. In May 1992, for example, it was revealed in the press in both the United States and Ireland that the amiable and much revered Bishop Eamonn Casey had fathered a child by a secret American lover, Annie Murphy, and that he had used diocesan funds for payments—essentially hush money—to the mother and her illegitimate child in Boston. When this cozy arrangement was compared with the Church's official intolerance, even meanness, toward all forms of "moral laxity" in the laity, the tide of public opinion throughout Ireland began to change. The contrast between the private sheltering of Bishop Casey and the official refusal of an abortion for a hapless fourteen-year-old girl who had been raped and was both pregnant and suicidal was often drawn following the revelation. Elsewhere, I have discussed the devastating effect of revelations of clerical sexual abuse on the morale of rural Irish and Irish-American Catholics (see Scheper-Hughes 1998).

17. Robin Fox (1978) has described the most extreme instance of "brother-sister" marriage in peripheral western Ireland, the pattern that allowed married couples to remain living in their natal homes with their adult siblings so as not to disrupt well-established living and work patterns. "Under ideal circumstances the woman would stay with her relatives and work and cook for them. Her husband likewise would remain with his. He would, however, be a privileged 'visitor' in his wife's household, taking some meals there and in the early days, at least, staying overnight for some nights" (p. 159). However, "if the marriage

was to be consummated, it had often to be in the fields at night" (p. 160) and children born of the union would be reared in the woman's natal household by herself and her kin.

18. Following Pierre Bourdieu (1977:173) a public secret refers to "the best-kept and the worst-kept secret (one that everyone must keep [so as not to break] the law of silence which guarantees the complicity of collective bad faith." There were a great many such secrets to be kept in Ballybran, among them the individual and collective nervousness about village endogamy which sometimes brought sexuality and marriage a little bit too close to home. Incestual themes crop up frequently enough in Irish and Irish-American literature, most recently in Jeannette Haien's elegant, complex, and sensitively rendered rural Irish morality tale, *The All of It* (1986).

19. According to K. H. Connell, in the seventeenth century the rural Irish were known for their sexual freedom, illegitimacy, early marriage, and large families. After that and "in the two or three generations following the 1780s peasant children, by and large, married whom they pleased. The opportunity to marry was contingent on the occupation of land that promised a family's subsistence [leading eventually to] . . . subdivision, earlier marriage, large families and more subdivision." The transformation of Irish sexuality and reproduction was brought about, Connell argued (1968: 115) in response to the famine: "The trend toward longer, if not lifelong celibacy probably set in with the imminence of the famine: it persisted among the people as a whole for the first half-century of civil registration."

But in some marginal, rural areas, illegitimacy was never considered a problem. On Tory Island, for example, "sex did not break up a [natal] family; neither did an illegitimate child. In any case, I was told, better an illegitimate child than an unsuitable marriage" (Fox 1978: 160).

INTRODUCTION

1. The interested reader is referred to Cusack (1871); Foley (1907); Hayward (1950); King (1931); and T. F. O'Sullivan (1931). Full citations can be found in the Bibliography.

2. The Thematic Apperception Test consists of a series of standardized pictures that reflect everyday characters in a variety of moods and human situations (see Appendix A). For each picture the subject is asked to make up a story with a definite plot and a final outcome. He is also encouraged to tell what each character is thinking and feeling. This psychological test has proven particularly well adapted to the needs and skills of the anthropologist: It is straightforward, relatively free of cultural bias, and suited to answering the

kinds of questions that the anthropologist has in mind regarding basic cognitive and normative orientations, appropriate role behaviors, and the quality of emotional life, etc., without having to venture into the deeper waters of technical personality assessment or symbolic analysis.

3. See, for example, the characterization of the English anthropologist in an Irish village from Honor Tracy's *The Straight and Narrow Path* (1956).

CHAPTER ONE

1. See "The Book of Invasions" from Proinsias MacCana's *Celtic Mythology*, London: Hamlyn (1970: 57–60).

2. Carl Selmer, ed. *Navagatio Sancti Brendani Abbatis*. Medieval Studies Series: University of Notre Dame (1959).

3. "Vitae Sancti Brendani," in Patrick Cardinal Moran, *Acta Sancti Brendani*, Dublin (1872). See also W. Stokes, ed. *Lives of the Saints from the Book of Lismore*, Dublin (1957).

4. Where some authors attribute the tradition of Irish asceticism and sexual repression to the seventeenth-century French Jansenist influence (see Blanshard 1953; Sheehy 1968; Whyte 1971), I take the position that the celibate and ascetic tendency extends back at least as far as the introduction of Christianity into Ireland by monastics, such as Brendan, who were culture bearers of Eastern Mediterranean "Desert Theology." Egypt and Syria gave birth to that specific form of monasticism that was to reappear a few centuries later in the Celtic west of Ireland. Unlike the Christian monastic tradition that developed on the continent of Europe, Desert Theology monasticism demanded a long period of ascetic discipline during which time each monk chose his own solitude, natural cave, or stone hut and applied to himself his own regime of fasting, self-mortification, and meditation. The interested reader is referred to Kathleen Hughes's *The Church in Early Irish Society* (1966: 12–20). See also chapter four, note 11.

5. Robin Flower (1947: 24) immortalized the first piece of whimsical Irish poetry, recorded in a ninth-century manuscript by a monk taking a breather from his weighty verses with the beguiling verse:

I and Pangur Ban my cat,
'Tis a like task we are at:
Hunting mice is his delight
Hunting words I sit all night.

6. Presently under excavation by a government archeologist.

7. Robert Graves. *The White Goddess*. London: Faber and Faber (1961: 51–53).

CHAPTER TWO

1. See K. H. Connell 1955: 82–103; 1968: 113–162.
2. For a full discussion of Irish emigration since the famine, see Robert Kennedy 1973, chapter 4, and K. H. Connell 1968.
3. In 1973 the average age of grooms in the Republic was 27.2, and of brides 24.8 (Ireland, *Report on Vital Statistics*, 1973: ix, courtesy of Robert Kennedy). However, this may be somewhat misleading. As there were no marriages in Ballybran for 1973, the age at marriage figures have been averaged from married couples spanning three generations in the parish. The figures represent an *overall* pattern among currently married villagers.
4. See Eugene Hammel and Peter Laslett 1974: 73–109.
5. Commins, H., and Kelleher, C., 1973, *Farm Inheritance and Succession*. Dublin: Macra na Feirme.
6. Jokes concerning bestiality, especially with sheep, are numerous in rural Ireland, but are particularly concentrated in the southwest. Professor Emmet Larkin of the University of Chicago, in conducting research in the Vatican Archives on confessional summations, found a surfeit of animal-contact confessions from Kerry and west Cork (John Messenger, personal communication).
7. *Gombeen man* is the disparaging term used in rural Ireland to refer to local capitalists or middlemen (often shopkeepers), in particular those who charge high interest rates. The term is thought to be a derivation of the Latin *cambiare* (to count, change money).
8. In 1844 J.C. Kohl notes in his book, *Ireland* (London: Chapman and Hall): "These Kerrymen enjoy the reputation throughout Ireland of great scholarship. 'Even the farmers' sons and labourers know Latin there' is a common saying." (P. 33)
9. Until very recently, suicide was punishable by automatic excommunication from the Catholic Church, and the remains were not granted a Christian burial. Seldom will a physician sign a death certificate indicating that suicide was the cause of death. Hence, Irish suicide statistics are very unreliable.
10. In the following discussion of the Irish language, I have relied on the following historical sources: O'Faolain 1949: 102ff.; Moody and Martin, eds., 1967; Curtis 1936. John Messenger (1969) first suggested that the Irish revival be considered a "nativistic" movement.

CHAPTER THREE

1. These statistics reflect only the prevalence of psychiatric hospitalization — specifically, the total number of mental patients in public and private psy-

chiatric hospitals under all diagnoses (including mental deficiency) on December 31, 1955, and December 31, 1965.

2. See World Health Organization 1968: 531–533.
3. The word *celibate* is used in the hospital census to refer to single persons; in this sense it implies neither permanent virginity nor religious vows.
4. See J. H. Whyte (1971: 377–398).
5. The interested reader is referred to Seán O'Súilleabháin's marvelous descriptions of Irish country wakes, 1967.

CHAPTER FOUR

1. "Seamas" and "Padraec" are based on true case histories. However, many identifying features have been altered to protect the anonymity of those concerned. They are not brothers, and neither is from the parish of Ballybran.
2. The greatest number of first admissions for schizophrenia in Ireland occur in the age bracket twenty-five to thirty-four (O'Hare and Walsh 1970, table 11, p. 32). Contrasting figures from Canada (courtesy of H. B. M. Murphy) indicate that there are approximately twice as many first admissions for schizophrenia among twenty-year-olds as there are among thirty-year-olds there. I should like to add a cautionary note, one pointed out to me by Professor H. B. M. Murphy. I do not suggest that celibacy necessarily *causes* schizophrenia. It is likely that for a large number the illness itself interferes with the forming of the romantic attachments or even the utilitarian kinship alliances necessary to contract a marriage. However, an alternate explanation offered in the following pages is that the rebelliousness of some young Irish schizophrenics to the norms of sexual repression in the rural west seems to contribute to the labeling of these men as "crazy" or "deviant." Hence, it is all right to withdraw from human contact as a village recluse, but it is all wrong to "make a fool" of oneself in an attempt to find a bride.
3. According to the sporadically kept Ballybran death register, there were 358 persons buried in the parish between 1928 and 1969. Of the 180 males, 87 were bachelors; of the 178 females, only 33 were spinsters.
4. Arensberg described this "west" room as the locus of honor, prestige, and power within the Irish cottage. However, my observations of the few old couples who, in fact, still inhabit such a room in the traditional two-rooms-plus-loft cottage seem rather to have been relegated to the "back ward" rather than to a place of authority in the home. The erosion of cultural values and the subjectivity and perception of the social scientist both come into play.
5. The Roman Catholic incest prohibitions impede marriage between all those persons descendant from a common great-great-grandparent, as well as

between a widow or widower and any of his or her deceased spouse's blood relations, and, finally, between any baptized Catholic and any of his or her ritual sponsors (i.e., "godparents"). See *Catholic Encyclopedia* article "Consanguinity" for fuller description.

6. The director of the district mental hospital in Kerry said that a sizeable proportion of married women patients are the casualties of unhappy marriages contracted in haste while in "culture shock" abroad.

7. The difficulty of female incorporation within patrilineal societies has been examined by Denich (1971) for the Balkans; by Hoffman (1970) for rural Greek society; and by Strathern (1972) for New Guinea Hagan society.

8. Seán O'Súilleabháin (personal communication) suggested that the origin of this custom was in the disregard of the Irish monks for Pope Gregory's revision of the calendar. On the Skelligs the monks observed a later Lenten and Easter schedule, which thereby lengthened the permissible period for marriage. The aspect of social control involved in the censure of bachelors and spinsters by the local Straw Boys is reminiscent of the custom of *cencerrada* practiced in Spain, where it is the remarriage of widows and widowers that violates folk morality (see Pitt-Rivers 1954: 170–175). Public mockings are also practiced in English villages (see Thomas Hardy's description of the "skimpty ride" in *The Mayor of Casterbridge*).

9. In 1995 the Irish electorate voted, by a tiny margin, in favor of the legalization of divorce in the Republic. In 1996 the government amended the Family Law Act to make divorce legally available in Ireland.

10. See J. G. Peristiany, ed., *Honour and Shame: The Values of Mediterranean Society* (London: Oxford University Press, 1966).

11. It is possible that the custom of "stations," or house masses, originated during Penal Times in Ireland, when the celebration of the Mass was forbidden, and priests mingled among the people in disguise as peasants. In Ballybran, stations occur twice a year, in spring and in autumn, at which time the local priest or curate visits one house in each townland of the parish. Confessions are heard in the parlor, and Mass celebrated in the kitchen. Parish dues (including "oat" money for the horse, which today is used for gasoline for the car) are collected, and both clergy and neighbors are entertained for breakfast. Sometimes an evening party concludes the station ritual, and is one of the few times when neighbors get together socially.

12. More recently, Jeannette Haien (1986) published an exquisite novel about the secret life of a brother and sister passing as a married couple in a distant parish where they escaped from the clutches of a brutal and abusive father.

13. In fact, the ascetic tradition in Ireland clearly predates Christianity, as can be

documented in the ancient Brehon Laws (codified about the time of Saint Patrick, but based on pagan "natural law" with some Christian reinterpretation). Throughout the *Senchus Mor*, the "Law of Distress," there is an emphasis on fasting and sexual continence. W. Neilson Hancock, in his preface to the 1865 edition of *Senchus Mor* (London: Longmans, Green) notes the parallels between the early Celtic practice of forcing compensation for a debt or wrongdoing by requiring the creditor or plaintiff to fast (until death) at the door of his debtor, and the Hindu law of Acharitan, also called the "Law of Distress." Whatever the origin of Celtic asceticism, it was quickly absorbed into a Christian ascetic tradition, largely through the efforts of the fifth- and sixth-century Irish penitentials, Brendan, Finian, and Columban. Even Saint Patrick was said to have been alarmed at the alacrity with which the pagan Celts embraced monastic Christianity, especially celibacy. Given its long penitential tradition, Ireland was fertile ground for the reception, many centuries later, of the heretical French Catholic movement called Jansenism, which found its way to Ireland through refugee clerics from Louvain during the French Revolution. Jansenism, a seventeenth-century reinterpretation of fifth-century Augustianism, placed great emphasis on sexual purity and interpreted human nature as weak and inclined toward evil, requiring acts of penance and self-denial. For background on the early penitential Christian tradition in Ireland, see Kathleen Hughes, *The Church in Early Irish Society* (Ithaca, 1966). Concerning the later development of Irish Jansenism, see J. H. Whyte, *Church and State in Modern Ireland* (Dublin, 1971), and John T. Noonan, Jr., *Contraception* (Cambridge, 1965: 316, 396–397). It is this unbroken penitential tradition in Ireland that most distinguishes Irish (and American) Catholicism from the Catholic tradition in the Mediterranean and Latin America, where the conflict between spirit and flesh is minimized.

14. Under guidelines from the *Documents of Vatican II*, Walter Abbot, ed. (London, 1966), regarding the sacredness of the body and the importance of conjugal love (see especially pp. 252–258), the Irish clergy has attempted to erase Irish puritanism. See, for example, Fr. O'Doherty in O'Doherty and McGrath, *The Priest and Mental Health* (Dublin, 1962).

15. The Values Hierarchy Scale was first developed by Diaz-Guerrero (1963) for the purpose of investigating values differences between Mexican and American youth.

16. See Maurice O'Sullivan's rendition of this folk belief in his autobiography, *Twenty Years A-Growing* (1957: 13–15).

17. Of the twenty-three essays I solicited from Ballybran secondary-school students on the topics "What Do Young People Expect from Marriage," and "How

Does an Idealized Image of Marriage Differ from the Reality of Married Life," over three-fourths of the girls and half the boys described marriage as a hardship, rarely resulting in the happiness hoped for. Of those who mentioned the physical aspect of marriage, all agreed that sex or "mere physical attraction" was the wrong reason for marrying. The well-indoctrinated students tended to stress the Christian duties of marriage, the procreation and education of children, yet concluded, ironically, that these very obligations made marriage a hardship, a "vale of tears," as one student dramatically phrased it. A desire to prolong youth and postpone parenting (without the availability of contraception) was expressed in the consensus that the "ideal" age at marriage would be in the late twenties.

CHAPTER FIVE

1. It might be noted that the clinging of malnourished *favela* babies was certainly exaggerated by their desperate condition.
2. Since this book was published I returned to northeast Brazil for a decade of intermittent field research that grappled with these issues. See *Death Without Weeping: the Violence of Everyday Life in Brazil* (University of California Press, 1993).
3. Criminal Law Amendment Act, Section 17; Ireland, *Public General Acts* 1935: 141. A lively and continuing debate on the efficacy and morality of natural methods of birth control (Billings and ovulation and temperature methods) can be followed in the *Irish Times* throughout the summer and fall of 1974.
4. While contraception is legal and widely accepted today, abortion is still prohibited.
5. An example of the impure status of the post-parturient woman comes from the seventeenth-century *Dunton Letters:* "Before I left Connaught, Mr. Flaghertie . . . conveyed me to a christening when he was gossip. I was much surprised to see the mother delivered but two days before about the house, but not suffered to touch either any of the meat or drink provided for the guests, because they deem her unhallowed until her churching or Purification be performed" (cited by Fleming 1953: 59). This ritual "churching" of mothers traditionally took place forty days after the birth of an infant. In the late 1960s Vatican Council reforms replaced the ancient Purification ceremony with a simpler Blessing of New Fathers and Mothers, which takes place immediately after the infant's baptism. Some traditional mothers in Ballybran, however, still request and receive the old "churching" blessing.
6. *A bhean, beir do leanbh*
   Mar rug Anna Muire,

Mare rug Muire Dia,
Gan mairtriú, gan daille
Gan easba coise ná laimhe.
—SEÁN O'SÚILLEABHÁIN (1974: 43)

7. Seán O'Súilleabháin (personal communication) tells of the famous trial in County Tipperary in 1875 in which a man and his blood kin were tried and convicted of burning the man's wife and infant son, who were believed to be changelings.

CHAPTER SIX

1. Jimmy Hennesy is a fictitious character, based on a true case history. He is not from the town of Dingle, and other identifying characteristics have been altered to preserve anonymity.
2. Robert Kennedy (1973) in his demographic study of marriage and fertility patterns in Ireland suggests that the subordinate status of Irish females seems to have increased their mortality levels from what they might otherwise have been over the past generation. The pattern of excess female mortality was especially marked in the decades before the 1940s and among rural females from early childhood until marriage, and then after the child-bearing period (see especially pp. 41–65).
3. Gregory Bateson, et al. (1956) define the necessary ingredients for a double-bind situation as follows:
   1. Two or more persons, one defined as victim and the other as the "binder."
   2. Repeated experience so that the double bind is a recurring theme in the experience of the victim.
   3. A primary negative injunction. This may have two forms: (a) "Do so and so, or I will punish you." (b) "If you do not do so and so, I will punish you."
   4. A secondary injunction conflicting with the first, at a more abstract level, and like the first enforced with punishment or signals that threaten survival.
   5. A tertiary negative injunction prohibiting the victim from escaping the field.

CONCLUDING OBSERVATIONS

1. "The Second Coming," in the *Collected Poems of W. B. Yeats*, New York: Macmillan (1970).
2. I might make mention here of the important distinction between those shamans and healers whose hysterical or epileptic symptoms are real, and those who simply mimic trance, hysteria, possession, or other ecstatic states in order to win an audience or demonstrate privileged status. See, for example, Claude Lévi-Strauss's description (1967) of a shaman pretender in "The

Sorcerer and His Magic." Schwartz (1968) has introduced the term "path-omimetic" to describe instances of shamanic mimicry. Brazilian *favelados* (hillside slum dwellers) of the shantytown in which I functioned as a public health worker, easily distinguished the money-grabbing fakers within the *Condomblé* cult from true mediums and healers. Evidently, charlatans exist in every society.

EPILOGUE: CREDITING AN CLOCHÁN

1. Michael Hout's excellent quantitative study (1989) of social mobility and industrialization in Ireland between 1959 and 1973 indicated that the "excess" sons of rural farm families did well and better in the Irish cities to which they migrated than did the urban-born children of the Irish working classes. Strong aspirations for achievement and social mobility were fueled in those same rural farm household sibling rivalries that produced the differential statuses of leave-taking and stay-at-home sons and daughters.

2. This section was inspired by a discussion between Seamus Heaney and Robert Haas on "the art of translating poetry" at the University of California, Berkeley, on 9 February 1999.

3. According to tradition in West Kerry, the "old ones" are expected to sense the approach of death, which was often personified as in the saying, "Death hasn't left Cork on its way to meet me yet!" or "He has struck me. I feel his blow in my heart." Many an older villager would tell with great satisfaction of the moment his old mother or father took to bed and sent for the priest with the words, "Today is my dying day" or "Sure, I won't last the night." A more discreet way of signaling that death was near was to ask for the final meal, what the old ones called the *Lon na Bais*. "Auntie" Anne explained it as follows: "One morning, about two weeks after I had returned from America, my father called me to his bedside and he asked me to bring him a large bowl of tea and two thick slices of fresh baked bread. 'Father,' says I, 'you must be mistaken. Our people haven't used bowls for more than a century. You must mean a large cup of tea.' 'It's a bowl I want,' he replied. I offered him some cognac to ease the pain, but he stopped me saying, 'No, my daughter, I have no more use for that — I had plenty enough when I was a boy. But today I am going to see my God.' So I did bring him the tea and the toast and I laid it next to his bed, but he never touched any of it. He just sat up in bed, smiling at it, anxiously waiting. He died that night. Wasn't that a beautiful death? It was what the old folks called the *Lon na Bais*, the death meal."

4. Even the most obedient scribes in the early Irish monasteries could not resist the lure and pleasure of writing. Deviating from the backbreaking work of

book copying, some monks would pause from time to time to comment in the margins of a text or to insert some earthy popular verses in between the learned Latin commentaries on classic and sacred texts. Sometimes they composed their own verses for the sheer enjoyment of it (see Cahill 1995:162-163). Consequently, the following four-stanza Irish poem, which was surreptitiously slipped into a ninth-century manuscript, has survived as a beloved commentary on the simple pleasures of 'mousing' and writing:

I and Pangur Ban my cat.
'Tis a like task we are at:
Hunting Mice is his delight,
Hunting words I sit all night.

'Tis a merry thing to see
At our tasks how glad are we
When at home we sit and find
Entertainment to our mind.

'Gainst the wall he sets his eye,
Full and fierce and sharp and sly;
'Gainst the wall of knowledge I
All my little wisdom try.

So in peace our task we ply,
Pangur Ban my cat and I.
In our arts we find our bliss,
I have mine and he has his.

5. I recall Eric Cross's conversation with "the Tailor" (1964: 167-168) in which he reports that "the book," *Tailor and Ansty* was placed on the banned list in Ireland:
"Tailor, I'm afraid the book is banned. . . . It isn't to be sold any more . . . . It's the law."
"The law!" exclaimed the Tailor. "But what has the law got to do with books?"
"The Board thinks [the book] is indecent."
"The book is nothing but the talk and the fun and the laughter which has gone on for years round this fireplace. . . . Did none of these men, or the Minister himself, never sit at an Irish fireside at night and join in the talk . . . or are they all a pack of jackaleens, aping the English?"

An Féach Blascaod Mór: The Great Blasket Island. The Blaskets comprise several tiny islands off the coast of the Dingle Peninsula, all uninhabited today. Once they were an epicenter of Irish Celtic culture and society.

aindeiseoir: an awkward, unfortunate, ungainly person or thing; a wretch; a miserable looking cow or person.

an gabha: a blacksmith.

bawneen: a white, woolen sack dress. *Bawne, bane, ban* are all variants of the word for white. The term, '*mo buacaill ban*,' my fair-haired boy, refers to the favorite and usually first born son.

bal, balli, bally, baile: a town (hence *Bally*bran).

beg, beag: small.

blas: skill with words.

bodhran: a goatskin drum.

bóithrín: a foot path, a little road.

Bran: the Celtic god of sea voyage, prototype for St. Brendan the Navigator with whom Bran is merged in the popular consciousness (hence *Bally*bran, the village of Bran or village of St. Brendan).

Brehon Laws: the customary law of the Celtic peoples. The term is derived from the Irish word for judge, *brithem.*

cairn: a mound of stones over a prehistoric grave.

ceilidhes (or *caeili*): an evening of musical entertainment; an evening visit, a friendly call.

clochán: a cluster of pre-Christian circular, stone "beehive" huts. An Clochán, the true Irish name of Ballybran. The name refers to its original Celtic settlement pattern.

Corca Dhuibhne: the Dingle Peninsula in County Kerry.

currach or *curragh:* a light canoe originally made of skins, in recent times of tarred canvas stretched over a wickerwork frame.

craic or *croiceann:* skin, hide, fleece. Colloquially, a kind of 'hiding' by teasing a person ruthlessly, as in "having a *craic*" at a person's expense. *Craic* is also used more simply to mean having a good time, making sport, making merry.

dun: a fort, usually made of stone.

dutcas: inherited dispositions passed along through the patriline to both sexes.

Fianna: also known as the Feninans. A band of warriors, a military elite, guards of the high king of Ireland; Fionn Mac Cumhail was their greatest leader.

lis, liss: a fort.

gaeltacht: Irish speaking areas of Ireland.

lough, loch: a lake or sea inlet.

Lugh: the Celtic Sun God.

meitheal: a collective work team, normally a group of fathers and sons attending to each man's field in turn.

naduir: nature, temperament, a quality of positive disposition, kindliness, passed through the matriline to both sexes, though boys are said 'to have' more of it.

piseogas: old beliefs and superstitions, usually relating to fairies.

Tuatha de Danaan: the original tribe of Mediterranean Celts who settled the west of Ireland around 350 B.C.

Abbott, Walter, S. J., ed. 1966. *The Documents of Vatican II*. London: Geoffrey Chapman.

Aberele, David F. 1952. Arctic Hysteria and Latah in Mongolia. *Transactions of the New York Academy of Sciences*, ser. 2, 22: 291–297.

Almeida Filho, Naomar. 1989. *Epidemiologia sem numeros*. Rio de Janeiro: Editoria Campus.

Altus, W. D. 1966. Birth Order and Its Sequelae. *Science* 151: 44–49.

Anonymous. 1850. Recent Publications on Insanity. *Dublin Quarterly Journal of Medical Science* (10): 415–445.

——. 1864. Comment on 13th Report of the Inspectors of Lunacy and Mental Hospitals, Ireland. *American Journal of Insanity* 4: 299–300.

Antonovsky, Aaron 1972. Breakdown: A Needed Fourth Step in the Conceptual Armamentarium of Modern Medicine. *Social Science and Medicine* 6: 537–544.

Arensberg, Conrad. 1968 (1937). *The Irish Countryman*. Garden City: Natural History Press.

Arensberg, Conrad, and Kimball, Solon T. 1968 (1940). *Family and Community in Ireland*. Cambridge: Harvard University Press.

Bachelard, Gaston. 1969. *The Poetics of Space*. Boston: Beacon Press.

Bagley, C., and Binitie, A. 1970. Alcoholism and Schizophrenia in Irishmen in London. *British Journal of Addiction* 65: 3–7.

Bahn, A. J., et al. 1966. Admission and Prevalence Rates for Psychiatric Facilities in Four Register Areas. *American Journal of Public Health* 56: 2033–2055.

Bailey, F. G., ed. 1973. *Debate and Compromise*. Totawa: Rowman and Littlefield.

Bales, Robert F. 1962. Attitudes towards Drinking in the Irish Culture. In Pittman and Snyder, eds., *Society, Culture and Drinking Patterns*. New York: Wiley.

Banfield, Edward C. 1958. *The Moral Basis of a Backward Society*. Glencoe: Free Press.

Barry, H., and Barry, H., Jr. 1967. Birth Order, Family Size and Schizophrenia. *Archives of General Psychiatry* 17: 435–440.

Basaglia, Franco. 1964. Silence in the Dialogue with the Psychotic. Paper presented at the Sixth Congress of Psychotherapy, London.

Bateson, Gregory, et al. 1956. Towards a Theory of Schizophrenia. *Behavioral Science* 1 (4): 251–264.

———. 1963. A Note on the Double Bind. *Family Process* 2: 154–161.

Becker, Howard S. 1973 (1963). *Outsiders*. New York: Free Press.

Beckett, Peter. 1972. Some Problems of Irish Psychiatry. *Psychiatric Opinion* 9 (2): 6–11.

Bell, Sam Hanna. 1974. *December Bride*. Belfast: Blackstaff.

Benedict, Ruth. 1928. Psychological Types in Cultures of the Southwest. *Proceedings of the Twenty-third International Congress of Americanists*, 572–581.

———. 1934. *Patterns of Culture*. Boston: Houghton Mifflin.

———. 1935. Culture and the Abnormal. *Journal of Genetic Psychology* 1: 60–64.

Berger, John. 1983. *Once in Europa*. New York: Pantheon.

Bieler, Ludwig. 1963. *Ireland: Harbinger of the Middle Ages*. New York and London: Oxford University Press.

Birdwell-Pheasant, Donna. 1998. Family Systems and the Foundations of Class in Ireland and England. *The History of the Family* 3 (1): 17–34.

Blanshard, Paul. 1953. *The Irish and Catholic Power*. Boston: Beacon Press.

Bleuler, Eugen. 1950 (1911). *Dementia Praecox: Or, the Group of Schizophrenias*. New York: International University Press.

Böll, Heinrich. 1967. *Irish Journal*. New York: McGraw-Hill.

Bourdieu, Pierre. 1962. Célibat et la condition paysanne. *Etudes rurales* 5/6 (April): 32–136.

———. 1977. *Outline of a Theory of Practice*. Cambridge: Cambridge University Press.

———. 1989. Reproduction interdit: La Dimension symbolique de la domination économique. *Etudes rurales* 113/114 (Jan.–June): 15–36.

Bourdieu, Pierre, and Waquant, Loïc J. D. 1992. *An Invitation to Reflexive Sociology*. Chicago: University of Chicago Press.

Bowlby, John. 1969. *Attachment*. New York: Basic Books.

———. 1973. *Separation*. New York: Basic Books.

Boyer, Bryce, et al. 1964. Comparison of the Shamans and Pseudo–Shamans of the Apaches of the Mescalero Indian Reservation: A Rorschach Study. *Journal of Projective Techniques and Personality Development* 28: 173–280.

Brody, Hugh. 1974. *Inishkillane: Change and Decline in the West of Ireland*. Harmondsworth: Penguin.

Brooke, E. 1967. *A Census of Patients in Psychiatric Beds*. London: Her Majesty's Stationery Office.

Bruhn, J. G., Brandt, E. N. and Shackelford, M. 1966. Incidence of Treated Mental Illness in Three Pennsylvania Communities. *American Journal of Public Health* 56: 871–883.

Cahill, Thomas. 1995. *How the Irish Saved Civilization*. New York: Anchor.

Carothers, J. C. 1953. *The African Mind in Health and Disease*. Monograph no. 17. Geneva: World Health Organization.

Caudill, William. 1958. *The Psychiatric Hospital as a Small Society*. Cambridge: Harvard University Press.

———. 1964. Sibling Rank and Style of Life Among Japanese Psychiatric Patients. *Folia Psychiatrica Neurologica Japonica*, Suppl. 7.

Central Statistics Office, Dublin. http://www.doh.ie/statistics/health_statistics/index.html [accessed 6/6/00].

Chadwick, Nora. 1970. *The Celts*. Harmondsworth: Penguin.

Colum, Padraic. 1954. *A Treasury of Irish Folklore*. New York: Crown.

Commins, H., and Kelleher, Carmel. 1973. *Farm Inheritance and Succession*. Dublin: Macra na Feirme.

Connell, K. H. 1955. Marriage in Ireland after the Famine: The Diffusion of the Match. *Journal of Statistical and Social Inquiry Society* 19: 82–103.

———. 1962. Peasant Marriage in Ireland. *Economic History Review* 14: 513–514.

———. 1968. Catholicism and Marriage in the Century after the Famine. In Connell, ed., *Irish Peasant Society*. Oxford: Clarendon Press.

Connolly, J. F., and Cullen, A. 1996. Suicide Trends in County Mayo: A Brief Report. *Crisis* 17 (1): 182–184.

Connolly, John F. 1977. Suicide and the Irish Problem: Comments on Under-Reporting. *Archives of Suicide Research* 3 (1): 25-29.

Cooley, Charles. 1956. *Human Nature and the Social Order*. Glencoe: Free Press.

Cooney, J. G. 1971. Alcohol and the Irish. *Journal of the Irish College of Physicians and Surgeons* 1(2): 50–54.

Cooper, Brian, and Brown, Alexander. 1967. Psychiatric Practice in Great Britain and America: A Comparative Study. *British Journal of Psychiatry* 1 13: 625–636.

Copeland, J., et al. 1971. Differences in Usage of Diagnostic Labels amongst Psychiatrists in the British Isles and America. *British Journal of Psychiatry* 1 18: 629–640.

Coulter, Carol. 1997. *The Hidden Tradition: Feminism, Women, and Nationalism in Ireland*. Cork: Cork University Press.

Cresswell, Robert. 1969. *Une Communauté rurale de l'Irlande*. Paris: Institute de Ethnographie.

Cross, Eric. 1942. *The Tailor and Ansty*. Cork: Mercier.

Crotty, Raymond. 1986. *Ireland in Crisis: A Study of Capitalist Colonial Under-development*. Dingle, County Kerry: Brandon.

Curtis, Edmund. 1936 (1970). *A History of Ireland*. London: Methuen.

Cusak, M. F. 1871. *A History of the Kingdom of Kerry*. London: Methuen.

Daly, J. 1976. The Irish Home as a Novitiate for Violence. *Irish Press*, June 6:2.

Danaher, Kevin. 1964. *Gentle Places and Simple Things*. Cork: Mercier.

Daube, David. n.d. The Duty of Procreation. MS, University of California, Boalt Hall.

Day, Richard, and Davidson, Ronald. 1976. An Ethnopsychiatric Study of Magic and Healing. *Psychoanalytic Study of Society*, vol. 7. New Haven: Yale University Press.

De Tocqueville, Alexis. 1970 (1835). *Journeys to England and Ireland*. Magnolia: Peter Smith.

Denich, Bette. 1971. Sex and Power in the Balkans. Paper presented at the 70th annual meeting of the American Anthropological Association, New York.

Department of Lands, Republic of Ireland. 1974. "Summary of Scheme for Implementation of EEC Directive 160 on Encouragement to Leave Farming" (February). Distributed by the Kerry County Committee of Agriculture. Mimeographed.

——. 1975. "New Voluntary Retirement Scheme For Farmers." Dublin: The Land Commission. Pamphlet.

Devereaux, George. 1977. *From Anxiety to Method in the Behavioral Sciences*. New York: Humanities Press.

Devereux, George. 1956. Normal and Abnormal: The Key Problem in Psychiatric Anthropology. In Casagrande and Gladwins, eds., *Some Uses of Anthropology: Theoretical and Applied*, pp. 23–48. Washington, D.C.: Anthropological Society of Washington.

DeVos, George. 1965. Transcultural Diagnosis of Mental Health by Means of Psychological Tests. In De Reuck and Porter, eds., *Transcultural Psychiatry*. Boston: Little Brown.

——. 1973. *Socialization for Achievement*. Berkeley and Los Angeles: University of California.

DeVos, George, and Wagatsuma, H. 1966. *Japan's Invisible Race*. Berkeley and Los Angeles: University of California.

Diaz-Guerrero, Roberto. 1963. Socio-Cultural Premises, Attitudes and Cross-Cultural Research. Paper presented at the 17th International Congress of Psychology, Washington, D.C.

Dinneen, Patrick. 1927. *Focloir Gaedilge Agus Bearla: An Irish-English Dictionary*. Dublin: Irish Texts Society.

Douglas, Mary. 1966. *Purity and Danger*. New York: Praeger.

———. 1970. *Natural Symbols*. London: Barrie and Rocklitt.

DuBois, Cora. 1944. *The People of Alor*. New York: Harper.

Dunham, H. Warren. 1965. *Community and Schizophrenia: An Epidemiological Analysis*. Detroit: Wayne State University Press.

Dunne, David. 1970. Lose the Heart—Destroy the Head. *The Corridor Echo*. Journal of St. Mary's Hospital Castlebar, February pp. 22–35.

Durkheim, Emile. 1951. *Suicide*. New York: Free Press.

Edgerton, Robert B. 1966. Conceptions of Psychosis in Four East African Societies. *American Anthropologist* 68: 408–425.

———. 1969. On the Recognition of Mental Illness. In Plog and Edgerton, eds., *Changing Perspectives in Mental Illness*. New York: Holt, Rinehart and Winston.

Eisenberg, L. 1968. Psychotic Disorders in Childhood. In Cooke, ed., *The Biologic Basis of Pediatric Practice*. New York: McGraw-Hill.

Erikson, Erik. 1953. Growth and Crisis of the Healthy Personality. In Murray, Kluckhohn, and Schneider, eds., *Personality in Nature, Society and Culture*, pp. 185–225. New York: Knopf.

———. 1963 (1950). *Childhood and Society*. New York: Norton.

Erlenmeyer-Kimbling, L. Van Den Bosch, E. and Denham, B. 1969. The Problem of Birth Order and Schizophrenia: A Negative Conclusion. *British Journal of Psychiatry* 115 (523): 659–678.

Evans, Estyn. 1957. *Irish Folk Ways*. London: Routledge and Kegan Paul.

Fantl, B., and Schiro, J. 1959. Cultural Variables in the Behavior Patterns and Symptom Formation of 15 Irish and 15 Italian Female Schizophrenics. *International Journal of Social Psychiatry* 4 (4): 245–253.

Farina, A. Barry, H. and Garmezy, N. 1963. Birth Order of Recovered and Non-recovered Schizophrenics. *Archives of General Psychiatry* 9: 224–228.

Favret-Saada, Jeanne. 1981. *Deadly Words*. Cambridge: Cambridge University Press.

———. 1989. Un-bewitching as Therapy. *American Ethnologist* 16 (1): 40–56.

Fennell, Nuala. 1974. *Irish Marriage—How Are You?* Cork: Mercier.

Ferreira, Antonio. 1963. Family Myths and Homeostasis. *Archives of General Psychiatry* 9 (5): 457–643.

———. 1965. Family Myths: The Covert Rules of the Relationship. *Confinia Psychiatrica* 8: 15–20.

———. 1966. Family Myths. *Psychiatric Research Report* 20: 85–90.

———. 1967. Psychosis and Family Myth. *American Journal of Psychotherapy* 21: 186–197.

Field, M. J. 1960. *Search for Security: An Ethnopsychiatric Study of Rural Ghana*. New York: W. W. Norton.

Fish, Frank. 1969. The Diagnosis of Acute Schizophrenia. *Psychiatric Quarterly* 43 (1): 35–45.

Fleming, John. 1953. Folklore, Fact and Fancy. *Irish Journal of Medical Science* 6 (326): 50–63.

Flower, Robin. 1945. *The Western Island*. Oxford: Clarendon.

——. 1947. *The Irish Tradition*. Oxford: Clarendon.

Foley, P. 1907. *History of the County of Kerry*. Dublin: Sealy, Bryers and Walker.

Fortune, Reo. 1963. *Sorcerers of Dobu*. New York: Dutton.

Foster, George. 1967. *Tzintzuntzan*. Boston: Little, Brown.

——. 1973. *Traditional Societies and Technological Change*. New York: Harper and Row.

Foucault, Michel. 1967. *Madness and Civilization*. New York: Mentor.

——. 1976. *Mental Illness and Psychology*. New York: Harper and Row.

Foulks, Edward. 1975. A Sociobiologic Model of Schizophrenia. Paper presented at the American Anthropological Association Meetings, San Francisco.

Fox, Robin. 1962. The Vanishing Gael. *New Society*, October, pp. 17–19.

——. 1963. The Structure of Personal Names on Tory Island. *Man* 192: 153–156.

——. 1968. Tory Island. In Burton Benedict, ed., *Problems of Small Territories*. London: Athlone.

——. 1978. *The Tory Islanders: A People of the Celtic Fringe*. Cambridge: Cambridge University Press.

Friedl, Ernestine. 1958. Hospital Care in Provincial Greece. *Human Organization* 16 (4): 27–36.

Goffman, Erving. 1959. *The Presentation of Self in Everyday Life*. New York: Doubleday.

——. 1961. *Asylums: Essays on the Social Situation of Mental Patients and Other Inmates*. New York: Doubleday.

——. 1963. *Stigma: Notes on the Management of Spoiled Identity*. Englewood Cliffs: Prentice-Hall.

Granville-Grossman, K. L. 1966. Birth Order and Schizophrenia. *British Journal of Psychiatry* 112: 1119–1126.

Graves, Robert. 1961. *The White Goddess*. London: Faber and Faber.

Greeley, Andrew M. 1972. *That Most Distressful Nation: The Taming of the American Irish*. Chicago: Aldine.

Gregory, I. 1959. An Analysis of Family Data on 1,000 Patients Admitted to a Canadian Mental Hospital. *Acta Genetica* 9: 54–96.

Gurland, Barry, et al. 1970. Cross National Study of Diagnosis of Mental Disorders: Hospital Diagnoses and Hospital Patients in New York and London. *Comprehensive Psychiatry* 11 (1): 18–25.

Haien, Jeanette. 1986. *The All of It: A Novel.* New York: Harper Perennial.

Haley, Jay. 1959. The Family of the Schizophrenic: A Model System. *Journal of Nervous and Mental Diseases* 129: 357–374.

Hallowell, A. I. 1934. Culture and Mental Disorders. *Journal of Abnormal and Social Psychology* 29: 1–9.

Hammel, Eugene, and Peter Laslett. 1974. Comparing Household Structure over Time and between Cultures. *Comparative Studies in Society and History* 16 (1): 73–109.

Hannan, Damian. 1972. Kinship, Neighborhoods and Social Change in Irish Rural Communities. *Economic and Social Review* 3: 163–188.

Harlow, H. F. 1958. The Nature of Love. *American Psychologist* 13: 673–685.

Harlow, H. F., and Harlow, M. K. 1965. The Affectional Systems. In Schrier, Harlow, and Stollnitz, eds., *Behavior of Nonhuman Primates.* New York: Academic Press.

Harris, Rosemary. 1972. *Prejudice and Tolerance in Ulster.* Manchester: Manchester University Press.

Hayward, Richard. 1950. *In the Kingdom of Kerry.* Dublin: Dundalgan Press.

Healy, David, n.d. Irish Psychiatry in the Twentieth Century: Notes Toward a History. MS. Department of Psychological Medicine, North Wales Hospital, Denbigh.

Healy, John. 1968. *The Death of an Irish Town.* Cork: Mercier.

Heaney, Seamus. 1966. Digging. In *The Death of a Naturalist.* New York: Farrar, Straus & Giroux.

———. 1995. *Crediting Poetry.* The Nobel lecture. Loughcrew, County Meath: Gallery.

———. 2000. *Beowulf: A New Translation.* New York: Farrar, Straus and Giroux.

Henry, Jules. 1965. *Pathways to Madness.* New York: Vintage.

Henry, P. L. 1974. *Language, Culture and the Nation.* Baile Átha Cliath: Comhdháil Náisiúnta na Gaeilge.

Henry, William. 1947. *The Thematic Apperception Technique in the Study of Culture-Personality Relations.* Genetic Psychological Monograph, 35.

Herr, Cheryl. 1990. The Erotics of Irishness. *Critical Inquiry* 17 (4): 1–34.

Hill, Lewis B. 1973 (1955). *Psychotherapeutic Intervention in Schizophrenia.* Chicago: University of Chicago.

Hoffman, Susannah. 1970. A Cultural Grammar of Peasant Society. Ph.D. diss., University of California, Berkeley.

Hollingshead, A., and Redlich, F. 1958. *Social Class and Mental Disorder: A Community Study*. New York: Wiley.

Holmes, T., and Rahe, R. 1967. The Social Readjustment Rating Scale. *Journal of Psychosomatic Research* 11 (2): 213–218.

Hooten, E. A., and Dupertuis, C. W. 1951. Age Changes and Selective Survival in Irish Males. *American Journal of Physical Anthropology, Studies in Physical Anthropology*, no. 2.

Hout, Michael. 1989. *Following in Father's Footsteps: Social Mobility in Ireland*. Cambridge: Harvard University Press.

Hughes, Kathleen. 1966. *The Church in Early Irish Society*. Ithaca: Cornell University Press.

Hughes, Nathanael E. 1999. *Playing Politics: W.B. Yeats' Nation and Theatre, 1919–1939*. M. Phil. Thesis in Irish Theatre Studies, The Samuel Beckett Center for Drama. Dublin: Trinity College.

Humphreys, A. J. 1966. *New Dubliners*. London: Routledge and Kegan Paul.

Hunt, Linda and Gary, and Scheper, Nancy. 1970. Hunger in the Welfare State. In Ramparts, ed., *Divided We Stand*. San Francisco: Canfield Press.

Illich, Ivan. 1982. *Gender*. New York: Pantheon.

Irish Times. 1974. All Irish Mothers Are Divided into Three Parts, *The Saint Crohane's Letters*, February 7.

——. 1974. Interview with Dr. Ivor Browne, November 14.

——. 1974. Leaving the Land, *Letters to the Editor*, November 20.

——. 1974. Fitzpatrick Defends Farm Retirement Scheme, November 24.

——. 1975. From Boherlahn to Brussels, February 8.

Jackson, Don, ed. 1960. *Etiology of Schizophrenia*. New York: Basic Books.

——. 1968. *Communication, Family and Marriage*. Palo Alto: Science and Behavior Books.

Jaco, E. G. 1954. The Social Isolation Hypothesis and Schizophrenia. *American Sociological Review* 19: 567–577.

Joyce, James. 1968. *A Portrait of the Artist as a Young Man*. New York: Viking.

Joyce, Patrick W. 1903. *A Social History of Ancient Ireland. 2 vols*. New York and Bombay: Longmans, Green and Company.

Jung, Carl G., ed. 1964. *Man and His Symbols*. New York: Doubleday.

Kane, Eileen. 1968. An Analysis of the Cultural Factors Inimical to the Development of the Nationalistic–Revivalistic Industrial Process of Rural Irish Gaeltachts. Ph.D. diss., University of Pittsburg.

Kardiner, Abram. 1939. *The Individual and His Society*. New York: Columbia University Press.

Kavanagh, Patrick. 1964. *The Great Hunger*. London: MacGibbon and Kee.

Keane, John B. 1974. *Letters of a Love-Hungry Farmer.* Cork: Mercier.

Keatinge, Carolyn. 1987. Schizophrenia in Rural Ireland: A Case of Service Overutilization. *International Journal of Social Psychiatry* 33 (3): 186–194.

Kelleher, M. J., and Copeland, J. R. M. 1973. Psychiatric Diagnosis in Cork and London: Results of a Cross-National Pilot Study. *Journal of the Irish Medical Association* 66: 553–557.

——. 1974. High First Rates for Schizophrenia in the West of Ireland. *Psychological Medicine* 4: 460–462.

Kellerher, Michael. 1998. Youth Suicide Trends in the Republic of Ireland. *Irish Journal of Psychological Medicine.* 13 (4): 199–197.

Kellerher, Michael, Corcoran, Paul, and Keeley, Helen. 1997. Suicide in Ireland: Statistical, Social, and Clinical Considerations. *Archives of Suicide Research* 3 (1): 13–24.

Kendler, Kenneth S., et al. 1993. An Epidemiologic, Clinical and Family Study of Simple Schizophrenia in County Roscommon, Ireland. *American Journal of Psychiatry* 151 (1): 27–33.

Keneally, Thomas. 1998. *The Great Shame and the Triumph of the Irish in the English-Speaking World.* New York: Doubleday.

Kennedy, John. 1973. Cultural Psychiatry. *Handbook of Social and Cultural Anthropology.* Chicago: Rand McNally.

Kennedy, Keiran. 1993. *Facing the Unemployment Crisis in Ireland.* Cork: Cork University Press.

Kennedy, Robert, Jr. 1973. *The Irish: Emigration, Marriage and Fertility.* Berkeley and Los Angeles: University of California Press.

Kerry County Committee of Agriculture. 1972. *County Kerry Agricultural Resource Survey.* Tralee: The Kerryman.

Kerryman, The. 1974. Rehabilitation Plans Going Ahead Despite Objections, October 14.

King, J. 1931. *County Kerry Past and Present.* Dublin: Hodges and Figgis.

Kirkpatrick, T. 1931. *A Note on the History of the Care of the Insane in Ireland.* Dublin: University Press.

Kirwan, P. 1991. Suicide in a Rural Irish Population. *Irish Medical Journal* 84 (2): 14–15.

Kohl, J. G. 1844. *Ireland.* London: Chapman and Hall.

Kohn, M. 1968. Social Class and Schizophrenia: A Critical Review. In Rosenthal and Kety, eds., *Transmission of Schizophrenia.* New York and London: Pergamon.

Kraemer, Morton. 1966. Some Implications of Trends in the Usage of Psychiatric Facilities for Community Mental Health Programs and Related Research.

U.S. *Public Health Service Publication* no. 1434. Washington, D.C.: U.S. Government Printing Office.

———. 1970. Marital Status, Living Arrangements and Family Characteristics of Admissions to State and County Mental Hospitals

———. 1970. Statistical Note 100. *U.S. Public Health Service Publications*. Washington, D.C.: U.S. Government Printing Office.

Laing, R. D. 1965. *The Divided Self*. Baltimore: Penguin.

———. 1969. *The Politics of the Family*. New York: Vintage.

Laing, R. D., and Esterson, A. 1964. *Sanity, Madness and the Family*. London: Tavistock.

Leighton, Alexander H. 1959. *My Name is Legion*. New York: Basic Books.

———. 1961. The Stirling County Study: Some Notes on Concepts and Methods. In Hoch and Zubin, eds., *Comparative Epidemiology of Mental Disorders*. New York: Grune and Stratton.

Leighton, Alexander, and Hughes, J. 1959. Culture as Causative of Mental Disorders. In *Causes of Mental Disorders: A Review of Epidemiological Knowledge*, pp. 341–383. Proceedings of round table (held at Arden House, Harriman, New York). New York: Milbank Memorial Fund.

Leighton, Alexander, et al. 1963. *Psychiatric Disorder Among the Yoruba*. Ithaca: Cornell University Press.

Lemkau, Paul, and Crocetti, Guido. 1958. Vital Statistics of Schizophrenia. In Leopold Bellak, ed., *Schizophrenia: A Review of the Syndrome*. New York: Logos.

Lévi-Strauss, Claude. 1961. *A World on the Wane*. New York: Criterion Books.

———. 1967. The Sorcerer and His Magic. In John Middleton, ed., *Magic, Witchcraft and Curing*. Garden City: Natural History Press.

LeVine, Robert and LeVine, Barbara. 1966. *Nyansongo: A Gusii Community in Kenya*. New York: John Wiley.

Lewis, Oscar. 1951. *Life in a Mexican Village: Tepozlan Restudied*. Urbana: University of Illinois Press.

Leyton, Elliott. 1975. *The One Blood: Kinship and Class in an Irish Village*. St. John's: Social and Economic Studies no. 5. Memorial University of Newfoundland.

Lidz, Theodore, et al. 1958. The Intrafamilial Environment of the Schizophrenic Patient: The Transmission of Irrationality. *Archives of Neurology and Psychiatry* 79: 305–316.

Lidz, Theodore, Fleck, S., and Cornelison, A. 1965. *Schizophrenia and the Family*. New York: International Universities Press.

Lin, Tsung-yi, et al. 1969. Mental Disorders in Taiwan and Fifteen Years Later: A Preliminary Report. In Caudill and Lin, eds., *Mental Health Research in Asia and the Pacific.* Honolulu: East-West Center Press.

Lindemann, Erich. 1941. Symptomatology and Management of Grief. *American Journal of Psychiatry* 101: 141–148.

Linton, Ralph. 1943. Nativistic Movements. *American Anthropologist* 45: 230–240.

Logan, Patrick. 1972. *Making the Cure: A Look at Irish Folk Medicine.* Dublin: Talbot.

Lynn, Richard. 1968. The Irish Brain Drain. Dublin: Economic and Social Research Institute.

———. 1971. National Differences in Anxiety. Dublin: Economic and Social Research Institute.

MacCana, Proinsias. 1970. *Celtic Mythology.* London: Hamlyn.

MacNeill, Marie. 1962. *The Festival of Lughnasa.* London: Oxford University Press.

Malzberg, Benjamin. 1964. Mental Disease among Native and Foreign Born Whites in New York State. *Mental Hygiene* 48: 478–499.

———. 1969. Are Immigrants Psychologically Disturbed? In Plog and Edgerton, eds., *Changing Perspectives in Mental Illness.* New York: Holt, Rinehart and Winston.

Malzberg, B., and Lee, E. S. 1956. *Migration and Mental Disease.* New York: Social Science Research Council.

Mazer, Milton. 1976. *People and Predicaments: Of Life and Distress on Martha's Vineyard.* Cambridge: Harvard University Press.

McCabe, Charles. 1980. Break Your Heart. *San Francisco Chronicle,* July 16, p. 49.

McCarthy, J. 1961. The 1961 Census of Population. *Journal of the Statistical and Social Inquiry Society of Ireland* 20: 174–197.

McCarthy, M. J. F. 1911. *Irish Land and Irish Liberty.* London: Robert Scott.

McNeill, William H. 1976. *Plagues and Peoples.* New York: Doubleday.

Mead, George H. 1934. *Mind, Self and Society.* Chicago: University of Chicago Press.

Mead, Margaret. 1928. *Coming of Age in Samoa.* New York: Morrow.

———. 1935. *Sex and Temperament in Three Primitive Societies.* New York: Morrow.

———. 1961. *New Lives for Old.* New York: Mentor.

Merriman, Brian. 1945. Cúirt an mheán oiche. The Midnight Court: A Rhythmical Bacchanalia from the Irish of Bryan Merryman, translated by Frank O'Connor. London and Dublin: M. Fridberg.

Merriman, Brian. 1961 (1780). The Midnight Court. In Frank O'Connor, ed., *Kings, Lords and Commons*. London: Penguin.

Messenger, John. 1969. *Inis Beag*. New York: Holt, Rinehart and Winston.

——. 1971. Sex and Repression in an Irish Folk Community. In Marshall and Suggs, eds., *Human Sexual Behavior*. New York: Basic Books.

Miller, Liam. 1977. *The Noble Drama of W. B. Yeats*. Dublin: Dolman.

Mills, C. Wright. 1959. *The Sociological Imagination*. New York and London: Oxford University Press.

Mishler, Elliot, and Waxler, Nancy. 1968. *Family Processes and Schizophrenia*. New York: Wiley.

Moody, T. W., and Martin, F. X., eds. 1967. *The Course of Irish History*. Cork: Mercier.

Moran, Patrick, Cardinal. 1872. Vitae Sancti Brendani. *Acta Sancti*. Dublin.

Mullen, Pat. 1940. *Come Another Day*. London: Faber.

Murphy, Gerard. 1961. *Saga and Myth in Ancient Ireland*. Cork: Mercier.

Murphy, H. B. M. 1959. Culture and Mental Disorder in Singapore. In Opler, ed., *Culture and Mental Health*, pp. 291–316. New York: Macmillan.

——. 1963. A Cross Cultural Survey of Schizophrenic Symptomatology. *International Journal of Social Psychiatry* 9: 237–249.

——. 1965. The Epidemiological Approach to Transcultural Psychiatric Research. In De Reuck and Porter, eds., *Transcultural Psychiatry*. Boston: Little, Brown.

——. 1967. Canadian Rural Communities and Their Schizophrenic Patients. Paper presented at the Basic Conference on Human Behavior, McGill University, Montreal.

——. 1968a. Mental Hospitalization Patterns in Different Canadian Subcultures. *Proceedings of the IV World Congress of Psychiatry* 4: 2512–2515.

——. 1968b. Cultural Factors in the Genesis of Schizophrenia. In Rosenthal and Kety, eds., *Transmission of Schizophrenia*. London: Pergamon.

——. 1975. Alcoholism and Schizophrenia in the Irish: A Review. *Transcultural Psychiatric Research Review* 9: 116–139.

Murphy, Jane. 1976. Psychiatric Labeling in Cross-Cultural Perspective. *Science* 191: 1019–1028.

Murphy, John. 1969. Priests and People in Modern Irish History. *Christus Rex* 23 (4): 235–259.

Newman, J., ed., 1964. *The Limerick Rural Survey*. Tipperary: Muintir na Tire Rural Publications.

Ni Dhomhnaill, Nuala. 1988. *Selected Poems: Rogha Danta*, translated by Michael Harnett. Dublin: Raven.

Ni Nuallain, M., O'Hare, A., and Walsh, D. 1987. Incidence of Schizophrenia in Ireland. *Psychological Medicine* 17: 943–948.

Noonan, John T., Jr. 1966. *Contraception: A History of Its Treatment by Catholic Theologians and Canonists.* Cambridge: Harvard University Press.

Norris, V. 1956. *Mental Illness in London.* London: Oxford University Press.

O Tuama, Sean. 1970. *Facts About Irish.* Baile Átha Cliath: Comhdháil Náisiúnta na Gaeilge.

O'Brien, Edna. 1976. *Mother Ireland.* New York: Harcourt Brace Jovanovich.

O'Brien, John, ed. 1954. *The Vanishing Irish.* New York: McGraw-Hill.

O'Brien, Liam. n.d. The Magic Wisp: A History of the Mentally Ill in Ireland. MS.

Ó'Conchúir, Doncha. 1973. *Corca Dhuibhne.* Baile Átha Cliath: Clodhanna Teoranta.

O'Connor, Frank. 1957. *My Oedipus Complex and Other Stories.* Harmondsworth: Penguin.

O'Connor, Frank. 1964. Introduction to the 1964 Edition. In Cross, *The Tailor and Ansty.* Cork: Mercier.

O'Crohan, Tomás. 1951. *The Islandman.* Oxford: Clarendon Press.

O'Doherty, E. F., and McGrath, E. D. 1962. *The Priest and Mental Health.* Dublin: Clonmore and Reynolds.

O'Faolain, Sean. 1949. *The Irish: A Character Study.* New York: Devin-Adair.

O'Hare, Aileen, and Walsh, Dermot. 1969. *Activities of Irish Psychiatric Hospitals and Units 1965–1969.* Dublin: Medico-Social Research Board.

———. 1970. *Activities of Irish Psychiatric Hospitals and Units 1970.* Dublin: Medico-Social Research Board.

———. 1974. *Irish Psychiatric Hospital Census, 1971.* Dublin: Medico-Social Research Board.

———. 1977, 1978, 1979, 1980, 1981. *Activities of Irish Psychiatric Hospitals and Units.* Dublin: Medico-Social Research Board.

O'Higgins, Kathleen. 1974. Marital Desertion in Dublin. Dublin: Economic and Social Research Institute.

O'Riordan, Sean. 1965. *Antiquities of the Irish Countryside.* London: Methuen.

O'Súilleabháin, Seán. 1963. *A Handbook of Irish Folklore.* Hartboro: Folklore Association.

———. 1967. *Irish Wake Amusements.* Cork: Mercier.

———. n.d. *Nosanna agus Piseoga na nGael.* Dublin: Cultural Relations Committee.

O'Sullivan, Maurice. 1957. *Twenty Years A-Growing.* London: Oxford University Press.

O'Sullivan, T. F. 1931. *Romantic Hidden Kerry*. Tralee: Kerryman.

O'Toole, Fintan. 1998. *The Lie of the Land: Irish Identities*. Dublin: New Island.

Odegaard, Oernulu. 1946. A Statistical Investigation of the Incidence of Mental Disorder in Norway. *Psychiatric Quarterly* 20: 382–388.

———. 1956. The Incidence of Psychoses in Various Occupations. *International Journal of Social Psychiatry* 2: 85–104.

Opler, Marvin. 1959. Cultural Differences in Mental Disorders: An Italian and Irish Contrast in the Schizophrenias. In M. K. Opler, ed., *Culture and Mental Health*. New York: Macmillan.

———. 1967. Cultural Perspectives in Research on Schizophrenia. In M. K. Opler (ed.), *Culture and Social Psychiatry*. New York: Atherton.

Opler, Marvin, and Singer, Jerome. 1956. Ethnic Differences in Behavior and Psychopathology: Italian and Irish. *International Journal of Social Psychiatry* 2 (1): 11–23.

Ozturk, Orhan. 1964. Folk Treatment of Mental Illness in Turkey. In Ari Kiev, ed., *Magic, Faith and Healing*. Glencoe: Free Press.

Pentony, P. 1965. Psychological Barriers to Economic Achievement. Dublin: Economic Research Institute.

Peristiany, J. G., ed. 1966. *Honour and Shame: The Values of Mediterranean Society*. London: Oxford University Press.

Piaget, Jean. 1954. *The Construction of Reality in the Child*. New York: Basic Books.

Piddington, Ralph. 1957. *An Introduction to Social Anthropology*. Edinburgh: Oliver and Boyd.

Pitt-Rivers, Julian. 1971 (1954). *People of the Sierra*. Chicago: University of Chicago.

Pollack, H. 1913. A Statistical Study of the Foreign-Born Insane in New York State Hospitals. *State Hospital Bulletin* (5): 10–25.

Powdermaker, Hortense. 1953. The Channeling of Negro Aggression by the Cultural Process. In Kluckhohn, Murray, and Schneider, eds., *Personality in Nature, Society and Culture*. New York: Alfred Knopf.

———. 1968. *Stranger and Friend: The Way of an Anthropologist*. New York: Norton.

———. 1970. Detachment and Estrangement. Plenary session keynote address, Krober Anthropological Society Meetings, University of California, Berkeley.

Power, Patrick C. 1974. *The Book of Irish Curses*. Cork: Mercier.

Redfield, Robert. 1930. *Tepoztlan: A Mexican Village*. Chicago: University of Chicago Press.

———. 1955. *The Little Community*. Chicago: University of Chicago Press.

Reider, Norman. 1950. The Concept of Normality. *Psychoanalytic Quarterly* 19 (6): 43–51.

Riordan, Siobhan. 1973. Popular Reaction to Government Policy in Irish Education, Past and Present. Master's thesis, University College, Cork.

Robins, Joseph. 1986. *Fools and the Mad: A History of the Insane in Ireland*. Dublin: Institute of Public Administration.

Rohan, Dorine. 1969. *Marriage Irish Style*. Cork: Mercier.

Rose, Kieran. 1994. *Diverse Communities: The Evolution of Lesbian and Gay Politics in Ireland*. Cork: Cork University Press.

Rosenthal, D. 1970. *Genetic Theory and Abnormal Behavior*. New York: McGraw-Hill.

Rosenthal, D., and Kety, S. S. 1968. *Transmission of Schizophrenia*. New York and London: Pergamon.

Ross, Miceal. 1969. Personal Incomes by County, 1965. Dublin: Economic and Social Research Institute, no. 49.

Saris, Jamie. 1995. Telling Stories: Life Histories, Illness Narratives, and Institutional Landscapes. *Culture, Medicine and Psychiatry* 19 (1): 39–72.

———. 1996. Mad Kings, Proper Houses, and an Asylum in Rural Ireland. *American Anthropologist* 98 (3): 539–554.

Sayers, Peig. 1962. *An Old Woman's Reflections*. London: Oxford University Press.

———. 1973. *Peig: The Autobiography of Peig Sayers*. Dublin: Talbot Press.

Scheff, Thomas. 1966. *Being Mentally Ill: A Sociological Theory*. Chicago: Aldine.

Scheper-Hughes, Nancy. 1973. Woman as Witch. *Popular Psychology* 1 (4): 57–65.

Scheper-Hughes, Nancy. 1987. The Best of Two Worlds, the Worst of Two Worlds—Reflections on Culture and Fieldwork among the Rural Irish and Pueblo Indians. *Comparative Studies in Society and History* 29 (1): 56–75.

———. 1992. *Death without Weeping: The Violence of Everyday Life in Brazil*. Berkeley and Los Angeles: University of California Press.

———. 1994. The Last White Christmas: The Heidleberg Pub Massacre. *American Anthropologist* 96 (4): 1–28.

———. 1995. Who's the Killer? Popular Justice and Human Rights in a South African Squatter Camp. *Social Justice* 22 (3): 143–164.

———. 1997a. Demography without Numbers: Counting Angel Babies in Brazil. In Fricke and Kertzer, eds., *Anthropology and Demography*. Chicago: University of Chicago Press.

———. 1997b. People Who Get Rubbished. *New Internationalist* (October): 20–22.

———. 1998. Institutionalized Sexual Abuse and the Catholic Church. In Scheper-Hughes and Sargent, eds., *Small Wars: The Cultural Politics of Childhood*. Berkeley: University of California Press.

———. 1999a. Sacred Wounds: The Body and the Violence *Theater Symposium* 7 (1): 7–30.

———. 1999b. Un-doing: Social Suffering and the Politics of Remorse. In Cox, ed., *Remorse and Reparation*. London: Jessica Kingsley.

Scheper-Hughes, Nancy, and Lovell, Anne M., eds. 1987. *Psychiatry Inside Out: Selected Writings of Franco Basaglia*. New York: Columbia University Press.

Schooler, C. 1961. Birth Order and Schizophrenia. *Archives of General Psychiatry* 4: 91–123.

Schwartz, Theodore. 1968. A Cargo Cult: A Melanesian Type Response to Change. In G. A. DeVos, ed., *Responses to Change: Adjustment and Adaptation in Personality and Culture*. Abstracts Symposia, VIIIth International Congress of Anthropological and Ethnological Sciences. Tokyo: Science Council of Japan.

Selmer, Carl, ed. 1959. *Navagatio Sancti Brendani Abbatis*. Medieval Studies Series. University of Notre Dame.

Senchus Mor (Anonymous). 1865. *Ancient Laws of Ireland: An Introduction to Senchus Mor, The Law of Distress*, vol. 1. London: Longmans, Green.

Sheehy, Michael. 1968. *Is Ireland Dying?* New York: Taplinger.

Singer, Margaret. 1963. Thought Disorder and Family Relations of Schizophrenics. *Archives of General Psychiatry* 9: 199–206.

Smith, C., and McIntyre, S. 1963. Family Size, Birth Rate and Ordinal Position. *Canadian Psychiatric Association Journal* 8: 244–248.

Smith, Charles. 1965 (1756). *The Ancient and Present State of Kerry*. Cork: Mercier.

Smyth, Ciaran, et al. 1997. Where To? A Survey of the Residual Population of a District Mental Hospital and Their Predicted Placement Needs. *Irish Journal of Psychiatric Medicine* 14 (3): 105–108.

Spindler, George. 1955. Sociocultural and Psychological Processes in Menomini Acculturation. *University of California Publications in Culture and Society*, vol. 5.

Spitz, R. A. 1946. Anaclitic Depression. *Psychoanalytic Study of the Child* 2: 313–342.

———. 1965. *The First Year of Life*. New York: International Universities Press.

Starn, Orin. 1992. Missing the Revolution: Anthropologists and the War in Peru. In Marcus, ed., *Rereading Cultural Anthropology*. Durham and London: Duke University Press.

Stein, L. 1957. Social Class Gradient in Schizophrenia. *British Journal of Preventive and Social Medicine* 11: 181.

Steiner, Margaret. n.d. Coaxing, Coercion, and Cooperation during Song Performances in a Northern Irish Community. MS. Folklore Program, Indiana University.

Stokes, W., ed. 1957. *Lives of the Saints from the Book of Lismore*. Dublin: Talbot.

Strathern, M. 1972. *Women in Between: Female Roles in a Male World*. New York: Seminar Press.

Streib, Gordon F. 1968. Old Age in Ireland: Demographic and Sociological Aspects. *Gerontologist* (8): 227–235.

Strole, Leo, et al. 1962. *Mental Health in the Metropolis: The Midtown Manhattan Study*. New York: McGraw-Hill.

Sullivan, Harry Stack. 1962. *Schizophrenia as a Human Process*. New York: Norton.

Sundararaj, N., and Rao, B. S. S. 1966. Order of Birth and Schizophrenia. *British Journal of Psychiatry* 112: 1127–1129.

Sweeney, Paul. 1998. *The Celtic Tiger: Ireland's Economic Miracle Explained*. Dublin: Oak Tree.

Synge, John M. 1935. *The Complete Plays of John M. Synge*. New York: Random House.

Szasz, Thomas. 1960. The Myth of Mental Illness. *American Psychologist* 15: 113–118.

———. 1961. *The Myth of Mental Illness*. New York: Doubleday.

Taussig, Michael. 1992. *The Nervous System*. New York: Routledge.

Taylor, Lawrence. 1996. There Are Two Things that People Don't Like to Hear about Themselves. The Anthropology of Ireland and the Irish View of Anthropology. *The South Atlantic Quarterly* 95 (2): 212–226.

Tooth, G. C. 1950. *Studies in Mental Illness in the Gold Coast*. Colonial Research Publication no. 6. London: Her Majesty's Stationery Office.

Torrey, E. Fuller, et al. 1984. Endemic Psychosis in Western Ireland. *American Journal of Psychiatry* 141 (8): 966–970.

Torrey, E. Fuller. 1994. The Prevalence of Schizophrenia in Ireland. *Archives of General Psychiatry* 51: 513.

Tracy, Honor. 1953. *Mind You, I've Said Nothing*. London: Methuen.

———. 1956. *The Straight and Narrow Path*. New York: Vintage.

Uris, Leon. 1975. *Ireland, A Terrible Beauty*. New York: Doubleday.

Ussher, Arland. 1949. *The Face and Mind of Ireland*. London: Gollancz.

Valarasan-Toomey, Mary. 1998. *The Celtic Tiger: From the Outside Looking In*. Dublin: Blackhall.

Viney, Michael. 1983. The "Yank" in the Corner: Why the Ethics of Anthropology are a Worry for Rural Ireland. *The Irish Times*, August 6, weekend section, p. 1.

Waddington, John, and Youssef, A. Hanley. 1994. Evidence for a Gender-Specific Decline in the Rate of Schizophrenia in Rural Ireland over a 50-Year Period. *British Journal of Psychiatry* 164: 171–176.

Wallace, Anthony F. C. 1952. The Modal Personality Structure of the Tuscarora Indians. Bulletin no. 150, *Bureau of American Ethnology*. Washington, D.C.: Smithsonian Institution.

——. 1956. Revitalization Movements: Some Theoretical Considerations for Their Comparative Study. *American Anthropologist* 58: 264–281.

——. 1960. The Biocultural Theory of Schizophrenia. *International Record of Medicine* 173: 700–714.

——. 1961. *Culture and Personality*. New York: Random House.

——. 1972. *The Death and Rebirth of the Seneca*. New York: Vintage.

Walsh, Brendan M. 1968. Some Irish Population Problems Reconsidered. Dublin: Economic and Social Research Institute, no. 42.

——. 1970. Marriage Rates and Population Pressure: Ireland, 1871 and 1911. *Economic History Review* 23 (1): 148–162.

Walsh, Dermot. 1994. Reply to E. Fuller Torrey. Letters to the Editor. *Archives of General Psychiatry* 51: 513–514.

Walsh, Dermot. 1968. Hospitalized Psychiatric Morbidity in the Republic of Ireland. *British Journal of Psychiatry* 114: 11–14.

——. n.d. *The 1963 Irish Psychiatric Hospital Census*. Dublin: Medico-Social Research Board.

Walsh, Dermot, and Kendler, Kenneth. 1995. The Prevalence of Schizophrenia in Ireland: Readdressing the Enigma. *Archives of General Psychiatry* 52 (June): 509.

Walsh, Dermot, and Walsh, Brendan. 1968. Some Influences on the Inter-county Variation in Irish Psychiatric Hospitalization Rates. *British Journal of Psychiatry* 114: 15–20.

——. 1970. Mental Illness in the Republic of Ireland: First Admissions. *Journal of the Irish Medical Association* 63: 365–370.

Ward, Peter. 1993. *Divorce in Ireland: Who Should Bear the Cost?* Cork: Cork University Press.

Whiting, Beatrice, ed. 1963. *Six Cultures: Studies of Child Rearing*. New York: John Wiley.

Whiting, John, and Child, I. 1953. *Child Training and Personality*. New Haven: Yale University Press.

Whiting, John, et al. 1966. *Field Guide for a Study of Socialization*. New York: Wiley.

Whyte, J. H. 1971. *Church and State in Modern Ireland*. Dublin: Gill and Macmillan.

Williamson, A. 1969. The Beginnings of State Care for the Mentally Ill in Ireland. *Economic and Social Review* 1: 281–290.

World Health Organization. 1961. *Statistics Reports*, 14: 221–245. Geneva: World Health Organization.

——. 1968. *Statistics Reports*, 21: 529–551. Geneva: World Health Organization.

——. 1973. *International Pilot Study of Schizophrenia*. Geneva: World Health Organization.

Yeats, W. B. 1970. *The Collected Poems of W. B. Yeats*. New York: Macmillan.

SUGGESTIONS FOR FURTHER READING

Ardagh, John. 1994. *Ireland and the Irish: Portrait of a Changing Society*. London: Hamilton.

Curtin, Chris. 1987. *Ireland from Below: Social Change and Local Communities*. Galway: Galway University Press.

Curtin, Chris, and Valery, A. 1991. Populism and Petty Capitalism in Rural Ireland. In Whatmore, Lowe, and Marsden, eds., *Rural Enterprises: Shifting Perspectives on Small Scale Production*. London.

Genet, Jacqueline, ed. 1996. *Rural Ireland, Real Ireland?* Irish Literary Studies 40. Gerrard's Cross: Colin Smythe.

Gibbons, Luke. 1998. *Transformations in Irish Culture*. Notre Dame: University of Notre Dame.

Kane, Eileen. 1968. Man and Kin in Donegal. *Ethnology* 7 (2): 245–258.

Russell, John C. 1984. Family Experience and Folk Catholicism in Rural Ireland. *Journal of Psychoanalytic Anthropology* 7 (2): 141–170.

Sheehan, Eugene P. 1996. The Social Consequences of Emigration from Ireland for Those Who Stay. *Irish Journal of Psychology* 17 (1): 13–22.

Taylor, Lawrence. 1987. The River Would Run with Blood: Commons and Community in Donegal. In McCay and Acheson, eds., *The Question of the Commons: The Culture and Ecology of Communal Resources*. Tucson: University of Arizona Press.

——. 1993. Peter's Pence: Catholic Discourse and Nationalism in Nineteenth-Century Ireland. *Journal of the History of European Ideas* 16 (1): 103–108.

——. 1995. *Occasions of Faith: An Anthropology of Irish Catholics*. Philadelphia and Dublin: University of Pennsylvania Press.

Viney, Michael, and Viney, Ethna. 1981. *Another Life Again*. Dublin. An Irish
    Times Publication.
Wilson, Thomas. 1994. Problems of Social Anthropology. In O'Muiri, ed. *The
    Unheard Voice: Social Anthropology in Ireland*. Belfast: Lagan Press.

Conradh na Gaeilge. See Gaelic
League
cooperatives, agricultural,
103–04, 304–05
"cooring," 110–11
corbelling, 83–84
corporal punishment, for children, 251–54, 279
counseling, psychiatric, 163, 305
courtship, absence of, 183
Cow, Giant (Glas Gyneth; Glas
Ghaibhneach), 186
craic. See ridicule
creamery, demise of, 16–17, *17,*
113–14
Cresswell, Robert, 23, 61, 122–23
Crom Dubh, 27–28, 28, 84,
86–87, 187, 321, 347n.8
cromlech (circle of monoliths),
80, 83
Cromwell, Oliver, 89, 90
Cross, Eric, 7, 9
Cuallacht an Scabaill, 130
Cuallacht Mhuire gan Smal, 130
*Cúirt an mheán oiche (The
Midnight Court)* (Merryman),
9
culture: decline of, 23, 60, 133,
300–301; and mental illness,
225, 298–305; revitalization of,
127
Cumann na Sagart (union of
Irish-speaking priests), 130, 131
curach (fishing boat), 77n, 114,
115

dairy farming, demise of, 104,
113–14
Dana (mother-goddess), 82
dancing, 26; as immoral, 3–4,
208
data, reliability of, 71–72
dating: as immoral, 183; women
as instigators of, 194
Daube, David, 10
death(s): accidental, of children,
247, 273, 274t; in Ballybran,
97, 98t, 353n.3 (ch.4); disease
and, 128t; in institutions, 148;
Kerry traditions about, 358n.3;
preoccupation with, 215, 217;
and sexuality, 215–21; *see also*
mortality rate
December Bride (Bell), 201
deformity, low tolerance for, 236
deinstitutionalization, 40,
348n.12
demography, imbalance in,
97–101, 97–103
demoralization: of children, as

discipline, 252; cultural, 125; in
rural areas, 108, 123, 305; *see
also* anomie
denial, and alcoholism, 160
deportment, defensive, 212–13
depression, 49, 124; and age,
126–27; among women, 126,
127, 141; endogenous, 126–27,
141, 142, 163; as hypochondria,
126, 207; as normal, 157; and
pregnancy, folk beliefs about,
233; and social change, 42, 46;
treatment of, 163
desertion, marital, 207
Desmond, earl of, 89–90
detribalization, and mental illness, 300
DeVos, George, 35
Dhomhnaill, Nuala ni, 346n.5
diagnosis, usages in, 136, 138,
145–47
Dingle Peninsula, 26, 78, 90
diploma. *See* certificate, school-
leaving
disease: and cultural decline,
300–301; rates of, 127, 128t
dis-ease, social, schizophrenia as,
36, 297–305
disintegration, "mazeway," 299
divorce, 32, 185
dole. *See* welfare
Dómash Crom Dubh (Crom
Dubh Sunday), 28, 86
double bind, 267, 281, 293, 298,
303, 315, 357n.3
doublespeak, Irish, 158
dowries ("fortunes"), 179
Draw-a-Person test, 64, 221
dress, 21, 212, 313
Druids, 85, 152
DSM-III. *See* Manual,
Diagnostic and Statistical
Dunne, David, 24
Dunton Letters, 235, 356n.3
dutcas (blood), folk traditions of
lineage and, 180, 270–71, 286,
288

Easter Rising, 29, 91
eccentricity, tolerance of, 36–37,
152, 153–54, 156–57
economics: of Ballybran,
104–06; EEC and, 116;
improvement in Irish, 31–32;
and Irish celibacy, 195
Economic and Social Research
Institute, Dublin, 288
education: corporal punishment
and, 253–54; government policy on, 112–13; of the lastborn

son, 91, 289–90; levels of, 112;
of the physically handicapped,
287
EEC. *See* European Economic
Community
egalitarianism, 317–18
elderly, care of, 35, 39, 95,
148–50, 281, 286, 294
electroplexy (shock treatment),
for mental illness, 163, 166
emigration: attitudes toward,
281–83; and birth order, 42;
forced, 25, 27, 49–50, 61, 97,
121, 170, 178, 286, 305; and lack
of local secondary schools, 113;
and the residual population,
34–35, 142–43, 305; statistics
on, 98t; and success, 28–29,
59–60, 318, 358n.1; of women,
100–103, 192, 281–83
employment, fishing industry, 115
England: birth order and mental
illness, 267; oppression of the
Irish by, 90, 91, 129, 347n.6;
primogeniture in, 317–18;
schizophrenia in, 140; tourists
from, 118–19
entrepreneurs, local. *See
gombeen* men
Erikson, Erik, 205
eroticism, suppression of, 53–54
ethnography, and truth, 318–20
ethnopsychiatry, 154
Europe, rural and urban sex
ratios in, 101t
European Economic
Community (EEC), 7, 15, 16,
31, 33, 61, 106–07
Exam, Present State, 40

familism: as a defense against
sexuality, 215; ideal of, 178; and
loyalty, 195; and marriage, 98,
196–202; and psychotherapy,
175; and social life, 96, 255;
and women, 191–92
family: as a blood tie, 196; disintegration of, 300; and mental
illness, 283–84, 298, 300, 303;
nuclear, 178, 239, 286; size of,
229–30, 230t; units of, as
exceptions, 177–78
*Family and Community in
Ireland* (Arensberg and
Kimball), 22
famine, and attitudes toward
food, 245; *see also* Great
Famine
farming: cooperative, 304–05;
and social values, 105–06, 226,

[385]

sin: differences in, by sex, 187–88; and heritage, 271; venial ("sineens"), 153, 187
Sinn Fein, 32
Skellig Lists (ballads), 185
Skellig rocks, 185, 354n.8
smoking, 127, 128t
social life, 96, 314; see also sexes, separation of
social services, availability of and use, 147–48
socioculture: and celibacy, 195; and madness, 24, 34–35
Sorcerers of Dobu (Fortune), 73
soul, beliefs about, 211–12, 238
souterrains, 83
spinsters: population of, 353n.3 (ch.4); public censure of, 184, 354n.8; as unexceptionable, 312; see also women
"stations." See Mass, house
statistics, and mental illness, 34, 39–40
status, social: land ownership and, 105, 192; occupation and, 119–21, 131; of psychiatry, 164; village customs and, 111; of women. See women, social position of
Stephens, James, 129
stoicism, and childbearing, 234–35
Straw Boys, 184–85, 354n.8
stress, social change and, 299–302
subjectivity, of ethnography, 53
subsidies, economic, 33, 61, 108, 116, 121, 131
suicide, 46–49; age and, 42, 126; on the pueblos, 50–51; rates of, 49, 51, 128t, 352n.9
Sweeny Astray (Heany), 34
Sweeny, king, 34
syncretism, traditional, 87, 88
Synge, J. M., 9, 23, 129

Tailor and Ansty, The (Cross), 7–9, 8, 322, 359n.5
tailor, the (Tailor Dean), 10, 15–16, 70, 79, 159
Talbot, Mat, 206
TAT. See Thematic Apperception Test
teachers, 120, 132
teasing (codding), 71, 193, 228, 236, 315
Tepotzlan, Mexico, 29, 73–74

Teresa the Little Flower, Saint, 206
testing, as informative, 65
thatching, 14
theft, as unknown, 313
Thematic Apperception Test (TAT), 64–66, 67, 350n.2; achievement and, 276–77; alienation and, 203–04; autonomy and, 278–80; competence and, 277–79; and definitions of "family," 196–98; guilt and, 280–83; hospitalized patients and, 35, 36, 147, 215, 217, 218–19, 221, 276–83 passim, 298; incest and, 52, 201–02; and a longing for intimacy, 203–04; and mother-child relationships, 258–60; patricide, 280; responses to, 30, 175–76, 204, 215, 243, 265, 276–83, 298; see also card, TAT
theology: desert, 351n.4; repressive moral, 207
therapy, psychiatric, 163, 164
tinkers, 121
Tir na nOg, 79
title, to land, 105
toilet training. See potty training
Tory Island, 26, 350n.19
touch: infants' needs for, 226–27, 239, 249–50; as permissible in death, 216–17; proscriptions against, 189, 260
tourism, 14, 18, 33, 96, 117–19, 306
trades: constriction of, 114–17; revival of, 11, 17, 131, 305; social status of, 119–21
Transcultural Psychiatric Research Group, McGill University, 301
Troubles, the, 89, 91
trust, erosion of, 205, 251, 255; see also psychotherapy
Tuatha de Danann, 80, 82–83

Une Communauté rurale de l'Irlande (Cresswell), 23
United States, mental illness in, 140, 267, 348n.13

vacation homes, market for, 118–19
values, changes in, 110–11
Values Hierarchy Scale, 64, 119, 208–10, 209t, 217, 355n.13

Viney, Michael, 11–12
violence: political, 30–31; symbolic, 42–43
violin (fiddle), as symbol, 124–26
Vitae Sancti Brendani, 84, 86
Voluntary Retirement Scheme, 109

wakes: ritual of, 212; separation of the sexes at, 188; as social occasions, 313
warehousing, of the unproductive population, 35, 40, 148–50
water-bailiff, 121, 160
weaving, attempted revival of, 131, 305
welfare: eligibility for, 104, 117, 149; as "the dole," 96
White Goddess, The (Graves), 86
widowers, remarriage of, 180
widows, attitudes of, toward their marriages, 199–200
witches, 17, 182
withdrawal: as punishment, 282; as a response, 41, 63, 124, 203, 255, 257, 260–61, 294
women: attitudes of, toward marriage, 192, 194, 198–200; depression and, 126, 127, 141; diagnosis of mental illness in, 161; disparagement of, 4; employment for, 115, 118; fathers' control over, 178–79; independence for, 192, 194, 312; independent income for, 118, 183; infertility of, as a fault, 227, 228–29; in-marrying outsiders, contempt for, 79, 100, 180–82, 354nn.6,7; and Irish patriarchy, 191–95; as landowners, 192, 312; maiden names of, 79, 183, 312; outsiders, contempt for, 79, 100, 180–82; physical safety of, 312; purity of, 187; schizophrenia among, 140, 177; social life of, 313; social position of, 100, 182–83, 312, 357n.2 (ch.6); treatment of, by mothers-in-law, 181; unmarried. See spinsters; violence against, 207
work ethic, and demoralization, 110, 114

Yeats, W. B., 23, 129, 300

DESIGNER: SEVENTEENTH STREET STUDIOS

COMPOSITOR: SEVENTEENTH STREET STUDIOS

TYPE: ELECTRA LH

Printed in the USA
CPSIA information can be obtained
at www.ICGtesting.com
JSHW021300110324
58990JS00002B/14

9 780520 224803